Responsible Technology and Intelligence: A Review Series

1. A Compendium of Responsible Artificial Intelligence
   Deepak Kumar Jain, Kirti Raj Bhatele, Deepak Garg and *Gaurav Dhiman (Editors), 2025*
2. Ambient Assisted Living: Technological Advances
   Rashmi Gupta, Shashi Shekhar, Jeetendra Kumar and *Gaurav Dhiman (Editors), 2025*
3. Industrial Internet of Things for Responsible Technology
   B.K. Mishra, Gaurav Dhiman, Hemant Kasturiwale, Sujata Alegavi and *Kusum Yadav (Editors), 2026*
4. Robust Biometric Systems and Efficient Data Preservation
   Brajesh Kumar Singh, Amrita Rai, Shamimul Qamar, Ravinder Kumar and Anil Kumar (Editors), 2026

Responsible Technology and Intelligence: A Review Series

Robust Biometric Systems and Efficient Data Preservation

Editors

Brajesh Kumar Singh
Assistant Professor
Department of Electronics, Rajdhani College
University of Delhi, India

Amrita Rai
Professor and Head
Department of Electronics and Communication Engineering
Galgotias College of Engineering and Technology, Greater Noida, India

Shamimul Qamar
Professor
Department of Computer Science & Engineering,
College of Sciences & Arts, Dhahran Al Janoub Campus
King Khalid University, Abha, Kingdom of Saudi Arabia

Ravinder Kumar
Associate Professor
Skill Faculty of Engineering & Technology
Shri Vishwakarma Skill University, Gurgaon, India

Anil Kumar
Assistant Professor
Department of Computer Science & Engineering
GL Bajaj Institute of Technology and Management, India

CRC Press
Taylor & Francis Group
Boca Raton London New York

CRC Press is an imprint of the
Taylor & Francis Group, an **informa** business
A SCIENCE PUBLISHERS BOOK

First edition published 2026
by CRC Press
2385 NW Executive Center Drive, Suite 320, Boca Raton FL 33431

and by CRC Press
4 Park Square, Milton Park, Abingdon, Oxon, OX14 4RN

CRC Press is an imprint of Taylor & Francis Group, LLC

Library of Congress Cataloging-in-Publication Data (applied for)

ISBN: 978-1-032-87452-4 (hbk)
ISBN: 978-1-032-90832-8 (pbk)
ISBN: 978-1-003-56001-2 (ebk)

DOI: 10.1201/9781003560012

Typeset in Times New Roman
by Prime Publishing Services

Preface

In today's digital age, the Internet of Things (IoT) and web applications have transformed the way we use technology. From smart homes and health monitoring to financial transactions and industrial automation, these networked systems produce huge amounts of sensitive information. But as technology improves, so do the issues of security, privacy, and data preservation. Unauthorized access, cyber attacks, and data breaches have created serious issues, necessitating strong security systems that protect identity and data integrity.

This book, *Robust Biometric Systems and Efficient Data Preservation*, discusses novel methods of securing IoT and web systems using biometric verification and advanced data preservation methods. It focuses on the use of multi-modal biometric recognition, cryptographic techniques, and AI-based security systems to improve verification and protect information from cyber attacks.

Some of the key topics discussed in this book are:

- Human Biological traits that can be used for security.
- Emerging Biometric methods used for person recognition.
- Multimodal Biometric security for enhancing performance and reliability.
- Cryptographic techniques for data preservation in IoT and web systems.
- Challenges and solutions for protecting sensitive information in networked environments.
- Real-world applications of biometric security.

This book is aimed at researchers, cybersecurity experts, IoT developers, and students interested in learning and implementing effective biometric security and data protection measures.

It is my hope this book is most useful for those who are working towards the security, safety, and privacy domain of research.

Brajesh Kumar Singh
Amrita Rai
Shamimul Qamar
Ravinder Kumar
Anil Kumar

Series Preface

The rapid pace of technological advancement in the 21st century has brought with it transformative capabilities and unprecedented possibilities across sectors. From artificial intelligence and ambient intelligence to industrial automation, technology is deeply embedded in our social, economic, and personal lives. While these innovations offer immense benefits, they also raise critical questions about ethics, equity, sustainability, and human well-being. It is within this context that the "Responsible Technology Series" has been conceived—a multidisciplinary initiative aimed at fostering technological progress that is not only intelligent and efficient but also inclusive, ethical, and accountable.

This series brings together thought leaders, researchers, and practitioners to explore how emerging technologies can be designed and deployed responsibly to serve both individual and collective good. Each volume in the series addresses a specific domain of technological innovation while upholding a common commitment: to highlight frameworks, practices, and case studies that emphasize responsible development, deployment, and governance.

The first volume, A Compendium of Responsible Artificial Intelligence, offers a comprehensive overview of the ethical, social, and regulatory challenges associated with AI systems. It explores fairness, transparency, accountability, and the societal impacts of machine learning and decision-making algorithms, laying the groundwork for sustainable AI applications.

The second volume, Ambient Assisted Living: Technological Advances, focuses on the intersection of healthcare, aging populations, and intelligent environments. It presents innovations in assistive technologies and smart living spaces, while foregrounding the need for privacy, user dignity, and human-centric design in care ecosystems.

The third volume, Industrial Internet of Things for Responsible Technology, examines how industrial automation and IoT can be harnessed responsibly. It covers foundational technologies, ethical considerations, sustainability, human-centered design, and resilience—demonstrating how IIoT can drive industrial efficiency without compromising societal and environmental values.

Together, these volumes reflect the core mission of the series: to enable a balanced narrative in which innovation and responsibility go hand in hand. By bringing diverse voices and insights to the forefront, this series aims to equip readers with the tools, perspectives, and inspiration needed to build a more equitable and conscientious technological future.

We invite scholars, professionals, students, and policymakers to engage with these works, contribute to this growing dialogue, and join us in shaping a future where technology serves humanity with foresight and integrity.

Contents

1 | Robust Biometric Systems and Characteristics

Brajesh Kumar Singh
Department of Electronics, Rajdhani College, University of Delhi, India

1. Introduction

Biometric technology has emerged as a modern security and identification system. This system uses unique biological and behavioral traits, such as fingerprints, facial features, iris patterns; voice, and gait; biometrics provides an unparalleled method for verifying and identifying individuals [1]. Unlike traditional security, modern security and identification systems now depend heavily on biometric technology which provides unique solutions for identification and verification tasks. The identification and verification of people is possible through the use of specific biological and behavioral characteristics including fingerprints, facial recognition, iris patterns, voice recognition and a human's walking style. Biometrics presents inherent security and convenience because they use the natural physical characteristics of individuals instead of traditional security tools such as passwords and tokens which can be stolen or forgotten [2]. Throughout the 20th century into the 21st century the market demand for biometric systems experienced a significant increase because digital devices and online services needed stronger security and multiple sectors like finance, healthcare, and government demanded more robust solutions. The global market for biometrics has experienced rapid growth because of progress in machine learning sensor technology and data processing technology. The applications of biometric authentication now extend from high-security environments to personal devices such as smartphones and online banking services as well as air travel screening thus demonstrating its increasing widespread use [3, 4]. The application of biometrics is rising everywhere now-a-days, but there are still some issues. So, a biometric system must have two characteristics: it must be able to verify the identity of the person accurately and it must be able to resist external and internal threats. A good biometric system maintains both: one it accurately identifies or recognizes the person, and other is its usability regardless of the operating conditions.

Email: brajeshsingh.dce@gmail.com

DOI: 10.1201/9781003560012-1

2. Biometric System

The biometric system is used to recognize biometrics characteristics of individuals built on their inherent physical and/or behavioral features that are unique for an individual and thus provide a genuine recognition solution. Biometric systems are currently used in many applications like attendance systems, security checks, and access to important documents in the bank. Thus, with the increased demand, many biometric systems are being developed.

It is observed that even sophisticated biometric systems suffer from numerous issues in the expression of data collection, algorithms designed, and system architecture. Noisy data, non-universality, and user acceptability are some of the issues faced in designing a biometric system [5]. Although biometric systems are designed to prevent these issues, some of the algorithms have high computational complexity, increased execution time, reduced recognition rate, and high error rates.

2.1 Basic Block Diagram of Biometric System

The biometric system, in the most basic sense, is a pattern recognition system that acquires a person's biometric data, extracts a master set of features from the data, matches this set of features to the set of features in the database, and finally decides based on the outcome of this match.

A basic block diagram of the Biometric System is given in Figure 1. It is majorly divided into following modules: (1) data acquisition, (2) pre processing, (3) matching, (4) feature extraction, and (5) database module [6].

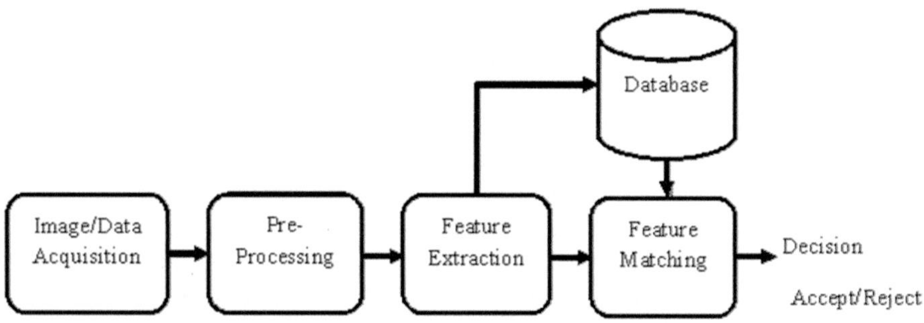

Figure 1: Biometric system block diagram.

1. **Data Acquisition:** The biological features of an individual can be acquired by the deployment of a camera or an appropriate sensor. The sensor should be able to capture high-quality images from the individual and then store this data in the database of a biometric system.
2. **Pre processing:** The primary function of this module is to analyze the quality of raw data acquired in the previous stage. Different pre processing algorithms can be applied on the raw data to enhance its quality and hence make it suitable for feature extraction.

3. **Feature Extraction:** In this phase, an appropriate algorithm is used to extract useful key points or features and their descriptions, which are needed for the identification of an individual. These extracted features are then stored as templates in the database of the system.
4. **Matching:** Features need to be extracted from the input test or query image and matched with the stored templates in the database to analyze and calculate the similarity measure between the template and test features of the claimant individual. A decision is then made as to whether the individual is genuine (authorized or registered user) or an imposter (unauthorized user), based on the closeness measure obtained.
5. **Database:** The collection of features extracted from the sample biometric is known as a template, and the need arises to store this template within the biometric system along with auxiliary information (e.g., name, Personal Identification Number (PIN), address, etc.) belonging to the user.

2.2 Biometric System Operation

The Biometric system is used in three modes of operation. One is Enrolment mode, second is Identification mode, and last is Verification mode [7]. It is explained as follows:

2.2.1 Enrolment Mode

A user needs to first register his individual biometric trait information in the biometric system before recognition. During this phase the sample data is acquired from the user, pre-processed and features are extracted [8]. The extracted features are then kept in the database as an original template together with other information like the name or ID of each of the users. This sample template is compared with the test template during recognition. The block diagram of the enrolment mode operation of the Biometric System is shown in Figure 2.

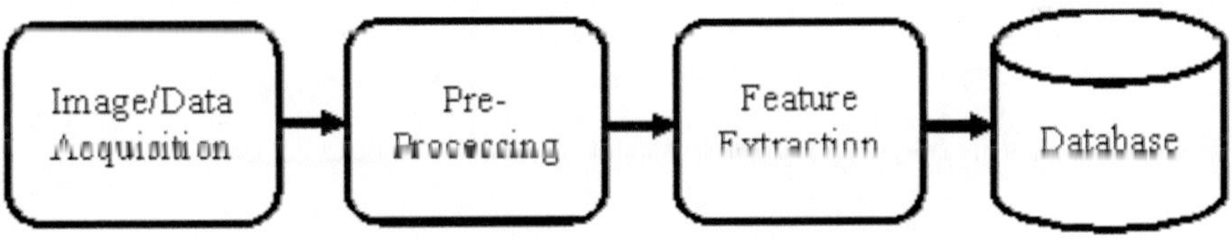

Figure 2: Enrolment mode operation of the biometric system.

2.2.2 Identification Mode

This is defined as the recognition of the registered person based uniquely on his/her biometric trait without any previous knowledge of the identity of the registered person [9]. In the identification process, a user goes through the same process as mentioned in the enrollment phase to provide the template which is called the test template. The test template is then matched with the master template which is available in the database. The matcher then decides whether to "Accept" or "Reject" based on the test image provided by the user which he registered himself in the biometric system or not, respectively. This is also referred to as one-to-many matching. The block diagram of the identification mode of a Biometric System is shown in Figure 3.

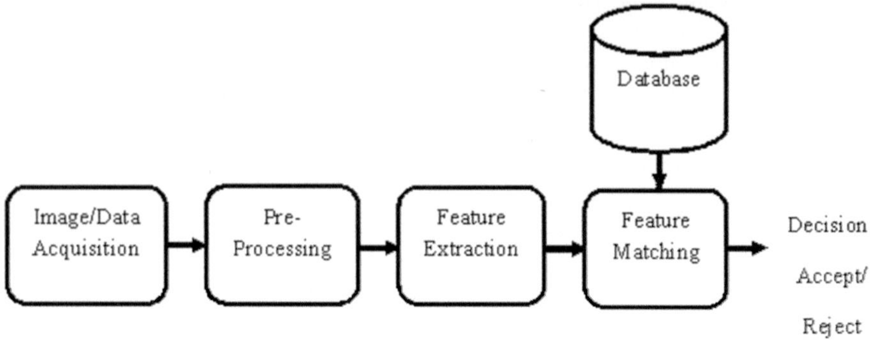

Figure 3: Identification mode operation of the biometric system.

2.2.3 Verification Mode

This requires an identity such as a smart card, an ID card, or an ID number to be affirmed by the user. The master template is then finally matched with the test template for recognition [10]. This is also called one-to-one matching. The block diagram of the verification mode of operation of the Biometric System is shown in Figure 4.

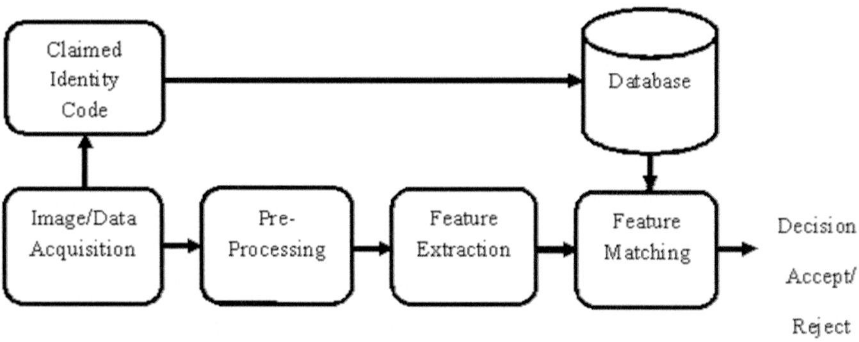

Figure 4: Verification mode operation of the biometric system.

3. Biometric System Evaluation Parameter

The code-based recognition (ID, PIN, password, etc.) needs to perfect the match to recognize a person, but in the case of biometric trait-based recognition, it is seldom that encounters of the two samples are identical feature sets. This is because of imperfect sensing conditions, inconsistent lighting conditions, and variation in user's interaction with the sensor. As a result, variability in the extracted feature is a set of biological traits.

This variability of the feature set between samples of the same individual is known as *intra-class* variation and it should be minimum for the biometric system to execute well. Similarly, the variability of the feature set between samples of the different individuals is known as *inter-class* variation, and it should be a maximum for a well-performing Biometric System.

- *Genuine Score:* If the matching score is calculated between the sample of the same person is called a Genuine matching Score or Genuine Score. It should be maximum.
- *Imposter Score:* The matching score calculated between the sample of different people is known as Imposter matching Score or Imposter Score. It should be minimum.

The calculated Matching Score (S) is compared with recognition Threshold (T) to decide. If $S > T$, then the system decides the claiming person is Genuine or matched. If $S < T$, then the system decides the claiming person is Imposter or Non-matched in the database. So, it is clear that the selection of T is a critical task for the biometric system to execute well.

The analysis of the Imposter and the Genuine Score distribution curve is helpful to understand the statically matching score data and also it assists in deciding about finding the best threshold value.

A general graph of Genuine and Imposter Score distribution curves are shown in Figure 5.

As the overlap part between the Genuine and Imposter distribution curve increases the possibility of errors also increases and vice versa [14]. The complete isolation between the curve of these two distributions reduces the error probability to zero. In Figure 5(a) the overlap part is shown by the red color which indicates a large error probability as compared to Figure 5(b) and in the case of Figure 5(c), there is complete isolation between the Genuine and the Imposter distribution curve so the error probability is reduced to zero. If the threshold value is selected between the curves and is in practice, it is very difficult to make a complete isolation between them. So, a T value is taken such that it can fulfill our purposes.

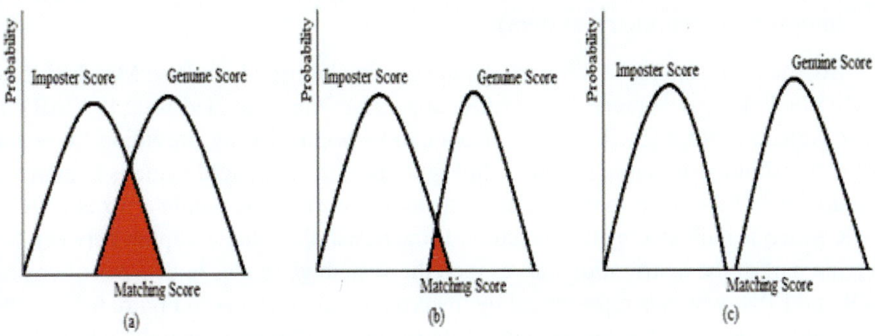

Figure 5: Genuine and the Imposter distribution graph.

The Binary Classification System has two classes of actual value, either True or False, and predicted outcome also has two classes, either True or False. It can be explained by a 2 × 2 Confusion matrix that depicts the four possible outcomes. A 2 × 2 Confusion matrix is given in Table 1.

Table 1: 2×2 Confusion matrix of a binary classifier

		Predicted outcome	
		True	**False**
Actual	True	True Positive (TP)	False Negative (FN)
	False	False Positive (FP)	True Negative (TN)

In the dataset, the total number of True Positives are 'P' and the total number of True Negatives are 'N'. The binary system predicted four types of outputs, two are correct outcomes, i.e., True Negative (TN) and True Positive (TP) and two are incorrect outputs, i.e., False Negative (FN) and False Positive (FP).

Correct Prediction

- *True Positive (TP):* True Positive is an outcome of a system where the system has correctly predicted a positive class (or an authorized person is correctly recognized as genuine by a biometric system).
- *True Negative (TN):* True Negative is an outcome of a system where the system has correctly predicted a negative class (or an unauthorized person is correctly recognized as an imposter by a biometric system).

Incorrect Prediction

- *False Positive (FP):* It is an outcome of a system where the system incorrectly predicted positive class (or an unauthorized person incorrectly recognized genuine by a biometric system). It is also called the Type-1 error of the null hypothesis.
- *False Negative (FN):* It is an outcome of a system where the system incorrectly predicted a negative class (or an authorized person was incorrectly recognized imposter by a biometric system).

So, the performance of a binary system can be described by False Matched Rate (FMR) or False Acceptance Rate (FAR) and False Non-Matched Rate (FNMR) or False Rejection Rate (FRR). These errors can be controlled by providing the value of the threshold as given in Figure 6. In Figure 6(a) the threshold value is kept at the extreme left of the overlap part of the distribution curves, the whole error is FAR or FMR which is indicated by the red color. If the threshold value is kept in between the overlap part of the distribution curves then the system generates both types of errors, FAR and FRR, which is represented by the red and green colors in Figure 6(b). If the threshold value is kept at the extreme right of the overlap part, then the whole error of a system is FRR or FNMR, which is indicated by the green color in Figure 6(c).

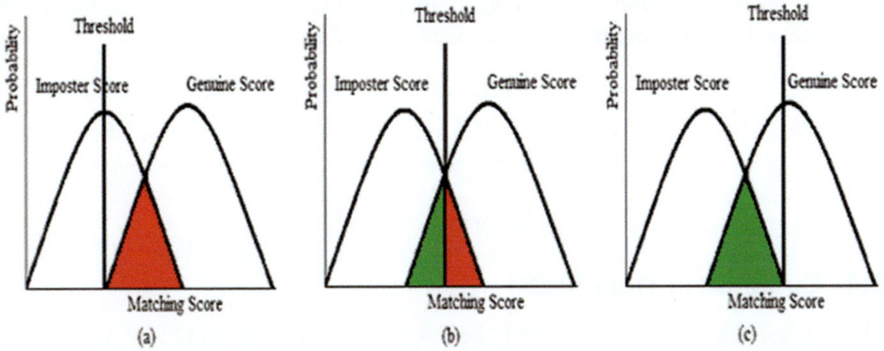

Figure 6: Genuine and imposter distribution graph with given threshold.

3.1 FAR or FMR

The ratio of the total number of falsely accepted to the total number of imposter attempts is called the False Matched Rate or False Acceptance Rate [11].

$$\text{FAR} = \frac{\text{Total False Acceptance}}{\text{Total Number of Imposter Attempt}} \tag{1}$$

$$\text{FAR} = \frac{\text{FP}}{\text{N}} = \frac{\text{FP}}{\text{FP} + \text{TN}} \tag{2}$$

3.2 FRR or FNMR

The ratio of the total number of falsely rejected to the total number of genuine attempts is represented by FRR or FNMR [12].

$$\text{FRR} = \frac{\text{Total False Rejected}}{\text{Total Number of Genuine Attempt}} \tag{3}$$

$$\text{FAR} = \frac{\text{FN}}{\text{P}} = \frac{\text{FN}}{\text{FN} + \text{TP}} \tag{4}$$

3.3 True Positive Rate (TPR)

The True Positive Rate is defined as the probability of detecting a true by the Binary Classification System.

$$\text{FRR} = \frac{\text{Total Positive Acceptance}}{\text{Total Number of Genuine Attempt}} \tag{5}$$

$$\text{TPR} = \frac{\text{TP}}{\text{P}} = \frac{\text{TP}}{\text{FN} + \text{TP}} = 1 - \text{FRR} \tag{6}$$

- *Zero False Rejection (ZFR):* Threshold value (T) at which the False Rejection Rate or FNMR becomes zero is defined as the Zero False Rejection.

$$ZER = T_{|at\ FRR = 0} \tag{7}$$

- *Zero False Acceptances (ZFA):* The value of Threshold (T) at which the False Acceptance Rate or FMR becomes zero is defined as the Zero False Acceptance.

$$ZA = T_{|at\ FAR = 0} \tag{8}$$

3.4 Equal Error Rate (EER)

The value of Threshold (T) at which the False Rejection Rate and False Acceptance Rate become equal or minimum then it is known as Equal Error Rate or Crossover Error Rate (CER) [13]. In other words, it is the point where Type-1 error and Type-2 error curves cross each other. To measure the biometrics' effectiveness, this is the best way. A system provides more accuracy with a lower CER value rather than a system having a higher CER value.

$$EER = T_{|at\ FAR = FRR} \tag{9}$$

4. FAR and FRR Graph

This graph is drawn between the value of FAR and FRR errors of a biometric system for the various values of thresholds between 0 to 1. The graph shows the expected value of FAR and FRR errors at any chosen threshold. This graph is often used by biometric researchers to understand the recognition performance. An example of such a graph is shown in Figure 7. The goal of a researcher is to minimize the cross over which reduces the EER of the system. This graph also gives information about how well a system handles imposters by the steepness of the FAR curve. The biometric system operator also used this graph to calculate the operating threshold value for system application.

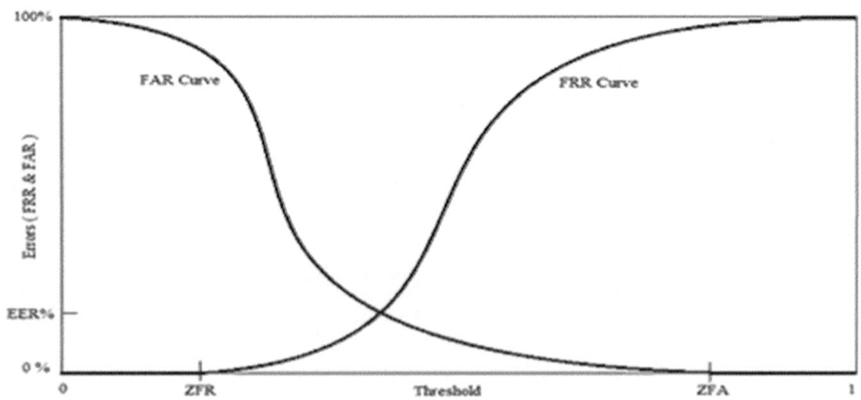

Figure 7: FAR and the FRR graph of a biometric system.

5. Detection Error Trade-off Graph (DET)

The DET graph is used to plot the error rate for a Binary Classification System. It is plotted between FRR versus FRR. The coordinate x and y-axis of the given graph are scaled non linearly (using a logarithmic transformation) which yields a more linear DET curve than a ROC graph. The image area highlights the critical operating region. Figure 8 shows the DET graph of the two systems. The green line shows the DET graph of Biometric-1 and the red line shows the DET graph of Biometric-2. Out of these two systems, Biometric-1 performs well as compared to Biometric-2, in terms of error.

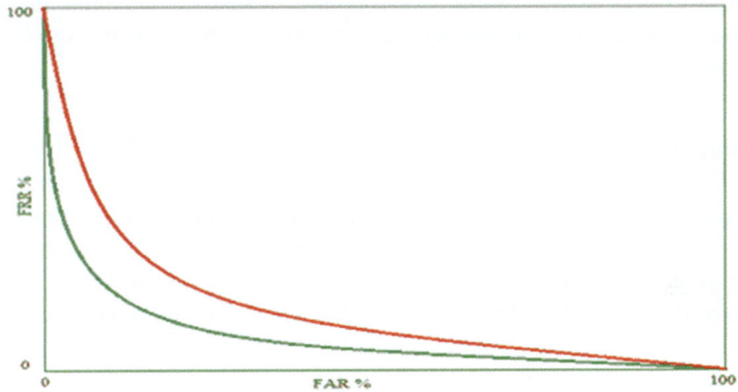

Figure 8: DET graph of two biometric systems.

6. Receiver Operating Characteristic Graph (ROC)

The ROC curve is used to describe the accuracy rate of a binary classification system. It is plotted between TPR and FPR and the accuracy of a system can be defined by the total area of a unit square under the curve of a system. As the area under the curve is increased, the accuracy of the system is also increased and vice versa. The ROC curves of the two biometrics are given in Figure 9, the green line shows the ROC

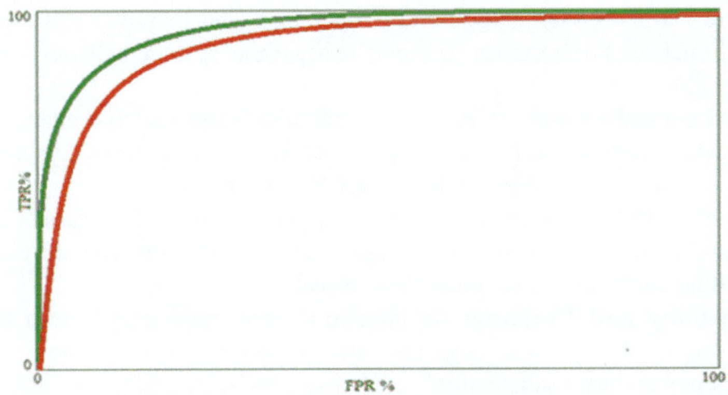

Figure 9: ROC graph of two biometric systems.

curve of System-1 and the red line shows the ROC curve of System-2. In Figure 9, the ROC curve of the two systems are given. System-1 covers more area under the curve as compared to System-2, hence the performance of System-1 is better as compared to System-2, in terms of accuracy.

7. Robustness in Biometric Systems

Robustness in biometric systems describes their capacity to be accurate, reliable, and operational under diverse and adverse conditions. Robustness ensures biometric systems are operational despite changes in the environment, user behavior, and potential security threats. A robust biometric system is essential in real-world applications where consistent and secure authentication reduces errors and maximizes performance.

The Key Features of Robust Biometric Systems are as follows.

- **Accuracy:** The system minimizes errors such as FAR and FRR with low EER. High accuracy is essential for accurate identification and authentication.
- **Resilience:** A robust biometric system operates well regardless of environmental fluctuations, such as changes in light, temperature, or noise. For instance, a face recognition system should work well in bright and dark light.
- **Adaptability:** Robust biometric systems accommodate physiological changes of users, such as aging, injuries, or medical issues. Adaptive learning algorithms allow the system to refine templates over time.
- **Security:** Robustness involves protection from spoofing and presentation attacks, such as false fingerprints or deep fake images. Anti-spoofing functions such as livens detection reinforce security.
- **Interoperability:** The capacity to operate across disparate devices, platforms, and environments ensures the system remains reliable across different environments.

8. Challenges of Robust Systems

- **Environmental Variations:** Biometrics operates in uncontrolled environments where variables such as lighting, temperature, and humidity can compromise performance. For instance, a facial recognition system will not work under low light.
- **Physiological Changes:** Over time, individuals can undergo changes in their biometric features due to aging, injuries, or medical conditions. Systems need to adjust to these fluctuations without sacrificing accuracy.
- **Spoofing Threats:** Impersonation attacks like spoofing fingerprints or images are authentic threats to biometric systems. Strong designs have developed anti-spoofing capabilities to counter these threats.
- **Scalability and Usability:** As biometrics gain popularity across the globe, systems need to process large amounts of data and heterogeneous users with efficiency and user satisfaction.
- **High Reliability:** Consistent accuracy under changing circumstances.

- **Error Minimization:** Minimizing false accept and false reject through sophisticated algorithms.
- **Adaptive Learning:** Machine learning algorithms to adaptively alter user profiles and learn changes.
- **Anti-Spoofing Measures:** Methods like livens detection to detect spoofing attempts.

All these factors combined make a biometric system robust for real-world applications

9. Real-world Applications

A robust biometric system is critical for delivering security, privacy, and convenience in contemporary applications. It fills the gap between security requirements and user-friendly experiences.

- **Border Security:** Automated gates at airports need to process heterogeneous populations and environmental conditions like varying lighting and high volume.
- **Healthcare:** Biometric patient identification ensures accurate record-keeping, even for unconscious or incapacitated patients.
- **Banking and Finance:** Secure biometric authentication secures financial transactions against fraud, providing secure alternatives to passwords or PINs.

10. Developing Challenges

Robustness remains a challenging task despite substantial advances. Key challenges are:

- **Data Quality:** Variations in input data due to environmental or physiological reasons.
- **Interoperability:** Compatibility between devices, platforms, and geographies.
- **Ethical Concerns:** Balancing security with user privacy and bias issues in biometric algorithms.
- **Resource Constraints:** Developing cost-effective and energy-efficient systems without sacrificing robustness

Addressing these challenges demands a multi disciplinary solution involving computer vision, machine learning, cyber security, and human-computer interaction expertise.

11. Conclusions

Biometric systems are playing a major role in new era security. It is offering security based on some physiological or behavioral characteristics of the human body. Their resilience is measured with respect to the variability of some parameters like environmental and physiological state changes. A robust biometric system reduces errors like FAR and FRR while providing high security against spoofing attacks. To increase robustness, biometric systems have to be based on adaptive learning, anti-spoofing, and scalable architectures. In the real world, the applications of biometric systems increase in various sectors such as border protection, healthcare, and finance, highlighting their increasing significance. Still, cost-efficient and effective biometric solutions call for a multi disciplinary framework that includes cyber security, artificial intelligence, and human-computer interaction. With ongoing developments, biometric systems are likely to be a key factor in determining secure and effective authentication processes globally.

References

1. Jain, A.K., P. Flynn, & A.A. Ross. (2007). *Handbook of Biometrics*. New York, NY, USA: Springer.
2. Prabhakar, S., S. Pankanti, & A.K. Jain. (2003, Mar.–Apr.). Biometric recognition: Security and privacy concerns. *IEEE Security & Privacy*, 1(2), 33–42.
3. Daugman, J. (1993, Nov.). High confidence visual recognition of persons by a test of statistical independence. *IEEE Trans. Pattern Anal. Mach. Intell.*, 15(11), 1148–1161.
4. Jain, A.K., K. Nandakumar, & A. Ross. (2016). 50 years of biometric research: Accomplishments, challenges, and opportunities. *Pattern Recognit. Lett.*, 79, 80–105.
5. Ross, Arun A., Karthik Nandakumar, & Anil K. Jain. (2006). *Handbook of Multibiometrics* (Vol. 6). Springer Science & Business Media.
6. Ross, Arun, & Anil K. Jain. (2007). Human recognition using biometrics: An overview. *Annales Des Telecommunications*, 62(1), 11–35. Springer-Verlag.
7. Ross, Arun, & Anil Jain. (2003). Information fusion in biometrics. *Pattern Recognition Letters*, 24(13), 2115– 2125.
8. Ross, A., & A.K. Jain. (2003, Sep.). Information fusion in biometrics. *Pattern Recognit. Lett.*, 24(13), 2115–2125.
9. Zhu, X., X. Li, S. Zhang, & L. Zhang. (1993, Dec.). Deep hashing network for efficient similarity retrieval. *IEEE Trans. Multimedia*, 20(12), 3370–3383.
10. Cappelli, R., D. Maio, & D. Maltoni. (2002, Aug.). Synthetic fingerprint-database generation. In: *Proc. Int. Conf. Pattern Recognit.*, pp. 744–747. Quebec City, Canada,
11. Jain, A.K., & U. Uludag. (2003, Nov.). Hiding biometric data. *IEEE Trans. Pattern Anal. Mach. Intell.*, 25(11), 1494–1498.
12. Bowyer, K., T. Boult, A. Kumar, & P. Flynn. (2010, Mar.). Challenges and research in fingerprint recognition. *IEEE Signal Process. Mag.*, 27(2), 150–152.
13. Galbally, J., J. Fierrez, F. Alonso-Fernandez, & M. Martinez-Diaz. (2010, Jun.). Evaluation of direct attacks to fingerprint verification systems. *Pattern Recognit. Lett.*, 31(8), 725–732.
14. Cappelli, R., M. Ferrara, & D. Maltoni. (2011, Jun.). Fingerprint indexing based on minutia cylinder-code. *IEEE Trans. Inf. Forensics Security*, 6(2), 502–512.

2 | Human Biological Traits and Biometric System Design Challenges

Brajesh Kumar Singh[1*], Ruchi Agarwal[2], Ranjana Kumari[3], Mohit Aggarwal[4]

[1] Department of Electronics, Rajdhani College, University of Delhi, India
[2] Department of Electronics and Communication Engineering, Pranveer Singh Institute of Technology, Kanpur, India
[3] Department of Electronics and Communication Engineering, Galgotias College of Engineering, Delhi NCR, India
[4] Noida International University, Delhi NCR, India

1. Introduction

Security is a necessity of society and day to day it has become more challenging due to increases in online works like e-Banking, e-Commerce, smart home security, attendance in educational institutes, industries, etc. The past decade used several traditional methods such as an Identification Document (ID) card, Password, Personal Identification Number (PIN) to recognize a genuine person but it is quite possible that the ID may be lost or stolen and misused by an unauthorized person and password may be forgetting or hacked using dictionary attacks [1]. This traditional method has also a major issue as the population is increasing day to day and it is tough to adhere to this traditional method to provide reliable security to all.

Now a days an automatic distinguishing and recognize system comes into practice to recognize individuals using some inherent human's biological trait [2] such as the face, fingerprint, hand geometry, ear, iris, retina, DNA, palm print, hand vein, Finger Knuckle Print (FKP), voice, gait, signature, keystroke dynamics, etc. The choice for the selection of biological traits must have the properties of distinctiveness, universality, permanence, acceptability, collectability, and security [3].

2. Biological Traits

The biological trait is one of the unique features of every human's body [4]. These unique features are used to recognize individuals, for example, fingerprint, finger knuckle print, DNA, ear, iris, gait, mole, signature, etc. These human's traits are

*Corresponding author: brajeshsingh.dce@gmail.com

DOI: 10.1201/9781003560012-2

broadly divided into three classes namely Physiological traits, Behavioural traits, and Soft traits as shown in Figure 1.

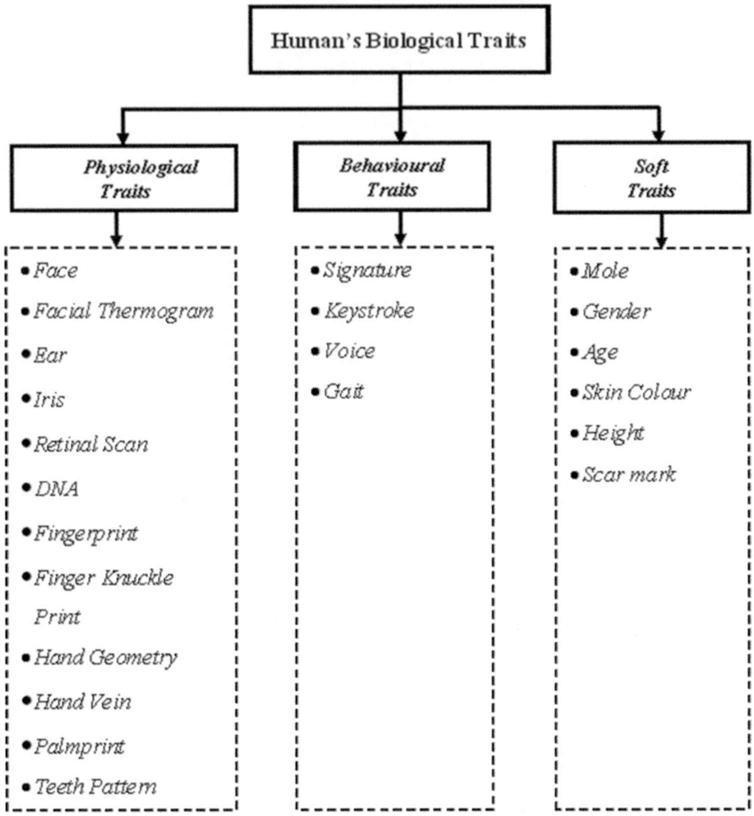

Figure 1: Classification of human's biological traits.

2.1 Physiological Traits

A human's biological trait which is based on the natural physical shape of a body is known as a Physiological Trait.

Face

The face is a commonly available biometric trait. It can be easily taken for record purposes using a normal resolution camera device in the presence of light. Face recognition was introduced in 1986 and suggested that seven different types of facial characteristics can be derived from faces such as pictorial, structural, visually derived semantic, identity-specific semantic, name, expression, and facial speech codes [5]. After that various authors introduced several facial feature algorithms like the shape and size of the nose, lips, eyes, ear, forehead, jaw edges, and some other facial peculiarities, and these facial features are used to recognize a person [6–8]. The face recognition method suffers from the difficulty that it requires the same face expression, the same background of the image, and also the same age sample of person, otherwise, the recognition accuracy may decrease. Also, identical twins will have the same face features, so it is very difficult to differentiate using face traits.

Facial Thermogram

In the mid-1990s, facial thermograms were initiated [9–11]. It is a visual display of the amount of infrared energy emitted by an object and converted into a temperature. This distributed temperature displayed in the form of an image is known as Facial Thermogram. It is formed using distinguishing heat designs made by branching of veins at the skin. These patterns are highly unique, as a consequence identical twins have different thermograms. So, it is used for person recognition/ identification.

Ear

The ear trait seems to be a good solution to person recognition/identification. Because it is a visible trait, easily captured, and also the structure does not change radically. The ear recognition is made by matching the landmark location of the ear such as Helix, Concha, Tragus, Lobule, Antitragus, etc., or a salient point on the pinna [12– 15].

Iris

The iris is a round shape pattern that lies in the centre region of the eyes and it is bounded by the sclera and around the pupil. The iris texture is modelled during fetal development and stabilizes within two years of the baby's life. It has an exceptionally remarkable visual surface example and remotely apparent organ of the human body and it tends to be effortlessly caught utilizing an imaging gadget from a little distance and used for personal identification [16–18]. Several countries have enrolled billions of people in the iris recognition system for the national ID program. A main problem is that people are not comfortable accessing iris recognition.

Retinal Scan

Retina scanning technology was developed in the 1980s and nowadays it is one of the most trusted biometric traits used for person recognition. It is basically a thin tissue made of a vascular pattern available at the posterior part of the eyes. This complex structure of capillaries supply blood to the retina. The network of blood vessels in the retina is so complex and unique to each person and remains constant for their whole life. To capture this unique vesicular pattern of the retina, a low-intensity low-energy infrared light is applied into the eye; the veins inside the retina assimilate light, then the encompassing tissue effectively can distinguish this interesting vesicular design and utilize it for individual acknowledgment [1]. Many authors use retina biometric traits for person recognition [19, 20].

DNA (Deoxyribonucleic Acid)

Jeffrey Glassberg in 1983, first time filed a patient to use DNA for forensic purposes. After that continuous interest increased in the field of biometric recognition purposes. Forensic DNA composing utilizing STR markers have been included in the criminal equity framework since 1998. At the forensic lab, the Human Identity Project Team has been working on the side of this local area with standard reference materials and the assessment of new advancements as well as giving preparatory and approval assets. With the help of FBI subsidizing, the DNA Biometrics Project Team is at present assessing strategies ordinarily utilized in the measurable local area for application to the field of biometrics.

Fingerprint

A fingerprint is a unique biological trait of every person and it is formed during fetal development within a seven-month period and remains constant for the whole life. A line that creates a fingerprint is known as a ridge and the space between the two ridges is known as a valley or wrinkle. These ridges and valleys make a pattern that is unique for every fingerprint. It is also shown that the fingerprint of identical twins and also different fingers of the same person are not identical. So, it is used for personal authentication purposes. Broadly, this fingerprint pattern is classified into three categories, namely, arc, loop, and whorl [1].

Finger Knuckle Print

The Finger Knuckle Print (FKP) is one of the rising hand-based biometrics for a person's identification. It is a unique skin pattern present at the backside of each finger joint. Every finger has three joints except the thumb, such as meta capo phalangeal joint, proximal interphalangeal joint (PIP), and distal interphalangeal joint.

The finger joint which connects the finger with the hand surface is known as the meta capo phalangeal joint, the middle joint is known as the proximal interphalangeal joint and the top of the finger joint (toward the tip of the finger) is known as distal interphalangeal joint.

The PIP joint creates a unique skin pattern on the back side of the finger that is mentioned as FKP [21].

Hand Geometry

Hand Geometry is also used as a biological trait to recognize a person. This method of recognition uses dimensional features like finger length, width, deviation angles, thickness, etc. to recognize a person [22–25]. This biological trait is not as highly unique as a fingerprint, palm print, hand vein, etc.

Hand Vein

Hand vein biometric identification technology has become a new research direction in the domestic and international identification system [26, 27]. The arrangement of hand vein picture obtaining gadgets was planned and the light source boundaries were improved by the picture mean and standard deviation. The fundamental standard of hand vein acquisition is that when haemoglobin in the blood carries oxygen and moves towards the tissues of the body by various arteries, and after delivering oxygen to the cell bloodstreams flow back to the heart using various arteries. Vein design acknowledgment utilizes this distinction among deoxidized and oxygenated haemoglobin. Deoxidized haemoglobin retains infrared light, making the vein design noticeable on the off chance that you utilize a scanner to enlighten it with infrared light. The image pre-processing algorithms are also used to improve picture quality. The threshold technique was utilized to eliminate the picture foundation, and the image grey was normalized. It is shown that top-notch pictures can be acquired by utilizing the optimized boundaries procurement gadget and picture pre-handling technique. The picture securing framework and pre-handling calculation give a decent stage to additional vein pictures including extraction and coordinating. Everybody has a different vein design in their palm. Reference focuses on the example can be put away and the example can be utilized as an ID and security method. Most frameworks that utilize vein design acknowledgment stores it as a picture, which might be encoded. With the Palm-ID, then once again, the examined reference focuses are put away straightforwardly as an encoded format, which implies that the vein design is converted into a code inside the actual scanner. This strategy for palm vein design acknowledgment, consequently, offers a very significant degree of safety.

Palm Print

A palm is an inner surface area that lies between the wrist and finger region of the hand. The palm print is defined as a unique line pattern available on the palm of every person's hand known as creases which are broadly divided into three major types namely, flexion creases, secondary creases, and wrinkles. Out of these three flexion creases, secondary creases are formed during fetal development of the baby and it is highly unique, even twins do not have the same lines. The surface area of this palm also is larger compared to other biometrics. Several literatures are also available to recognize a person using this biometric [28–31].

Teeth Pattern

The teeth pattern is a unique identity of every person, even identical twins do have identical teeth patterns. So, dental records can be beneficial in identifying humans.

A dental radiograph method is often used to extract dental information such as tooth contours, teeth shape, and neighbouring teeth information [32]. The extracted teeth information is used to identify people.

2.2 Behavioural Traits

A human's trait which is based on the natural behavior of a human is known as Behavioural traits such as Signature, Keystroke, Voice, Gait, etc. It is also used for human identification/recognition.

Signature

The writing style of every person is a unique identity and it is treated as a trait for the purpose of recognition. A person signs their name on a paper, special tablet, and the tablet utilizes an uncommon sensor to record the movement of a pointer to animate the production of signature. The signature investigation looks at the actual provisions found inside the signature, including such qualities as letter size, separating, points, strokes, and inclination [33]. Signatures are social biometrics that change throughout some undefined time frame like the physical or emotional states of the person. Lamentably, signature examination frameworks can be simpler to trick since they are defenceless to the utilization of mechanical multiplications or the handicraft of experienced, proficient counterfeiters. By and large, signature investigation frameworks have possibly moderate precision when contrasted with different sorts of biometric pointers. This is maybe because of the elements like weakness, ailment, fretfulness, and climate which will decide how an individual signs his/her name in some random occurrence.

Keystroke

The way of typing over a computer keyboard is an individual identity and it can be also used for identity verification [34]. The keystroke dynamics include observing clients as they type on a console and estimating the speed, duration, latencies, mistakes, power, and time frames of individual keystrokes. Most computer clients can repeatedly type certain known examples with a consistency that can be repeated and estimated, in this manner making it normal for biometric use. The general exactness of this system can be highly variable, contingent upon the strategy for estimation utilized and the sort of information mentioned by the client. However, many factors can influence the exactness, including the client's typing capability and even the utilization of a different keyboard.

Voice

Voice biometrics is a blending of both behavioural and physiological qualities. The peculiarities focus around the mouth, nasal cavity, vocal tract, and lips. Consequently, the shape and size of the extremity are used as a part of the sound combination. The physiological uniqueness of human verbal communication is non-changeable for a person [35]. However, the behavioural component of communication changes because of age, emotional state, and medical conditions. The voice is particularly different including twins and cannot be precisely copied. Voice is additionally not proper for careful validation of an individual since it isn't extremely different. The inconvenience with the voice biometric framework is that the peculiarities of speech may shift because of introducing noise into the system.

Gait

The Gait biometric trait is basically a walking way of a person and this trait is used for low-security applications [36]. This method is often used for surveillance purposes to recognize a person from a distance. Hence, it is important to capture a good and natural walking video for better recognition performance.

2.3 Soft Traits

Soft biometric characteristics refer to physical and social qualities, like sexual orientation, stature, and weight, which are not interesting to a particular subject but rather are valuable for distinguishing proof, confirmation, and depiction of human subjects. These biometrics characteristics are used for the distinguishing proof of people and can be joined with biometric confirmation systems to build the exactness of acknowledgment [39]. An example is visual surveillance, and soft biometric data can assist with recognizing individuals during the irregularities when faces are caught ineffectively on camera.

Mole Mark

Mole marks are concentrations of pigment-producing cells (melanocytes) on the skin. People with light skin tend to have more moles. The technical name for a mole is nevus. Facial soft biometrics of this kind is often used for personal verification and identification [37].

Gender

The gender information is used as a piece of secondary information along with the physiological trait to increase the recognition rate of a biometric system [38]. Gender recognition is fundamental for some applications in the business spaces also like utilization of human-computer association and computer-assisted physiological or mental investigation since it contains a wide scope of data concerning the qualities distinction among males and females. Some have proposed different methodologies for automatic gender classification using the components obtained from human bodies as well as practices.

Age

The age information of a person is also used to enhance the feature to increase the recognition rate of a biometric system. An age information extraction algorithm is proposed by the author [40].

Skin Color

The skin color information of a person is also used to enhance the feature to increase the recognition rate of a biometric system. Gonzalez-C. et al. [41] use skin color information to detect a face.

Height

The height feature information of a person is also used to increase the recognition rate of a biometric system. Koide and Miura [42] use height information for the person following the robot.

Scar

The scare information on the face is also used to enhance the feature parameter to recognize a person. Lee et al. [43] use scar information to recognize a person. The scare mark image is given in Figure 1.

3. Biometric Deformations

The working performance of a biometric system is highly dependent on the collected biometric sample and the environmental condition in which the samples are accumulated. It might be possible some of the samples are deformed which can affect the biometric system performance and taking into consideration it can increase the system performance [44].

(i) Fingerprint
- (a) Cut on a finger
- (b) Fractured finger

(c) Parched finger
(d) Increased or decreased humidity

(ii) **Speech Recognition**
(a) Cough and cold
(b) Interception devices
(c) Background noise

(iii) **Face Recognition**
(a) Change of the facial hair
(b) Change of the hairstyle
(c) Lighting conditions

(iv) **Iris Scanning**
(a) Movement of head and eyes
(b) Lenses
(c) Colored contact lenses

(v) **Hand Geometry**
(a) Jewelry
(b) Weight change
(c) Swelling of the joints

(vi) **Scan the Signature**
(a) Marking too fast
(b) Various marking positions

(vii) **Finger Knuckle Print (FKP)**
(a) Ring
(b) A fracture of the finger

The performance of many biometric systems varies depending on the population. In addition, the problem may also occur if significant time has passed after registration, then physiological changes may complicate the recognition [45].

4. Biometric Trait Properties

All biometric traits have their strength as well as weakness. Therefore, the selection of a biometric trait for a particular application is conditional and it depends on several parameters, in addition to the complementing performance. The author has recognized seven parameters that determine the fitness of a particular behavioural or physical methodology for use in a biometric application [4]. These parameters are described below:

- **Universality:** Each individual accessing the implementation should own this characteristic of universality. This is essential for the user to be registered in the system so that the registered user can make use of the available facility.
- **Uniqueness:** The characteristic of no two individuals must have any resemblance in them. This improves the discrimination capability thus aiding in improving the performance rate.
- **Permanence:** The features of an individual should be unchanging over a long duration of time. This is essential for the inclusion of that particular trait in the biometric system.

Table 1: Biometric trait comparison

	Biological Trait Properties						
Trait	**Universality**	**Distinctiveness**	**Permanence**	**Collectability**	**Performance**	**Acceptability**	**Circumvention**
Face	H	L	M	H	L	H	H
Facial Thermogram	H	H	L	H	M	H	L
Ear	M	M	H	M	M	H	M
Iris	H	H	H	M	H	L	L
Retinal Scan	H	H	M	L	H	L	L
DNA	H	H	H	L	H	L	L
Fingerprint	M	H	H	M	H	H	M
Finger Knuckle Print	M	H	M	H	H	H	M
Hand Geometry	M	M	M	H	M	M	M
Hand Vein	M	M	M	M	M	M	L
Palm Print	M	H	H	M	H	M	M
Signature	L	L	L	H	L	H	H
Keystroke	L	L	L	M	L	M	M
Voice	M	L	L	M	L	H	H
Gait	M	L	L	H	L	H	M

Notes: H = High, M = Medium and L = Low.

- **Collectability:** It must be possible to acquire the raw data from the individual without any constraints. The data must be useful for further processing so that useful information can be selected and stored as templates.
- **Performance:** The biometric system must adhere to the operating speed, accuracy, and other conditions imposed by the application. The design of hardware and software and their interaction plays a vital role in this case.
- **Acceptability:** Individuals must be willing to provide that characteristic without being hesitant.
- **Circumvention:** This cites the ease with which the features can be duplicated to deceive the system.

5. Comparisons of Biometric Traits

The biometric trait can be compared based on the biometric trait property [29]. The comparison of biometric traits is given in Table 1.

6. Conclusions

This chapter gives an introduction of the human biological trait, its application areas, challenges, and the issues associated with identifying a person using these traits. It also gives a brief overview of the biometric system, challenges of biometric systems, and their standard evaluation parameters which are often used by the research community. At the end of the chapter are given the motivation and issues addressed along with the organization of the thesis.

References

1. Jain, Anil, Lin Hong, & Sharath Pankanti. (2000). Biometric identification. *Communications of the ACM*, 43(2), 90–98.
2. Anil K., Arun Ross, & Sharath Pankanti. (2006). Biometrics: A tool for information security. *IEEE Transactions on Information Forensics and Security*, 1(2), 125–143.
3. Jain, Anil K., & Ajay Kumar. (2010). Biometrics of next generation: An overview. *Second Generation Biometrics*, 12(1), 2–3.
4. Jain, Anil K., Arun Ross, & Salil Prabhakar. (2004). An introduction to biometric recognition. *IEEE Transactions on Circuits and Systems for Video Technology*, 14(1), 4–20.
5. Bruce, Vicki, & Andy Young. (1986). Understanding face recognition. *British Journal of Psychology*, 77(3), 305–327.
6. Hu, Haifeng, & Jianquan Gu. (2016). Multi-manifolds discriminative canonical correlation analysis for image set-based face recognition. *Cognitive Computation*, 8(5), 900–909.
7. Mi, Jian-Xun, Chao Li, Cong Li, Tao Liu, & Ying Liu. (2016). A human visual experience-inspired similarity metric for face recognition under occlusion. *Cognitive Computation*, 8(5), 818–827.

8. Kumar, Neeraj, Alexander Berg, Peter N. Belhumeur, & Shree Nayar. (2011). Describable visual attributes for face verification and image search. *IEEE Transactions on Pattern Analysis and Machine Intelligence*, 33(10), 1962–1977.
9. Prokoski, Francine J., & Robert B. Riedel. (2008). Infrared identification of faces and body parts. In: *Biometrics*, pp. 191–212. Springer, Boston, MA, 1996.
10. Wu, Shiqian, Weisi Lin, & Shoulie Xie. (2008). Skin heat transfer model of facial thermograms and its application in face recognition. *Pattern Recognition*, 41(8), 2718–2729.
11. Wu, Shi-Qian, Wei Song, Li-Jun Jiang, S-L. Xie, Feng Pan, Wei-Yun Yau, & Surendra Ranganath. (2005). Infrared face recognition by using blood perfusion data. In: *International Conference on Audio-and Video-Based Biometric Person Authentication*, pp. 320–328. Springer, Berlin, Heidelberg. .
12. Malathy, C., K. Annapurani, & M. AbdulKarim Sadiq. (2013). Analysis of fusion methods for ear biometrics. *International Journal*, 3(1).
13. Chen, Hui, & Bir Bhanu. (2007). Human ear recognition in 3D. *IEEE Transactions on Pattern Analysis and Machine Intelligence*, 29(4), 718–737.
14. Emersic, Ziga, Vitomir Struc, & Peter Peer. (2017). Ear recognition: More than a survey. *Neurocomputing*, 255, 26–39.
15. Yuan, Li, & Zhi-chun Mu. (2007). Ear recognition based on 2D images. In: *2007 First IEEE International Conference on Biometrics: Theory, Applications, and Systems*, pp. 1–5. IEEE.
16. Sanderson, S., & J.H. Erbetta. (2000). Authentication for secure environments based on iris scanning technology. 2000, 8–8.
17. Ma, Li, Tieniu Tan, Yunhong Wang, & Dexin Zhang. (2004). Efficient iris recognition by characterizing key local variations. *IEEE Transactions on Image Processing*, 13(6), 739–750.
18. Sruthi, T.K., & Jini, K.M. (2013). A literature review on iris segmentation techniques for iris recognition systems. *IOSR Journal of Computer Engg.*, 11(1), 46–50.
19. Borgen, Halvor, Patrick Bours, & Stephen D. Wolthusen. (2008). Visible-spectrum biometric retina recognition. In: *2008 International Conference on Intelligent Information Hiding and Multimedia Signal Processing*, pp. 1056–1062. IEEE.
20. Delac, Kresimir, & Mislav Grgic. (2004). A survey of biometric recognition methods. In: *Proceedings. Elmar-2004. 46th International Symposium on Electronics in Marine*, pp. 184–193. IEEE.
21. Zhang, Lin, Lei Zhang, & David Zhang. (2009). Finger-knuckle-print verification based on band-limited phase-only correlation. In: *International Conference on Computer Analysis of Images and Patterns*, pp. 141–148. Springer, Berlin, Heidelberg.
22. Ross, Arun, Anil Jain, & S. Pankati. (1999). A prototype hand geometry-based verification system. In: *Proceedings of 2nd Conference on Audio and Video Based Biometric Person Authentication*, pp. 166–171.
23. Fabregas, Joan, & Marcos Faundez-Zanuy. (2009). Biometric recognition performing in a bioinspired system. *Cognitive Computation*, 1(3), 257–267.
24. El-Alfy, El-Sayed M., & Radwan E. Abdel-Aal. (2013). Abductive learning ensembles for hand shape identification. *Cognitive Computation*, 6(3), 321–330.
25. Faundez-Zanuy, Marcos, Jiri Mekyska, & Xavier Font-Aragones. (2014). A new hand image database simultaneously acquired in visible, near-infrared, and thermal spectrums. *Cognitive Computation*, 6(2), 230–240.
26. Im, Sang-Kyun, Hyung-Man Park, Young-Woo Kim, Sang-Chan Han, Soo-Won Kim, Chul-Hee Kang, & Chang-Kyung Chung. (2001). A biometric identification system by extracting hand vein patterns. *Journal - Korean Physical Society*, 38(3), 268–272.

27. Kumar, Ajay, & K. Venkata Prathyusha. (2009). Personal authentication using hand vein triangulation and knuckle shape. *IEEE Transactions on Image Processing*, 18(9), 2127–2136.
28. Zhang, David, Wai-Kin Kong, Jane You, & Michael Wong. (2003). Online palmprint identification. *IEEE Transactions on Pattern Analysis and Machine Intelligence*, 25(9), 1041–1050.
29. Zhang, David D. (2004). *Palmprint Authentication*. Springer Science & Business Media.
30. Zheng, Ping. (2010). Gaussian shape descriptor for palmprint authentication. *Cognitive Computation*, 2(4), 303–311.
31. Darini, Mojtaba, & Houshmand Amiri Doumari. (2015). Personal authentication using palm-print features: A Survey. *International Journal of Innovative Research in Science, Engineering, and Technology*, 4(9), 21–25.
32. Pretty, I. A., & D. Sweet. (2001). A look at forensic dentistry – Part 1: The role of teeth in the determination of human identity. *British Dental Journal*, 190(7), 359–366.
33. Jain, Anil K., Friederike D. Griess, & Scott D. Connell. (2002). On-line signature verification. *Pattern Recognition*, 35(12), 2963–2972.
34. Monrose, Fabian, & Aviel D. Rubin. (2000). Keystroke dynamics as a biometric for authentication. *Future Generation Computer Systems*, 16(4), 351–359.
35. Chibelushi, Claude C., F. Deravi, & J.S. Mason. (1994). Voice and facial image integration for person recognition. In: *Multimedia Technologies and Future Applications*, pp. 155–161. Pentech Press Publishers, London.
36. Gafurov, Davrondzhon. (2007). A survey of biometric gait recognition: Approaches, security and challenges. In: *Annual Norwegian Computer Science Conference*, pp. 19–21. Norway: Annual Norwegian Computer Science Conference.
37. Kumar, Neeraj, Alexander Berg, Peter N. Belhumeur, & Shree Nayar. (2011). Describable visual attributes for face verification and image search. *IEEE Transactions on Pattern Analysis and Machine Intelligence*, 33(10), 1962–1977.
38. Ng, Choon Boon, Yong Haur Tay, & Bok Min Goi. (2012). Vision-based human gender recognition: A survey. arXiv preprint arXiv:1204.1611.
39. Tome, Pedro, Julian Fierrez, Ruben Vera-Rodriguez, & Mark S. Nixon. (2014). Soft biometrics and their application in person recognition at a distance. *IEEE Transactions on Information Forensics and Security*, 9(3), 464–475.
40. Dehshibi, Mohammad Mahdi, & Azam Bastanfard. (2010). A new algorithm for age recognition from facial images. *Signal Processing*, 90(8), 2431–2444.
41. Chaves-Gonzalez, J.M., M.A. Vega-Rodriguez, J.A. Gomez-Pulido, & J.M. Sanchez-Perez. (2010). Detecting skin in face recognition systems: A colour spaces study. *Digital Signal Processing*, 20(3), 806–823.
42. Koide, Kenji, & Jun Miura. (2016). Identification of a specific person using colour, height, and gait features for a person following robot. *Robotics and Autonomous Systems*, 84, 76–87.
43. Lee, Jung-Eun, Anil K. Jain, & Rong Jin. (2008). Scars, marks and tattoos (SMT): Soft biometric for suspect and victim identification. In: *2008 Biometrics Symposium*, pp. 1–8. IEEE.
44. Hayashi, J., M. Yasumoto, H. Ito, & H. Koshimizu. (2002, Aug.). Age and gender estimation based on wrinkle texture and colour of facial images. In: *Proceedings of the Sixteenth International Conference on Pattern Recognition*, pp. 405–408. Quebec City, Canada.
45. Jain, Anil K., Arun Ross, & Umut Uludag. (2005). Biometric template security: Challenges and solutions. In: *2005 13th European Signal Processing Conference*, pp. 1–4. IEEE.

3 | Machine Learning and Deep Learning for Person Recognition

S. Mehra*, V. Ranga, R. Agarwal

Department of Information Technology, Delhi Technological University, Delhi, India

1. Introduction

The real, well-established physical characteristics used in biometric technologies include fingerprints, iris patterns, and DNA (deoxyribonucleic acid) due to their constancy, universality, uniqueness, and invariance. Meanwhile, speech recognition—also known as voice biometrics—falls under another emerging biometrics pillar [1]. Voice characteristics offer several appealing advantages compared to other biometric technologies. They are omnipresent, dynamic, adaptive, non-intrusive, and can be implemented remotely. Like traditional biometric technologies, voice biometrics can provide valuable information for forensic investigations, intelligence gathering, patient identification, and other purposes [2]. They are increasingly being used to enhance security measures in financial services [3] and border control [4], as well as serving as an additional layer for access control and authentication. Furthermore, speech contains health-related data, which could open the door to new biometric applications such as wearables for non-invasive early disease detection and emotional state analysis [5]. The importance of biological traits in resolving criminal cases has increased recently. Biometrics—such as voiceprints, faces, fingerprints, and DNA—have become indispensable tools in criminal investigations due to their distinctiveness and uniqueness, and they are now maintained as ministerial-level databases [6]. Traditionally, authentication methods relied on passwords. However, many people do not change their passwords often, use the same ones, or select easy-to-guess passwords. Some users fail to take precautions to secure their passwords, such as using a password manager or storing them in an encrypted file. As a result, passwords are vulnerable to hacking attempts, and there is always a risk that users may forget or misplace them.

In this context, biometric-based authentication systems shown in Figure 1 are becoming increasingly popular due to their widespread availability in computers, cell phones, and other devices. 'Biometrics' refers to biological traits or measurements used to verify an individual's identity.

*Corresponding author: mehra.sunakshi623@gmail.com

DOI: 10.1201/9781003560012-3

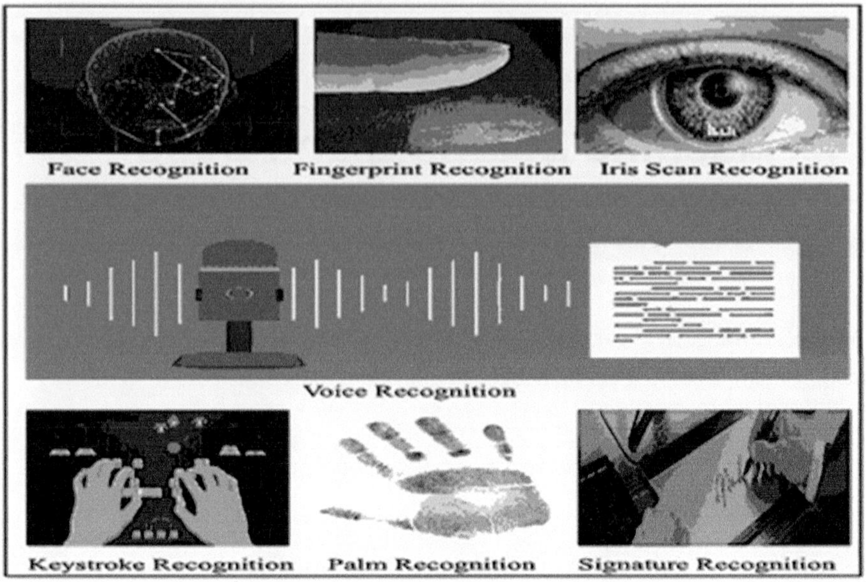

Figure 1: Biometric recognition methods.

However, it has been found that biometrics-based authentication techniques can pose security concerns related to presentation attacks (PAs), even though they seem to be safer than passwords [7]. A PA system evaluates whether a collected biometric feature is authentic or not [8]. To address these security challenges, complementary equipment must be deployed. Consequently, the model becomes more sophisticated, and the authentication process takes longer [6].

Although using biometrics has many advantages, storing raw biometric data poses privacy and security risks, including identity theft, privacy invasion, and data breaches [9]. Raw biometric templates, if stored without adequate security measures, could compromise the original biometric data. Hackers targeting biometric databases may obtain registered users' biometric information and use it to impersonate them, gaining access to associated authentication systems [10]. Unlike passwords, biometric information cannot be altered once compromised, which exacerbates the situation as the data is lost forever. Cancellable biometrics is a widely used and successful strategy for biometric security, but there are other methods to protect biometric data as well. The same irreversible modification is applied to query data during the verification or identification stage. The modified template and the query data match in the transformed domain [7]. In other words, cancellable biometrics utilize the modified biometric data rather than the original data for authentication [8]. If it is discovered that a set of biometric data was altered, it may be revoked, and a new set obtained. Certain essential standards for cancellable biometrics are established in the ISO/IEC 24745 standard [11]. They are listed in the following order:

1. **Renewability:** The capacity to remove a compromised biometric template and replace it with a new one is a critical component of cancellable biometrics.

2. **Non-inevitability:** To protect the privacy of biometric data, unique templates made from a user's biometrics should be application-specific. It is prohibited to use the same modified template in more than one application.
3. **Performance:** Template protection approaches should not make biometric systems less effective at recognizing identities. That is, recognition accuracy for cancellable biometrics should be comparable before and after feature transformation.

In order to achieve excellent recognition performance in cancellable biometrics while maintaining the privacy of biometric data, we focus on feature extraction and learning methodologies in our survey work. Different perspectives on the taxonomy of feature representations are explored. The survey delves deeply into three main topics: types of cancellable transformation functions, feature extraction and learning strategies, and performance evaluations of cancellable biometric systems using these techniques. Secure voice-based communication is illustrated in Figure 2.

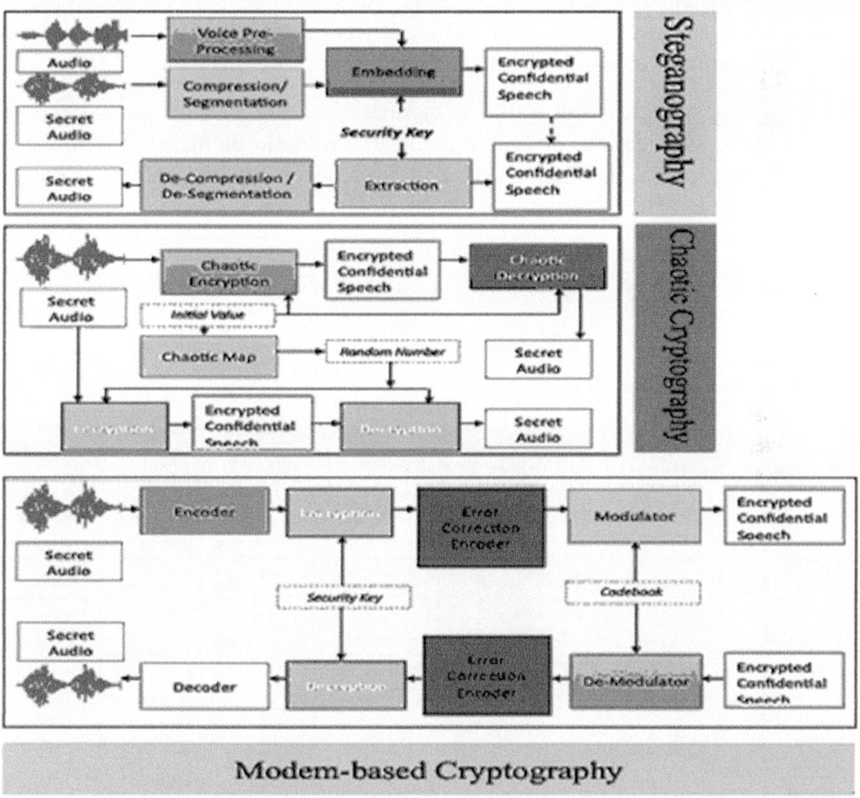

Figure 2: Secure voice communication based on: (a) steganography, (b) chaotic cryptography, (c) modem-based cryptography technique.

1. **Steganography:** Steganography is a technique that secures covert communication in voice-based systems by embedding secret information in

non-secret data. Steganography allows for private communication without raising red flags, as it encodes messages into sound waves.

2. **Chaotic Cryptography:** Chaotic cryptography harnesses the complex behavior of chaotic systems to encrypt voice data. This technique utilizes chaotic maps or systems to generate cryptographic keys and algorithms, enhancing the security of voice-based communications against unauthorized access.
3. **Modem-based Cryptography:** Modem-based cryptography employs advanced modulation techniques to secure voice transmissions over communication channels. By integrating cryptographic protocols into modem signals, this method ensures data integrity and confidentiality, safeguarding voice communication from eavesdropping and interception.

2. Attacks

Biometric-based authentication attacks target vulnerabilities in systems that rely on biometric characteristics for identity verification as shown in Figure 3. These attacks can exploit various weaknesses in the authentication process, such as:

1. **Spoofing Attacks:** Access to a biometric system can be gained through the theft, duplication, or reproduction of synthetic biometric features [12]. Spoofing attacks, in which an attacker fabricates biometric features or data, or

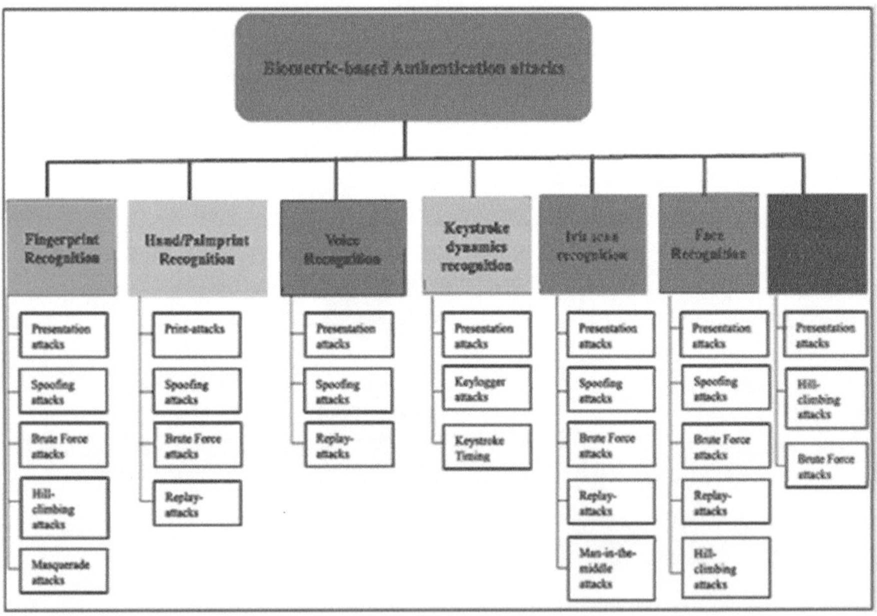

Figure 3: An examination of the various forms of biometric authentication and the associated threats they could encounter is presented in "A Classification of Attacks on Biometric Authentication Methods".

reconstructs the original biometric image using the biometric hash code, can also be used to circumvent biometric authentication systems.

2. **Presentation Attacks:** An alternative form of impersonation or spoofing attack, known as a presentation attack, is typically conducted with the use of Presentation Attack Instruments (PAIs). These can include silicone fingerprint impersonators, lenses, masks, and other devices. Attackers may exploit PAIs in various ways to circumvent biometric systems. Presentation attacks can target most biometric modalities, such as voice, fingerprint, face, and signature identification systems.
3. **Brute-force Attacks:** Attacking a biometric system by repeatedly attempting to fool it occurs mostly due to the system's inability to distinguish between similar samples, stemming from a lack of trustworthy data [13].
4. **Hill-Climbing Attacks:** In one type of brute force attack, the attacker fabricates biometric data and submits it repeatedly, gradually refining the results. Ultimately, this strategy may enable the attacker to gain acceptance or illegal access to the biometric system.
5. **Masquerade Attack:** One type of spoofing attack spoofs the channel between the sensor and the feature extractor module by using readily available bogus data, such as digitized latent fingerprints or digital face photographs [14, 15].
6. **Replay Attack:** An attacker intercepts and retransmits biometric data in a replay attack, a kind of man-in-the-middle assault. Since the attacker only needs to intercept the data and then decode or process it further, this attack does not require specialized knowledge.
7. **Man-Made Attack:** When an attacker intercepts or modifies sensor data while it is being sent between the biometric feature extractor, biometric template generator, or matcher on the application device, it is known as a 'man-in-the-middle' attack. The attacker can acquire biometric traits to launch further attacks by intercepting this data.
8. **Keylogger Attack:** Installing malicious software or hardware on a victim's device to record keystrokes is known as a keylogger attack [16]. Sensitive data such as credit card details, passwords, usernames, and private communications may be included in the collected data. The attacker obtains this data to steal personal information, commit identity theft, or gain illegal access to accounts. Keyloggers can be installed on a device physically, through malicious downloads, or via phishing emails. They pose a serious security risk because they operate surreptitiously, making them difficult to detect.

3. Speech Recognition Systems

In this section, we discuss modern speech recognition systems (SRS) that demonstrate remarkable resilience against various performance-degrading factors, such as linguistic accents and dialects. Creating voice datasets is a fundamental step in developing these systems. Especially for specialized applications, unique speech datasets must be constructed, as the required data is often not readily available. During the creation of voice databases, some variabilities that impact SRS performance—like room reverberation, channel mismatch, and individual vocal variations—are typically addressed. But when designing and developing the SRS, other important elements such as background noise, emotional tones, and linguistic accents and dialects need to be taken into account [17]. An ongoing project at the National Institute of Standards and Technology (NIST), known as the Speaker Identification Evaluation (SRE) programme, aims to advance speaker identification technology and explore innovative concepts in this field [18]. The primary goals of the programme include developing large-scale speech datasets and state-of-the-art SRS capable of handling a wide range of variance and mismatch. Another notable initiative, RedDot [19], gathers speech data from mobile devices to identify speakers. The database comprises voice samples from 45 native and non-native English speakers across 16 different countries. It includes brief test phrases demonstrating significant intra- and inter-speaker variability and a diverse range of phonetic content. Capturing a broad spectrum of speaker variance is the primary objective of the RedDot database.

Speakers from around the world were chosen, and information was gathered from them in 91 different sessions to accomplish the main objective. The research community can test their systems using the rich datasets and opportunities provided by the RedDot and NIST speech recognition assessments; however, the variability of the data is limited by the evaluations' primary focus on controlled data gathering using landline or mobile phones [20]. "Speakers in the Wild (SITW)" is a new speech dataset created to overcome some of the shortcomings of earlier datasets, particularly NIST-SRE with the aim of capturing a wider range of variability, SITW is a speaker recognition database specifically designed for text-independent speaker identification applications [21]. The public can access the extensive audio-visual speaker identification dataset VoxCeleb2 [22], which was compiled from open-source media and comprises approximately a million words spoken by over 6,000 individuals. Besides its scale, the dataset was intentionally created to address issues observed in previous datasets, including recordings in controlled environments, size limitations due to manual annotations, and restricted accessibility for the scientific community [23]. Accent and dialect recognition systems have proven highly beneficial in mitigating the variability associated with accents and dialects and in developing reliable SRS (Figure 4).

A weighted accent classification algorithm was developed using a variety of phrases [24]. This study employed support vector machines (SVMs) and extreme learning machines (ELMs) to address the accent and dialect classification challenge, utilizing the TIMIT dataset, which includes 630 speakers from eight different dialect regions in the US. Research into accent and dialect classification is crucial for enhancing speaker and speech recognition systems tailored to specific regions, as well as for developing databases that encompass regional accents. For instance, to facilitate research in voice recognition, an Algerian speech corpus was established, comprising 300 native speakers of Algerian Modern Standard Arabic (MSA)[25]. In the Philippines, a method for categorizing accents was developed using audio recordings of 150 native Filipino residents [26]. MLP and k-NN classifiers were trained with features extracted from Mel-frequency cepstral coefficients (MFCC). The MFCC-MLP-based accent classification system achieved a recognition accuracy of 56.19%. Additionally, a small-scale database included 11 speakers with distinct Canadian accents and fluency in French [27].

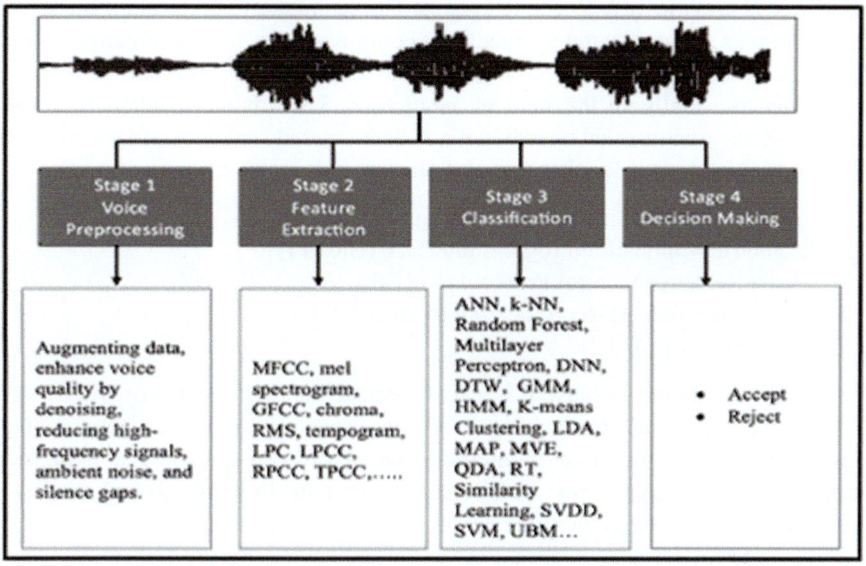

Figure 4: A comprehensive framework for voice authentication systems.

Among these speakers were 7 men and 4 women, ranging in age from 19 to 36 years. Voice samples were recorded in two different locations: a lively college cafe and a conference room.

4. Advancements in Voice Authentication Technology

For every speech recognition system, there are two main stages of operation: enrollment and verification. The technology records the speaker's voice during enrollment to produce a unique voice print, template, or model that captures specific speech elements necessary for recognition. The system compares a fresh speech sample or utterance with the previously created voice print during the verification stage. Speech recognition systems come in two flavors: text-dependent and text-independent. The same predetermined text or passphrase is used for both enrollment and verification in a text-dependent system. This consistency ensures that the system uses the speaker's unique pronunciation of that specific sentence to identify them. Text-independent systems, on the other hand, offer flexibility by using different speech samples for enrollment and verification. This approach is often employed in forensic contexts where enrollment may occur accidentally or without explicit user consent. These systems are crucial for security, authentication, and forensic investigations as they utilize advanced technology to identify individuals based on their speech patterns.

Finding the speaker among a recognized collection of voices is the goal of speaker identification, or SIS (Speaker Identification System). It involves analyzing voice wave data to identify the source of a particular utterance. Speaker identification typically employs a 1:N matching technique, where a match is found between the speech and N previously recorded templates. This technology is crucial for numerous applications as it can accurately identify people based on their distinctive speech characteristics. Standards are crucial for the development and maintenance of technology, especially in the field of biometrics. The advancement of biometric technologies is greatly aided by national and international standardization initiatives. Important initiatives for speaker recognition standards include:

1. Speaker Verification Application Program Interface (SVAPI)
2. Biometric Application Program Interface (BioAPI)
3. Media Resource Control Protocol (MRCP)
4. Voice Extensible Markup Language (VoiceXML)
5. Voice Browser (W3C)

BioAPI stands out because it is a fundamental standard created by the BioAPI Consortium, an alliance comprising over 120 companies and organizations. This consortium aims to promote biometrics innovation and commercial expansion through standardized practices. Additionally, other notable standards and initiatives contributing to speaker recognition advancements could include:

1. ISO/IEC 19794-7 (Speaker Recognition Biometric Data Interchange Format)
2. NIST (National Institute of Standards and Technology) Speaker Recognition Evaluations
3. ITU-T (International Telecommunication Union: Telecommunication Standardization Sector) standards related to voice and speech processing
4. IEEE (Institute of Electrical and Electronics Engineers) standards on biometric technologies.

These assessments and standards provide SRS with frameworks and benchmarks that ensure correctness, reliability, and interoperability, promoting their broad use and usefulness in a range of applications. Speech recognition technology is versatile and ever-evolving, finding applications across various domains. Voice biometric systems are predominantly employed in phone-related functionalities. They serve critical roles in sectors such as public services, healthcare, finance, call centers, e-commerce, and customer authentication for service requests. Additionally, these systems play a significant role in verifying identities for home confinement and probation purposes.

5. Evaluating Biometric System Effectiveness: Performance Metrics and Insights

The effectiveness of speaker recognition and biometric systems is influenced by a number of factors, including:

1. **Equal Error Rate (EER):** The formula FAR = FRR = EER is commonly used in biometric systems to determine the Equal Error Rate (EER). The False Acceptance Rate (FAR) represents the percentage of fraudulent attempts that the system mistakenly accepts, while the False Rejection Rate (FRR) indicates the fraction of legitimate attempts that the system erroneously rejects. The EER, which is the point where the system achieves a balance between

accepting legitimate users and appropriately rejecting imposters, is marked by the equality of FAR and FRR.

2. **Relative Operating Characteristic (ROC) Curve:** Plotting the ROC curve often involves using the True Positive Rate (TPR) and False Positive Rate (FPR).
3. **FAR:** The FAR in a biometric system is typically calculated using the following formula as mentioned in Eq. 1:

$$\text{FAR} = \frac{\text{Number of impostor attempts accepted}}{\text{Total number of impostor attempts}} \times 100\% \quad (1)$$

To put it another way, FAR calculates the proportion of false attempts that the biometric system mistakenly recognizes as authentic.

4. **False Rejection Rate (FRR):** The FRR in a biometric system is calculated using the following formula:

$$\text{FRR} = \frac{\text{Number of genuine attempts rejected}}{\text{Total number of genuine attempts}} \times 100\% \quad (2)$$

FRR calculates the proportion of legitimate attempts that the biometric system mistakenly rejects as fraudulent attempts.

5. **Template Capacity:** Template capacity is often determined by the available storage divided by the size of each template, taking into account any overhead or management considerations. Therefore, the formula to estimate template capacity could be represented as:

$$\text{Template Capacity} = \frac{\text{Total storage capacity}}{\text{Size of each biometric template}} \times 100\% \quad (3)$$

This provides an approximate measure of how many unique biometric templates the system can handle based on its storage resources and operational constraints.

6. Classification Models for Voiceprint Recognition and Authentication Security

After extracting voice features (MFCCs), several well-known machine learning methods were tested on a test set and trained on a training set of feature vectors. These methods included Support Vector Machines (SVM), Artificial Neural Networks (ANN), k-NN, and Random Forest (RF) [28] (Khan et al., 2019) (Table 1). Ten-fold cross-validation (TFCV) was employed in constructing and evaluating the learning models. In the TFCV technique, the original feature vector is randomly divided into approximately ten equal subsamples. Ten subsamples are used as training feature vectors, and one subsample is randomly selected as the test feature vector. This process repeats until each of the ten subsamples has been used as the test feature vector [29].

The supervised machine learning model SVM is utilized for both regression and classification by analyzing data and identifying patterns [30]. This widely used discriminative classifier effectively distinguishes the genuine speaker from a group of imposters by simulating a boundary line. The Sequential Minimal Optimization (SMO) algorithm [31] was employed to train the SVM classifier. The k-NN algorithm belongs to a family of instance-based, slow-learning algorithms. It identifies the k most similar samples in the training dataset to classify an unknown data sample from a test dataset. Implementing instance-based classification algorithms is crucial for successful k-NN application [32]. In our implementation, we utilized a methodology based on Euclidean distance [33].

RF, a supervised learning model used for both regression and classification problems, constructs numerous decision trees during training and aggregates their outputs to determine the mode class. It is a robust and highly accurate classifier that effectively avoids overfitting issues [34]. The bootstrapping of samples technique was employed to implement RF in this study. ANNs are simplified models of the human brain, composed of interconnected nodes [35]. Typically, an ANN comprises three layers: input, hidden, and output. Its primary function is processing inputs and transforming them into useful outputs. The neuron activation function used in this study was the log-sigmoid function. Additionally, we constructed the Multilayer Perceptron (MLP) algorithm using a back-propagation feed-forward method to categorize instances [36].

Table 1: Classification models for voiceprint recognition and authentication security

References	Classification methods
Khan et al., 2019 [28]	ANN
Khan et al., 2019 [28]	k-NN
Jiang & Chen, 2016 [29]	TFCV
Breiman, 2001 [34]	Random Forest
Yee & Ahmad, 2008 [36]	Multilayer Perceptron
Narendiranath et al., 2018 [37]	DNN
Cengiz & Arıoz, 2016) [38]	DWT
Mporas et al., 2007 [39]	GMM
Gofman et al., 2016 [40]	HMM
Hua et al., 2013 [41]	K-means Clustering
Li et al., 2020 [42]	MAP
Lu et al., 2019 [43]	SVDD
Singh, 2018 [30]	SVM
Platt, 1998 [31]	SMO
Chauhan et al., 2022 [44]	UBM
Zhang et al., 2020 [45]	VAD
Isyanto et al., 2022 [46]	CNN

In their 2016 work on feature-level biometric fusion for mobile devices, Gofman, Smith, and Mitra developed a multimodal biometric system that utilized Hidden

Markov Models (HMMs) to combine facial and vocal data [40]. They suggested that integrating multiple biometric modalities could enhance recognition accuracy. This system was implemented on a Samsung Galaxy S5 (SG5) and tested under real-world conditions. In the same year, Singh, Gencaga, and Raj recognized the need to address voice imitation and decided to investigate vocal impersonations by mimicry experts [47]. Their focus was on analyzing formants and formant-related features to assess the extent and nature of these manipulations. The ability of Deep Neural Networks (DNNs) to model complex relationships in speech features has recently enhanced the performance of HMMs compared to traditional Gaussian Mixture Models (GMMs) in speech recognition. In their study, "Comparison of Speech Features on the Speech Recognition Task", the authors evaluated various speech parameterization techniques within HMM-based speech recognition systems [39, 48]. They also reviewed parameterization methods cited by other researchers. Additionally, Winda et al. [49] introduced an innovative Arduino-based system that enables motorbike owners to start or stop their vehicle with a simple voice command, eliminating the need for a traditional mechanical key. ANNs and RNNs are considered less reliable than CNNs. Furthermore, machine learning methods such as GMM, GMM-UBM, GMM-HMM, and HMM have limitations in processing complex data and are only capable of analyzing smaller datasets effectively.

ANNs and DNNs are deep learning techniques that are generally less reliable compared to RNNs and CNNs [37]. Although RNNs are designed for sequential data modeling, they are less compatible with features compared to CNNs. One of the major issues with RNNs is the problem of gradient loss. To address the gradient vanishing problem, Long Short-Term Memory (LSTM) networks are often integrated with RNNs. However, a notable drawback of LSTMs is their higher memory requirements during training. In addition, while CNNs are generally more reliable than ANNs and RNNs, employing GMMs, GMM-Universal Background Model (GMM-UBM), GMM-Hidden Markov Model (GMM-HMM), and HMM techniques presents challenges in processing complex data, as they are only capable of handling smaller datasets effectively [44]. SVDD is a classification technique that eliminates impostor components, while UBM is a method for identifying human-specific traits [43]. SVMs, a statistical classification technique, separates feature sets using a hyperplane.

A deep learning speech biometric model was developed using CNN Residual networks and a hybrid feature extraction method combining Discrete Wavelet Transform (DWT) and Mel-Frequency Cepstral Coefficients (MFCC) [46]. The CNN Residual networks enhance classification accuracy and streamline the training and validation processes. Meanwhile, the hybrid extraction method, utilizing DWT and MFCC, effectively removes noise interference, identifies voice pattern shapes based on individual characteristics, and selects the essential voice features [38]. To improve voice recognition accuracy, various classification techniques such as DTW, MAP [42], MVE, and VAD have been developed. Dynamic Time Warping (DTW) is a time series analysis technique that measures the similarity between voice samples at different speeds. The Maximum A Posteriori (MAP) technique reduces noise components in speech signals. Minimum Verification Error (MVE) minimizes speaker verification errors. Additionally, Voice Activity Detection (VAD) identifies the presence or absence of human speech.

7. Navigating Challenges in Voice Verification Systems

Even while speech biometric technology has advanced to the point that it can now automatically identify people by their voices, factors such as stress, illness, medicine, and other physical difficulties might negatively affect this automated system [50]. The following is a list of the issues that negatively impact voice verification performance. One of the most significant issues with speech verification systems is background noise. According to Pal et al. [51] this might have an impact not only on matching performance but also on the quality of the template that was gathered in such a noisy environment.

1. **Device Quality:** Tovarek et al. [48] emphasize that the quality of equipment significantly impacts the fidelity of recorded audio. High-end devices often feature superior microphones capable of capturing exceptionally clear sound. Key factors used to assess microphone quality include maximum sound pressure level, frequency response, and sensitivity.
2. **Age-related Variability:** As individuals age, their vocal characteristics naturally evolve. This poses a challenge for maintaining accuracy in databases over time, as children grow into adults and young adults experience noticeable changes in their voices.
3. **Emotional State:** A person's emotional state can significantly alter their voice characteristics, rendering it difficult for a system to accurately identify or verify their identity. Whether experiencing excitement or depression, these emotional states can manifest in distinct vocal patterns.
4. **Replay Attack:** A straightforward yet effective method known as a replay attack involves recording and replaying voice samples from individuals in the database to gain unauthorized access to an Automatic Voice Identification System (AVIS).

8. Conclusions

This study reviewed recent research on the application of machine learning and deep learning in biometric authentication and identification processes, emphasizing security considerations.

1. The study focuses on two main objectives: Ensuring the secure storage of biometric traits and mitigating risks associated with biometric applications.
2. Machine learning techniques play dual roles in biometric applications: Providing a secure foundation for these applications and enhancing the recognition and authentication processes.
3. In biometric recognition-authentication processes, enrollment and authentication represent pivotal stages. The secure acquisition of biometric

traits during these phases is critical. Protecting these acquired characteristics drives the development of transformation-based methods and biometric cryptosystems aimed at enhancing security.

4. Biometric recognition-authentication processes utilizing machine learning algorithms consist of two key stages. Initially, biometric traits are identified for feature investigation and analysis. Subsequently, machine learning techniques such as SVM, KNN, NB, ANN, etc., are employed to train the system using the collected characteristic features. These phases remain consistent, with variations occurring in the methodologies employed within each phase.
5. Ensuring a secure platform for biometric applications involves addressing vulnerabilities arising from usage and the environment. Table 1 outlines machine learning approaches across these pivotal stages.
6. Recent research highlights two primary biometric methodologies: Machine learning methods and statistical approaches. The combination of specific techniques yields varying levels of success with machine learning technologies. In biometric applications, the effectiveness of hybrid techniques is generally observed to surpass that of single techniques.
7. Based on usage preference, fingerprint recognition systems are the most commonly employed biometric methods. Several factors contribute to this preference. Fingerprint features offer high discriminatory power, making them highly reliable. Moreover, obtaining fingerprints is simpler compared to techniques such as iris, retina, or gait recognition. Additionally, evaluating the validity of certain biometric traits, such as retina scans, can pose risks to individuals. For these reasons, fingerprint recognition stands out as one of the most dependable biometric techniques.
8. Biometric applications require datasets for testing purposes. Fingerprint datasets are extensive, whereas datasets for gait analysis are comparatively limited.

This chapter explores recent advancements in biometric applications, focusing on secure login methods and machine learning techniques as discussed in the literature. By providing detailed descriptions of these methodologies, the study benefits researchers interested in exploring biometric authentication and identification processes, and in developing secure biometric platforms using machine learning. Our findings also offer valuable insights for system and application developers aiming to innovate in software development. Ultimately, end users need to be aware of cutting-edge preventive techniques for secure storage of biometric data and effective countermeasures, which our recommendations aim to facilitate.

References

1. Babu, A., E. Raoul, G. Kassahun, I. Dufour, D. Mandal, & D. Thuau. (2024). Programmable polymeric-interface for voiceprint biometrics. *Advanced Materials Technologies*, 9(4), 2301551.

2. Wu, Y., J. Han, Z. Jian, & W. Xu. (2024). Human voice sensing through radio-frequency technologies: A comprehensive review. *IEEE Transactions on Instrumentation and Measurement*, 73, 1–20.
3. Alkaseasbeh, M.M., B.R. Shammout, & T.A.K. Alqurran. (2024). Biometric authentication in fintech and its role in increasing security of financial services. *Migration Letters*, 21(S4), 885–900.
4. Hasan, M.K., Z. Weichen, N. Safie, F.R.A. Ahmed, & T.M. Ghazal. (2024). A survey on key agreement and authentication protocol for Internet of Things application. *IEEE Access*, 12, 61642–61666.
5. Vakulenko, D., L. Vakulenko, & O. Hevko. (2024). Prospect of creating a virtual reality system with feedback for the correction of the patient's psychological state based on the results of the analysis of arterial pulsations registered during blood pressure measurement using the Oranta-AO information system. In: *Arterial Oscillography: New Capabilities of the Blood Pressure Monitor with the Oranta-AO Information System*. Nova Science Publishers.
6. Toygar, O., F.O. Babalola, & Y. Bitirim. (2020). FYO: A novel multimodal vein database with palmar, dorsal, and wrist biometrics. *IEEE Access*, 8, 82461–82470.
7. Vishwakarma, A.K., S. Chaurasia, K. Kumar, Y.N. Singh, & R. Chaurasia. (2024). Internet of things technology, research, and challenges: A survey. *Multimedia Tools and Applications*, 1–36.
8. Mahmood, K., Z. Ghaffar, M. Farooq, K. Yahya, A.K. Das, & S.A. Chaudhry. (2024). A security enhanced chaotic-map based authentication protocol for internet of drones. *IEEE Internet of Things Journal*, 11(12), 22301–22309.
9. Karampidis, K., M. Rousouliotis, E. Linardos, & E. Kavallieratou. (2021). A comprehensive survey of fingerprint presentation attack detection. *Journal of Surveillance, Security, and Safety*, 2(4), 117–161.
10. Dong, X., J. Park, Z. Jin, A.B.J. Teoh, M. Tistarelli, & K. Wong. (2024). On the security risk of preimage attack on cancelable biometrics. *Journal of King Saud University - Computer and Information Sciences*, 36(5), 102060.
11. Sumalatha, U., K.K. Prakasha, S. Prabhu, & V.C. Nayak. (2024). A comprehensive review of unimodal and multimodal fingerprint biometric authentication systems: Fusion, attacks, and template protection. *IEEE Access*, 12, 64300–64334.
12. Biggio, B., Z. Akhtar, G. Fumera, G.L. Marcialis, & F. Roli. (2012). Security evaluation of biometric authentication systems under real spoofing attacks. *IET Biometrics*, 1(1), 11–24.
13. Mihailescu, P. (2007). The fuzzy vault for fingerprints is vulnerable to brute force attack. arXiv preprint arXiv:0708.2974.
14. Karimovich, G.S., & K.Z. Turakulovich. (2016, November). Biometric cryptosystems: Open issues and challenges. In: *2016 International Conference on Information Science and Communications Technologies (ICISCT)*, pp. 1–3. IEEE.
15. Roberts, C. (2007). Biometric attack vectors and defences. *Computers and Security*, 26(1), 14–25.
16. Bhardwaj, A., & S. Goundar. (2020). Keyloggers: Silent cyber security weapons. *Network Security*, 2020(2), 14–19.
17. Saquib, Z., N. Salam, R.P. Nair, N. Pandey, & A. Joshi. (2010, December). A survey on automatic speaker recognition systems. In: *International Conference on Multimedia, Computer Graphics, and Broadcasting*, pp. 134–145. Springer Berlin Heidelberg.
18. Kozlov, A., O. Kudashev, Y. Matveev, T. Pekhovsky, K. Simonchik, & A. Shulipa. (2013). SVID speaker recognition system for NIST SRE 2012. In: *Speech and Computer: 15th International Conference, SPECOM 2013*, Pilsen, Czech Republic, September 1–5, 2013. *Proceedings* 15, pp. 278–285. Springer International Publishing.

19. Lee, K.A., A. Larcher, G. Wang, P. Kenny, N. Brummer, D. Van Leeuwen, ... & J. Perez. (2015, September). The RedDots data collection for speaker recognition. In: *Interspeech, 2015.*
20. McLaren, M., L. Ferrer, D. Castan, & A. Lawson. (2016, September). The 2016 speakers in the wild speaker recognition evaluation. In: *Interspeech*, pp. 823–827.
21. McLaren, M., L. Ferrer, D. Castan, & A. Lawson. (2016, September). The speakers in the wild (SITW) speaker recognition database. In: *Interspeech*, pp. 818–822.
22. Chung, J.S., A. Nagrani, & A. Zisserman. (2018). Voxceleb2: Deep speaker recognition. arXiv preprint arXiv:1806.05622.
23. Fisher, W. (1986). The DARPA speech recognition research database: Specifications and status. In: *Proc. DARPA Workshop on Speech Recognition*, pp. 93–99.
24. Rizwan, M., & D.V. Anderson. (2018). A weighted accent classification using multiple words. *Neurocomputing*, 277, 120–128.
25. Selouani, S.A., & M. Boudraa. (2010). Algerian Arabic speech database (ALGASD): Corpus design and automatic speech recognition application. *Arabian Journal for Science and Engineering*, 35(2), 157–166.
26. Danao, G., J. Torres, J.V. Tubio, & L. Vea. (2017, December). Tagalog regional accent classification in the Philippines. In: *2017 IEEE 9th International Conference on Humanoid, Nanotechnology, Information Technology, Communication and Control, Environment and Management* (*HNICEM*), pp. 1–6. IEEE.
27. Thullier, F., B. Bouchard, & B.A.J. Menelas. (2017). A text-independent speaker authentication system for mobile devices. *Cryptography*, 1(3), 16.
28. Khan, S., H. Ali, Z. Ullah, N. Minallah, S. Maqsood, & A. Hafeez. (2019). KNN and ANN-based recognition of handwritten Pashto letters using zoning features. arXiv preprint arXiv:1904.03391.
29. Jiang, P., & J. Chen. (2016). Displacement prediction of landslide based on generalized regression neural networks with K-fold cross-validation. *Neurocomputing*, 198, 40–47.
30. Singh, S. (2018). Support vector machine-based approaches for real time automatic speaker recognition system. *International Journal of Applied Engineering Research*, 13(10), 8561–8567.
31. Platt, J. (1998). *Sequential Minimal Optimization: A Fast Algorithm for Training Support Vector Machines*. ResearchGate.
32. Aha, D.W., D. Kibler, & M.K. Albert. (1991). Instance-based learning algorithms. *Machine Learning*, 6, 37–66.
33. Guo, G., H. Wang, D. Bell, Y. Bi, & K. Greer. (2003). KNN model-based approach in classification. In: *On The Move to Meaningful Internet Systems 2003: CoopIS, DOA, and ODBASE: OTM Confederated International Conferences*, CoopIS, DOA, and ODBASE 2003. Catania, Sicily, Italy, November 3–7, 2003. *Proceedings*, pp. 986–996. Springer Berlin Heidelberg.
34. Breiman, L. (2001). Random forests. *Machine Learning*, 45, 5–32.
35. Nagy, H.M., K.A.N.D. Watanabe, & M. Hirano. (2002). Prediction of sediment load concentration in rivers using artificial neural network model. *Journal of Hydraulic Engineering*, 128(6), 588–595.
36. Yee, C.S., & A.M. Ahmad. (2008, December). Malay language text-independent speaker verification using NN-MLP classifier with MFCC. In: *2008 International Conference on Electronic Design*, pp. 1–5. IEEE.
37. Narendiranath Babu, T., A. Aravind, A. Rakesh, M. Jahzan, D. Rama Prabha, & M. Ramalinga Viswanathan. (2018). Automatic fault classification for journal bearings using ANN and DNN. *Archives of Acoustics*, 43.

38. Cengiz, Y., & Y.D.U. Arioz. (2016, November). An application for speech denoising using discrete wavelet transform. In: *2016 20th National Biomedical Engineering Meeting* (*BIYOMUT*), pp. 1–4. IEEE.
39. Mporas, I., T. Ganchev, M. Siafarikas, & N. Fakotakis. (2007). Comparison of speech features on the speech recognition task. *Journal of Computer Science*, 3(8), 608–616.
40. Gofman, M.I., S. Mitra, & N. Smith. (2016, November). Hidden markov models for feature-level fusion of biometrics on mobile devices. In: *2016 IEEE/ACS 13th International Conference of Computer Systems and Applications* (*AICCSA*), pp. 1–2. IEEE.
41. Hua, J., J. Zheng, H. Xiong, & E. Zhan. (2013, November). Voiceprint identification based on model clustering. In: *2013 3rd International Conference on Consumer Electronics, Communications, and Networks*, pp. 727–730. IEEE.
42. Li, H., C. Xu, A.S. Rathore, Z. Li, H. Zhang, C. Song, ... & W. Xu. (2020, November). Vocalprint: Exploring a resilient and secure voice authentication via mmwave biometric interrogation. In: *Proceedings of the 18th Conference on Embedded Networked Sensor Systems*, pp. 312–325.
43. Lu, L., J. Yu, Y. Chen, H. Liu, Y. Zhu, L. Kong, & M. Li. (2019). Lip reading-based user authentication through acoustic sensing on smartphones. *IEEE/ACM Transactions on Networking*, 27(1), 447–460.
44. Chauhan, D., E. Anyanwu, J. Goes, S.A. Besser, S. Anand, R. Madduri, ... & A.R. Patel. (2022). Comparison of machine learning and deep learning for view identification from cardiac magnetic resonance images. *Clinical Imaging*, 82, 121–126.
45. Zhang, X., D. Cheng, P. Jia, Y. Dai, & X. Xu. (2020). An efficient android-based multimodal biometric authentication system with face and voice. *IEEE Access*, 8, 102757.
46. Isyanto, H., A.S. Arifin, & M. Suryanegara. (2022). Voice biometrics for Indonesian language users using algorithm of deep learning CNN residual and hybrid of DWT-MFCC extraction features. *International Journal of Advanced Computer Science and Applications*, 13(5).
47. Singh, R., D. Gencaga, & B. Raj. (2016, March). Formant manipulations in voice disguise by mimicry. In: *2016 4th International Conference on Biometrics and Forensics* (*IWBF*), pp. 1–6. IEEE.
48. Tovarek, J., G.H. Ilk, P. Partila, & M. Voznak. (2018). Human abnormal behavior impact on speaker verification systems. *IEEE Access*, 6, 40120–40127.
49. Winda, A., W.R.E. Byan, D.L. Zariantin, & B.G. Josep. (2017, March). Motorcycle start-stop system based on intelligent biometric voice recognition. In: *IOP Conference Series: Materials Science and Engineering*, 187(1), 012039. IOP Publishing.
50. Latinus, M. (2011). Human voice perception. *Current Biology*, 21(4), R143–R145.
51. Pal, M., D. Paul, & G. Saha. (2018). Synthetic speech detection using fundamental frequency variation and spectral features. *Computer Speech and Language*, 48, 31–50.

4 | Biometric System Based Data Security Analysis Using Fuzzy Machine Learning with Cloud Edge Computing Model

Hashim Elshafie[1], Ashwag Alsmari[2], Shamimul Qamar[2*], Haroon Bengali[1], Mohammed Inamurrahman[2], Syed Asif Basha[1], Firdouse Banu[3], Ajay Roy[4], Amrita Rai[5]

[1] Department of Computer Engineering, College of Computer Science, King Khalid University, Saudi Arabia
[2] Computer Science, College of Arts & Sciences, Dhahran Al Janoub, King Khalid University, Saudi Arabia
[3] Department of Applied Information System, Applied College, Khamis Mushaiyt, King Khalid University, Saudi Arabia
[4] Lovely Professional University, Jalandhar, Punjab, India
[5] Department of Electronics and Communication Engineering, Galgotias College of Engineering and Technology, Greater Noida, India

1. Introduction

Biometric addresses a science through which a framework can distinguish in a novel manner an individual in view of his physiological (face, unique mark, iris, hand calculation, retina, and so forth), and behavioral (voice, step, signature, keystroke, and so forth) traits. Because of the rich utilizations and frameworks that happen right now and are available, the verification innovation is exceptionally broad from web-based business applications, entryway access, and brilliant city advances to Internet of Things (IoT) advances as well as applications. When these arrangements were pronounced as giving better security in validation, consequently issues with protection safeguarding and information honesty had been found and didn't stop to happen. To be sure, biometrics frameworks become more helpful when utilized as contrasted with different exemplary confirmation frameworks, for example, token-based (e.g., ID vehicles) or information-based [1]. A biometric-based confirmation framework is utilizing two various working modes: distinguishing proof and confirmation modes. These two distinct modes are vital as they address security loopholes, which are

*Corresponding author: sqamar@kku.edu.sa

DOI: 10.1201/9781003560012-4

taken advantage of by undesirable clients (e.g., programmers/wafers). Creating and carrying out validations modules for programming as well as web applications, utilizing biometric qualities, can be a difficult errand for typical (work area) conditions. Assuming we are moving to distributed computing, map decrease, huge information, Hadoop advances, we can encounter genuine assignments that are hard to achieve with standard cryptographic crude in the event that they are not improved as well as certain additional security boundaries are added. Cancelable biometrics plans are utilized altogether these days. By and large, a cancelable biometric plot relies upon extricating different facial, iris, and unique finger impression highlights to verify people in a constant way [2]. These separated highlights of acquired biometrics structure the cancelable biometric formats. A cancelable biometric, for the most part, comprises two center stages, i.e., enrollment and verification. In the enrollment stage, biometrics obtained from sensors for explicit clients are put away in a data set. Nonetheless, during the confirmation stage, a question layout is produced to be contrasted and the biometrics that are put away in the data set. The client is validated assuming both the put-away biometrics as well as the given question formats match. A cancelable biometric plan can be either uni-biometric-based or multi-biometric-based [3]. Uni-biometric based plans send solitary information like the face, iris, or finger impression to verify people, while the multi-biometric-based plot takes advantage of at least two information sources. Be that as it may, multi-biometric-based plans are viewed as safer since it is difficult to hack a bunch of biometrics simultaneously. Typically, examined biometrics are put away in a dataset during the enlistment stage. Indeed, even on account of conveying encryption methods on the put-away biometrics, this requires carrying out unscrambling during the validation stage. Hence, the first biometrics may be uncovered. Thus, an ideal cancelable biometric plan ought to think about forestalling unapproved admittance to the first biometric layouts while keeping up with the biometric plan's elite exhibition. Besides, the cancelable biometric plan ought to ensure that approved clients can undoubtedly get to the framework with high acknowledgment execution. Cancelable biometric methods should meet International Organization for Standardization/International Electrotechnical Commission (ISO/IEC) 24745:2022 standards in addition to ensuring high recognition [4]. Preventing biometric template cross-matching, regardless of whether the templates were derived from the same or different biometrics, is the first prerequisite. Stated otherwise, it ought to be impossible to correlate distinct templates across separate databases. Assuring irreversibility—that is, making it impossible to recover original biometrics given a cancelable biometric template—is the second prerequisite. An additional requirement limits the creation of new cancelable templates before eliminating the previous iterations to safeguard the database in the event that it has been hacked. In the biometric recognition process, machine learning techniques are employed for many objectives in addition to feature extraction. A few examples of these diverse goals include improving speed as well as reliability in a developed biometric technique, detecting liveness in biometric traits, and classifying biometric data sets for analysis as well as classification to enhance the statistical method utilized in biometric authentication [5]. The procedure reveals that the primary vulnerabilities are related to biometric features' storage, protection, and issues that arise when using biometric apps. As a result, in this chapter, the biometric recognition process is examined in light of utilization areas, user-friendliness, and biometric application vulnerabilities. The trustworthy biometric system may be installed on platforms thanks to the protection strategies and procedures we have already discussed. Furthermore, some variables may still compromise data security, integrity, and availability despite all safety measures. A direct attack on data and an individual's privacy results from breaking this guideline. What can be done depends on who can imagine what to do if someone's biometric data is hacked [6].

2. Literature Review

In recent years, biometric validation has become pivotal, particularly in security as well as protection safeguarding applications, for example, monetary exchanges, observation framework, visa handling, basic conditions, etc. Be that as it may, because of the inborn impediments inside each biometric, no single biometric strategy can accomplish a high accuracy and unwavering quality of people's confirmation. In this way, in exceptionally basic applications, a solitary biometric may not be adequate to ensure security, but rather performing solid confirmation by joining a few biometrics might be vital. Siddiqui et al. [7] reviewed various user authentication schemes using machine learning methods, emphasizing their potential for improving biometric reliability and adaptability. Kim et al. [8] have proposed a facial acknowledgment technique in the light of PCA as well as backpropagation NN (neural network). Every facial picture in the preparation is addressed precisely by a direct mix of eigenfaces. A review directed by Sindhuja and Srinivasan [9] showed that the heaviness of the picture when contrasted and the test pictures can be utilized to recognize facials. For the same goal, Hossain et al.'s method [10] combines two different approaches: (1) Fisher linear discriminant (FLD) method to obtain fusion feature space; (2) PCA (principal component analysis) method to obtain feature space of the training set; and (3) both methods are used to train and recognize projected facial in feature space. Their research showed that the method based on PCA and FLD features can perform better than currently used facial recognition techniques. Agrawal et al. [11] suggested a four-step face recognition method. The localization of the faces is the first stage; feature extraction is the second; classification is the third; and the back propagation method is the fourth step in identifying the faces. The LDA (linear discriminant analysis) strategy is a mathematical procedure that can be utilized to order and further develop the information portrayal. The subsequent blends are normally utilized as direct classifiers. This calculation cuts every facial into a direct mix prior to grouping it. The subsequent arrangements of new aspects are called fisherfaces after LDA technique. Because of its intricacy, LDA calculation isn't generally so powerful as different strategies. Sedik et al. [12] proposed a technique that includes gathering pictures of similar and various classes. The subsequent arrangement of facials is then ordered by the nearest preparing pictures. The review's outcomes uncovered that the proposed calculation is altogether better compared to the current techniques. Prassetha et al. [13] consolidated both direct LDA as well as Fragmentary LDA procedures, and calculations can be utilized for little example sizes. It can likewise characterize the facials as indicated by the nearest preparing pictures. After effects of the investigations on two information bases upheld the adequacy of proposed calculation. Support vector machines (SVMs) are usually utilized in AI to tackle issues connected with separation and relapse.

Despite the fact that they are not generally so effective as probably the most well-known calculations, their true capacity is still extremely encouraging. In their review, Barros et al. [14] proposed a calculation in view of a changed SVM learning plan that utilizes the SVM and molecule swarm streamlining strategies. Consequences of examinations showed that the proposed strategy has preferable precision over the current techniques. Furthermore, Hathaliya et al. [15] introduced a survey of the strategies utilized for 2D facial acknowledgment utilizing SVM procedure. The creators broke down acknowledgment results as per methods used to remove data like facial elements, design classifiers, and information bases. Another strategy that utilizes the SVM calculation to identify facials in grayscale pictures was introduced by Banson et al. [16]. They then identified the appearances utilizing sizes as well as places of eyes as well as lips. Likewise, Rajasekar et al. [17] utilized PCA as well as SVM to work for building a facial acknowledgment model. Liu et al. [18] introduced an outline of successful utilization of AI, especially with regard to involving SVMs in facial acknowledgment. In this manner, the creators give a broad overview of facial acknowledgment and its applications. The creators, Brown et al. [19], prescribed utilizing biometric recognizable proof to get to a focal well-being record information base with protection strategies. DeRidder et al. [20] examined a novel approach to Multi-Criteria Decision-Making (MCDM). The MCDM technique was used to rank each set of items using an integrated strategy for the order of preference by similarity (TOPSIS) as well as analytic hierarchy process (AHP). Additionally, K-means clustering was used to determine which elements in each group were crucial. A novel hybrid strategy that might be utilized to EMR (Electronic Medical Record) methods was created [21]. This approach will help EMR systems be more reliable, secure, and integrated.

Many deep learning architectures are used, including CNN (Convolutional Neural Network), RBM (Restricted Boltzmann Machine), RNN (Recurrent Neural Network), DBN (Deep Belief Network), and stacked autoencoders. A three-dimensional CNN was utilized to extract spatiotemporal data from inputs for the purpose of identifying anomalous events in films [22]. The SVM's probabilistic outputs were used to design sparse-layered coding and intra-frame classification algorithms for identifying rare events in multimedia, including movies. Using a CNN, anomalies in crowded activity can be found [23]. By examining input frames, researchers investigated the effects of anomaly detection approaches on high-level feature aggregation and the performance of convolutional autoencoders (CAEs) [24]. To identify anomalies in video data, Motion as well as Appearance DeepNet approach combined a number of one-class SVM techniques with a DNN. Patterns of video events were examined using a deep Gaussian mixture technique, feature learning was achieved using PCANet for anomalous event recognition utilizing DL methods [25].

3. System Model

Figure 1 illustrates how authentication systems are classified into three types of solutions: knowledge-based, physiological biometric, and behavioral biometric. In order to verify an individual's identity, knowledge-based authentication specifically asks the user to input credentials such as a password, graphical PIN, and personal identification number (PIN). Physiological biometric-based authentication uses machine learning techniques to distinguish between user identities based on biological characteristics. Additionally, behavioral biometrics like keyboard patterns, walking motion, and touchscreen dynamics are employed for user verification.

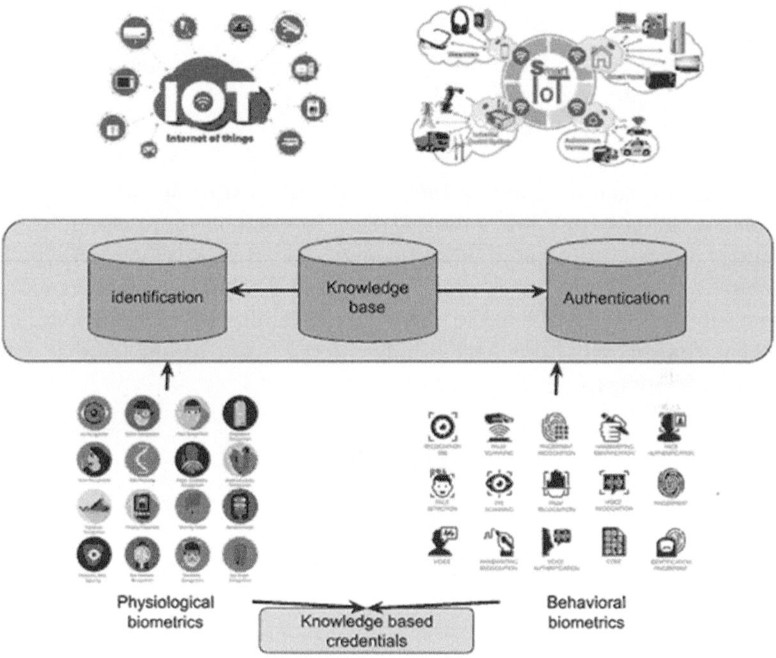

Figure 1: Biometric authentication modeling.

Using a classification function $f_m : R^n \rightarrow \{x_1,..., x_c\}$ on the feature vector $v = (v_1,..., v_n) \in R^n$, the input will be classified. The result is $x_{c*} = f_m(v)$, where $c^* \in \{1,..., c\}$; x_{c*} is the class in which v falls, according to model m. In this instance, every biometric piece of data that the classification data is applied to is represented by the feature vector by Eq. (1).

$$v = (v_1, ..., v_n) \in R^n$$

$$\text{biometric vector} = (b_v) = (b_{v_1}, \ldots, b_{v_n})$$

$$f_m : R^n \rightarrow \{x_1, \ldots, x_c\} \text{ over } b_v \text{ and the output is } x_{c*} = f_m(v) \text{ where } c^* \in \{1, \ldots, c\} \quad (1)$$

Based on model m, the class in which b_v belongs is represented by the x_{c*}. The hyperplane decision-based classifier and Naïve Bayes are two significant classification methods.

Inexperienced Bayes: This classifier's model m is built on probabilities: $\{p(X = x_i)\}$

$c_i = 1$ is the likelihood that class x_i occurs, and v_j is the probability that an element of v exists in that specific class x_i. The role of classification is by Eq. (2).

$$x_{C*} = \max_{i\in\{1,\dots,c)} p(X = x_i \mid V = v) = \max_{i\in\{(1,\dots,c)} p(X = x_i, V_1 = v_1, \dots, V_n = v_n) \quad (2)$$

Bayes principles were used to obtain the second equality. The Naïve Bayes algorithm in biometrics will aid in the classification of biometric data and enable speedier processing times. The biometric features provide the basis for the classification.

Hyperplane choice: The classification function is and the model $m = \{m_i\}\ c_i = 1$ comprises c vectors in R^n by Eq. (3).

$$x_{c*} = \max_{i\in\{(1,\dots,c)} \langle m_i, v \rangle \quad (3)$$

The hyperplane decision in biometrics will greatly aid in the identification and classification of the biometric 3D face recognition representations. Figure 2 illustrates a fingerprint-based identification system in a cloud setting. Because biometric templates are stored in the centralized database, it becomes a prominent target in this situation. Due to the restricted availability of each biometric modality, any compromise will have far-reaching effects. As a result, there is interest in cancelable biometrics.

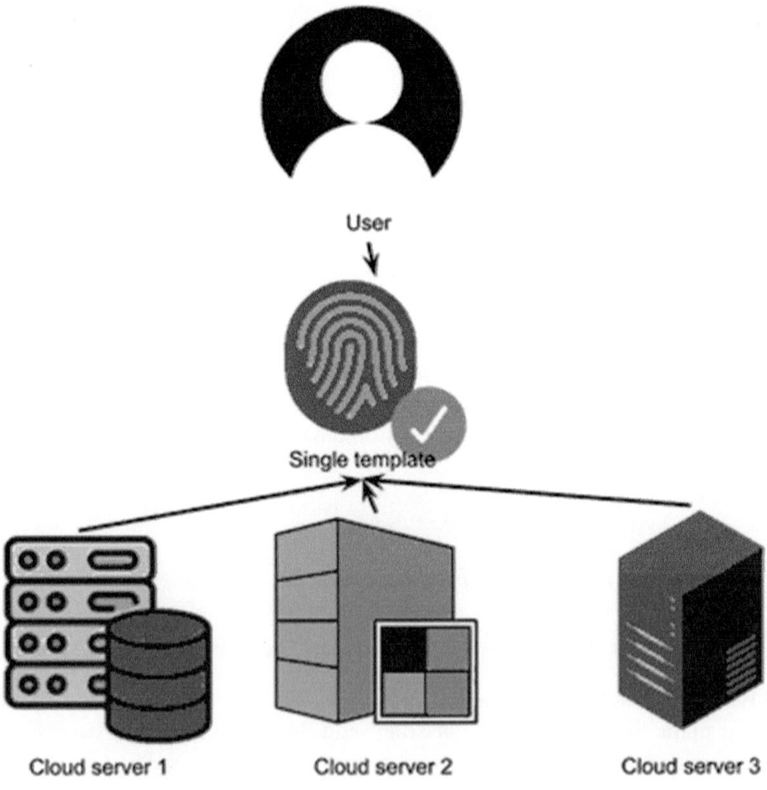

Figure 2: Biometric authentication in cloud computing environments.

Facial Biometric is otherwise called the most unmistakable key credits for biometric validation because of their uniqueness and strength. This innovation is typically founded on estimation of facial elements like mouth, eyes, nose, lips, face structure. In this specific situation, a few methods can be utilized to remove significant highlights from the face picture like variety examination and brain organization. In this work, we have dealt with the face biometrics extraction using Luxand FaceSDK 3, a powerful and efficient technique. The cross-platform face location and recognition library Luxand FaceSDK provides the orientations of over 70 facial component focuses, such as the nose, eyes, mouth, eyebrows, and face forms. A client photo is taken during the enrollment process, and Luxand SDK is used to extract the client's details into an arrangement that will be stored with their finger format. The facial layout needs to be used for correlation and cannot be changed. Age and orientation are extracted as supplementary elements from the given face image and analyzed with the help of the Computerised Persona SDK, which provides a certainty level. The age result, for instance, might be "Female: 3.0001% and Male: 96.9999%". After that, the age result is standardized so that the AI calculation can use it in conjunction with the client's orientation from the data set. While the age and orientation data can be erased on the fly, it is not necessary to store the finger and facial layouts created during the enrollment step. Instead, they are preserved in a MySQL dataset. In addition to such components, extra client-related data, such as his name, ID, and accolades, is also stored. Throughout this endeavor, an ASP Web 2.0 Programming interface was developed to complete all exchanges with the MySQL dataset.

3.1 Fuzzy Graph Based Boltzmann Q-spatial Neural Network

Largest classification interval is similar to minimizing the normal vector of the classification plane, which is represented by the symbol ω. To accurately categorize all samples, however, a classification plane is necessary. Constraint condition is by Eq. (4).

$$y_i(\dot{\omega} \cdot x_i + b) - 1 \geq 0 \tag{4}$$

For $\sigma \in [0, 1]$, the resulting IT2FM ($\varphi_0(\sigma)$) can be expressed as follows by Eq. (5).

$$\varphi_0(\sigma) = P\sigma k(\sigma) \tag{5}$$

Where $k(\sigma)$ is described as:

$$k(\sigma) = \frac{1}{2}\left(\frac{1}{\alpha + \sigma - \alpha\sigma} + \frac{-1+\alpha}{-1+\alpha\sigma}\right) \tag{6}$$

A type-2 fuzzy set $M^{\sim Q}_{ij}$ is given as:

$$M^{\sim Q}_{ij} = \left\{\left(p_{ij}, \mu_{M^Q_{ij}}\right), \mu_{M^Q_{ij}}\left(p_{ij}, \mu_{M^Q_{ij}}\right) \forall p_{ij} \in I, \forall \mu_{M^Q_{ij}} \in Jp_{ij} \subseteq [0,1]\right\} \tag{7}$$

Where p_{ij} is the input image I, μM | pixel centered at (i, j) inside a window of size $(2Q + 1) \times (2Q + 1)$. The type-2 membership function is Q_{ij}. The mean of the k-middle is computed for an element set $X\,Q_{ij} = \{x_1, x_2, x_3,..., x_n\}$ that was taken from a window of size $(2Q + 1) \times (2Q + 1)$ centered at (i, j), where $\forall\, 1 < i, j \leq (2Q + 1)$ by Eq. (8).

$$m_k\left(X_{ij}^{Q}\right) = \left\{\frac{1}{2k-1}\sum_{i=q-k+1}^{q+k-1} x_i \text{ for add } n \frac{1}{2k}\sum_{i=q-k+1}^{q+k} x_i \text{ for even } n\ (n = 2q).\right.$$

$$\mu_{M_{ij}}^{(Q,k)}(x_n) = e^{-(x_n - v_{ij}^{(Q,k)})^2} \Big/ 2(\sigma_{ij}^{Q})^2 \tag{8}$$

Related GMFs for the elements in a window are calculated using the GMF parameters mean $v\ (Q, k)\ ij$ and standard deviation $\sigma\ Q_{ij}$. Next, q distinct means are produced using the k-middle mean as Eq. (9).

$$v_{ij}^{(Q,k)} = m_k\left(X_{ij}^{Q}\right), k = 1, 2, 3, \ldots q \tag{9}$$

For k-middle means in a window, the standard deviation is calculated as Eq. (10).

$$\sigma_{ij}^{Q} = m_h\left(\Omega_{ij}^{Q}\right)$$

$$\Omega_{ij}^{Q} = \left|x_n - v_{avg}\right|, \forall x_n \in X_{ij}^{Q}$$

$$v_{avg} = \frac{1}{q}\sum_{k=1}^{q} v_{ij}^{(Q,k)} \tag{10}$$

Matrix Δ_{ij} can be stated mathematically as Eq. (11).

$$\Delta_{ij} = \Big[\mu_{M_{ij}}^{(Q,1)}(x_1)\mu_{M_{ij}}^{(Q,1)}(x_2)\ldots\mu_{m_{ij}}^{(Q,1)}(x_n)\mu_{M_{ij}}^{(Q,2)}(x_1)\mu_{M_{ij}}^{(Q,2)}(x_2)\ldots \tag{11}$$

$$\mu_{M_{ij}}^{(Q,2)}(x_n)\ldots\ldots\ldots\ldots\mu_{M_{ij}}^{(Q,q)}(x_1)\,\mu_{M_{ij}}^{(Q,q)}(x_2)\ldots\mu_{M_{ij}}^{(Q,q)}(x_n)\Big]$$

Interval Type-2 Fuzzy Membership is by Eq. (12).

$$\bar{u}_j(x_i) = \left\{\frac{\sum_{k=1}^{C}\left(\left(d_{ji}/d_{ki}\right) + \alpha\left(d_{ji}/d_{ki}\right)\delta\right)^{2/(m_i-1)}}{\sum_{k=1}^{C}\left(\left(d_{ji}/d_{ki}\right) + \alpha\left(d_{ji}/d_{ki}\right)\delta\right)^{2/(m_i-1)}}, \text{if } \frac{1}{\sum_{k=1}^{C}\left(d_{ji}/d_{ki}\right)} <\right.$$

$$\frac{1}{C}, \frac{\sum_{k=1}^{C}\left(\left(d_{ji}/d_{ki}\right) + \alpha\left(d_{ji}/d_{ki}\right)\delta\right)^{2/(m_j-1)}}{\sum_{k=1}^{C}\left(\left(d_{ji}/d_{ki}\right) + \alpha\left(d_{ji}/d_{ki}\right)\delta\right)^{2/(m_2-1)}}, \text{otherwise}, \underline{u}_j(x_i) =$$

$$\left\{\frac{\sum_{k=1}^{C}\left(\left(d_{ji}/d_{ki}\right) + \alpha\left(d_{ji}/d_{ki}\right)\delta\right)^{2/(m_i-1)}}{\sum_{k=1}^{C}\left(\left(d_{ji}/d_{ki}\right) + \alpha\left(d_{ji}/d_{ki}\right)\delta\right)^{2/(m_i-1)}}, \text{if} \frac{1}{\sum_{k=1}^{C}\left(d_{ji}/d_{ki}\right)} \geq\right.$$

$$\frac{1}{C},\frac{\sum_{k=1}^{C}\left(\left(d_{ji}/d_{ki}\right)+\alpha\left(d_{ji}/d_{ki}\right)\delta\right)^{2/(m_i-1)}}{\sum_{k=1}^{C}\left(\left(d_{ji}/d_{ki}\right)+\alpha\left(d_{ji}/d_{ki}\right)\delta\right)^{2/(m_2-1)}},\text{ otherwise} \tag{12}$$

Type reduction and hard-partitioning is given as follows by Eq. (13).

$$u_j(x_i)=\frac{u_j^R(x_i)+u_j^L(x_i)}{2}, j=1,\ldots,C, u_j^R(x_i)=\frac{\sum_{l=1}^{M}u_{jl}(x_i)}{M} \tag{13}$$

Where

$$u_{jl}(x_i)=\{\overline{u}_j(x_i),\text{ if } x_{il} \text{ uses} \overline{u}_j(x_i) \text{for } v_j^R, \underline{u}_j(x_i), \text{ otherwise}, \tag{14}$$

and

$$u_j^L(x_i)=\frac{\sum_{l=1}^{M}u_{jl}(x_i)}{M} \tag{15}$$

Where

$$u_{jl}(x_i) = \{\overline{u}_j(x_i), \text{if } x_{il} \text{ uses } \overline{u}_j(x_i) \text{ for } v_j^L, \underline{u}_j(x_i), \text{otherwise.} \tag{16}$$

Utilizing an empirical approach, the function of Upper Membership values is choosed. Our solution offers an additional set of configurable parameters for the Type-2 Fuzzy Logic Systems (FLS) reduction technique, which is dependent on the Centroid-type. Probability that a susceptible agent in age group g and patch i will get disease is represented by the value of $\Pi_i^g(t)$. Given the assumptions of the model, this probability is determined by Eq. (17).

$$\Pi_i^g(t)=\left(1-p^g\right)P_i^g(t)+p^g\sum_{j=1}^{N}R_{ij}^g P_j^g(t) \tag{17}$$

In this sense, the likelihood of getting the disease within the dwelling patch is indicated by the first term in the r.h.s. of Eq. (8), while contagions occurring in any of the surrounding areas are included in the second term. Moreover, we assume that a monotonically growing function f governs the relationship between the number of interactions and the density of each area. Using criteria given above, P_i^g reads by Eq. (18).

$$\frac{\partial\phi_i}{\partial t}=|\nabla\phi_i|\left(\mu\nabla\cdot\left(\frac{\nabla\phi_i}{|\nabla\phi_i|}\right)-\text{sign}(\phi_i)\left(p_i-p_{i_i}\right)\right) \tag{18}$$

The exponents show how many times an agent in age group g in patch i came into contact with infectious people in age group h living in patch j (i.e., compartments A and I, respectively). As a result, the double product represents the likelihood that a person in age group g will remain uninfected while residing in patch I. In Eq. (9), the term $C(t) = \{x(t)\in\Omega:\phi(x(t),t)$ accounts for normalization factor z^g, which is derived as follows. It also reflects the total number of contacts, which grows with density of patch i according to function f by Eq. (19).

$$z^g=\frac{N^g}{\sum_{i=1}^{N}f\left(\frac{n_i^{eff}}{s_i}\right)\left(n_i^g\right)^{eff}} \tag{19}$$

Where patch *I*'s effective population is determined by Eq. (20).

$$n_i^{eff} = \sum_{g=1}^{N_G} \left(n_i^g\right)^{eff} \tag{20}$$

It is dispersed throughout size-based age groupings by Eq. (21).

$$\left(n_i^g\right)^{eff} = \sum_j \left[\left(1 - p^g\right)\delta_{ij} + p^g R_{ji}^g\right] n_j^g. \tag{21}$$

According to author [33], function *f*(*x*) controlling impact of population density has been chosen as follows by Eq. (22).

$$f(x) = 1 + \left(1 - e^{-\xi x}\right) \tag{22}$$

The likelihood that these contacts are contagious is contained in the final term of exponents in Eq. (9) and is proportional to $n_{j\to i}^{m,h}$, which is the predicted number of people in age group h who have moved from area j to region i in specified infectious condition m (either A or I) by Eq. (23).

$$n_{j\to i}^{m,h}(t) = n_j^h \rho_j^{m,h}(t)\left[\left(1 - p^h\right)\delta_{ij} + p^h R_{ji}^h\right], m \in \{A, I\} \tag{23}$$

This model's discrete time feature makes it simple to calculate time evolution of all the pertinent variables, offering regionally relevant data. One useful metric to measure the effectiveness of the policy is the likelihood that a single person residing in a home inside a particular municipality is free of infection. φ is set to be negative inside *C* and positive outside *C* in order to make a normal point outward. The zero level set continues to depict a contour as it changes over time by Eq. (24).

$$C(t) = \{x(t) \in \Omega : \phi(x(t), t) = 0\} \tag{24}$$

Equation (25) can be differentiated to get $\varphi t + \nabla\varphi \cdot xt = 0$. Only a contour's speed in the normal direction is taken into account while monitoring it over time; speed of a contour in tangential directions is not significant.

$$\nu(x(t), t) = x_t \cdot \frac{\nabla\phi}{|\nabla\phi|} \tag{25}$$

Chan and Vese based constraints on reduction of an energy functional for vector-valued pictures ($m > 1$) by Eq. (26),

$$F_{n,m}^{CV}\left(C_0, \ldots, C_{n-1}, c_0, \ldots, c_{2n-1}\right) = \mu \sum_{i=0}^{n-1}$$

$$\text{surface}\left(C_i\right) + \frac{1}{m} \sum_{i=0}^{2n-1} \sum_{j=0}^{m-1} \lambda_{i,j} \int_{\Omega_i} \left(u_j - c_{i,j}\right)^2 dx \tag{26}$$

in which $C = \bigcup_{i=0}^{n-1} C_i$. The set C_i consists of *n* simple closed hypersurfaces $\{C_0, \ldots, C_{n-1}\}$ that divide Ω/C into 2*n* subdomains $\{\Omega_0, \ldots, \Omega^{2n-1}\}$. Area of a surface or hypersurface is represented as surface(C_i), where $C_i \in [0, 1]$. The user can adjust the parameters m, which are constants that indicate the image's intensity on each subdomain.

The function $\varphi_i : \Omega \rightarrow R$'s zero level set, Eq. (27), represents hypersurface C_i. In the event that n exceeds one, the level set functions are amalgamated into a vector:

$$\Phi : \Omega \rightarrow R, \Phi = \left(\phi_0, \ldots, \phi_{n-1}\right) \tag{27}$$

To abbreviate notation, $\{c_0, \ldots, c_{2n-1}\}$ is expressed as a $2n \times m$ matrix c. One way to rewrite energy Eq. (28) is using the level set functions.

$$F_{n,m}^{CV}(\Phi, c) = \mu \sum_{i=0}^{n-1} \delta\left(\phi_i \left|\nabla \varnothing i\right| dx\right) + \frac{1}{m} \sum_{i=0}^{m-1} \sum_{i=0}^{n-1} \lambda_{i,j}\, \delta\left(\phi_i \left|\nabla \varnothing i\right| dx\right) \tag{28}$$

The Euler-Lagrange Eq. is used to minimize this energy in relation to Φ by Eq. (29).

$$\delta\left(\phi_i \left|\nabla \varnothing i\right| dx\right).n = 0 \tag{29}$$

Index of subdomain to which x belongs is $I(x)$, index of subdomain that is located in opposition to subdomain $I(x)$ with respect to the hyper surface is ˘$Ii(x)$.1. Outlining the Penalty Functions to explain why points in Ω shouldn't be Ω_i, use p_i: $\Omega \rightarrow R$ by Eq. (30)

$$\nabla \phi_i \cdot n = 0 \forall i \in \{0, \ldots, n-1\} \tag{30}$$

Euler-Lagrange equations Eq. (31) become

$$\frac{\partial \phi_i}{\partial t} = \left|\nabla \phi_i\right| (\mu \nabla \cdot \left(\frac{\nabla \phi_i}{\left|\nabla \phi_i\right|}\right) v \tag{31}$$

The evolution equation for a contour moving in a normal direction is obtained by substituting $|\nabla \varphi_i|$ for $\delta(\varphi_i)$. Then, using a speed function, Eq. (32) is applicable.

$$v_i = \text{sign}(\phi_i \left(p_I - p_{I_i}\right) - \mu \nabla \cdot \left(\frac{\nabla \phi_i}{\left|\nabla \phi_i\right|}\right) \tag{32}$$

So,

$$\frac{\partial \phi_i}{\partial t} = \left|\nabla \phi_i\right| \left(\mu \nabla \cdot \left(\frac{\nabla \phi_i}{\left|\nabla \phi_i\right|}\right) - \text{sign}\left(\phi_i\right)\left(p_i - p_{i_i}\right)\right) \tag{33}$$

Neumann boundary conditions

$$\nabla \phi_i \cdot n = 0 \forall i \in \{0, \ldots, n-1\} \text{ on } \partial\Omega. \tag{34}$$

It is possible to obtain the feature matrix Q selection that yields subset of features with lowest criterion score:

$$Q = \arg\min_{Q} \frac{Tr\left(Q' f(P) M I_w f'(P) Q\right)}{Tr\left(Q' f(P) M I_b f'(P) Q\right)} \tag{35}$$

Unfortunately, the lack of closed-form solutions has made it difficult to directly address the trace-ratio problems mentioned above. Thus, rather than addressing trace-ratio problems directly. Many occupations aim to switch to comparable trace-various problems in order to obtain a global optimisation solution. Considering that the standard score for the subset-level in Eq. (5) increases to global lowest λ^* fulfilling by Eqn.(36).

$$\lambda^* = \arg\min \frac{Tr\left(Q'f(P)MI_w f'(P)Q\right)}{Tr\left(Q'f(P)MI_b f'(P)Q\right)} \tag{36}$$

This is to show that

$$\frac{Tr\left(Q'f(P)ML_w f'(P)Q\right)}{Tr\left(Q'f(P)MI_b f'(P)Q\right)} \geq \lambda^*, \forall Q \Rightarrow Tr\left(Q'f(P)\left(MI_w - \lambda^* MI_b\right)f'(P)Q\right) \geq 0, \forall Q$$
$$\Rightarrow \min_Q Tr\left(Q'f(P)\left(MI_w - \lambda^* MI_b\right)f'(P)Q\right) = 0 \tag{37}$$

At this point, we can use others as constants like: to represent the function of λ.

$$R(\lambda) = \arg\min_Q Tr\left(Q'f(P)\left(MI_w - \lambda MI_b\right)f'(P)Q\right) \tag{38}$$

Therefore, solving the equation's root (λ) = 0 instead of searching for the global optimal λ is a trace-variance problem. Observe that (λ) is a monotonically increasing function. We equate our ultimate aim function as follows by putting forth trace variance optimization problem, which is shown above in Eq. (8) within auto-encoder's hidden layer updating:

$$\min_{W_{\text{in}}, W_{\text{out}}, v_{\text{in}}, v_{\text{out}}, \lambda} m = \frac{1}{2} \| P - g(f(P)) \|_F^2 + \frac{\gamma}{2} Tr\left(Q'f(P)\left(MI_w - \lambda MI_b\right)f'(P)Q\right) \tag{39}$$

In this case, the autoencoder term and feature selection are separated by the balancing parameter, γ. λ is ratio of the trace's score following acquisition of optimization Q, where Q is trace ratio of most recent issue.

The following are the detailed steps: The on-board sensors are actively searching for the moving obstruction at each time step. The dynamic Q-learning of the upper layer will be engaged as soon as a moving obstacle is recognized within sensor range. Identifying the location of the closest moving barrier and the desired direction. Then, all of the upper layer's Q-values for the present state are recovered. All of the bottom layer's Q-values for the present state are likewise retrieved at the same time. The action with the highest Q-value will be developed after carefully taking into account the Q-values of both the higher and lower layers, and this action is the best option at the moment. Till the objective is accomplished, repeat the process. Let x represent the segmented form of y_t and t the segmentation of video sequence y. In a similar vein, x_{st} denotes a site's label in the *th* frame. Assume for the moment that X_t stands for the MRF, of which x_t is a realization. The following posterior probability distribution can be maximized to predict the label field for any feature extraction challenge by Eq. (40).

$$\hat{x}_t = \arg\max_{x_t} P(X_t = x_t \mid Y_t = y_t)$$

$$\hat{x}_t = \arg\max_{x_t} \frac{P(Y_t = y_t \mid X_t = x_t) P(X_t = x_t)}{P(Y_t = y_t)} \tag{40}$$

Where estimated labels are indicated by $\hat{x}_t$. Since (41) reduces, prior probability $P(Y_t = y_t)$ is constant.

$$\hat{x}_t = \arg\max_{x_t} P(Y_t = y_t | X_t = x_t, \theta) P(X_t = x_t, \theta); P \cdot (X_t = x_t) \tag{41}$$

Where θ is a parameter vector connected to x_t's clique potential function. The MAP estimate in this case is $\hat{x}_t$. $P(X_t = x_t)$ is prior probability, and $P(Y_t = y_t \mid X_t = x_t, \theta)$ is likelihood function, which makes up Eq. (42).

Prior probability $P(X_t = x_t)$ is given as:

$$P(X_t = x_t, \theta) = \frac{1}{z} e^{\frac{-U(x_t)}{T}} = \frac{1}{z} e^{\frac{-\{\sum_{c \in C} V_c(x_t)\}}{T}} \tag{42}$$

Where $U(X_t)j$ is the energy function (a function of clique potentials), and z is the partition function, defined as $z = \sum_{x_t} e^{\frac{-U(x_t)}{T}}, U(X_t)j$. The clique potential function in the spatial domain is represented by $V_c(x_t)$. It is characterized by the bonding parameter of the MRF model as Eq. (43).

$$V_c(x_t) = \{+\alpha \text{ if } x_{st} = x_{qt} - \alpha \text{ if } x_{st} \neq x_{qt}, V_{sc}(x_{st}, x_{qt})$$
$$= \{+\alpha \text{ if } x_{st} \neq x_{qt} \text{ and } (s,t),(q,t) \in S - \alpha \text{ if } x_{st} = x_{qt} \text{ and } (s,t),(q,t) \in S \tag{43}$$

If q is a site that is next to s and α is the bonding parameter of the MRF method. After passing the identity authentication process, users can get the necessary information access privileges, ensuring their privacy is protected. An edge computing node randomly chooses $(t - 1)$ devices from other edge computing when it receives a request to perform identity authentication. In order to finish gathering user permission data, two devices work together using secret sharing homomorphism technology and combine the compute results through a cloud computing center.

3.2 Experimental Analysis

The evaluation of the fully integrated system as well as the component systems is listed in this part. A Lenovo U31-70 computer equipped with an Intel Core i7 processor and 8 GB of RAM is used for the experiment.

3.2.1. Dataset Description

To prepare and test the method, three datasets were utilized, which were SDUMLA-HMT, IT Delhi, and FERET (Fluorescence Forster Resonance Energy Transfer),

IIT Delhi and FERET were utilized for beginning investigations on iris and face unimodal methods, individually. To accomplish the targets of the review, particularly as it utilizes profound learning, we embrace a standard FKP (finger knuckle point) picture dataset called IIT Delhi Finger Knuckle Dataset version1.0.20. Size of this dataset as well as its different FKP pictures arrangement with layered network for profound engineering plan. This assists with beating the impediments related with submitting constants as this dataset is freely accessible for research in the local area. Accordingly, our test was completed on IIT Delhi Finger Knuckle Dataset version1.0.20. IIT Delhi Finger Knuckle Dataset contains 790 pictures for 161 subjects, 5 pictures each. Size of every picture is 80 × 100 pixels.

The test misfortune esteem in the organization preparing process diminishes continuously. At the point when the quantity of cycles is 50,000, the misfortune esteem diminishes to the base, and afterward continuously becomes steady. During the time spent network preparing, the model test precision increments with the increment of the quantity of cycles. At the point when the quantity of emphases is 50,000, the test precision arrives at the most extreme, and afterward continuously becomes steady, and the convolutional brain network preparing is effective. Altogether, 3,000 sets of face information in these pictures are positive models, set apart as 1, excess pictures are from various items and are set apart as 0. Prepared convolution brain network is utilized to remove component vectors of 6,000 sets of appearances in informational index. As per the particular circumstance of element vectors, cosine likeness between component vectors is determined as well as standardized to the [0, 1] stretch. Various edges somewhere in the range of 0.2–0.8 are chosen to ascertain the exactness of 6,000 sets of face checks under various limits.

Table 1 shows comparatives for various biometric dataset based on deep learning techniques. Here parametric analysis is carried out in terms of accuracy, precision, recall, RMSE. with the increment of the edge esteem from 0.2 to 0.8, the precision pace of face confirmation first increments and afterward diminishes. At the point when the limit esteem is 0.51, the precision of face check arrives at the greatest worth, which is 92.46%, which additionally demonstrates that the exactness of face confirmation of the keen framework planned in this review can reach 92.46%,

Table 1: Comparative for various biometric dataset

Dataset	Techniques	Accuracy	Precision	Recall	RMSE
SDUMLA-HMT	LSTM	84	67	57	61
	CNN	90	69	61	67
	FGBQSNN	91	80	62	69
IIT Delhi	LSTM	88	75	63	62
	CNN	91	79	62	64
	FGBQSNN	95	84	69	66
FERET	LSTM	90	77	67	69
	CNN	95	83	69	71
	FGBQSNN	98	90	71	80

which is a long way past the acknowledgment strength of natural eyes, showing that proposed plan can essentially expand security of shrewd framework.

3.2.2. Result Discussion

The security examination of the proposed strategy is talked about in this part. The cloud server in our framework is viewed as "fair yet inquisitive", and that implies that the cloud server will complete the convention that you determine; in any case, it will dissect and continue to observe all around delicate data about face information. Hence, face information that is transferred to the cloud server should be appropriately secured. The *n* edge processing servers we utilized in the framework are characterized as noncolluding and autonomous with one another. Consequently, we should ensure that edge processing servers cannot acquire any data about face information exclusively by the mystery shadow they get from other edge figuring servers.

Figure 3 (a)–(d) shows comparatives for the SDUMLA-HMT dataset. Here proposed technique accuracy 91%, precision 80%, recall 62%, RMSE 69%. Existing technique KNN attained accuracy 84%, precision 67%, recall 57%, RMSE 61%; while LSTM accuracy 90%, precision 69%, recall 61%, RMSE 67%.

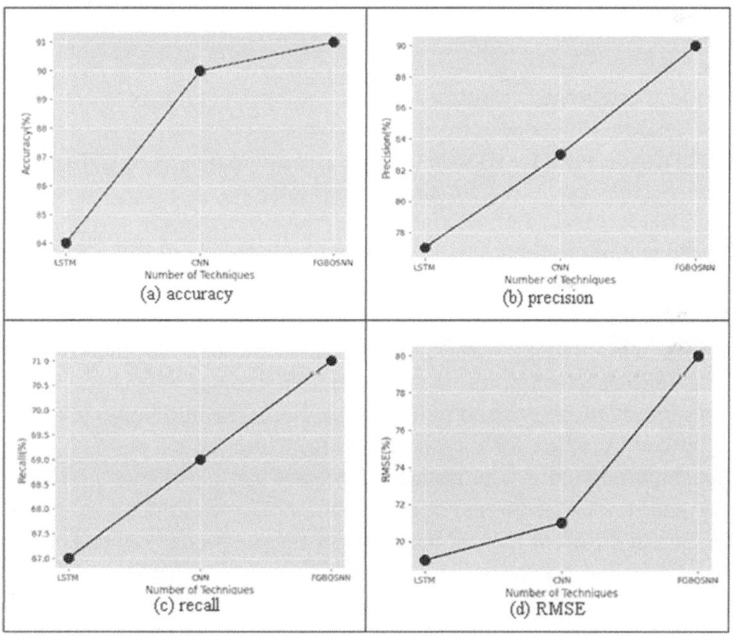

Figure 3: Comparative for SDUMLA-HMT dataset in terms of: (a) accuracy, (b) precision, (c) recall, (d) RMSE.

Figure 4 (a)–(d) comparative carried out. Proposed technique accuracy 95%, precision 84%, recall 69%, RMSE 66% for IIT Delhi dataset. Existing KNN attained accuracy 88%, precision 75%, recall 63%, RMSE 62%, LSTM accuracy 91%, precision 79%, recall 62%, RMSE 64%.

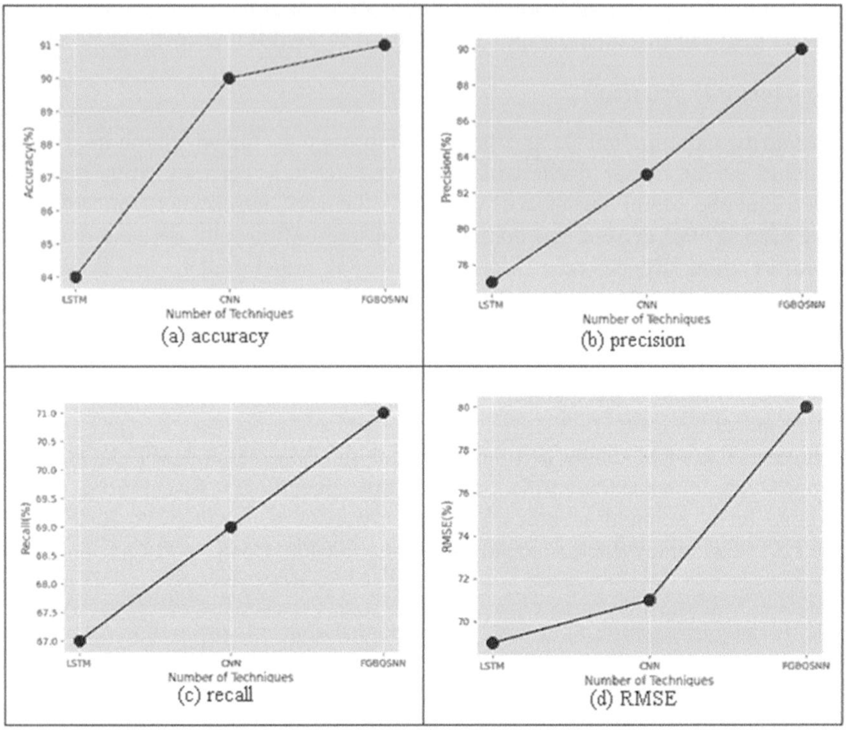

Figure 4: Comparative for IIT Delhi dataset in terms of: (a) accuracy, (b) precision, (c) recall, (d) RMSE.

Proposed technique accuracy 98%, precision 90%, recall 71%, RMSE 80% for FERET dataset. Existing technique accuracy 90%, precision 77%, recall 67%, RMSE 69% by KNN and LSTM attained accuracy 95%, precision 83%, recall 69%, RMSE 71% as shown in Figure 5 (a)–(d). The client can't send a similar picture without fail. Thus, in the verification explorer, the pictures used to decide the character of a client are not the same as those utilized in the preparation. The initial two pictures of each and every client are taken for the confirmation, while the excess eight pictures are utilized for the preparation. The testing pictures of various clients which shows that the testing pictures shift from one client to another. For example, Client 2 has a side development and different look in the first and second pictures. Client 6 is grinning in the second picture, however not in the primary picture. Additionally, the look of Client 1 varies in the two pictures as well as a variety of light is noticed. Initially two clients are wearing glasses, while the last client is without glasses. Such variety in testing pictures is great to notice the power of the created confirmation model.

We can make that opportunity utilization of these three strategies practically straight to the quantity of face pictures in the data set. Notice that, time utilization of face acknowledgment with face includes vectors safeguarded by the solid closest neighbor is practically equivalent to that with the plain text of face highlight vectors. In this way, performing secure closest neighbor conspire on edge processing server

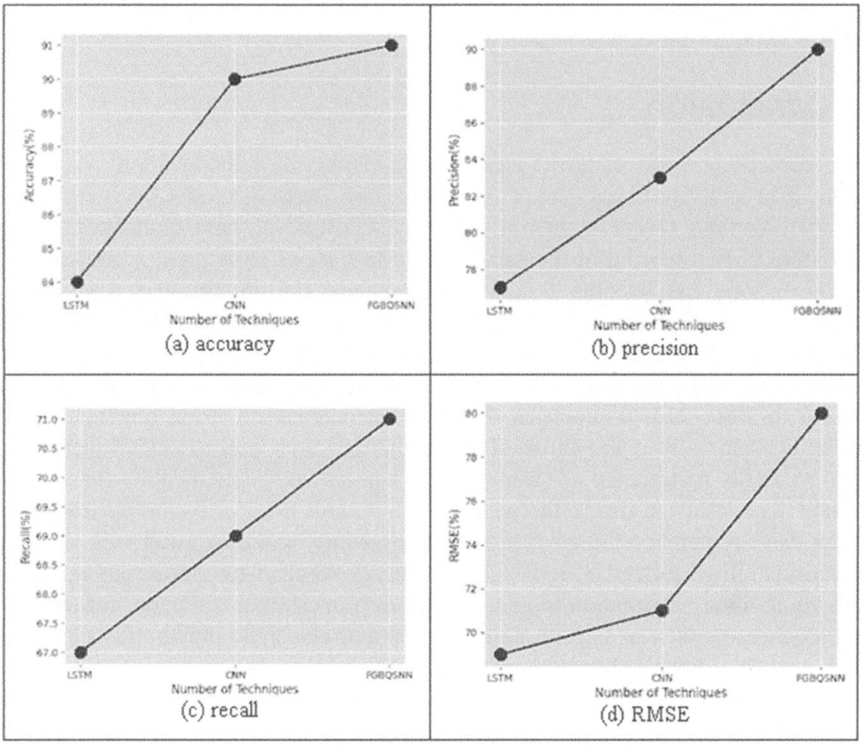

Figure 5: Comparative for FERET dataset in terms of: (a) accuracy, (b) precision, (c) recall, (d) RMSE.

can safeguard face information of clients enlisted on it from being taken by foes and won't burn through an excessive amount of time simultaneously. We can likewise see that the time utilization of face acknowledgment with the face includes vectors that are safeguarded by secret sharing plan is under an adequate reach. Although the time cost of the mystery sharing plan is somewhat longer, it can accomplish cross-confirmation among all the edge processing servers on the reason of safeguarding protection of all face information. In addition, most often for clients' demand for personality validation on edge processing servers that they enlisted on in a large portion of situations. Hence, personality verification can be finished exclusively on edge figuring servers without extra correspondence troubles in this situation so a great deal of time could be saved. For example, over 70% of online clients access the web across various gadgets. 90% utilize various screens consecutively to achieve an undertaking over time 2. The intricacy of multi-gadget, multi-client connection presents critical difficulties for cross-gadget persistent validation. Earlier examinations accept the balanced planning among client and gadget, and predominantly centre around the client verification in the single device situation. Be that as it may, the connections among clients and devices in multi-client, multi-device situations is many-to-many. Because of the heterogeneity of gadgets, moving one pretrained client ID model from source space to target area is seldom examined. There are tremendous contrasts in communication methodology among heterogeneous gadgets. For gadgets with comparable connection modalities, move learning is one promising arrangement.

4. Conclusion

This research proposes a novel technique in biometric authentication systems in secure data analysis based secure fuzzy machine learning model by fuzzy graph based Boltzmann Q-spatial neural network (FGBQSNN) and cloud computing. Validating clients to control their admittance to various structures, frameworks or administrations has become fundamental nowadays. Biometric-based validation draws near, including faces, iris, fingerprints, are vigorously utilized in such settings. Be that as it may, guaranteeing the classification of these biometrics is vital to ensure effectiveness of the given confirmation administrations. Many existing frameworks attempt to store these biometrics scrambled to keep away from any unattended revelation that could make abuse of these biometrics as well as permit interlopers gain unlawful admittance to frameworks and assets. Nonetheless, the current methodologies shift in their effectiveness with regards to security and intricacy. The model can't remember the gave models if by some stroke of good luck a subset of information is utilized. It is feasible to survey whether overfitting is happening utilizing leftover information inputs. The level of overfitting is determined utilizing the exactness as well as accuracy of the prepared plan. The preparation technique takes up 80% of the split; 10% of tests are utilized to check the information all through the preparation stage, and the excess 10% is used as the testing information contribution to survey the precision and execution of the now-prepared strategy. By adding different changes to the approaching information, the end-product can be worked on much more. These alterations will help the classifier in adjusting to genuine settings, permitting it to upgrade the precision and execution much further. Discoveries from our review are utilized to exhibit potential for proposed ways to deal with be conveyed in genuine settings. Both hypothetical as well as trial examinations recommend that the proposed approach has an insignificant equivalent error rate contrasted with those of the cutting edge strategies. Additionally, the proposed method is demonstrated to consume less time, making it reasonable for IoT conditions.

Acknowledgment

The authors extend their appreciation to the Deanship of Scientific Research at King Khalid University for funding this work through a large group Research Project under grant number RGP2/469/44.

References

1. Prakash, A.J., K.K. Patro, M. Hammad, R. Tadeusiewicz, & P. Plawiak. (2022). BAED: A secured biometric authentication system using ECG signal based on deep learning techniques. *Biocybernetics and Biomedical Engineering*, 42(4), 1081–1093.

2. Kim, S.K., C.Y. Yeun, & P.D. Yoo. (2019). An enhanced machine learning-based biometric authentication system using RR-interval framed electrocardiograms. *IEEE Access*, 7, 168669–168674.
3. Al Alkeem, E., S.K. Kim, C.Y. Yeun, M.J. Zemerly, K.F. Poon, G. Gianini, & P.D. Yoo. (2019). An enhanced electrocardiogram biometric authentication system using machine learning. *IEEE Access*, 7, 123069–123075.
4. Piugie, Y.B.W., J. Di Manno, C. Rosenberger, & C. Charrier. (2022, September). Keystroke dynamics based user authentication using deep learning neural networks. In: *2022 International Conference on Cyberworlds (CW)*, pp. 220–227. IEEE.
5. Almomani, I., W. El-Shafai, A. AlKhayer, A. Alsumayt, S. Aljameel, & K. Alissa. (2023). Proposed biometric security system based on deep learning and chaos algorithms. *Comput. Mater. Contin.*, 74(2), 3515–3537.
6. Punithavathi, P., S. Geetha, M. Karuppiah, S.H. Islam, M.M. Hassan, & K.K.R. Choo. (2019). A lightweight machine learning-based authentication framework for smart IoT devices. *Information Sciences*, 484, 255–268.
7. Siddiqui, N., L. Pryor, & R. Dave. (2021). User authentication schemes using machine learning methods: A review. In: *Proceedings of International Conference on Communication and Computational Technologies: ICCCT 2021*, pp. 703–723. Springer Singapore.
8. Kim, S.K., C.Y. Yeun, E. Damiani, & N.W. Lo. (2019). A machine learning framework for biometric authentication using electrocardiogram. *IEEE Access*, 7, 94858-94868.
9. Sindhuja, R., & S. Srinivasan. (2020). Efficient fusion based multi-modal biometric authentication system using machine learning. In: *Electronic Systems and Intelligent Computing: Proceedings of ESIC 2020*, pp. 119–131. Springer Singapore.
10. Hossain, M.S., M.T. Islam, & Z. Akhtar. (2022). Incorporating deep learning into capacitive images for smartphone user authentication. *Journal of Information Security and Applications*, 69, 103290.
11. Agrawal, V., M. Hazratifard, H. Elmiligi, & F. Gebali. (2023). ElectroCardioGram (ECG)-based user authentication using deep learning algorithms. *Diagnostics*, 13(3), 439.
12. Sedik, A., M. Hammad, A.A. Abd El-Latif, G.M. El-Banby, A.A. Khalaf, F.E. Abd El-Samie, & A.M. Iliyasu. (2021). Deep learning modalities for biometric alteration detection in 5G networks-based secure smart cities. *IEEE Access*, 9, 94780–94788.
13. Praseetha, V.M., S. Bayezeed, & S. Vadivel. (2019). Secure fingerprint authentication using deep learning and minutiae verification. *Journal of Intelligent Systems*, 29(1), 1379–1387.
14. Barros, A., P. Resque, J. Almeida, R. Mota, H. Oliveira, D. Rosario, & E. Cerqueira. (2020). Data improvement model based on ECG biometric for user authentication and identification. *Sensors*, 20(10), 2920.
15. Hathaliya, J.J., S. Tanwar, & R. Evans. (2020). Securing electronic healthcare records: A mobile-based biometric authentication approach. *Journal of Information Security and Applications*, 53, 102528.
16. Bansong, C., K.K. Tseng, K.L. Yung, & W.H. Ip. (2022). Hierarchical attention network of multi-modal biometric for a secure cloud-based user verification. *IEEE Internet of Things Magazine*, 5(3), 122–127.
17. Rajasekar, V., M. Saracevic, M. Hassaballah, D. Karabasevic, D. Stanujkic, M. Zajmovic, & P. Jayapaul. (2023). Efficient multimodal biometric recognition for secure authentication based on deep learning approach. *International Journal on Artificial Intelligence Tools*, 32(03), 2340017.
18. Liu, S., W. Shao, T. Li, W. Xu, & L. Song. (2022). Recent advances in biometrics-based user authentication for wearable devices: A contemporary survey. *Digital Signal Processing*, 125, 103120.

19. Brown, R., G. Bendiab, S. Shiaeles, & B. Ghita. (2021). A novel multimodal biometric authentication system using machine learning and Blockchain. In: *Selected Papers from the 12th International Networking Conference: INC 2020 12*, pp. 31–46. Springer International Publishing.
20. DeRidder, Z., N. Siddiqui, T. Reither, R. Dave, B. Pelto, M. Vanamala, & N. Seliya. (2022, November). Continuous user authentication using machine learning and multi-finger mobile touch dynamics with a novel dataset. In: *2022 9th International Conference on Soft Computing & Machine Intelligence* (*ISCMI*), pp. 42–46. IEEE.
21. Fu, S., D. Qin, G. Amariucai, D. Qiao, Y. Guan, & A. Smiley. (2022, May). Artificial Intelligence meets Kinesthetic Intelligence: Mouse-based user authentication based on hybrid human-machine learning. In: *Proceedings of the 2022 ACM on Asia Conference on Computer and Communications Security*, pp. 1034–1048.
22. Pryor, L., R. Dave, J. Seliya, & E.S. Boone. (2021, December). Machine learning algorithms in user authentication schemes. In: *2021 International Conference on Electrical, Computer and Energy Technologies* (*ICECET*), pp. 1–6. IEEE.
23. Rayani, P.K., & S. Changder. (2023). Sensor-based continuous user authentication on smartphone through machine learning. *Microprocessors and Microsystems*, 96, 104750.
24. Gornale, S.S., S. Kumar, A. Patil, & P.S. Hiremath. (2021). Behavioral biometric data analysis for gender classification using feature fusion and machine learning. *Frontiers in Robotics and AI*, 8, 685966.
25. Prabu, S., M. Lakshmanan, & V.N. Mohammed. (2019). A multimodal authentication for biometric recognition system using intelligent hybrid fusion techniques. *Journal of Medical Systems*, 43, 1–9.

5 | Enhancing Data Communication Security with Advanced Deep Learning Techniques

Sanjay Kumar[1*], Naresh Kumar[2], Anil Kumar[1], Kuldeep Singh Kashwan[3]

[1] Computer Science Engineering Department, Galgotias College of Engineering and Technology, Gr. Noida, India

[2] Department of CS (AIML), GL Bajaj Institute of Technology and Management, Gr. Noida, India

[3] School of Computing Science and Engineering, Galgotias University, Gr. Noida, India

1. Introduction

Data communication is the backbone of modern-day infrastructure, permitting information to be transferred smoothly between devices, networks, and systems in this virtual age. From easy e-mail conversation to complicated worldwide economic transactions, reliance on efficient and reliable information conversation structures has accelerated exponentially. But as the scope and scale of data communication grow, so do the challenges associated with securing these systems [1]. The modern age is steadily seeing an increase in cyber threats, whether it is data breaches, ransomware attacks, advanced persistent threats, or denial-of-service (DoS) attacks, all of which put the confidentiality, integrity, and availability of the data in question as well as the trust and reliability in the systems that depend on them. All this calls for a paradigm shift towards innovative and adaptive security mechanisms in the face of increasing network complexity and evolving cyber threats.

1.1 Overview of Data Communication and Its Security Challenges

The data connection is increasing and allowing them in the instruments, almost only through the Digital website. The structure, such as healthcare, financial, educational, and government and so on, is important where the transportation of the information is essential to import, 5G/6G communications, cloud computing speeds up digital innovation. He provides other weak groups in these developments [2].

*Corresponding author: skhakhil@gmail.com

DOI: 10.1201/9781003560012-5

Modern data communication systems face several security challenges:

- **Cyber-dmalaki Vikas:** The attackers regularly expand the attackers in the corners, spreading to the arrangement in the building arrangement. These include fishing, Gaya-inset (Maltah), and malware.
- **Completeness:** In the Communion Device incensements in the Odd, Protocols and structures, this page cannot adapt to a more difficult task.
- **Data Privacy and Compliance:** As the data-driven services are increasing, the protection of sensitive information and compliance with regulations like GDPR and HIPAA are becoming very critical concerns.
- **Scalability and Real-Time Security:** Providing real-time threats and responses cannot be easily established because networks are larger and more complex. Traditional solutions for security frequently fail to comply with these demands owing to their inefficiency in scalable and dynamic systems.

These challenges call out for intelligent, adaptive, scalable security solutions that can keep pace with the dynamic nature of modern data communication systems. To this end, deep learning features are a possible solution.

1.2 Role of Deep Learning in Addressing Communication and Security Issues

Deep learning, an artificial intelligence technique, has changed the face of so many technical fields. This could be attributed to the ability of machines to understand, analyze, and learn voluminous amounts of data. Deep learning models find patterns and relationships in any data much better than the old machine learning methods, which require manual feature extraction [3]. This is particularly helpful in a very high dimensional, dynamic environment. Therefore, in the field of security for data communication, deep learning advantages are:

- **Real-Time Threat Detection:** Deep learning models, such as CNNs and RNNs, can process data streams in real time, detect anomalies and intrusions, and other malicious activities as they occur.
- **Pattern Recognition:** The deep gaining knowledge of fashions can understand the patterns related to cyber threats consisting of phishing attempts or malware signatures and use that know-how to be expecting and save you future assaults via reading historical information.
- **Apted Education:** Depth models learn new information and thus become the easiest of the thriving Ceber and Dmahaki.
- **Multiple Information:** Modern communications systems are from various means, including words, paintings, ears, and local trees in deeper teachings to precede the security of many records that provide protection for security.
- **I SHE AASARRA BRILY:** The deep benefits of the Dancy are genetics worthy of scales. They are useful for a legerity of change in an extremely large facility in the recording of reports.

The statistics that support the combination of the maths cycle help increase the power of escape, and the asylum, and the conquerors must be well-published by the Dhlamini's. Even today, it depends on construction and on the streets.

1.3 Importance of Architectures and Frameworks for Secure and Efficient Data Communication

In deep study and architectural art, their chinch selection is the most important thing in order to develop knowledge of the safety and skill of the signs in the signs. Architectural CNNs, RNN, and Transformer Modeler have identified it as a good demonstration of safety lessons.

- **Chordate Nerve Networks:** CN is really skilled in planning. It includes the Logs, the lack of perfection, and the website. Their local affairs are of great benefit to music and communications research [4]. They are mainly for merely the series of articles; thus, in an introduction on the introduction where chronic events are very important, good is good. LSM devices are more like phones, they expand their power to pass through the long delivery.
- **Transformer Models:** Transformer models are growing, for it is a screen and it is also skillfully killing the great aggregates. Applications such as Encrypted Communication are the introduction to language crime.

This system influences the depth of the deeper example of the lesson and the use of this system. The Depth Education Room fosters development through stormflow, Pytch, and keras, training, and swelling.

Ease of Development: Pre-constructed modules and APIs (application programming interfaces) have made the creation and checking out of deep studying fashions very smooth.

- **Scalability:** The frameworks are optimized for large-scale facts' processing, so they may be suitable for great communication networks.
- **Compatibility with Current Systems:** Frameworks ensure some degree of integration of deep analysis fashions with the current conversation systems with minimal disruption.
- **Advanced Architectures and Frameworks:** Create a good platform for building secure and inexperienced data communication structures. Nonetheless, forcing these solutions onto something is not being honest; as an illustration, there might be issues that involve some computational overhead, issues of private information of the record, and other vulnerabilities against attack.

1.4 Scope of the Chapter

The proposed chapter should ideally provide in-depth exploration as regards how deep advanced learning techniques, architectures, and frameworks could improve data communication security. Specifically, it is divided into:

- Foundations based on theories of deep learning; and their use and applications in securing communications.
- Comprehensive elaboration concerning suitable architectures and suitable frameworks in safe systems of communications.
- Concrete case studies describing the practice via real-time usage of deep getting to know in conditions: Internet of things (IoT), as an example; in addition to 5G/6G networks.

Challenges and restrictions to be used in deeper solutions and the guidelines of the future research. The conclusion of the material, the researchers, nurses, and morality has the mind and tools that can be placed behind the system that can represent fate.

2. Fundamentals of Deep Learning in Data Communication

2.1 Basics of Deep Learning and Neural Networks

"Deep getting to know" is a subset of machine getting to know, that is a department of artificial intelligence (AI). At its center, deep getting to know focuses on training synthetic neural networks (ANNs) with more than one layer (therefore the term 'deep') to analyze huge volumes of statistics and apprehend patterns. Neural networks are inspired by the human brain's structure, consisting of interconnected nodes or 'neurons' that process information [5].

Every neuron in a deep learning model accepts input, passes it through weighted connections, and produces an output. The layers of neurons are usually arranged as an input layer, several hidden layers, and then an output layer. Deep learning algorithms can automatically learn to make predictions or decisions with the use of vast amounts of labeled data, without needing to be explicitly programmed for every case.

The power of deep learning lies in the fact that it models extremely complex relationships in data to enable applications such as automatic speech recognition, image processing, and natural language understanding.

2.2 Applications of Deep Learning in Data Communication Protocols

Deep learning has successfully found transformative applications in the arena of data communication, especially in developing efficiency and reliability within data transmission, as well as network performance. Important applications include the following:

- **Traffic Classification and Management:** Deep learning algorithms can be employed to analyze data traffic patterns and classify network traffic real-time. He helps to determine how the networks can and assists in stopping the narrow tasks properly.
- **Signal Processing:** You can use a deeper study for data communication. For example, the promotion is a noise destroyed in the media, so that when transferred, it reduces the defects and breaks the law [6].
- **Network Optimization:** Neurons can also be used in predicting network crashes, optimizing usage of resources, managing bandwidth dynamically, and many others. These kinds of predictive models help in holding the stability in data networks using real-time solutions for traffic.
- **Criminals are Alternate:** A balanced analysis must, at the same time, both

review the positives and weaknesses of such advancements in order to provide a fair view in real time.

2.3 Key Challenges in Implementing Deep Learning for Secure Communication

Although deep study promises to improve discipline, many challenges are there to protect the communications:

- **Mystery and Protection:** Large data groups may need to be deeper in a further education. Such data groups are often easy to report. Thus, in the law of GDP, it must be very difficult to hear deep pictures of the buildings. From there, deep examples are easily attacked by the competition, and some changes from the introductions.
- **Example Definition:** Excessive doctrine or a clear teaching of "kala-Box". This is one of the main concerns of the deeper [7]. This is a problem for a strict or a safety of communication where the process can be seen and accepted. Lack of talks without a proliferation in security programs can be hindered based on deep study.
- **Computaticization Complicity:** What Education Model, mainly in deep arrays, wishes to be trained to train the finest computer device, for schooling and minds. Similar to IoT, the use of utilizing mack can't be employed in the deep, heavy, because these sophisticated deep learning architectures need sophisticated neural network layers and lots of computational resources, much more than lightweight hardware can offer.
- **Real-Time Processing:** Data communication protocols often have a need to provide low latency in order to ensure quality of service. Processing information in the cases of multilayer deep learning models takes rather long and is not of use in real time unless optimized.
- **Scalability:** Because communication networks have scale, large-scale data sources become available to train deep models. It poses a challenge to develop models scalable to handle large-scale datasets with similar levels of high accuracy and efficiency.

3. Deep Learning Architectures for Data Communication

3.1 Overview of Deep Learning Architectures

In profound doctrines, by means of a particular artery, such as many places as signals and data communication. Each one of the Architectures is specific and based on various taxes and incorporating of plans, circulation and absorption. This example can increase the number of communications in communication, to increase the communications in the communications, to rise in the description of depth Architecture, CNN, Transformers, and Autoencoder.

3.1.1 Convolutional Neural Networks (CNNs)

CNNs are a type of deep learning architecture that shine in processing grid-structured data such as images and video data. The architecture has several layers of convolution followed by pooling, then fully connected layers, intended to automatically detect hierarchical features in input data [8]. Although they were designed for CNN, it is easy to use communication plans and communication. CNNs can be used in data communications:

- **Signal Detection:** CNNs can classify and detect signals from noisy environments. They can learn the underlying features of communication signals to differentiate between valid and invalid signals.
- **Modulation Recognition:** CS can just identify moderation programs, an important part of most communication programs. This reminds the buyers of the actual accuracy of the moderation system, which improves the media and reduces the mistakes.
- **Chanel Assessment:** CNNs can be used for the real time on the road and the nature of the method of working so that the statistics can be more effective.

3.1.2 Recurrent Neural Networks (RNNs)

The idea is that RNNs are processing sequential data based on the state and memory of past inputs. For this reason, RNNs are very helpful in applications of time-series data or sequential patterns, which data communication systems generally experience. Among key uses for RNNs, some of these in data communication include:

- **Network Traffic Forecast:** RNNs can make use of previous knowledge to forecast traffic in a network, hence help optimize routing and balancing loads inside a network. It is thus an important aid for managing congestions and also provides fair use of resources.
- **Error Correction:** RNNs may be applied to coding schemes that can predict errors to be made and correct them during the process of transmitting data. The pictures of the turbulence can be seen at times to make the mistakes on the basis of vital reasons in real time.
- **Chanel Modeling:** RNN can set the pattern of communication. In the literal interaction system, people adapt to RNNs in the first steps, exercising effective work in the system.

3.1.3 Transformers

Transformers, at first advanced for herbal language processing (NLP) tasks, have tested substantial ability inside the subject of verbal exchange. Unlike RNNs, which procedure information sequentially, transformers use self-interest mechanisms to simultaneously technique all parts of the input information. This is appropriate to acquire quick education and first issues. Verbs are used in any way in revolution. Transformer is used:

- **Encoding and Decoding:** Transformer Oral Exchictures, especially in which it is the greatest, Throop and coffee-lateen-laten-laten-laten-Lerten Formulation needs, so that they can explain and translate it. Both records and series can be kept, Transformer, which was announced as a journal and the inscription of the text.

- **Strong Earthly Relationship in the Main Side of the Terrorists in the Transportation of Terrorists:** Transformer will allow the right mistakes to be reformed and adaptation.
- **Wires Communications:** Future Brief Communication Program, 5G, Transformer, Induction Processioning, and Intervention Resolves.

3.1.4 Autoencoders

Autoencoders are neural networks designed to compress and reconstruct the data by forcing the network to learn the most efficient representation of the input data from a bottleneck layer [9]. In data communication, autoencoders may be applied for:

- **Data Compression:** Autoencoders can compress the data prior to sending them through. That helps to save the bandwidth associated with the transmission process. Data encoding into lower dimensions ensures effective communication of the data with minimum information loss.
- **Anomaly Detection:** Autoencoders have also been put to use for anomaly detection while transmitting data as well wherein they learn what the normal data looks like, and anomalies correspond to error states or security issues.
- **Noise Reduction:** Autoencoders can be trained to reduce noise in communication signals, improving the clarity and quality of transmitted data.

3.2 Use of Architectures for Enhancing Data Transmission Efficiency

To attain profound construction knowledge, the deep construction program reduction is required.

- **Optimized Resource Allocation:** CS and Transformers, etc. With the in-depth research of the study, network-sources, help, it can be allowed to depend on real-life territories provided by the visitors. This will lessen congestion and ensure higher throughput for customers.
- **Compression Techniques:** Autoencoders can compress information earlier prior to sending it. Thus, you can actually ship more records via the identical bandwidth. This could be very useful in systems where bandwidth is both costly and constrained, like in satellite communication or IoT networks.
- **Better Channel Estimation:** With models of deep learning, CNNs and RNNs are being trained to predict the state of a communication channel; systems have opportunities to adapt to changing conditions to establish data transmission at its best. It is indispensable for maintaining communication reliability in those environments where interference or noise tends to vary.
- **Error-Free Transmission:** RNNs and transformers can help in error detection and correction that may happen during transmission, thus reducing the number of retransmissions and improving the overall efficiency of the communication system.

3.3 Case Studies/Examples of Architecture Implementations in Real-World Systems

Many real worldly systems have been injured in the deep architecture to encourage the greatest communications and security.

- **5G Network:TR:** 5G in Ordinary Exchange, CNNs, and Transformers used to promote oversight of the aid. Such techniques play an essential role in maximizing the allocation of resources, such as frequency bands and transmission power, to optimize energy utilization and support critical applications like diabetes management. They optimize how resources like frequency bands and transmission power are allocated at some unspecified time in the future of the network for maximum throughput and minimum delays.
- **Wi-Fi Networks:** In Wi-Fi networks, CNNs are deployed to enhance the beautification of sign detection and interference. This permits for indicators to be transmitted with little degradation and with a clearer exception, especially in noisier or busier environments.
- **Wireless Sensor Networks (WSNs):** Autoencoders were implemented in WSNs for information compression and anomaly detection. Since low-energy gadgets are used in such networks, autoencoders help to lessen the quantity of records to be transmitted thereby growing the gadget's performance and extending the battery lifestyles [10].
- **Satellite Communication:** In the PC that moves around for Sine Processing and Blanket Reforms, the weather is a weather in these wings, and the deep Architecture helps to correct the deep Architecture. It helped to reduce the expansion, which can be more valuable and timely.
- **IoT Network:** It is used in a profound doctrine in IoT in order to expect the communication to continue and adjust things more than more than more. In such an IoT conference, the RNN group can be useful in articles on series, as they are about singular words, the best for equipment, and the communication of Ahahan.

4. Frameworks for Deep Learning in Security

4.1 Popular Frameworks and Libraries for Deep Learning in Security

Depth Teaching lines and Libraries' are the methods of the AI Model, especially in safety activity. This fragrance creates a difficult situation, a skill in construction, training, and research. Some of the most famous expansion in deep study, such as a bigger tensor, MXNET PyTorch have transformed the region, allowing complex training and deployment of AI systems. They were introduced, the sprinkling of the body and the introduction [11].

4.1.1 TensorFlow

TensorFlow, developed by Google, is among the most commonly used deep learning libraries in research and industry. It provides an open, flexible, comprehensive ecosystem to build machine learning models and deploy them to production environments. Keras, its high-level API, makes the design of neural networks easier [12]. Its lower-level API offers more flexibility for customization.

In the context of security, TensorFlow can be used for:

- **Intrusion Detection:** It constructs deep learning models that can predict intrusion or unusual system or network activities.
- **Malware Classification:** TensorFlow can be used to develop models that classify files or behaviors as benign or malicious by learning from large datasets of labeled security incidents.
- **Spam Filtering:** Using textual content-based deep gaining knowledge of models, TensorFlow may be applied in e-mail protection structures to filter out phishing and spam messages.

4.1.2 PyTorch

The PyTorch, developed via Facebook, is another popular framework for deep mastering. It is more intuitive and flexible to construct models compared to TensorFlow. Hence, it has been a famous preference among researchers [13]. PyTorch also provides awesome support for GPU (graphics processing unit) acceleration, making it best for big-scale safety applications.

In security, PyTorch is often used for:

- **Outlier Detection:** PyTorch is provided by creating the auto encoder or recurrent network that can sense the normal function of a network system and the anomaly deviation resulting from possible dangerous threats.
- **Behavioral Analysis:** Malicious behavior in cybersecurity is often detected by identifying patterns over time. PyTorch's RNNs and LSTMs (long short-term models) are great for sequential analysis, such as analyzing time-series data from system logs or network packets.
- **Fraud Detection:** PyTorch is applied in financial security systems for fraud detection through the modeling of patterns of transactions and identification of suspicious activity.

4.1.3 Keras

Keras is the epi in the high group. It is built to keep the deep images going to heaven. Keras is a very high-level library deep learning model, and it is easy, and runs on top of either TensorFlow, Microsoft Cognitive Rock, Theon.

Keras helps with safety plans.

- **In the Killing of Actual Humans:** In the very Odds itself, the instance of depth is straightforward in Keras, which performs a very special role within the safety of the surprising table.
- **Encryption Systems:** Neural networks can be developed using Keras to layout the encryption and decryption systems in a manner that provide automated protection for sensitive information.
- **Security-Related Classification Tasks:** Whether it is phishing websites, malicious software programs, or unauthorized "get right of entry to attempts",

Keras is a handy framework for growing awesome category fashions for security duties.

4.1.4 MXNet

Apache Mxnet is a profound opportunity to support all the symbols and order of all arrangements, making it a good routine. For this reason, the training that is distributed can be many GPUs, a suitable way to maintain a greater safety work.

In the Security Field, MXnet is often used for:

- **Threat Intelligence:** The first example of the ultimate investigation in threats, Mxnet Udayan Cyber—can help to do the Dhimmi and the possibility.
- **Security Authority:** Mxnet can play a major role in one's own life activities such as safety planning, care, and actual analysis of statistics.

4.2 Customizing Frameworks for Secure Communication Protocols

The profound lesson can be adjusted to support Protocols. Things in the system of things are widespread in the aspects of these sections of the proponents of safety communications, truth, and privacy.

4.2.1 Neural Network-based Encryption

The neural network encryption technique employs an advanced deep learning technique to protect communication software effectively. The method uses neural networks to mimic complex encryption and decryption processes, enhancing the security and robustness of data transmission. The prowess of this method is its adaptive nature, which can withstand cryptanalysis by dynamically changing encryption patterns. Using this method, neural networks can encrypt encryption keys and transmission protocols to guarantee a secure and effective way of safeguarding confidential data.

4.2.2 Key Management and Generation

Deep learning can be applied to generate cryptographic keys for secure communication. By customizing frameworks to handle secure key exchanges, neural networks can improve the process of key generation, distribution, and storage. Deep learning can also help develop secure key management protocols, where the key generation and management systems are decentralized and more resilient against attacks.

4.2.3 Secure Authentication Systems

Deep learning can be used to generate cryptographic keys to enable secure communication. Neural networks can improve the generation, distribution, and storage process through customization frameworks that handle secure key exchanges. Deep learning can help develop secure key management protocols where the key generation and management system are decentralized, more resilient against attacks, and quite broad.

4.2.4 Intrusion Detection Systems (IDS)

Since authentication protocols can have deep learning architectures such as CNNs, RNNs, and transformers, they can be made customizable through frameworks to apply them in biometric authentication systems such as facial recognition or voice recognition, which provide an additional layer of security to communication protocols [14]. Such systems may be more adaptive to environmental changes and improve with time as they begin to recognize different types of users or abnormal behaviors over a sequence of interactions.

4.3 Framework-based Methods for Threat Detection and Prevention

Deep learning frameworks provide strong methods for threat detection and prevention in cybersecurity. Using different deep learning techniques, security professionals can build systems that predict, detect, and prevent a wide array of security threats.

4.3.1 Intrusion Detection Systems (IDS)

Deep learning frameworks such as Tensor Flow and PyTorch are commonly used to build IDS that detect and prevent unauthorized access to systems. The example of deep study can be trained in the larger data groups in frequently emotionally and negative groups and car travel. From there, these programs can lead to a website program, or a fair, or uncertainty. For example, the mystery muscle can be used to mirror the connection. The relaxing roots and lSM can also be made for the time system in the treasury interactions.

4.3.2 Malware Detection

A deep study vow is also beneficial to Mammary and introductions. They know that the CNNs, RNNs, and Auto Encoders are aware of the characteristics of a sting-moving Analysis and Dances from Keras and tensors that can be used for filing, making plans, or planning. An example of characteristics of the differences between the malwareware differences in the most powerful.

4.3.3 Phishing Detection

Phishing attacks are among the most prevalent and perilous security threats of the day, especially in the form of fake emails and websites. Phishing attacks try to make people provide sensitive information by pretending to come from credible sources. Unlike other cyber-attacks, phishing targets human trust, so detection becomes difficult. They are different from fishing efforts.

4.3.4 Distributed Denial-of-Service (DDoS) Attack Prevention

Depth Education Ward can use Debility and DDoS attacks. You can create a Model by using the Mxnet or Tensor flow to detect DDos's attack on the symptoms. Once he sees these attacks, he can adjust his own plans so that the plans can prevent the burdens and ensure that the ministry prevents it.

5. Integration of Deep Learning and Cybersecurity

The profound computerized teaching has opened up new ways to deal with the strong modern Dashikis. The traditional safety system is often based on a pre-religious system, which is not enough for what has been done and has been reduced in the present Dijinal conditions. Deep learning, because of its capabilities to learn through vast amounts of data and identify patterns, is of utmost importance in improving cybersecurity practices. This section looks into the integration of deep learning into cybersecurity, including intrusion detection, anomaly detection, encryption models, and adversarial attacks.

5.1 Deep Learning for Intrusion Detection and Anomaly Detection

Traditional IDs are very important to prevent computer attacks, and the computer attacks, relying on myths or unknown attacks. Deep education has shown great promise to increase the highest muscles and the introduction of the introduction.

5.1.1 Intrusion Detection Systems (IDS)

A deeper example of teaching examples, such as Kansolve Network and the revival of the arts of network, the travel, Log, and the plan based on a measurement of examples based on the study. Large matching and data groups can be trained to learn such examples on the website.

- **CNNs for IDS:** CNNs are very powerful in gaining knowledge of spatial hierarchies in records, which could be very useful for network visitor's evaluation. CNNs can robotically come across complicated styles that correspond to security breaches, inclusive of uncommon packet sequences, without having guide feature engineering [15].
- **RNNs for Time-Series Data:** Many cyber attacks are sequential in nature, which encompass a sequence of failed login attempts or bizarre get right of entry to patterns. RNNs, particularly LSTM networks, are amazing for studying time-series records, which lets them select anomalous conduct over time and flag capability threats.
- **Anomaly Detection with Autoencoders:** Autoencoders may be used to apprehend a compressed model of normal network behavior. Then, the version could decorate alarms on capability intrusions or anomalies with every prevalence whilst fed clean information as it detects deviations from the found out regular sample.
- These deep "getting-to-know-based" totally IDS answers can offer tremendous actual-time analysis and identify formerly unseen or novel threats, thereby improving the overall security posture of a device.

5.1.2 Anomaly Detection

This is a subdomain of intrusion detection where deviation from normal behavior has been sought after. With autoencoders and unsupervised learning, deep learning models can be employed to identify deviations in network traffic or system behavior that could indicate security incidents [16].

- **Autoencoders:** Autoencoders are trained on normal data and are designed to reconstruct the input. If the model fails to reconstruct a given input accurately, that is, a deviation from normal behavior, then it may be an anomaly, which could represent a malicious activity or intrusion.
- **Unsupervised Anomaly Detection:** Deep mastering models can be applied to unsupervised mastering methods, where the version identifies anomalies without the want for classified information. This method is particularly useful when categorized attack records are sparse or unavailable.

Anomaly detection can be carried out through the usage of deep "getting-to-know" fashions which can be deployed in extensive-ranging structures such as network protection and endpoint safety to reveal for any deviation that can suggest a potential chance.

5.2 Securing Communication through Encryption Models Powered by Deep Learning

One of the essential concepts of cybersecurity is the steady transmission of sensitive facts over networks. Encryption is extensively used to ensure that information is blanketed from unauthorized "get right of entry" to at some point of communique. Traditional cryptographic techniques are regularly deterministic and rely upon predefined algorithms. However, deep learning introduces the opportunity of the usage of neural networks to increase more adaptive and robust encryption models.

5.2.1 Deep Learning-based Encryption Models

Deep studying may be used to supplement or perhaps supplant traditional encryption schemes. Neural networks can learn how to encrypt and decrypt facts in methods which might be resistant to standard cryptanalysis. These models use a technique of mastering to encrypt based on schooling information, in which the neural community learns a characteristic that maps plaintext to cipher textual content and vice versa.

- **Generative Models for Encryption:** Generative Adversarial Networks (GANs) may be used to create novel encryption schemes. The generator, a part of a GAN, can discover ways to produce encrypted facts, even as the discriminator guarantees that the encryption scheme cannot be deciphered without difficulty.
- **End-to-End Encryption using Deep Learning:** Deep mastering fashions may also additionally aid in using an end-to-cease encryption process wherein facts are encrypted on the resource aspect and only a selected party, the goal consumer, is going to be in a position to decrypt. Application of deep gaining knowledge of on give up-to-stop encryption enables the key usage to be quite robust with lower possibilities to usual assault tactics.

Deep mastering-based encryption models have large benefits in phrases of flexibility and resistance to attacks. They adapt to new threats and update their encryption technique in real time with information obtained, thereby making the communication channel safer.

5.2.2 Secure Communication in IoT Systems

It is particularly challenging to secure communication between devices in the context of IoT, given that the computational resources are limited and that the devices are diverse. Deep learning can be applied to design lightweight encryption models suitable for IoT devices, which allows them to securely communicate without wasting too many resources [17]. Lightweight deep learning models can be optimized for overall performance, making sure that encryption can still be performed successfully on low-power gadgets.

5.3 Overview of Adversarial Attacks on Communication Systems and Defenses

While deep learning models have shown great promise in improving cybersecurity, they are not immune to adversarial attacks. Adversarial attacks involve manipulating the input data in a way that misleads the deep learning model into making incorrect predictions or decisions. These attacks can have serious implications for communication systems, especially in critical areas such as intrusion detection and encryption.

5.3.1 Adversarial Attacks on Deep Learning Models

The promise proven by means of deep "getting-to-know" models in enhancing cybersecurity isn't always without being immune to opposed attacks. The manipulation of enter statistics can also lead a deep mastering model to be misled into generating incorrect predictions or selections. Criticality applies to subjects like intrusion detection and encryption, in which excessive implications relate to conversation systems [18].

Adversarial Examples: As the safety applications of CNNs, RNNs, and autoencoders, adversarial examples can deceive the models, making them fail to detect threats. For instance, an attacker might regulate the community packets or malicious payloads so subtly that they escape the detection of the model.

- **Model Inversion Attacks**: Model inversion, where an attacker reconstructs sensitive information, like encryption keys or plaintext, from a compromised model, is any other context in which deep learning-powered encryption could be used to release adverse attacks.

5.3.2 Defenses against Adversarial Attacks

To counter these attacks, researchers have recommended numerous techniques to develop robustness in deep getting to know models used in protection packages. The most promising methods encompass:

- **Adversarial Training:** In this, the deep learning models are trained on hostile examples so that the version learns to pick out and face up to these varieties of attacks. The model can discover ways to come across and reject manipulated inputs all through schooling by exposing it to antagonistic inputs.

- **Defensive Distillation:** This method trains a version to supply softened output possibilities that are less prone to antagonistic perturbations. Defensive distillation has been used to make models greater resilient to small enter modifications.
- **Input Preprocessing:** It can be a great protection by means of preprocessing inputs to do away with adverse perturbations earlier than feeding into the version. Image demising and gradient protecting strategies can mitigate the outcomes of adverse assaults.

5.4 Secure Models for Communication Systems

In secure communication systems, adversarial attacks could compromise the integrity of encrypted messages or breach IDS. Techniques such as model assembling, using multiple models to verify predictions, and robust optimization can secure the communication process against adversarial manipulation.

6. Case Studies and Applications

Deep studying has been integrated into cybersecurity and verbal exchange systems, which has led to giant advancements in securing digital environments. In this segment, we explore real-global case research and applications of deep gaining knowledge in securing information transmission, improving verbal exchange in rising technology like IoT and 5G/6G, and utilizing block chain-based structures for secure conversation [19].

Case Study 1: Secure Data Transmission in IoT Using Deep Learning

The IoT has transformed the way devices communicate, but security of such devices and their data transmission is a major concern. IoT networks usually consist of a large number of heterogeneous devices with limited computational resources, making it challenging to implement traditional security measures. However, deep studying affords a progressive technique closer to securing communication in such systems by permitting intelligent anomaly detection, adaptive encryption, and efficient resource management.

Problem: IoT gadgets are fairly susceptible to cyberattacks like unauthorized access, information interception, and denial-of-provider (DoS) attacks in general due to the fact most IoT gadgets have limited computational electricity. In addition, the range of the devices and complexity in their communication styles make the challenge of securing their statistics transmission even more challenging.

Solution: In a research case study on IoT security, a deep learning-based intrusion detection system (IDS) was implemented for monitoring communication between IoT devices in a smart home network. The system used CNNs to analyze the patterns in the network traffic to identify anomalies, which are signs of potential security threats. The large dataset consists of normal and malicious behavior, which the deep learning model was trained on to, for instance, spot aberrant activities such as spikes in access pattern or traffic or unauthorized access from a device.

In addition, autoencoders were applied to anomaly detection. These autoencoders learn normal network traffic and can flag data packets that are abnormal or deviate from the normal, thus identifying a potential intrusion in real-time [20]. The result was a great reduction in false positives and enhanced accuracy in detection of attacks, such as Man-in-the-Middle (MITM) and DoS.

Results: Deploying deep learning to secure IoT communication meant that real-time adaptive anomaly detection did not require any sophisticated rule-based system. High accuracy in discovering novel attack patterns was established for the IoT network, greatly improving the security and reducing resource usage on the devices.

Case Study 2: Use of AI Models in 5G/6G Secure Communication

These features hold much promise, such as increased improvements in terms of speed, latency, and connectivity due to the 5G network roll-out and then especially due to the planned shift towards 6G. At the same time, they create new security challenges, like a larger surface for attacks, vulnerabilities brought about by the high density of connected objects, and mm Wave communication for securing purposes [12]. Deep learning models are increasingly being integrated into 5G and 6G networks to ensure secure communication to address these challenges [21].

Problem: With the broad deployment of 5G and the imminent 6G networks, communications will guide extremely-low latency, excessive bandwidth, and huge device connectivity. This expands the possibilities of applications which include self-sustaining automobiles and smart towns however also will increase the threat of cyber attacks. A significant challenge would be to ensure safe communication in a hyper-connected high-speed environment.

Solution: A case study was conducted by one of the leading telecommunication companies in integrating deep learning models into their 5G secure communication protocols to improve encryption, intrusion detection, and traffic management. The system is based on a composition of RL (reinforcement learning) and GANs dynamically adjusts security measures in real time relative to network conditions and detected threats.

- **Adaptive Security Deployed the usage of Reinforcement Learning:** RL have become implemented to constantly experiment the community surroundings and adjust protection strategies, such as encryption algorithms and visitors routing, based on detected threats and anomalies. This manner of communication remained strong while the community setup and site visitor's styles changed.
- **GANs for Encryption:** In this, the GAN generated new encryption schemes. The generator network in the GAN produced the brand new encryption keys, and the discriminator community became used to charge their energy as opposed to regarded assault strategies, for that reason helping in the formation of more secure verbal exchange channels.

Results: AI-based models integrated into the 5G communication system provided adaptive, dynamic security features that could adjust quickly to new threats. Models were enhanced not only for encryption schemes but also for real-time monitoring and response to potential intrusions. The introduction of deep learning made the network better suited to handle the complexities and vulnerabilities of high-speed, highly connected environments like 5G and 6G.

6.1 Applications of Deep Learning in Block Chain Based Secure Communication

Block chain generation is being adopted extensively for securing the instantaneous messaging element of transactions and information garage, due to its decentralized characteristics and immutability. However, securing communique channels within block chain-based systems, together with transactions and consensus mechanisms, remains a problem. Deep learning is a key location being explored for improving the security of block chain networks by improving fraud detection, computerized transaction validation, and defending in opposition to diverse styles of attacks.

6.1.1 Deep Learning for Fraud Detection in Block Chain Transactions

Fraudulent sports in block chain systems consist of double-spending and Sybil assaults, which compromise the integrity of network practices. Deep getting to know fashions can pick out styles of bizarre transactions or validate sequences of the transactions using RNNs and automobile encoders.

- **RNNs for Validation of Transaction Collection:** RNNs can test conventional styles in sequences of transactions over the years. Once a strange transaction is made, together with double spending or reversal, the RNN flags the ambiguity and alerts the community.
- **Auto Encoders for Fraud Detection:** Auto encoders may be used to examine a compressed representation of everyday transaction styles. Any transaction that deviates from this located out behavior can be flagged as potentially fraudulent.

6.1.2 Enhancing Consensus Mechanisms with Deep Learning

Mechanisms such as proof of work and proof of stake in block chains give way to mechanisms for validating a transaction and achieving a consistent ledger state. Deep learning improves these with predictive attacks towards the network so that the validations can be improved in terms of optimizing the entire validation process in a network.

- **Prediction of Consensus Failures:** Deep learning models can predict when a particular consensus mechanism might fail due to malicious activities, network congestion, or node behavior anomalies. Block chain networks can, therefore, increase their resilience against attacks and become more efficient with the integration of predictive models.

6.1.3 Block Chain Based Secure Communication in Decentralized Networks

Block chain may be used to stable verbal exchange among nodes in a decentralized network. Smart contracts and deep studying may be used to establish steady and automatic verbal exchange channels. For instance, smart contracts can put into effect protection guidelines, and deep learning fashions can continuously reveal communique for suspicious activities, ensuring that only authorized messages are allowed through the network.

6.1.4 Securing Identity and Authentication in Block Chain Systems

Authenticating and handling the identities in block chain-based systems is the most important. In such systems, deep learning may also be used to improve identity verification through the use of biometric authentication-possible facial recognition or voice recognition-or behavioral biometrics-user behavior pattern analysis.

- **Secure Access through Biometric Authentication:** Block chain structures can combine deep gaining knowledge of totally based biometric authentication with a view to authenticate simplest authorized users, consequently stopping unauthenticated access to sensitive statistics or even transactions. For instance, the totally deep learning-based facial reputation systems may be incorporated for the authentication of customers' identities earlier than letting them get right of entry to the block chain community.

Results: Block chain-based secure communication is enhanced through deep learning by more accurate fraud detection, improvement of mechanisms of consensus, and automation of identity verification. Deep learning integration leads to improvement of block chain networks with resilience against attacks and is better-equipped to deal with further complexity in the transactions of digital deals and decentralized applications.

7. Challenges and Future Directions

The growth of deep learning has been dramatic in improving communications systems and cybersecurity. The rapid evolution of technology, the complexity of highly interconnected systems to be secured, and the growing need for integrating deep learning into quantum communication security are both its limitations and the new opportunities to be explored further [22]. This section briefly discusses the existing limitations of the architectures and frameworks, emerging trends and research gaps, and what lies ahead in deep learning and quantum communication security integration.

7.1 Limitations of Existing Architectures and Frameworks

Many of the present-day architectures and frameworks in communication and protection also have boundaries approximately their promising packages using deep mastering.

7.1.1 Computational Overhead and Resource Requirements

Deep getting to know fashions, especially the ones utilized in complicated applications which includes intrusion detection, anomaly detection, and encryption, require pretty excessive computational energy. Deep neural networks require powerful computing hardware, such as high-performance GPUs and high memory capacity, to train from large-scale datasets. In systems like IoT devices or edge computing environments, these resource requirements will be more of a bottleneck because many devices are resource-constrained and cannot support deep learning models efficiently [23]

7.1.2 Lack of Explain Capability and Transparency

One of the largest worrying situations in deep analysis is that many models are black packing containers. Deep mastering may also additionally attain immoderate overall performance in detecting assaults or anomalies, but it is hard to give an explanation for why a model made a specific decision. In vital safety programs, including intrusion detection structures (IDS) or automatic encryption, the incapacity to provide clean reasoning for selections can avert acceptance as true with and adoption, especially in regulated industries [24]. This loss of transparency complicates the manner of debugging models, information vulnerabilities, and improving their overall performance.

7.1.3 Vulnerability to Adversarial Attacks

Deep studying fashions are also at risk of antagonistic assaults, where slight carefully crafted perturbations in the entered facts can deceive the model in making faulty predictions. In cybersecurity contexts, hostile assaults can affect security measures, consisting of intrusion detection and anomaly detection structures. Increasing the sophistication of such adversarial techniques makes ensuring robustness for deploying deep learning models in real-world security scenarios very challenging.

7.1.4 Data Privacy and Ethical Concerns

Data which could be vast with sensitive information might be collected during training in large amounts. Since data privacy matters a lot, especially for any form of cybersecurity, or communication purposes; in this aspect, raising ethical problems can be avoided and thus development for deep learning models that ensure that the outputs or the working algorithms are sound for applicability and adherence to the policy would be essential. In such a case, models trained with biased data could lead to poor discriminatory outcomes, especially concerning applications such as biometric authentication or fraud detection [25].

7.2 Emerging Trends and Research Gaps in Deep Learning for Communication and Security

As the combination of deep analyzing into communique and cybersecurity continues to evolve, many rising tendencies may be seen that allows you to form future research guidelines.

7.2.1 Federated Mastering for Privacy-retaining Protection Fashions

Federated learning is a rising paradigm that enables a machine reading model to study know-how at some stage in decentralized gadgets or edge nodes without absolutely sharing the sensitive records with a critical server. This technique has super implications, specifically in the geographical areas of communication and cybersecurity, as it permits the education of sturdy deep analyzing models at the same time as maintaining statistics privateers [26]. The consciousness of studies is on the manner to correctly implement federated gaining knowledge in aid-constrained environments like IoT devices that can offer a manner to steady communications on the same time as respecting privateers' concerns.

7.2.2 Lightweight Deep Learning Models for Edge and IoT Security

Deep learning models applied for safety responsibilities very often require heavy computational belongings. This makes them a motive to get wrong for things like gadgets or IoT packages. For this reason, there may be a developing trend in the path of developing light-weight deep studying models optimized for deployment on low-energy gadgets. Model compression techniques, which includes pruning, quantization, and knowledge distillation, are an increasing number of important for making deep mastering viable in resource-restricted environments. Future studies will probably focus on the way to make these lightweight models extra efficient and effective without sacrificing safety [27].

7.2.3 Explainability and Interpretability of Deep Learning Models

As discussed above, the scarcity of interpretability in deep studying models makes them a massive hurdle in their adoption in safety applications. Researchers are increasingly focused on developing techniques for making those models more apparent and interpretable. Techniques such as Shapley values, saliency maps, and community surrogate fashions are being explored to provide perception into how deep gaining knowledge of models make decisions, which might enhance their trustworthiness and cost in cybersecurity structures.

7.2.4 Cross-domain Security Solutions

The security challenges will be more advanced, and a cross-domain solution is very evident. For example, deep learning with block chain technology for the secure communication of block chain, AI with 5G/6G networks for a more efficient method of communication in order to gain stronger defenses against evolving cyber threats [28]. The idea of research will be on hybrid models with the strengths of different technologies that combine to offer the best security, scalability, and efficiency.

7.3 Future Possibilities in Quantum Communication Security with AI Integration

The destiny of steady verbal exchange is going to be fashioned by using quantum computing and quantum communication technology, and deep studying is in all likelihood to have a vital position to play in this space. Quantum communication systems are based on quantum cryptographic protocols, which can be theoretically immune to eavesdropping and therefore offer extraordinary security. However, the mixture of deep studying with quantum communication in addition to decorative protection opens up quite a few exciting opportunities.

7.3.1 Quantum Key Distribution and Deep Learning

One of the essential building blocks of quantum conversation is Quantum Key Distribution (QKD), which enables stable key trade. Deep getting to know may be carried out to improve the efficiency and robustness of QKD structures. For example, deep gaining knowledge of fashions may want to optimize the method of key distribution, thereby growing the velocity of steady communication whilst preserving excessive safety ranges. This may be complemented with deep learning for the detection of quantum channel assaults by way of anomaly in the key alternate method and security features adjustment.

7.3.2 AI-driven Quantum Cryptanalysis

This advance can potentially crack existing cryptographic algorithms being used by modern communication systems. Researchers have taken the opportunity to develop novel schemes for new cryptographic models through deep learning techniques to resist such quantum attacks. Quantum-resistant encryption techniques can thus be designed through AI models in support of building secure future communication systems.

7.3.3 Quantum Machine Learning for Secure Communication

Quantum machine learning (QML) represents a new frontier that combines the field of quantum computing with the learning paradigm. In continual dialogue, QML can be applied to optimize encryption, improve anomaly detection and intrusion prevention capabilities. Quantum systems can also supply unique properties in accelerating the education of deep understanding models in true time to be able to determine safety in extremely difficult conversation environments.

7.3.4 Quantum Communication Networks and AI Integration

Given the large-scale propagation of quantum communication networks, deep learning models can be combined with the quantum network to ensure such networks' safety. AI models can monitor the quantum conversation community for anomalies, detect potential eavesdropping tries, and optimize using quantum sources for max security. In the destiny, the aggregate of quantum verbal exchange and AI-driven safety ought to provide a new paradigm of extremely-steady communication, presenting safety towards even the most sophisticated cyber threats.

8. Conclusion

This chapter has discussed the transformative position of deep getting to know in improving contemporary facts, conversation, and protection systems. With the evolving nature of verbal exchange technologies and growing sophistication of cybersecurity threats, the need for superior answers is at its maximum compelling point ever. Deep learning is a process of processing huge data, pattern recognition, and making real-time decisions, which has shown to be quite effective in handling the security issues related to modern communication systems. We start by covering the basics of deep learning and some of its key architectures, like CNN, RNN, and autoencoders, which have shown incredible promise in making the data transmission efficient, reliable, and secure. These architectures were accomplished in diverse domain names, from IoT security to 5G/6G communications, in which they facilitate secure conversation with the aid of detecting intrusions, enhancing encryption strategies, and ensuring the confidentiality and integrity of transmitted records. The bankruptcy additionally covered the numerous frameworks and equipment—which incorporates Tensor Flow and PyTorch—that empower researchers and practitioners to increase deep studying primarily based solutions for securing communique systems. These frameworks, in combination with AI models that have been integrated into block chain and quantum communication systems, open avenues toward much more robust and adaptive security mechanisms for highly complex networks. In this work, through case studies and real-world applications, we showcased the deployment of deep learning toward the successful protection of IoT networks, 5G/6G infrastructure, and block chain-based communication systems. This case research verified the capability of deep studying in dealing with particular protection threats, together with intrusion detection, statistics tampering, and unauthorized access. However, regardless of its several benefits, the chapter additionally emphasized the challenges going through the combination of deep mastering in communique and safety systems. Issues along with computational overhead, loss of giving an explanation for ability, vulnerability to adversarial assaults, and information privateers' worries want to be addressed for deep mastering to attain its full ability. Emerging trends along with federated learning, light-weight models, and the combination of quantum communication with AI-driven safety solutions factor in the direction of exciting future opportunities in this discipline. Finally, the destiny of constant statistics verbal exchange is based upon further improvement in deep gaining knowledge of strategies. They are sure to play an important function in the next technology of conversation networks, which might encompass quantum-secured structures. The persisted evolution of the era would supply an extra enormous integration of deep analysis with the newly growing field of quantum computing to further improve the sturdy and adaptive nature of communication and security mechanisms.

References

1. Al-Garadi, M.A., A. Mohamed, A.K. Al-Ali, X. Du, I. Ali, & M. Guizani. (2020). A survey of machine and deep learning methods for internet of things (IoT) security. *IEEE Communications Surveys and Tutorials*, 22(3), 1646–1685.
2. Santhosh Kumar, S.V.N., M. Selvi, & A. Kannan. (2023). A comprehensive survey on machine learning-based intrusion detection systems for secure communication in Internet of Things. *Computational Intelligence and Neuroscienc*e, 2023(1), 8981988.
3. Benzaid, C., & T. Taleb. (2020). AI-driven zero touch network and service management in 5G and beyond: Challenges and research directions. *IEEE Network*, 34(2), 186–194.
4. Abed, A.K., & A. Anupam. (2023). Review of security issues in Internet of Things and artificial intelligence-driven solutions. *Security and Privacy*, 6(3), e285.

5. Selem, M., F. Jemili, & O. Korbaa. (2025). Deep learning for intrusion detection in IoT networks. *Peer-to-Peer Networking and Applications*, 18(2), 22.
6. Wu, B., J. Xu, Y. Zhang, B. Liu, Y. Gong, & J. Huang. (2024). Integration of computer networks and artificial neural networks for an AI-based network operator. arXiv preprint arXiv:2407.01541.
7. Mistry, H.K., C. Mavani, A. Goswami, & R. Patel. (2024). Artificial intelligence for networking. *Educational Administration: Theory and Practice*, 30(7), 813–821.
8. Ahmad, J., M.U. Zia, I.H. Naqvi, J.N. Chattha, F.A. Butt, T. Huang, & W. Xiang. (2024). Machine learning and blockchain technologies for cybersecurity in connected vehicles. *Wiley Interdisciplinary Reviews: Data Mining and Knowledge Discovery*, 14(1), e1515.
9. Li, Z., Q. Chen, J. Li, J. Huang, W. Mo, D.S. Wong, & H. Jiang. (2024). A secure and efficient UAV network defense strategy: Convergence of blockchain and deep learning. *Computer Standards & Interfac*es, 90, 103844.
10. Javeed, D., M.S. Saeed, I. Ahmad, M. Adil, P. Kumar, & A.N. Islam. (2024). Quantum-empowered federated learning and 6G wireless networks for IoT security: Concept, challenges, and future directions. *Future Generation Computer Systems*, 160, 577–597.
11. Rzym, G., A. Masny, & P. Cholda. (2024). Dynamic telemetry and deep neural networks for anomaly detection in 6G software-defined networks. *Electronics*, 13(2), 382.
12. Hussain, A., A. Mehdi, & C.H. Kim. (2024). A communication-less islanding detection scheme for hybrid distributed generation systems using recurrent neural network. *International Journal of Electrical Power & Energy Systems*, 155, 109659.
13. Lilhore, U.K., S. Dalal, & S. Simaiya. (2024). A cognitive security framework for detecting intrusions in IoT and 5G utilizing deep learning. *Computers & Security*, 136, 103560.
14. Zhao, C., H. Du, D. Niyato, J. Kang, Z. Xiong, D.I. Kim, ... & K.B. Letaief. (2025). Generative AI for secure physical layer communications: A survey. *IEEE Transactions on Cognitive Communications and Networking*, 11(1), 3–26.
15. Kumar, S., G. Gupta & K.R. Singh. (2015). 5G: Revolution of future communication technology, In: *International Conference on Green Computing and Internet of Things* (*ICGCIoT*), pp. 143–147. Greater Noida, India, 2015. doi: 10.1109/ICGCIoT.2015.7380446.
16. Abd Elaziz, M., M.A. Al-qaness, A. Dahou, S.H. Alsamhi, L. Abualigah, R.A. Ibrahim, & A.A. Ewees. (2024). Evolution toward intelligent communications: Impact of deep learning applications on the future of 6G technology. *Wiley Interdisciplinary Reviews: Data Mining and Knowledge Discovery*, 14(1), e1521.
17. Blika, A., S. Palmos, G. Doukas, V. Lamprou, S. Pelekis, M. Kontoulis, ... & D. Askounis. (2024). Federated learning for enhanced cybersecurity and trustworthiness in 5G and 6G networks: A comprehensive survey. *IEEE Open Journal of the Communications Society*, 6, 3094–3130.
18. Khaleel, Y.L., M.A. Habeeb, A.S. Albahri, T. Al-Quraishi, O.S. Albahri, & A.H. Alamoodi. (2024). Network and cybersecurity applications of defense in adversarial attacks: A state-of-the-art using machine learning and deep learning methods. *Journal of Intelligent Systems*, 33(1), 20240153.
19. Sanagana, D.P.R., & C.K. Tummalacheruvu. (2024, May). Securing cloud computing environment via optimal deep learning-based intrusion detection systems. In: *2024 Second International Conference on Data Science and Information System* (*ICDSIS*), pp. 1–6. IEEE.
20. Shinde, R., S. Patil, K. Kotecha, V. Potdar, G. Selvachandran, & A. Abraham. (2024). Securing AI-based healthcare systems using blockchain technology: A state-of-the-art

systematic literature review and future research directions. *Transactions on Emerging Telecommunications Technologies*, 35(1), e4884.

21. Ghubaish, A., Z. Yang, & R. Jain. (2024, May). HDRL-IDS: A hybrid deep reinforcement learning intrusion detection system for enhancing the security of medical applications in 5G Networks. In: *2024 International Conference on Smart Applications, Communications, and Networking* (*SmartNets*), pp. 1–6. IEEE.
22. Dong, R., B. Wang, K. Cao, J. Tian, & T. Cheng. (2024). Secure transmission design of RIS enabled UAV communication networks exploiting deep reinforcement learning. *IEEE Transactions on Vehicular Technology*, 73(6), 8404–8419.
23. Okafor, E.S., O. Akinrinola, F.O. Usman, O.O. Amoo, & N.A. Ochuba. (2024). Cybersecurity analytics in protecting satellite telecommunications networks: A conceptual development of current trends, challenges, and strategic responses. *International Journal of Applied Research in Social Sciences*, 6(3), 254–266.
24. Awad, A.I., A. Babu, E. Barka, & K. Shuaib. (2024). AI-powered biometrics for Internet of Things security: A review and future vision. *Journal of Information Security and Applications*, 82, 103748.
25. Karthikeyan, M., D. Manimegalai, & K. RajaGopal. (2024). Firefly algorithm based WSN-IoT security enhancement with machine learning for intrusion detection. *Scientific Reports*, 14(1), 231.
26. Damaraju, A. (2024). The future of cybersecurity: 5G and 6G networks and their implications. *International Journal of Advanced Engineering Technologies and Innovations*, 1(3), 359–386.
27. Mishra, K.N., V. Bhattacharjee, S. Saket, & S.P. Mishra. (2024). Security provisions in smart edge computing devices using blockchain and machine learning algorithms: A novel approach. *Cluster Computing*, 27(1), 27–52.
28. Gonaygunta, H., G.S. Nadella, P.P. Pawar, & D. Kumar. (2024, May). Enhancing cybersecurity: The development of a flexible deep learning model for enhanced anomaly detection. In: *2024 Systems and Information Engineering Design Symposium* (*SIEDS*), pp. 79–84. IEEE.

6 | Security Threats to Cloud Computing and Cloud Services

Mohan Singh[1*], Arti Joshi[2], Kapil Dev Tyagi[3], Vaibhav Bhushan Tyagi[4]

[1] Department of ECE, G.L. Bajaj Institute of Technology and Management, Greater Noida - 201308, India
[2] Department of Geography, D.S.B. Campus, Nainital, Uttarakhand - 263002, India
[3] Department of ECE, Jaypee Institute of Information Technology, Noida - 201309, India
[4] Department of ECE, ISBAT University, Kampala, Uganda

1. Introduction

The extraordinary integration of on premise and cloud-based systems is known as cloud computing. It enables the creation of a hybrid platform that fosters business expansion without regard for investments or the perfect environment. The methods used in modern cloud computing are more flexible and agile. It helps businesses of all sizes and sectors fulfil their infrastructure, software, and hardware demands. Recent advances in cloud computing have increased the technology's adaptability and scalability. This helps give companies more control over their data. It also helps each data centre's security to be better. The latest cloud computing solutions include well-organized key components. Therefore, without needing active and direct user administration, cloud computing enables processing power and data storage. Clients of cloud computing are able to access servers, apps, and storage facilities through their utilization of the Internet. There are several benefits to using these combined resources. Due to their high cost, dedicated data centres are not accessible to many businesses. However, with cloud computing, they can make use of these resources to the most degree possible. The sharing of digital files and media storage through Google Drive is a well-known application of cloud computing. You may share a link to a Drive folder so that both of you can view and edit it.

A new form of computing known as "cloud computing" refers to the provision of resources that are rapidly scalable and frequently integrated as offerings through the Internet. Cloud computing is the term for network sharing of computer resources depending on demand. Other organizations typically provide these resources, and

*Corresponding author: mohansingh571@gmail.com

DOI: 10.1201/9781003560012-6

they simply need minimal supervision. There are several relevant models and frameworks for cloud computing that may be employed with additional resources and approaches to design [1–3]. Cloud computing is ranked as one of the most significant ten technologies that will disrupt the foreseeable future by Gartner [4]. It represents the long-held ambition of realizing computation as a provider of services [5], where the fundamentals of capitalism and economies of scale assist in significantly lowering the cost of the infrastructure used for computing. Cloud technology has emerged as a key technological pipeline, and numerous analysts predict that it will drastically alter IT operations and the IT industry. The use of cloud computing technological advances allows users to access software, retrieval, and application-development frameworks through the Internet using a range of gadgets, notably desktops, notebooks, cell-phones, and PDAs (personal digital assistants). Reduced expenses, a high level of availability, as well as straightforward scalability, are benefits of cloud computing technological advancements. The six main stages of paradigms for computing are depicted in Figure 1, which has undergone modifications by Voas and Zhang [6]. They range from the dummy value mainframes/terminals through PCs, collaborating computing, computing on a grid, and the use of cloud computing.

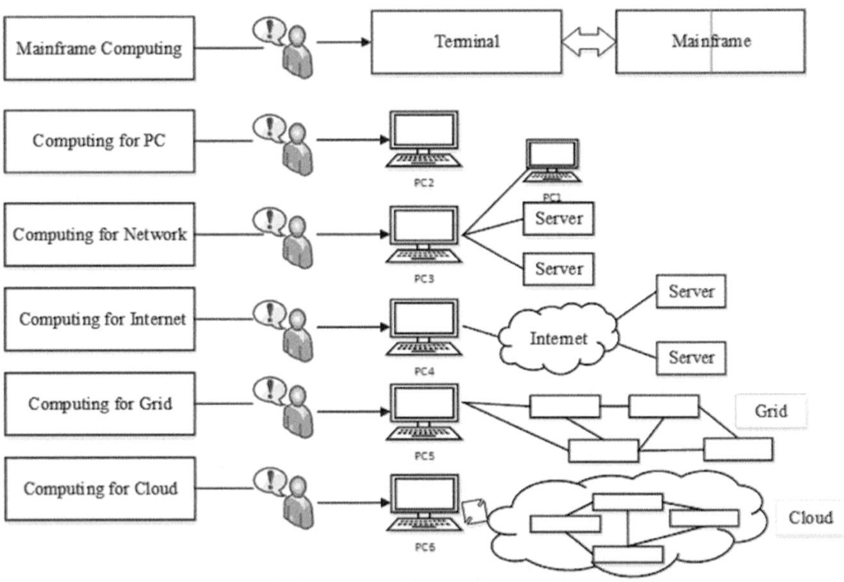

Figure 1: Six different approaches to computing exist, ranging from computing mainframe to Internet computing, as well as computing on a grid, and computing in the cloud.

During Phase 1, plenty of people utilized fake terminals to share robust mainframes. Phase 2 saw the development of standalone PCs that were capable of serving the bulk of user requirements. Phase 3 involved connecting notebooks, personal computers, and servers over local networks in order to collaborate on resources and improve functionality. To access overseas applications and amenities, regional networks were linked together in Phase 4 to create a global network similar to the Internet. Through the use of the distributed computational architecture, Phase 5 grid computing offered pooled processing resources and storage. Phase 6 of cloud computing continues to offer a flexible and user-friendly collaboration of resources over the Internet. It appears that cloud computing is an amendment to the classical mainframe technological paradigm when compared to these other six computing paradigms. These two paradigms do differ in a number of significant ways, though. Although cloud computing offers nearly endless power and computing on mainframes has limited computational capability. Additionally, fake terminals were used as user interface devices in mainframe computers, but in cloud computing, sophisticated PCs might offer local processing power and financial assistance.

The following are the top five features needed to provide security threats to cloud computing, according to NIST:

1. **Self-service Available on Demand:** Without involving a person, cloud resources may be accessed or supplied. Customers can sign up for this model and have instant access to cloud services. The ability to access their own resources and cloud services on interest and in accordance with preset logic without going via IT services is another capability that organizations may develop.
2. **Extensive Network Access:** If they have an authorization, users are able to utilize cloud resources and other services from any networked location using any device.
3. **Pooling of Resources:** Numerous tenants access the infrastructure of the cloud service provider, yet particular clients' data is kept private from the rest of the customers.
4. **Quickly Elastic:** Contrary to within the premises computer equipment and software, computing resources in the cloud can be quickly raised, lowered, or changed in any other way in response to the changing demands of the cloud user.
5. **Assessed Service:** Corporations and other cloud clients only have to make payments for what capabilities they actually use during a given billing period since cloud resource usage is metered.

The whole chapter is divided into four sections as shown in Figure 2: Section I is for cloud computing technology and systems, in which the cloud computing systems and technologies are elaborated in terms of the role of networks and service-oriented workflows. In Section II, the architecture of cloud computing has been covered in detail including load distribution. All the cloud computing services including types and scalability over the cloud are covered in Section III. In Section IV, all the utilization possibilities are introduced with an enhanced computing paradigm. Eventually, the chapter concludes with cloud computing potential in future trends from a professional standpoint.

2. Cloud Computing Technologies and Systems

The most recent technology, cloud computing, has made it simpler for businesses to organize their data and provide seamless access to their distant staff. Removing the

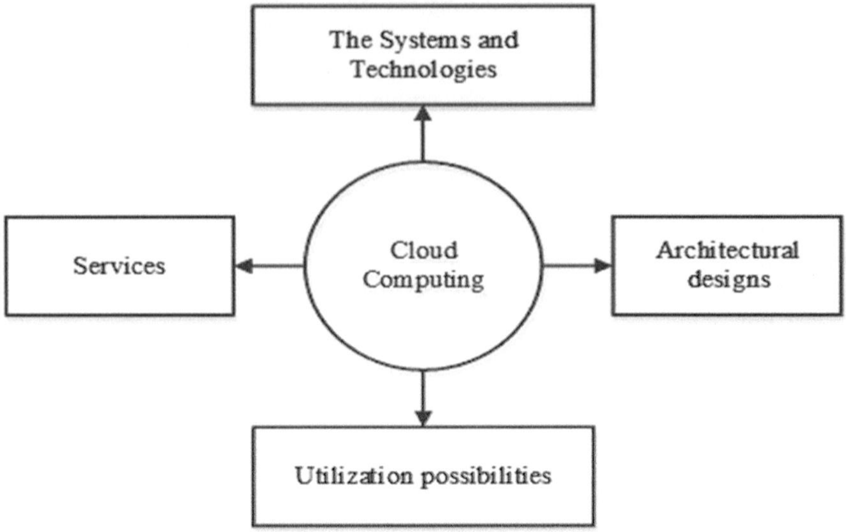

Figure 2: Basics of cloud computing.

need for any physical components and storage arrangements, it also aids in cost reduction. You receive a more secure cloud network that allows all team members to remain connected to one another and collaborate regardless of where they are physically located. Different cloud technologies must collaborate to create a more secure cloud network. All of these essential parts are hosted by the CNCF (Cloud Native Computing Foundation), which also provides infrastructure to the process's subscribers, technical staff, and developers. The many hybrid computing features that support cloud computing technologies are what make cloud services successful in execution. Every organization has different demands, thus altering the cloud computing architecture is necessary to accommodate all of them. Only a specialist can assist with the adaptations that the cloud specialists provide because they are based on cloud technology. The optimum cloud technology for a particular cloud application is better understood by the specialists. They can assist with speedy implementation because they have an in-depth understanding of each kind. Let's go further and comprehend the technologies that each cloud specialist would study and use in their professional careers.

Technological Advances: The cloud-based computing tools that businesses may use to create their cloud frameworks are listed below.

> **Virtualization:** It is a procedure for building a virtual environment that will allow several operations to operate on a single server. It might be a virtual replica of servers, a network of cloud services, and storage devices. However, a mix of these resources is another possibility. By doing so, you may grant access to a group of users while allowing numerous virtual apps to share a single physical source. The virtual networks that a real-world application produces are referred to as guests, while the actual application itself is the host computer.

Virtualization is a popular technique among cloud users and works well for all sorts of computing clouds.

Deployment of Virtualization: Following are the deployment virtualization of cloud computing.

(i) The benefits of virtualization are innumerable.
(ii) Decreases the expense of establishing and maintaining an IT system.
(iii) Enables the running of many operating systems on both real and virtual computers.
(iv) Employees may access the system remotely, which helps the business run more efficiently.
(v) It provides effective resource allocation, which aids in scalability.

The functionality of many different kinds of real-world infrastructure may be obtained using virtualization technology, together with all the advantages of a virtualized environment. In your virtual surroundings, you may build an assortment of virtual resources in addition to virtual computers.

Server Virtualization: A real server is divided into several virtual servers through a technique known as server virtualization. It is a productive and economical approach to employ server resources and offer IT services to a company. Without server virtualization, physical servers only utilize a small portion of their computing power, leaving equipment inactive.

Storage Virtualization: SAN (Storage Area Network) and NAS (Network-Attached Storage) are two examples of physical storage systems whose functionalities are combined by storage virtualization. Even if it comes from many suppliers or is of various sorts, you may still pool the storage gear in your data centre. Utilizing management software, you may allocate and administer a sizable virtual storage unit created by storage virtualization utilizing all of your physical storage for data. Because they can essentially integrate numerous network storage devices into one storage device, IT administrators may simplify storage tasks like archiving, backup, and recovery.

Network Virtualization: Hardware components including routers, switches, and firewalls are present in all computer networks. The corporate network of a company with offices spread across numerous different regions can be built using a variety of different network technologies. All these network resources are combined through the procedure of network virtualization, which centralizes administrative chores.

Data Virtualization: Modern businesses get data from many sources and store it in a variety of ways. They could also save data in several locations, like a local data centre and a cloud infrastructure. Through the use of software, data virtualization establishes a barrier between the data and the applications that use it. An application's data request is processed by data virtualization technologies, and the results are returned in the appropriate format. Therefore, organizations utilize data virtualization technologies to enhance the cross-functional evaluation of data and boost flexibility for data globalization.

Application Virtualization: The virtualization of applications extracts an application's functionality so that it may operate on an operating system that's different from the one for which it was originally created. For instance, users don't need to modify the computer's setup to run a Microsoft Windows program on a Linux machine.

Service-Oriented Architecture: An application called SOA separates the services into distinct business functions and everyday operations. This particular cloud application component provides cloud-related arrangements that may be changed and amended as needed based on business requirements. A service-oriented system consists of two main parts: software as a service, and quality as a service. Identifying a service's behaviour and operation from a distinct perspective is its primary purpose. A new software delivery model known as "software as a service" is offered and is derived from the world of application service providers.

Grid Computing: In order to accomplish a shared objective, several servers are connected through this method. By breaking enormous issues down into smaller ones, servers are broadcast to and placed inside the grid through the use of grid computing. It is mostly used in e-commerce and is designed to share resources on massively parallel cluster computing. Folding@home is a well-known grid-computing project. The initiative seeks to identify disorders connected to protein folding and misfolding. It entails using the computing capacity of idle computers to resolve challenging scientific puzzles.

Utility Computing: The pay-per-utilize approach is utilized in this procedure. For a metered benefit, it offers computational services on demand. Lowering the initial expenditure, it mostly aids in cost reduction. The billing changes in accordance with changes in a business's computing needs without incurring any additional costs. The cost of charging likewise decreases in line with a decrease in customer utilization.

3. Architectural Design of Cloud Computing

An Architecture for computing is created by combining a number of different parts and subparts. Along with an integration of the event-driven framework and the service-oriented design in cloud computing, security design is categorized into frontend and backend components in this technology. Frontend architecture is oriented towards users and clients. Applications and client-side user interfaces are included that are required to use cloud computing systems. Through a network, such as the Internet, the frontend and backend may communicate. Additionally, using the middleware, the user experience sends inquiries to the backend (examples include web servers, smartphones, thin clients, tablets, and fat clients).

The cloud itself is referred to as the backend, on the other hand. It is a collection of cloud computing resources that service providers (sometimes referred to as hosts) employ to administer and run cloud services. It provides security for the data of cloud users. Middleware is another feature offered by the backend that facilitates communication and device connection. The backend replies to requests appropriately while also safeguarding the data that is received from the frontend. This section of cloud architecture design handles traffic control in addition to security management (Examples include the use of virtual devices, traffic management systems, and massive storage of data). All researchers may learn more about the cloud by seeing the architectural Figure 3 for cloud computing.

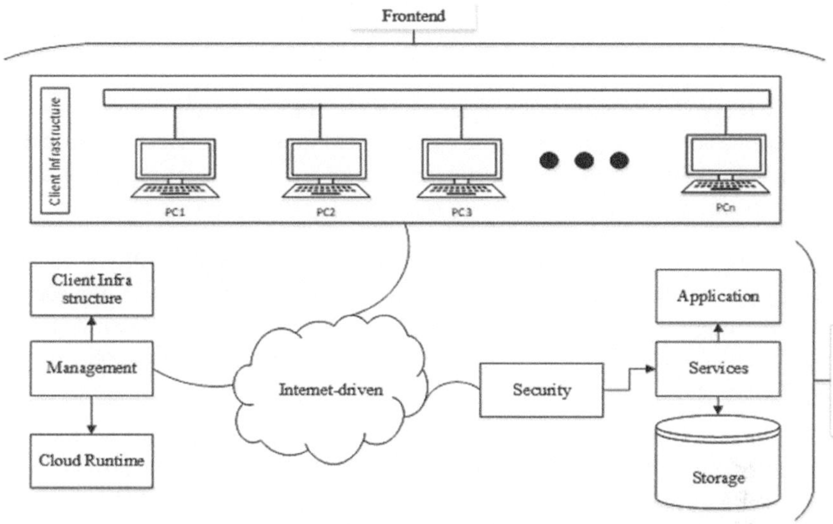

Figure 3: Framework for cloud computing.

Numerous loosely linked components make up cloud computing. It carries out activities with the aid of these digital infrastructure design components and subcomponents. The user interactions, client-side apps, and client devices or networks that let users communicate with and use remote computing applications are all included in frontend technologies in cloud computing. For instance, you might edit a Google Doc while the cell phone's web browser is open. These three terms all refer to elements of frontend cloud architecture. The backend, contrary to popular belief, refers to the cloud architectural components that comprise the cloud itself, such as computing resources, retrieval, security methods, management, and so on.

The frontend and the backend are the two core elements of the cloud computing architecture. In this design, the frontend serves as the client and connects with the backend via an internet connection or network. The client-side, or frontend, of a cloud computing framework, is made visible to external entities, while the backend is kept hidden from any outside contacts but it is still able to connect with the client directly via a specified protocol. Important data is protected by the backend of cloud computing systems from the demands of client-facing technologies.

Backend Architectural Design for Cloud Computing

The frontend's functionality is made possible by the backend. Hardware and storage are included in it. The whole burden of carrying out the backend of cloud computing falls on a cloud service provider. As it keeps the whole thing together, the backend of the cloud architecture should ideally be strong. The following are the main elements of the backend architecture:

Application: The backend software or program that the client uses to coordinate or complete client requests and needs.

Service: The service, which manages all the actions carried out on a cloud computing system, is the brain of the cloud architecture. It controls which resources, such as storage, developing application surroundings, and web-based applications.

Runtime Cloud: The runtime cloud acts as an operating system to organise and execute service activities, providing the environment in which services are operated. Runtimes build hypervisors using virtualization technologies that represent all of your services, including applications, storage spaces, servers, and connectivity.

Storage: Data needed to run apps is saved in a storage system on the back end. Although there are many cloud storage choices available depending on the service provider, the majority of cloud service providers offer adaptable, scalable storage services that can accommodate enormous volumes of data. Storage options include persistent discs, solid-state drives, and hard drives in server bays.

Infrastructure: The part of cloud architecture that is arguably the most well-known is the infrastructure. You could have even assumed that cloud architecture included cloud infrastructure. However, the CPU, graphics processing unit (GPU), computer networks, and other gear required for systems to function properly are all included in the cloud infrastructure, that powers cloud services. In every aspect, the software required to operate and control everything is referred to as infrastructure as well.

Management: Resources must be handled in real-time in accordance with user needs for cloud service models. To organize communication between the frontend and backend cloud design components and distribute resources for certain activities, management software, sometimes referred to as middleware, is crucial. In addition to middleware, management software will provide features for data emancipation application deployment as well, use monitoring, and disaster recovery.

Security: Implementing cloud privacy safeguards and solutions is essential to protecting data, apps, and platforms as more businesses utilize cloud computing. To give visibility, guard against data loss and interruptions, and provide redundancy, it is crucial to plan and integrate data security and security for the network. Regular backups as needed, debugging tasks, and virtual firewalls may all be part of this.

Frontend Architectural Design for Cloud Computing

The entirety of a user's interactions are represented at the front end of the cloud computation framework. A user interface is made up of several different subcomponents put together in combination. These are the main frontend elements:

User Interface: All the activities an end user carries out to access a platform are represented by a user interface. Sheets from Google, Gmail, and other tools have some of the more well-known user interfaces. The advantage of the cloud is that it can handle the full workload without bothering clients about space or other limitations.

Client Infrastructure: A graphical user interface (GUI) is a frontend feature of cloud computing that makes it possible for people to communicate with the cloud.

Software: It illustrates the user-facing cloud software design. It focuses mostly on browsers and on the client side software.

Network or Client Device: Client devices are essential for connecting cloud services across the network. Here, the frontend and the backend communicate with one another using the Internet as an interconnected medium. Hardware is the party that stands up for end consumers. Additionally, the network may be offered as a utility, allowing users to choose their own protocol and network path.

Working Behaviour of Cloud Computing

In cloud architectural design, all of the elements come together to provide a framework for cloud computing that gives users access to various services and resources as needed. All of a cloud service provider's assets, amenities, storage of information, and applications are located on the backend. The frontend and backend cloud computing components are linked via a network, allowing data to be exchanged back and forth between layers. The frontend, also known as the client-side user interface, uses middleware to transmit queries to the backend, where the services model handles the specific job or request. There are a few typical cloud architectural models, even though no two clouds are the same.

Multi-cloud Architectural Design: Numerous public cloud services are utilized in a multi-cloud architecture. A multiple cloud platform's environment's benefits include more freedom in selecting and deploying the cloud services that are most probable to meet various organizational needs. Reduced dependence on any one provider of cloud services allows for higher cost reductions and a decreased risk of vendor lock-in. Furthermore, multi-cloud architecture could be necessary to enable containerized systems based on small-scale services where services are located on different clouds.

Hybrid Cloud Architectural Design: A hybrid cloud infrastructure combines the individual cloud's data security features with the public cloud's operational efficiency. Hybrid clouds let organizations consolidate their information technology assets while facilitating workload migration between environments based on their IT and data security needs. Hybrid clouds use both public and private cloud infrastructures.

Private Cloud Architectural Design: A private cloud is one that is privately operated and controlled, typically in a business's own on-site data centre. However, an individual cloud can also incorporate rented space in geographically dispersed colocation facilities or numerous server sites. Private cloud platforms can offer stricter data compliance and safety choices while often costing more than public cloud alternatives.

Public Cloud Architectural Design: Computing facilities are owned and managed by a cloud services provider in a public cloud framework. Through the Internet, these resources are pooled and disseminated across many tenants. Reduced operational expenses, simple scalability, and minimal to no upkeep are benefits of the public cloud.

Benefits of Cloud Architectural Design

The framework for cloud computing is created in a way that offers a number of advantages. The design of cloud computing has a number of benefits, some of which include:

- Enhancing data processing needs and resolving delay difficulties.
- Lowering IT operational expenses and ensuring optimal data and digital tool accessibility.
- Facilitating simple scaling up and scaling down of an organization's cloud resources.
- Offering adaptability as a feature gives organizations a competitive edge.
- Higher security and improved catastrophe recovery.
- Automatically updating services.
- Remote employment and enhanced teamwork.

4. Cloud Computing Services

Cloud computing is a popular buzzword in today's society. The majority of IT companies, including Google, Salesforce, Microsoft, and Amazon, are adopting cloud computing security because it is a new infrastructure that has many advantages over those existing ordinary service providers, including incredible fault-tolerance competence, high availability, reduced expenditures, infinite adaptability, potential performance, and more [7]. Governments and businesses employ the services of cloud computing to address a range of application and architecture demands, including databases, CRM, storage of data, and computation. The following characteristics are shared by all cloud-computing offerings: multi-tenancy, on-demand, elastic network access, metering/chargeback, and virtualization. Large corporations are collaborating to build cloud services, including Microsoft in the software sector, Google, and Amazon in the internet technology sector [8, 9]. IaaS (Infrastructure as a Service), PaaS (Platform as a Service), and SaaS (Software as a Service) are the three cloud computing services that are most frequently provided both internally and by outside suppliers as shown in Figure 4.

IaaS (Infrastructure-as-a-Service): IaaS is a method of providing cloud-based computing infrastructure—storage, servers, networks, and operating systems—as a service on-demand. Clients purchase these resources as a completely outsourced service on demand rather than purchasing servers, data centre space, software, or networking hardware. IaaS is the most fundamental service paradigm, according to the IETF (Internet Engineering Task Force). Users can access networks via virtual machines and this paradigm is coupled to a virtual engine [10, 11]. As providers release technologies as part of IaaS that assist with implementation, including the capability to install several types of clouds, the distinction between IaaS and PaaS continues to get more hazy. It is widely acknowledged that IaaS complies with the following:

- Distribution of resources is done as a service.
- Consists of several people using a single piece of gear.

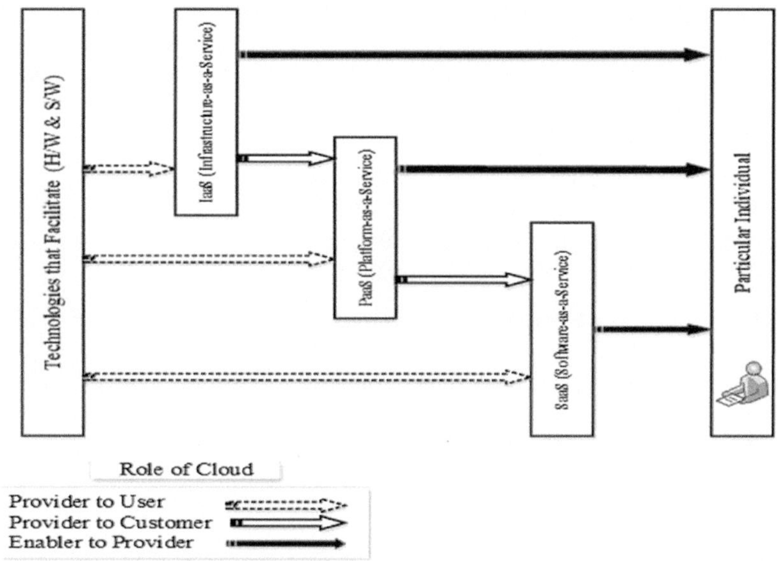

Figure 4: Role of cloud and its services.

- Has a utility-based pricing model with variable costs.
- Permits adaptive scaling.

PaaS (Platform-as-a-Service): The phrase "platform as a service" refers to a computer platform that enables the process of developing web-based programs quickly and easily without the headache of having to buy and maintain expensive software and hardware. PaaS is a platform for the creation of software that is delivered through the internet as an alternative to actual software, much like SaaS. Here, the corporation's service offers fundamental regulations for development and advice on how to successfully disseminate them. In this case, the environment would include an OS, a database, a setting for running programs, and a web server. On the same framework that their end-user customers use to execute the program, this enabled the developer to create, test, and build their individual software. This service concept is well illustrated by Microsoft Azure and the Google App Engine.

Basic PaaS properties include:

- The provision of load balancing and resilience are included in the implemented software's integrated scalability.
- Tools for creating user interfaces on the web make it easier to design, edit, test, and deploy various UI scenarios.
- Using standard protocols for integration with databases and online services.
- Support for cooperation among development teams.

SaaS (Software-as-a-Service): Software that is made available online is referred to as "Software as a Service" or SaaS. In software as a service (SaaS), a provider licenses a software program to users either as a service on consumer demand, through an agreement to be charged based on their usage, or for free where there is a potential to generate money from sources other than the ordinary user, such as through advertising or user list sales. As a result, the cost of assistance and upkeep is effectively reduced. SaaS will soon be used by every organization, according to recent studies; therefore, it is critical for purchasers and technology users to comprehend what it is and when it makes sense to utilize it. Among the salient features of SaaS are:

- Delivering software via a "one to many" paradigm,
- Users are exempt from handling software updates,
- Access to commercially available software over the web,
- Centralized management of the software, and
- APIs enable the integration of different software components.

BDaaS (Big-Data-as-a-Service): BDaaS offers businesses a cloud-based architecture that offers comprehensive big data solutions. DaaS (Data-as-a-Service), HDaaS (Hadoop as a Service), and DAaaS (Data Analytics as a Service) are all bundled into one structure. One of the main forces at play in this market is the massive expansion of data. At a CAGR of 37.3% during the projection period, the worldwide Big-Data-as-a-Service (BDaaS) market is anticipated to increase from $7 billion in 2020 to $11.2 billion by 2023. The following submarkets based on the sort of solutions will be BDaaS:

HaaS (Hadoop-as-a-Service): Many big data initiatives and applications use Hadoop as their foundational technology. This system for handling data storage makes it possible to store data, share files, analyse data, and more. Hadoop is widely employed by businesses from Facebook to Yahoo as the use of social networks and Internet communication both develop. In accordance with the research firm Research and Markets, from 2018 to 2022, the market for Hadoop-as-a-Service would expand by almost 89% annually. As an alternative to on-premises Hadoop, HaaS has developed. The following characteristics aid in differentiating the range of HaaS alternatives.

- The requirements of data professionals and data centre administrators must be met.
- Data at rest: Should be stored in HDFS by HaaS.
- HaaS must offer elasticity.
- HaaS must facilitate continuous operations.
- HaaS must adapt on its own.

Companies who provide Hadoop as a service provide it "fully baked". Their customized Hadoop release generally adheres closely to the initially released Apache Hadoop release. Here is a list of HaaS's advantages.

- No requirement for employing a system administrator with managed Hadoop.
- Easy to use: Designed for rapid setup.
- No infrastructure or hardware: Simply add or remove server hardware as necessary.
- Each business has a group of Hadoop specialists on hand to provide assistance as needed.

DaaS (Data-as-a-Service): DaaS, SaaS's fraternal twin brother, assists in integrating high-quality data into corporate and promotional initiatives while SaaS continues to dominate the technology industry with new offerings and ground-breaking software frameworks. Technology-based DaaS services offer real-time consumer and market data. DaaS separates data from its connected apps without taking into account the platform or location in order to provide consumers with relevant data. The technologies required to obtain data from diverse sources, including operational data warehouses, database servers, enterprise resource planning (ERP) infrastructure, and CRM (customer relationship management) tools, are brought together by DaaS. The DaaS strategy offers the following advantages:

- Ability to transfer data quickly between platforms.
- The protection of data integrity with access control methods.
- Collaboration and administration made simple.
- Interoperability between varieties of systems.
- Being able to access worldwide.

DAaaS (Data-Analytics-as-a-Service): Through the process of a cloud-based distribution approach, DAaaS, or Analytics as a Service, makes expandable analytical tools attainable [12]. To analyze heterogeneous statistics, this service provides a number of analytical tools. Individuals of the online service submit information about their businesses to the cloud, which has been constructed up of analytical methods and algorithmic learning principles, and get the data that has been analysed and is pertinent for business reasons via the cloud. In DAaaS, big data and the cloud are integrated. It explains how to create an extensible framework with cloud-based analytical capabilities that include a wide variety of features from gathering statistics to end-user visualization, disclosure, and collaboration. Analytics as a service allows information workers to have personalized access to pertinent data sets. This suggests that information users, such as business people and data scientists, may engage with information in order to analyse it and swiftly get deeper insights. The advantage of DAaaS is that it reduces obstacles to entry for higher levels of analytical power without needing customers to devote a large amount of organizational and administrative resources to the execution of the endeavour.

Instead of a complicated bespoke project, the client takes these few actions:

- The data analysts who work for the company search the AppStore for a data visualization app that addresses the issue.
- They hire a statistical app for a certain amount of time or data.
- They adjust the Statistical App to its requirements.
- After that, the statistical app receives the data from the systems that are internal.
- Results are provided for all other applications.

DBaaS (Database-as-a-Service): DBaaS is a type of cloud computing paradigm that gives customers access to databases without requiring them to install programs, set up physical infrastructure, or optimize throughput. Customers are paid for using features, capabilities, and database management tools in DBaas. The DBaaS database administrator module uses an API (Application Programming Interface) to manage all underpinning database instances. This API is accessible to the user through the administration interface, Web application, resulting in the user can use it to administer and set up the database as well as provide and de-provision records instances. Demographics & Demographics expects the cloud database and DBaaS market will grow from $15.6 billion in 2018 to $17.05 billion by 2023, with an average annual growth rate (CAGR) of 73.30% from 2015 to 2022. With the DBaaS industry expected to reach $6.8 billion by 2022, the necessity for an agile data layer on the cloud has grown critical.

INaaS (Information-as-a-Service): Information as a Service (INaaS) is the ability to provide consistent and secure ways to generate, manage, distribute, and extract pertinent information from all available data in the proper format at the appropriate time. This enables any program to use any kind of centrally housed data and gives any application access through API to any kind of relevant data. Businesses use data from several sources in a single service or 'mashup' [13]. Through INaaS, the data belonging to the client is "decoupled from the essential sophistication of the statistical landscape". irrespective of the kind or whereabouts of the data, it provides a framework for managing the conversion of data into information and producing useful business insights.

BPaaS (Business-Process-as-a-Service): Businesses are using process optimization to boost productivity and specify precise business goals. Business Process as a Service (BPaaS) refers to business operations such as payroll administration, the printing press, and e-commerce that are provided as a service via the Internet and accessed by one or more accessible via Internet interfaces including PCs, smartphones, and tablets. There are several publicly accessible services, including advertising services like Google Adsense and IBM Blueworks Live for business procedure management, but there are also many services that IT departments now offer to their customers behind a firewall or to reliable collaborators. The BPaaS market has a wide range of solutions for businesses that assist customers and businesses in efficiently adapting to the new, shifting business conditions, and lowering labour expenses. Customer service, HR activities (payroll, motivational compensation), acquisition, sales operations, and industry operation procedures are among the best-liked services provided under the BPaaS umbrella. At a CAGR of 26.7% from 2016 to 2022, the BPaaS market is predicted to grow from $2.10 billion in 2016 to $6.73 billion by 2022. More BPaaS suppliers are starting this thrilling cloud adventure. According to analyst firm Gartner, the market's yearly growth will reach 15.72% by 2022, and there will likely be high demand for all kinds of cloud service products.

INaaS (Integration-as-a-Service): An integration service provision paradigm in the cloud is called Integration as a Service (INaaS). By implementing clear interfaces, web services, and interactions between programs and data sources, integration-as-a-service offers an integrated solution that connects to operational apps, sources, documents, and systems at the back end. Leading companies such as Dell Boomi, MuleSoft, CloudSwitch, and others offer integration as a service.

SECaaS (Security-as-a-Service): Users who access the Internet over relatively unprotected roadways are vulnerable to security assaults. SECaaS can act as a buffer against the most persistent internet attacks in this situation. Software as a Service (SaaS) is the paradigm on which SECaaS is built, however, it is only applicable to certain security-critical services. This security management outsourcing strategy. SECaaS refers to apps like anti-virus software that are distributed over the Internet, but the phrase can also apply to security management services that are offered internally by a third-party company. In order to meet corporate objectives and maintain the integrity, accessibility, and protectionism of information assets, SECaaS provides security for systems of information. The benefits of security-as-a-service are numerous and include:

- Continual virus description updates independent of compliance among users.
- Accelerated provisioning for users.
- More advanced security knowledge than is generally present in an organization.
- Administrative responsibilities like log management are outsourced.
- A cloud-based safeguard also avoids the expense of hiring security analysts and professionals.

TaaS (Testing-as-a-Service): TaaS for clouds, SaaS, and cloud-based applications is made possible by cloud computing. TaaS is an approach to outsourcing where testing tasks related to company operations are delegated to a third party with expertise in mimicking real-world testing circumstances in accordance with client needs. TaaS may employ specialists to assist and counsel staff members or only outsource a portion of testing to a service provider. This creates new economic opportunities, difficulties, and requirements for creative service models, testing strategies, and QoS standards [14].

5. Utilization Possibility of Cloud Computing

The worldwide market for cloud computing is expanding at that rate as the demand for cloud services rises so quickly. Because of the numerous advantages that cloud computing offers, many businesses from a variety of industries are increasingly favouring cloud services. Numerous businesses use cloud computing for a variety of functions, and as a result, providers of cloud computing services provide a wide range of applications in numerous industries. By offering a wide range of cloud applications at the same time, cloud computing has now impacted every industry according to cloud service providers (CSPs).

Online Data Retention: Organizations must store a large amount of data, and this data grows larger over time. Any format, including text, images, audio, and video, can be used for this data. Organizations no longer need to put up physical database systems in order to hold and handle this enormous volume of data. They can keep their data in the cloud. A company's whole data set may be divided into two categories: current data and data from the past. Current data refers to information that is commonly needed to carry out certain daily tasks. Historical data, on the other hand, is information that is not currently being used but still has worth and must be kept. Therefore, we have two storage alternatives at our disposal to store these two different kinds of data separately:

- *Hot Storage:* This type of storage is used to keep data that must be accessed immediately or regularly.
- *Cold Storage*: Data that doesn't need regular or quick access is kept in cold storage.

Data that is stored in the cloud is also more readily available since you may access it from any location in the globe with only a connection to the internet.

Backup and Restoration: Numerous solutions are available for data recovery from cloud service providers. They provide numerous rehabilitation programs at varied prices. Depending on their needs, businesses may choose the type of plan they want. The cloud service provider offers the option of offering redundancy, which involves storing a duplicate of the data in many locations. A new server, data facility, or even a different country might be the culprit. This redundant storage solution was chosen in order to protect data and provide users with options when accessing it. Data may be quickly retrieved from alternative storage places if the original location becomes unreachable for whatever reason.

Developing and Testing: Testing is crucial for completing a product after development and preparing it for release. A product must undergo thorough testing before distribution. Because the final user of that product might be located everywhere, it needs to be tested on a variety of devices with a variety of infrastructures. It also has to pass a load-balancing test. Load balancing: How a product's performance changes when a lot of consumers utilize it at once. Testing needs various IT resources and computer systems to do these duties. These testing functionalities may now be offered in a single location via a cloud. Businesses may quickly assess how well their product performs against a big user base on the cloud.

Medical Fields Using Cloud Computing: Since cloud computing enables data storage and internet access without the need for a physical setup, it is now also employed in the medical industry for data access and storage. It makes it simpler for patients and different medical professionals to access and distribute information. Similar to how physicians conducting emergency house calls and ambulances can easily retrieve and modify information remotely without having to wait until they can reach a hospital with a computer system, cloud computing enables off-site buildings as well as healthcare facilities like labs.

Big Data Evaluation: Dealing with enormous volumes of data that range in size from gigabytes to zettabytes is what big data analysis entails. Now, maintaining this quantity of data would be quite challenging for any conventional database management system. Large data collections, including both structured and unstructured data, from many sources, ranging in size from terabytes to zettabytes, may be stored using cloud computing. In addition to providing us with storage, these technologies enable us to analyse this large data. Because getting anything out of large data is the major reason for storing it, Big Data analytics can benefit from the cloud's adaptability.

Entertainment Software: Today, the internet is a great source of entertainment, whether it be videos from YouTube, Netflix streaming television episodes, or online games. Users from practically every country in the globe make extensive use of this data. Having a wonderful client experience is also essential. In order to make this content downloadable. For this, entertainment firms use a multi-cloud approach to connect with their audience. The cloud is enabling the entertainment sector to grow to new heights.

Social Networking Sites: Platforms for social networking are crucial in daily life. They have altered how people connect and communicate. These platforms are excellent candidates for cloud computing adoption since they have a significant global user base. Social networking sites can slow down the entire network since they frequently post large amounts of multimedia information, such as photographs and videos. This is where cloud storage comes into play. Social networking apps benefit from cloud storage.

Anti-virus Programmes: These days, cloud-based security programmes outperform older versions of antivirus software in terms of performance. Cloud-based antivirus maintains malware information on the cloud as opposed to on the user's PC, which is the major cause of this. Traditional antivirus programs are used to keep malware information from entering the user's system, which might negatively impact the user's system's productivity.

Application of Accounting: Applications for cloud-based accounting make it easier, cheaper, and more labor-efficient for businesses to handle their accounting and finances. Without sacrificing data security, it enables businesses to control their funds from anywhere in the entire globe. Accounting software or apps that are hosted in the cloud are scalable because they enable businesses to grow without having to invest in new infrastructure. The cloud makes it simple to upgrade this software because we are no longer concerned about our system's requirements and resources.

Management Programmes: 'Evernote' and other management applications are cloud-based. Notes may be formatted, saved, and shared through the cloud. Evernote stores user data via the cloud computing technology's storage service. The data may be accessed at any moment, from any location, and on any device, because it is stored on the cloud. The cloud's security service aids in maintaining the data's security. Additionally, there are no concerns about data loss thanks to Evernote's utilization of a redundant storage solution in cloud computing.

6. Top Cloud Security Risks and Issues for Modern Cloud Computing

To varied degrees, almost all businesses have incorporated cloud computing into their operations. However, as more businesses utilize cloud computing, they must be sure that their cloud security plan can fend off the most common threats to cloud security as shown in Figure 5.

Misleading Setup: One of the main reasons for the cloud theft of information is incorrect cloud security setup arrangements. The cloud-based infrastructure of many organizations is not sufficiently protected by their cloud security program management procedures.

Unlicensed Entry: The resources of a company's cloud-based installations are instantly available from the general Internet and are situated beyond the network circumference, in contrast to their premises-based systems. This facilitates workers' and client's access to the physical structures, but it also makes it simpler for an attacker to obtain unauthorized access to a company's cloud-based resources. Unauthorized entry may be made possible by inadequate authentication or credential breaches, perhaps without the awareness of the company.

Vulnerable APIs and Interfaces: For its clients, cloud service providers (CSPs) frequently offer a variety of user interfaces and APIs. Generally speaking, these programming interfaces are extensively documented making a CSP's clients find them simple to use. This might cause problems, though, if a customer hasn't adequately protected connectivity for their infrastructure that is hosted on the cloud. Cybercriminals can also utilize customer-designed documentation to find and take advantage of potential ways to access and extract highly sensitive information from an organization's cloud infrastructure.

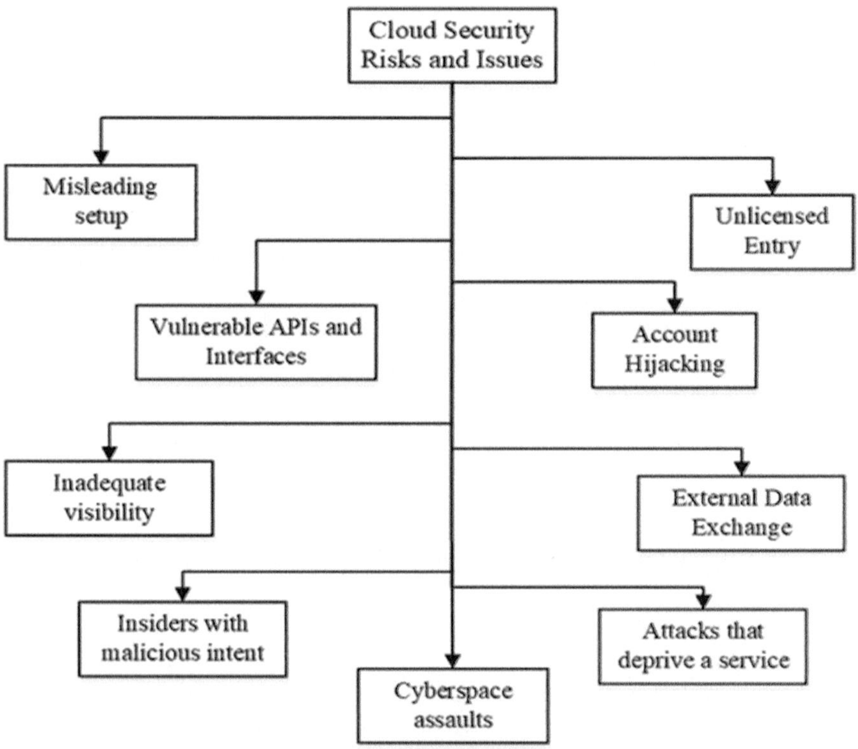

Figure 5: Modern cloud security risks and issues.

Account Hijacking: Numerous individuals have extremely inadequate security credentials, including the usage of fragile passwords and password repetition. Because it allows just one compromised password to be used on several accounts, this issue exacerbates the effect of phishing attempts and data breaches. As organizations increasingly rely on cloud-based networks and apps for critical business processes, hijacking accounts is one of the most significant cloud security challenges. An attacker possessing access to a staff member's credentials can get access to critical data or performance and weakened customer credentials grant complete authority over their user account on the internet. Furthermore, organizations in the cloud frequently lack the capacity to recognize and respond to these risks with the same effectiveness as within the premises equipment.

Inadequate Visibility: Cloud-based assets utilized by an organization operate on an infrastructure that is not owned by the firm and are situated elsewhere in the corporate network. Because of this, a lot of conventional methods for obtaining network visibility do not perform well in cloud settings, and some businesses do not have cloud-focused security products or services. This may make it more difficult for a company to keep an eye on and defend against attacks on its cloud-based services.

External Data Exchange: Sharing information is made simple by the design of the cloud. A lot of clouds convey the ability to share links to resources that allow anybody with the URL to view the resource being shared or to specifically invite someone to collaborate via email. This simple data exchange has its benefits, but there may be serious cloud security risks as well. It is challenging to manage access to the shared resource when link-based sharing is used, while being a popular choice because it is simpler than directly requesting each targeted collaborator. Unauthorized access to the shared resource may be possible if the shared link is intercepted by a cybercriminal, communicated to another person, or taken as part of a hack. Furthermore, access to a shareable link cannot be revoked for a single recipient due to link-based hosting.

Insiders with Malicious Intent: An important security concern for every organization is insider threats. A malevolent insider already has authorized access to a corporation's network and certain critical resources. Most attackers are exposed to their target when they attempt to obtain this degree of access, which makes it challenging for an unprepared organization to identify a hostile insider. Finding an illegal insider on the cloud is considerably harder. Businesses that use cloud deployments lose authority over the infrastructure that underlies them, which reduces the efficacy of many conventional security measures. This makes it considerably harder to identify malevolent insiders, in addition to the fact that infrastructure running on the cloud is frequently plagued by security vulnerabilities and is easily accessed from the global Internet.

Cyberspace Assaults: Since cyberattacks are an enterprise, the projected financial gain of an attack determines which targets the internet hackers choose to attack. A lot of sensitive and important data is stored on an infrastructure that is cloud-based, which is readily accessible from the public Internet and frequently has inadequate security. In addition, a large number of different businesses use the cloud, which implies that a successful assault has a significant chance of being replicated repeatedly. Consequently, cloud deployments by businesses are frequently the target of assaults.

Attacks that Deprive a Service: The capacity of many organizations to conduct business depends on the cloud. They operate vital internal and external apps and save vital corporate data in the cloud. This implies that several businesses are likely to be significantly impacted in the event of a successful Refusal of Service assault on cloud infrastructure. Because of this, refusal of service assaults that involve an attacker demanding a ransom to end the attack represents a serious risk to a corporation's resources stored in the cloud.

7. Top Cloud Security Threats for Modern Cloud Computing

Organizations were questioned about their top security worries in relation to cloud environments for the Cloud Security Research. Numerous organizations have chosen to migrate critical apps as well as confidential data to the cloud, but there are still numerous questions about how to secure such information there as shown in Figure 6.

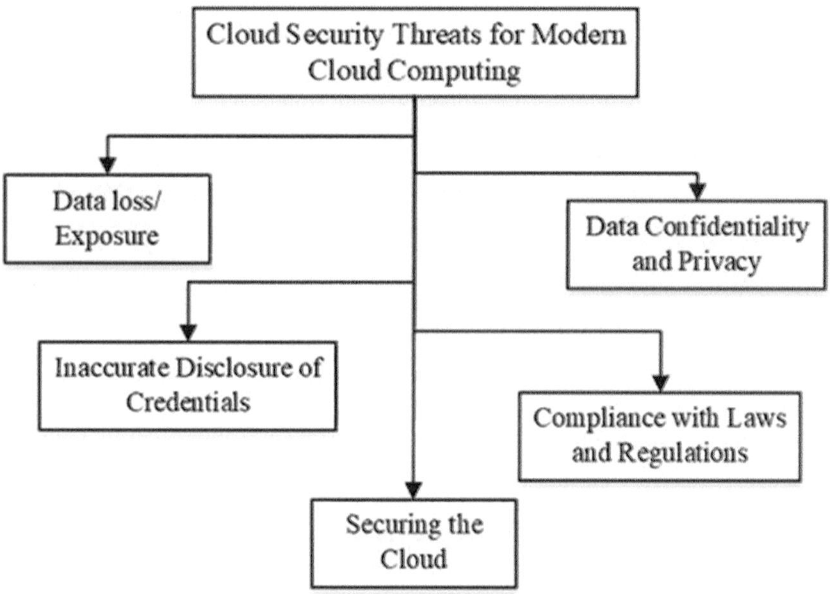

Figure 6: Modern Cloud security threats.

Data Loss/Exposure: Data saved in cloud-based systems may be shared with ease. The aforementioned environments may be accessed straight from the worldwide Internet and facilitate the exchange of data with third parties through public links or direct email invites. Though a great benefit and essential to cloud partnership, the ease of exchanging data in the cloud raises severe questions about losing information or leakage. As a matter of fact, 71% of businesses cite this as their top worry regarding secure cloud storage. Anybody with an understanding of the link can access data shared over public links or make publicly traded in a cloud-based repository. There are tools designed to find these unprotected instances of the cloud on the global web.

Data Confidentiality and Privacy: For many organizations, data confidentiality and security are top priorities. While there are benefits to storing sensitive data in the cloud, 69% of organizations have expressed serious security concerns. Although a lot of businesses have embraced cloud computing, they don't know enough to make sure that their staff members are utilizing it safely. Sensitive data is hence vulnerable to disclosure, as seen by the numerous cloud data breaches.

Inaccurate Disclosure of Credentials: Cloud infrastructures and apps are frequently used by phishers as a pretext for their assaults. The increasing prevalence of cloud-based email platforms (Microsoft 365, G-Suite, etc.) along with offerings (Google Drive, OneDrive, and Dropbox) has made it common for staff members to receive emails containing links that may require them to verify their login credentials in order to access an individual file or website. Because of this, it is simple for fraudsters to get an employee's cloud service login credentials. Because it may jeopardize the integrity and confidentiality of their stored information in the cloud as well as other resources, 47% of organizations express great worry over the unintentional disclosure of cloud credentials.

Compliance with Laws and Regulations: Organizations are required by data protection rules such as HIPAA, DSS, and PCI to provide proof that they have restricted access to confidential data (credit card information, medical records, etc.). To do this, it could be necessary to divide off a portion of the company's network, either physically or conceptually, so that only staff members with a valid reason to access the data can access it. It may be more challenging to achieve and prove regulatory compliance when transferring data covered by these and related laws to the cloud. Organizations that use cloud deployments can only see and manage a portion of their infrastructure. Consequently, 44% of organizations view complying with legal and regulatory requirements as a serious cloud security risk, necessitating the use of specialized compliance with cloud regulations solutions.

Securing the Cloud: Although the cloud offers many benefits to businesses, there are security risks and issues of its own. The security of the servers hosted in the cloud is not always achievable with typical security tools and tactics since it differs greatly from an information centre on-premises centre.

8. Cloud Computing Challenges

In conclusion, many organizations are embracing the novel approach of cloud computing since it offers a variety of advantages and benefits over the older paradigms of computing. However, many issues still need to be resolved, and researchers and industry professionals are doing so right now. Cloud computing is the real-time, on-demand delivery of resources like data and storage. With the market valuation expanding quickly, it has been demonstrated to be innovative in the IT business. Cloud development has shown to be advantageous for both large public and commercial corporations as well as small-scale firms since it reduces expenses. More than 94% of organizations are predicted to boost their cloud investment by more than 45%. As a result, there are now more high-paying opportunities available, especially for cloud developers. Although deployment of cloud services and usage were already booming before the epidemic, they have suddenly increased during the lockdown. The fact that classes have been moved online, virtual office meetings take place on video chatting platforms, conferences are held electronically, and on-demand streaming applications have a large user base may all be attributed to the enormous increase. Only cloud computing is responsible for making all of this feasible. It is reasonable to say that the cloud is a significant aspect of our lives today, regardless of whether we are businesses, students, developers, or anybody else who relies significantly on it. However, given this reliance, it is also crucial that we consider the problems and difficulties that come with cloud computing. In light of this, we present to you today the most typical difficulties encountered while using cloud computing. Let us take a closer look at each of them individually:

Performance: Performance is a crucial consideration when looking at cloud-based solutions. If the cloud's performance is subpar, consumers may stop using it and businesses may suffer. A small amount of delay while loading an app or website might cause a significant decrease in the number of users. Ineffective load balancing may be the cause of this delay since the server is unable to divide incoming traffic effectively for the optimum user experience.

Privacy and Security: Security concerns for businesses employing cloud computing remain. Customers worry that when information and essential IT resources are outside the firewall, they are vulnerable to assaults. The answer to security presupposes that cloud computing service providers adhere to accepted security procedures.

Control: Many IT departments are concerned because cloud-based corporations have total control over the operating systems. Cloud computing companies often don't develop systems specifically for certain organizations and their processes.

Diverse Cloud Environments: Due to the increased number of options available to them, businesses today rely on several cloud service providers along with employing a single cloud. The bulk of these organizations use hybrid cloud methods, and about 84% of them are dependent on several clouds. The infrastructure team regularly encounters management challenges with this. The process frequently ends up being rather hard for the IT team due to the differences between different cloud providers.

Cost of Bandwidth: Although almost all cloud hosting companies use a "Pay As You Go" model, which reduces the overall cost of the hardware and software utilized, there are times when a firm adopting cloud computing will face considerable costs. When capabilities are not optimized, such as when machines are not being used to their full potential, the hidden costs rise. If there are sudden spikes in use or poor application functionality, the overall cost rises. Abandoned resources are another major driver for cost increases.

Reliability: When a company utilizes one cloud service provider and decides to migrate to another, it can be a time-consuming process since applications are created for one cloud and its application stack must be recreated for the other cloud. Due to the difficulties involved, migrating from one cloud to another is not flexible. When switching cloud solutions, problems with handling data transfer, establishing security from start, and networks also arise, limiting flexibility. Even now, 24-hour availability is not always guaranteed by cloud computing. There have been instances where cloud-computing services experienced brief outages.

Flexibility and Interoperability: When a company employs a certain cloud service provider and wishes to migrate to another cloud-based solution, it can be a time-consuming process since apps created for one cloud using the application stack must be rewritten for another cloud. Because of the intricacies involved, migrating from one cloud to another is inflexible. Handling data transfer, establishing security from scratch, and network challenges all contribute to the issues experienced when switching cloud options, and diminishing flexibility.

High Reliance on the Network: Cloud computing manages enormous amounts of information that flows to and from computer systems because it uses real-time resource procurement. The only thing that makes this conceivable is the availability of the rapid connectivity network. Although this information and other assets are exchanged through the network, there may be instances where there is an unanticipated outage or a bandwidth problem.

Knowledge and Skill Deficit: Because of its intricate nature and significant demand for research, working with the cloud usually proves to be a very time-consuming task. It requires deep subject knowledge and competence. Despite the fact that the business has a large number of professionals, they nonetheless need to continually improve their abilities. Salaries are particularly expensive in the profession of cloud computing due to the significant supply and demand imbalance.

9. Trends and Future Research Directions

Cloud computing is one of the IT trends that is now receiving the most attention. This occurs regularly because cloud computing has allowed many firms to dramatically reduce expenses while also improving consumer comfort. In recent years, there have been substantial changes in the cloud computing industry as a whole. Modern technology, which now makes it possible for individuals to be closely connected throughout the world, has also driven the fast acceptance and move towards cloud computing technologies. The amount of personnel, resources, and research costs required to ascertain the future breadth and depth of cloud computing has also increased. This clarifies the reason why cloud computing has so many interesting developments. This chapter will discuss the potential applications of security threats to cloud computing as well as how this technology is ready and prospering to revolutionize enterprises all over the world. Let us talk about a few technological trends that will demonstrate how its use will grow significantly in the upcoming years.

Better Cloud Services: First, the use of cloud computing in education and associated industries will demonstrate the power of dependable cloud computing services. Better cloud services may be categorized into three groups:

(i) Service-based software

(ii) Software as a Platform
(iii) Technological Innovation as a Service.

These constitute the three main services used by reputable, approachable organizations. When new services can support these facilities, businesses may relocate more readily. More institutions and colleges will eventually start to gain from cloud computing.

Integrity: One of the most important issues that are inherent in cloud computing is security. Service providers must ensure the data is stored safely and securely. This calls for a higher level of cloud computing proficiency and understanding. Consequently, careers in cloud computing have a bright future. Businesses will seek competent professionals who can ensure security across the whole lifetime of cloud services. Furthermore, it is critical for service providers to ensure the prevention of cyberattacks. If security is not a top priority, even small enterprises need to change their operating procedures.

Module-based Software Development: The future growth of cloud computing technology is thought to depend heavily on the success of modular software development. This is because in order for enterprises to utilize cloud technology, code, and apps must be divided into smaller, loosely coupled portions. As a result, developers now find it easier to upload their work to the cloud. It also makes it simpler for people to get material from far-off places. However, reliability and functionality availability rise when programming is adaptable. Businesses that put modular code investment first will eventually save more money.

Market Development: By the end of 2018, the market's capitalization of cloud computing had topped 128 billion USD. As cloud computing utilization is anticipated to increase, a consistent value is forecast for the next few years. Even Fortune 500 companies and household names are migrating their services and products to the cloud. In the meanwhile, businesses' spending patterns on premise infrastructure have dropped. These are signs of a more promising and safe cloud future. The market and long-term prospects for cloud computing are undeniably inevitable.

The Use of Virtualization: It will now discuss the virtualization possibilities of cloud computing. This intriguing relationship has a lot of space for further research and development. To begin with, combining cloud computing and virtualization requires a unique design. There is a chance that this evolution matches the traits of the computing cell. The computer cells are recognized for their continuing demand for more complicated software design, which is integrated with characteristics like encryption, dependable and efficient division of network organizing information, and third-party authentication.

Cloud Computing's Potential from a Professional Standpoint: The potential for a career in cloud computing is very strong. According to a study report, there is a high need in this sector for positions that are specialized in:

(i) Engineer for Cloud Infrastructure
(ii) Cloud Technologist

(iii) Enterprise Cloud Architect
(iv) Engineer for cloud software.

With such a predicted development, it is clear how fantastic the career opportunities are for individuals working in cloud computing. In India, an entry-level employment in the cloud-computing sector now pays between 6 lakh and 8 lakh per year. As your expertise and talents increase, you may anticipate earning more money. Mid-level managers in this sector might make up to 20 lakh per year, while senior cloud professionals with more than 15 years of expertise earn more than one crore.

The industry also faces difficulties due to a serious scarcity of qualified and gifted workers. The same poll reports that there are more than 1.8 million open cloud jobs globally due to a shortage of qualified people. Typically, just 1.2% of candidates have the necessary qualifications to work in the cloud. Simply put, a cloud computing education can assist you in developing the skills necessary to operate in an area where you will be in high demand. Cloud computing is an everlasting technology. This technology must be embraced by businesses so that they can advance. Impressive and inspiring technology. Large and small enterprises alike find it to be a cost-effective way to provide services over time.

10. Conclusion

Cloud computing will have an influence on a substantial segment of the IT industry, including programmers and internet service vendors. Cloud computing renders it exceedingly simple for business enterprises to deliver their products to end consumers since it eliminates the need to worry about computer hardware specifications or extra requirements. By delegating all control plane duties connected to the creation, management, and maintenance of the virtual environment to a computerized layer known as an API along with the functions of cloud servers, digitalization and cloud computing are distinguished from one another. Virtualization, to put it straightforwardly, is a kind of cloud computing that uses human administration to interact with a virtualization system. On the other hand, cloud computing enables users to self-consume cloud-based offerings by managing their own activities by employing an API. The growth of the consumer Internet has spawned a brand-new approach to using and providing IT services termed security threats to cloud computing. The cloud-computing paradigm, which integrates rapid scalability, pervasive Internet usage and Internet-connected devices, unmatched self-service, and the emergence of enticing web-based apps, continues the evolution of the World Wide Web. Users may accomplish sophisticated computational activities via the cloud without having to comprehend the underlying technology. The emergence of cloud computing with security threats comes at a crucial time for the IT sector. There is a rising awareness that infrastructure, systems, and physical and IT assets are quickly approaching their breaking point. Both digital and physical foundations on which growth depends are struggling to keep up as the speed of business and society as a whole continues to quicken for the following reasons:

(i) The current IT framework and operations are under pressure due to the growth of data, interactions, and digitally aware gadgets.

(ii) The exponential growth of communications users and services can be considered as a cause of bandwidth and data retention limitations.
(iii) Energy and utility networks are under strain from inefficient supply and demand increases.

A fundamental component of IBM's and others' Smarter Planet vision, the growing cloud computing paradigm takes advantage of better technology. This cloud model is distinguished by cutting-edge Internet-driven economics that makes use of the technology's enormous inherent scaling potential. By addressing expectations for immediate accessibility as well as dynamic access to novel new services, cloud computing offers the possibility of enhanced service (not only high availability and quality of current services). Through virtualization, optimization, energy management, and flexible procurement, cloud computing also enables cost reduction—not simply cost containment—and the achievement of ground-breaking productivity increases.

Of course, there are difficulties with cloud computing security threats. Productivity and capacity factors must be given crucial investigation throughout the design, delivery, and administration of cloud-based systems due to the complicated nature of cloud computing and its rising reliance on the Internet, and virtualization, which is on-demand supporting technology.

A cutting-edge technology, cloud computing gives users online access to high-speed computers, networking, storage, and infrastructure. Security of cloud computing is becoming a bigger aspect of IT, and many enormous organizations are likely to use it. Many of them provide IaaS, PaaS, and SaaS, while others only offer one of those. While Google Apps offers software as a service, Amazon.com, Sun, and IBM provide storage services. Future work on data science, machine learning services, and artificial intelligence within cloud providers will protect and secure customer-sensitive data, such as login credentials, through encryption techniques and other password protection techniques inside the security groups, to increase efficiency and accuracy and make the data more secure.

References

1. Sadashiv, N., & S.D. Kumar. (2011, August). Cluster, grid and cloud computing: A detailed comparison. In: *2011 6th International Conference on Computer Science & Education* (*ICCSE*), pp. 477–482. IEEE.
2. Liu, F., J. Tong, J. Mao, R. Bohn, J. Messina, L. Badger, & D. Leaf. (2011). NIST cloud computing reference architecture. *NIST Special Publication*, 500, 1–28.
3. Jansen, W., & T. Grance. (2011). Guidelines on security and privacy in public cloud computing.
4. Trends, G.E. (2008). Technologies roadshow. *Gartner Identifies Top Ten Disruptive Technologies for 2008 to 2012*. Posted by Insurance-Canada.ca.
5. Armbrust, M., A. Fox, R. Griffith, A.D. Joseph, R.H. Katz, A. Konwinski, ... & M. Zaharia. (2009). *Above the Clouds: A Berkeley View of Cloud Computing* (Vol. 17). Technical Report UCB/EECS-2009-28, EECS Department, University of California, Berkeley.

6. Voas, J., & J. Zhang, J. (2009). Cloud computing: New wine or just a new bottle? *IT Professional*, 11(2), 15–17.
7. Zhou, M., R. Zhang, D. Zeng, & W. Qian. (2010, October). Services in the cloud computing era: A survey. In: *2010 4th International Universal Communication Symposium*, pp. 40–46. IEEE.
8. Qian, L., Z. Luo, Y. Du, & L. Guo. (2009). Cloud computing: An overview. In: Proceedings 1, *Cloud Computing: First International Conference, CloudCom 2009*, pp. 626–631. Beijing, China, December 1–4, 2009. Springer Berlin Heidelberg.
9. Lin, G., D. Fu, J. Zhu, & G. Dasmalchi. (2009). Cloud computing: IT as a service. *IT Professional*, 11(2), 10–13.
10. Xiong, K., & H. Perros. (2009, July). Service performance and analysis in cloud computing. In: *2009 Congress on Services-I,* pp. 693–700. IEEE.
11. Moschakis, I.A., & H.D. Karatza. (2011, June). Performance and cost evaluation of gang scheduling in a cloud computing system with job migrations and starvation handling. In: *2011 IEEE Symposium on Computers and Communications* (*ISCC*), pp. 418–423. IEEE.
12. Güemes, C., J. Janeczko, T. Caminel, & M. Roberts. (2013). Data analytics as a service: Unleashing the power of cloud and big data. *Ascent Thought Leadership from Atos*. White paper.
13. Linthicum, D.S. (2009). *Cloud Computing and SOA Convergence in Your Enterprise: A Step-by-step Guide*. Pearson Education.
14. Gao, J., X. Bai, W.T. Tsai, & T. Uehara. (2013, March). Testing as a service (TaaS) on clouds. In: *2013 IEEE Seventh International Symposium on Service-Oriented System Engineering*, pp. 212–223. IEEE.

7 | Network Security Issue and Data Privacy on Online Social-Media

Ramesh Kumar[1*], S.P. Singh[1], Brajesh Kumar Singh[2], Vivek Kumar[3]

[1] Department of Computer Science & Engg, Nims University Rajasthan, Jaipur, India
[2] Department of Electronics, Rajdhani College, University of Delhi, India
[3] Department of Computer Science, NIET, Gr. Noida, AKT University Lucknow, India

1. Introduction

In this age of digital communication, there has been a dramatic rise in the amount of information that is being shared. Every piece of information that is either being transmitted or received is susceptible to a variety of active and passive assaults. As a result, ensuring the safety of the data while it is being sent is the primary issue. Cryptography plays a critical part in the process of securing the communication that takes place inside a network, and it provides an incredible solution to meet the need for adequate data security from unauthorized users. Over a considerable period, data encryption methods have undergone substantial evolution to ensure a robust level of connection security, transitioning from straightforward techniques to intricate mathematical computations. Cryptographic algorithms are vulnerable to a wide variety of assaults, even though they are notoriously tough to crack. This chapter will cover a range of symmetric key encryption techniques, comparing them with asymmetric key encryption, and delving into their individual strengths, weaknesses, limitations, and susceptibility to attacks. Additionally, the proposed methodology to enhance protection and reduce the impact of attacks will be explored.

2. Cryptography

Cryptography involves transforming information from a readable form to an unreadable form to meet security requirements. Its purpose is to safeguard data, verify user identities, and provide authentication services. In simple terms, data in its unencrypted form is known as plaintext, and once encrypted, it becomes ciphertext. Encryption is the process of converting plaintext into ciphertext and decryption is the process of converting ciphertext to plaintext [1]. Cryptography is further classified

*Corresponding author: rks208@gmail.com

DOI: 10.1201/9781003560012-7

into two groups: Symmetric Key Cryptography and Asymmetric Key Cryptography. In the context of cloud computing [2], where data is transmitted over the internet for storage, cryptography plays a vital role. Without encryption, data becomes vulnerable to attackers who can easily locate and access it. To protect data stored in cyberspace, a robust encryption algorithm must be applied to ensure its security [1].

2.1 Objectives of Cryptography

There are four objectives that, when met, make it very difficult for attackers to succeed in their attempts to steal, modify, or otherwise exploit specific data [3]. These objectives are:

i. **Confidentiality:** It is the process to safeguard sensitive data, personal information, financial records from unauthorized access, disclosure of messages, and privacy to prevent misuse. By ensuring confidentiality, organizations and individuals can trust their sensitive data to try to remain secure and is only accessible to authentic users who have a legitimate right to access [4].

ii. **Data Integrity:** It is the procedure that ensures the data will be transferred in its whole and without any changes being made to it. There are some different ways that the data may be modified: replacement, deletion, and insertion [3, 5].

iii. **Authentication:** A service that is closely connected to identification is called authentication. This function applies to information as well as the things that it describes. It is important for people who are going to communicate with each other to identify themselves. It is compulsory to verify the origin date, data content, time communicated, and other aspects of information that is sent through a channel. Because of these factors, this facet of cryptography is often broken down into two key categories: authentication of entities and authentication of the source of data. Data integrity is ensured implicitly by data origin authentication; if a message is altered, this indicates that the source has been altered.

iv. **Non-repudiation:** Non-repudiation is the process of information security system and digital communication that ensures the sender's message or the initiator of any valid transaction cannot deny their involvement or the authenticity of the action in the future. It provides a way to prove the originality and integrity of data, making it a critical aspect of securing communication and reliable transactions in the digital era.

2.2 Cryptography Mechanisms

Cryptography mechanisms are techniques and processes used to secure and protect information in various ways. These mechanisms guarantee the privacy, integrity, genuineness, and non-rejection of data. Some common cryptography mechanisms are [1]:

- Encryption/Decryption
- Asymmetric Key Cryptography Algorithm
- Message Authentication Codes (MAC)
- Symmetric Key Cryptography Algorithm

- Digital Signatures
- Key Exchange Algorithms
- Hash Functions.

These cryptographic techniques to secure communication channels, ensuring the confidentiality, integrity, and authenticity of data during transactions across diverse applications, including secure messaging, online banking, e-commerce, and beyond.

3. Plaintext Processing Methods

Plaintext processing methods refer to the techniques and operations used on raw, readable data (plaintext) before or after encryption. These methods are typically applied to ensure data is in the correct format, enhance security, or provide additional functionalities [1, 6]. Some common plaintext processing methods are:

Padding: Padding is a technique applied in symmetric encryption algorithms to align the plaintext to a specific block size mandated by the encryption method. Since many encryption algorithms operate on fixed block sizes. Frequently used padding schemes, such as PKCS#5 and PKCS#7, are utilized in block ciphers like AES.

Compression: Sometimes, before encryption, plaintext data is compressed to decrease its size, leading to enhanced efficiency and reduced data transmission over networks or storage on disk. However, it is crucial to understand that while compression can have its benefits, it may not always bolster security as compressed data might be vulnerable to specific attacks.

Salting: In the context of hashing, salting is a technique used to add a unique, random value (the salt) to the plaintext before hashing. This prevents attackers from using precomputed rainbow tables to perform a brute-force attack on hashed passwords or data. Salting ensures that even identical plaintexts produce different hash values.

Normalization: In certain applications, it's crucial to ensure that plaintext data is consistently formatted to avoid data discrepancies and improve accuracy. Text normalization methods, such as converting all characters to lowercase, removing extra whitespace, or replacing accented characters with their base counterparts, are often used in natural language processing and text-based applications.

Escape Characters: In programming and data storage contexts, special characters or sequences may need to be escaped in plaintext to prevent misinterpretation by parsing systems. Common escape characters include backslashes (\) and quotes (", ").

Encoding: Encoding converts plaintext data into a specific format suitable for transmission or storage. Common encoding schemes include Base64 encoding, which represents binary data in an ASCII string format, and URL encoding, which encodes special characters in a URL-safe format.

Preprocessing and Normalization: In natural language processing and machine learning tasks, plaintext data may undergo preprocessing and normalization steps, such as tokenization, stemming, or lemmatization, to extract meaningful information and reduce word variations to their base forms.

Filtering and Sanitization: In web applications and database management, plaintext data is often filtered or sanitized to eliminate potentially harmful or malicious content, effectively thwarting. These days SQL injection and Cross-Site Scripting (XSS) attacks are common and potentially dangerous in web applications. Plaintext processing methods are crucial for ensuring data is correctly prepared for further operations, including encryption, storage, and analysis, while also maintaining security and data integrity [1, 7].

4. Key Distribution

Key distribution is the process of securely and reliably delivering cryptographic keys from the sender (or key generator) to the intended recipients (or users) in a communication system. The distribution of keys is a critical aspect of cryptography because without secure key distribution, encrypted communication cannot take place effectively [1, 8].

Some existing key methods are:

Symmetric Key Distribution: Pre-shared keys: In some scenarios, especially in small-scale systems or closed environments, keys can be distributed manually before communication starts. This method is known as pre-shared keys (PSK) distribution. However, it becomes impractical as the number of users or devices increases.

Key Distribution Centers (KDC): In more extensive systems, a centralized entity known as the Key Distribution Center (KDC) can be employed to securely disseminate keys. The KDC has the role of creating and distributing session keys between two parties engaged in communication. The Needham-Schroeder symmetric key protocol is a widely recognized method used for this specific purpose.

Asymmetric Key Distribution: Public Key Infrastructure (PKI) is a framework used in information security to manage the generation, distribution, storage, and validation of digital certificates and public-private key pairs. PKI enables secure communication and authenticity over public networks, such as the internet. Certificate Authorities (CAs) issue digital certificates, which associate public keys with specific identities. Users can obtain each other's public keys from these certificates or a trusted repository.

Diffie-Hellman Key Exchange: It is widely used in various secure communication protocols, such as TLS/SSL for secure web browsing, VPNs (Virtual Private Networks), and secure email encryption, to establish secure and private channels for data transmission.

Key Derivation: In certain scenarios, cryptographic keys are obtained from other shared secrets or passwords using key derivation functions (KDFs). The KDF takes the shared secret as input and generates a cryptographic key suitable for encryption or decryption.

Quantum Key Distribution (QKD): QKD is an emerging technology that harnesses the principles of quantum mechanics to distribute keys in a secure manner. QKD guarantees that any attempt to eavesdrop or intercept the key exchange will be detected, as quantum principles prohibit copying or measuring quantum states without altering them.

The process of key distribution is of utmost importance, and the protection of the communication system greatly depends on the efficacy of the chosen approach. The primary objective in all instances is to guarantee that cryptographic keys are shared solely with the intended recipients, preventing any unauthorized access or interception. To uphold the confidentiality and integrity of the communication system, it is crucial to utilize trusted and secure channels for key distribution.

5. Cryptanalysis

Cryptanalysis, often referred to as "codebreaking", is the study of examining cryptographic systems and techniques with the goal of deciphering encrypted messages or breaking the security of a cryptographic algorithm. Cryptanalysts aim to find weaknesses, vulnerabilities, or flaws in cryptographic schemes to recover plaintext from ciphertext or discover the encryption keys [9].

Symmetric Cryptanalysis: The main objective of symmetric cryptanalysis is to study and break the security of symmetric cryptographic systems. Cryptanalysts used various techniques to attempt to discover the secret key or to recover the plaintext from the ciphertext without knowing the correct key. The process of symmetric cryptanalysis typically revolves around attempting to discover the secret key through various techniques, including:

- **Brute-Force Attack:** The attacker can try all possible combinations of the secret key until finding the correct one. Brute-force attacks can be computationally demanding, especially for long and complex keys, but they are successful when the key space is limited.
- **Known-Plaintext Attack:** The attacker possesses both the ciphertext and the corresponding plaintext for certain messages encrypted with the same key. By scrutinizing these known plaintext-ciphertext pairs, they can infer details about the key or the encryption algorithm.

Cryptanalysis is an essential aspect of cryptography as it helps identify weaknesses and vulnerabilities in cryptographic systems. By discovering these weaknesses, cryptographers can develop stronger encryption algorithms and protocols that withstand modern attacks and ensure data security and privacy [19]. It is a constant battle between cryptographers who design robust algorithms and cryptanalysts who attempt to break them, leading to continuous advancements in both encryption techniques and cryptanalysis methods [1, 10].

6. Classifications of Cryptography

Cryptography can be classified in various ways, including the types of keys used, the quantity of keys involved in encryption and decryption, and the specific application of the encryption process [1, 11]. Some common categorizations of the cryptography process are:

- **Symmetric Key Cryptography:** It is using a single secret key for encryption and decryption, requiring secure key exchange. Examples: AES, DES, 3DES.
- **Asymmetric Key Cryptography:** Two mathematically related keys for encryption (public) and decryption (private). No key exchange needed. Examples: RSA, ECC.
- **Hybrid Cryptography:** It combines approaches for symmetric and asymmetric approaches for efficiency and security.
- **Stream Ciphers:** It encrypts data one bit/byte at a time. Example: RC4.
- **Block Ciphers:** It divides plaintext into fixed-size blocks for independent encryption. Examples: AES, DES.
- **Cryptographic Hash:** These Functions produce fixed-size hash values, used for data integrity, digital signatures, passwords.
- **Homomorphic Encryption:** It allows computations on encrypted data without decryption. Outcome remains encrypted.

7. Symmetric Key Cryptography

It is often known as secret key cryptography, a symmetric key cryptographic technique where a single secret key is used to both encrypt and decrypting data. This method, one of the oldest and widely adopted forms of encryption, is favored for its efficiency in handling large volumes of data. To ensure secure communication, the sender and receiver must be exchanging the secret key before initiating any data exchange [1, 12]. Here's how symmetric key cryptography works:

- **Key Generation:** A confidential key is created through a trustworthy key generator or a secure key exchange protocol. The key generator ensures that the key is both random and safeguarded from unauthorized individuals.
- **Encryption:** It is the process to convert plaintext into the ciphertext using cryptographic algorithms and keys. The purpose of encryption is to protect data from unauthorized access.
- **Decryption:** It is the process to convert ciphertext to plaintext using the appropriate cryptographic key. It is the inverse operation of encryption. Decryption is essential for authorized parties to access and understand the original information securely.

7.1 Characteristics of Symmetric Key Cryptography

- **Speed:** It is faster than asymmetric key cryptography because it is associated with simpler mathematical operations.
- **Security:** It is effective and depends significantly on the secrecy of the shared key. If an attacker gains access to the secret key through unauthorized methods like interception or brute-force attacks, the security of the communication becomes compromised.
- **Key Distribution:** Securely distributing the secret key to all communication parties poses a key challenge in symmetric key cryptography. If an eavesdropper

gains access to the key during distribution, they can decrypt all messages encrypted with that key.

- **Key Management:** As the number of users communicating grows, the requirement for a distinct secret key for each pair of users adds complexity to key management, especially in large-scale systems.
- **Perfect Forward Secrecy:** It is commonly used in protocols such as Transport Layer Security (TLS), which is the foundation for secure communication on the internet (e.g., securing HTTPS connections). By using ephemeral key exchanges like Diffie-Hellman, the TLS protocol ensures that each session's encryption keys are unique and unrelated to the server's long-term private key [13].

7.2 Frequently Employed Symmetric Key Encryption Algorithms

- **Advanced Encryption Standard (AES):** In fact, encryption standard used in various industries, healthcare, e-commerce, and government applications, including financial services, for securing sensitive data and protecting information from unauthorized access or interception. It is considered one of the most secure and widely adopted encryption algorithms worldwide.
- **Data Encryption Standard (DES):** An antiquated symmetric key algorithm, currently deemed weak due to its limited key size. It has mostly been supplanted by AES.
- **Triple Data Encryption Standard (3DES):** 3DES finds extensive usage in older systems and applications, particularly when maintaining compatibility with DES is essential. Nonetheless, its relatively slow processing speed and restricted effective key length have led contemporary cryptographic systems to favor AES for superior security and improved performance.

In summary, symmetric key cryptography is a fast and efficient method of encryption that relies on the use of a shared secret key between communicating parties. While it has its advantages, the key distribution and management aspects pose significant challenges, especially in large-scale systems. To address some of these challenges, hybrid cryptography, which combines symmetric and asymmetric key techniques, is often used in modern secure communication systems [14].

7.3 Advantages and Disadvantages of Symmetric Key Cryptography

Advantages

- **Efficiency:** Symmetric-key algorithms, in comparison to asymmetric-key algorithms (public-key cryptography), are generally faster and demand fewer computational resources. This characteristic makes them highly suitable for swift encryption and decryption of substantial volumes of data.
- **Simplicity:** Symmetric-key encryption is more straightforward because it is using the same key for encryption and decryption.
- **Strong Security:** When the key length is sufficiently large, symmetric-key cryptography can provide strong security against brute-force attacks. Modern

symmetric algorithms, such as AES, offer high levels of security, and their security is well-established through years of scrutiny by experts.

- **Perfect Forward Secrecy:** In certain scenarios, such as secure communication sessions, symmetric keys can be generated on-the-fly and discarded after use. This approach ensures perfect forward secrecy because even if an attacker compromises the key, they cannot decrypt past or future communications.
- **Data Integrity:** Symmetric-key encryption not only provides confidentiality (privacy) but can also be used to ensure data integrity. By using symmetric encryption together with a cryptographic hash function, data can be protected against tampering or unauthorized modifications.
- **Key Distribution:** While key distribution is a challenge in symmetric-key cryptography (since both parties need the same key), it can be more manageable in certain scenarios. For instance, in closed systems or situations where the number of participants is limited, key distribution can be easier to accomplish.
- **Compatibility:** Many legacy systems and applications still rely on symmetric-key cryptography. Using symmetric encryption allows for easy integration and compatibility with these existing systems.

Disadvantages

- In a big network, there are likely to be numerous pairs of keys, and it is essential that these keys be maintained effectively. Because of this, the administration of the effective key requires the use of a TTP (tactics, techniques, and procedures) that can be trusted in any circumstance.
- To guarantee the secure execution of cryptographic operations, it is crucial to periodically update the key, ideally before each unique communication session.

Digital signature systems have evolved from symmetric-key encryption methods and often require either the utilization of a TTP or large key sizes to facilitate public verification.

8. Asymmetric Key Cryptography

Asymmetric-key cryptography, also referred to as public-key cryptography. These key pairs consist of a public key and a private key. The public key is disseminated to the general public, whilst the private key is utilized during the decryption process to transform encrypted text into plain text. To ensure the confidentiality of information sent over the internet, asymmetric keys are used extensively. We make use of the RSA (Rivest, Shamir, Adleman) method for the encryption of asymmetric keys in order to provide improved and more secure transactions over the internet. Because of the calculations required to decrypt an asymmetric key, asymmetric cryptography is noticeably more time-consuming than symmetric encryption. A well-known example of an application that makes use of an asymmetric key to ensure the safety and confidentiality of online communications is SSL (secure sockets layer). In this article, we present a method for maintaining authentication and the secrecy of information while it is being transported. This method involves implementing the RSA algorithm, which will guarantee that the confidentiality of the information is maintained. Keep in mind that authentication refers to the process in which the receiver must be assured as to the identity of the sender, while confidentiality refers to the protection of the communication from being observed.

8.1 Advantages of Asymmetric Key Cryptography

- **Secure Key Exchange:** This is especially valuable in scenarios where establishing a shared secret key through a secure channel is impractical or not possible.
- **Digital Signatures:** Asymmetric cryptography allows individuals to create digital signatures using their private keys. These signatures offer authentication, integrity, and non-repudiation. In this case the sender of the message cannot deny sending it and that the message remains unaltered during transmission.
- **Public-key Distribution:** Asymmetric encryption relies on the distribution of public keys, which can be openly shared and does not require a secure channel. This is particularly useful in PKI systems, where trusted authorities issue digital certificates that bind an entity's identity to its public key, enabling secure communication over the internet.
- **Enhanced Security:** Asymmetric algorithms are based on complex mathematical problems, making them resistant to brute-force attacks. Breaking the security of asymmetric encryption requires significant computational resources, providing a higher level of security compared to many symmetric-key algorithms.
- **Perfect Forward Secrecy (PFS):** If ephemeral key pairs are utilized, asymmetric encryption can attain perfect forward secrecy. This signifies that in the event of an attacker compromising a private key, they would still be unable to decrypt previous communications that were encrypted with previously employed ephemeral keys.

8.2 Disadvantages of Asymmetric Key Cryptography

- **Computational Overhead:** Asymmetric encryption algorithms tend to be slower and computationally more demanding than symmetric encryption algorithms. Encrypting and decrypting data using asymmetric keys can be relatively slow, which is a concern for applications requiring high-performance data encryption.
- **Key Management:** Asymmetric cryptography necessitates the handling of key pairs (public and private keys) for every user or entity. Key management can become cumbersome in large-scale systems, particularly when dealing with a considerable number of users and devices.
- **Key Size:** Asymmetric encryption algorithms usually demand longer key lengths compared to symmetric algorithms to attain an equivalent level of security system. Longer key lengths result in larger encrypted data and can lead to heightened computational overhead.
- **Vulnerable to Certain Attacks:** While asymmetric encryption withstands brute-force attacks, it could be susceptible to other forms of attacks, such as side-channel attacks or those leveraging quantum computing algorithms (for traditional asymmetric algorithms). To address this concern, post-quantum cryptography is currently under development.
- **Lack of Secrecy:** The public key can be openly shared to all users, but the private

key must be kept confidential. If the private key is compromised, it can result in significant security breaches, potentially jeopardizing the confidentiality and authenticity of encrypted communications. Limited encryption capacity.

- **Asymmetric Encryption:** It is not optimal for encrypting large volumes of data due to its computational overhead and longer key lengths, making it less efficient for bulk data encryption when compared to symmetric encryption. Consequently, hybrid encryption schemes are frequently employed to combine the advantages of both asymmetric and symmetric encryption.

9. Data Encryption Standard (DES) Algorithm

Figure 1 illustrates a symmetric-key block cipher algorithm that gained widespread use for secure data encryption and decryption. While initially considered secure, advancements in technology exposed vulnerabilities to brute-force attacks. The relatively short key length of 56 bits allows for a manageable number of possible keys, making it susceptible to exploration using modern computing power. Consequently, DES is no longer recommended for encrypting sensitive data [15]. As a result, NIST officially retired DES in 2005. It has been supplanted by more robust and secure encryption algorithms like Triple DES and AES, which provide significantly stronger security with larger key lengths. AES is currently the most widely used symmetric-key encryption standard for various security applications.

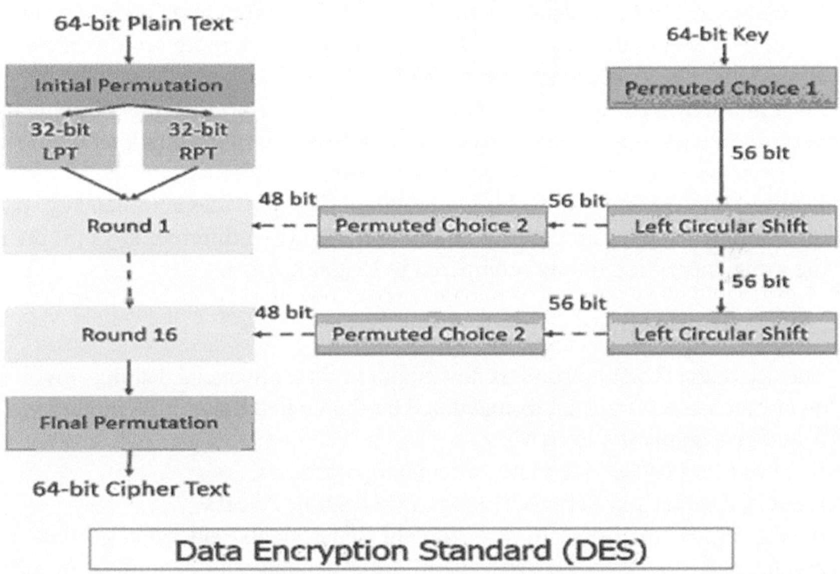

Figure 1: DEC encryption algorithm.

9.1 Advantages of DES

- **Historical Significance:** DES was the first widely used encryption standard and played a crucial role in advancing the field of cryptography. Its adoption set the foundation for modern encryption standards.

- **Simplicity:** DES has a relatively simple structure and algorithm, making it easy to understand and implement in software and hardware.
- **Efficient Hardware Implementation:** DES was designed during a time when hardware implementations were more common, and it can be efficiently implemented in hardware, which was beneficial for certain applications and devices.
- **Wide Acceptance:** At its peak, DES was widely adopted as the encryption standard for various applications, ensuring compatibility between systems that used it.

9.2 Disadvantages of DES

- **Key Length:** DES key size is 56 bit long, which renders it susceptible to brute-force attacks. With advancements in computing power, it has become feasible to exhaustively search the key space to find the correct key.
- **Security Concerns:** DES has been shown to be susceptible to several cryptographic attacks, such as differential and linear cryptanalysis, which significantly weaken its security. As a result, it is no longer considered a secure encryption standard for sensitive data.
- **Block Size:** The 64-bit block size of DES limits its ability to handle larger data sets efficiently. This can be a concern for certain applications that require encryption of large files or data streams.
- **Retirement:** DES is officially retired as a standard encryption algorithm due to its security vulnerabilities. It has been substituted with more secure encryption algorithms, like Triple DES and the AES.
- **Slow in Software Implementations:** While DES can be efficiently implemented in hardware, it can be relatively slow in software implementations due to the high number of rounds and complex operations involved.
- **Limited Key Space:** The 56-bit key length of DES provides a limited key space, resulting in a higher probability of key collision (two different keys producing the same encryption output) compared to longer key lengths.

9.3 DES Application

- The use of the DES algorithm is now required for all financial dealings involving electronic money transfer, as mandated by the United States government.
- Rapid processing in the ATM
- It is used for private video teleconferencing purposes.
- Used in Routers and Servers That Provide Remote Access
- It is available for usage by government departments and agencies that need cryptographic security for sensitive information and may be utilized in certain situations.

10. Triple Data Encryption Standard (3DES)

Figure 2 illustrates a symmetric encryption algorithm created to offer a higher level of safety compared to the original DES algorithm. While DES was widely used in the 1970s and 1980s, its 56-bit key size became susceptible to brute-force attacks as computing power increased [16]. Triple DES was introduced as a solution to enhance security by applying DES encryption three times with different keys. It operates by encrypting the data three times in succession: encrypt, decrypt, and then encrypt again. This process is often referred to as Encrypt-Decrypt-Encrypt (EDE) [17].

The three key option provides an effective key size of 168 bits (56 bits × 3) and significantly improves the security level compared to the original DES. However, 3DES has gradually become less popular due to its relatively slow performance and the emergence of more advanced encryption algorithms like AES.

As a result, modern systems and applications tend to use AES for symmetric encryption due to its better performance and comparable security with shorter key lengths. Nevertheless, 3DES is still used in some legacy systems or where compatibility with older implementations is necessary. In most cases, AES is considered the preferred choice for symmetric encryption in current applications.

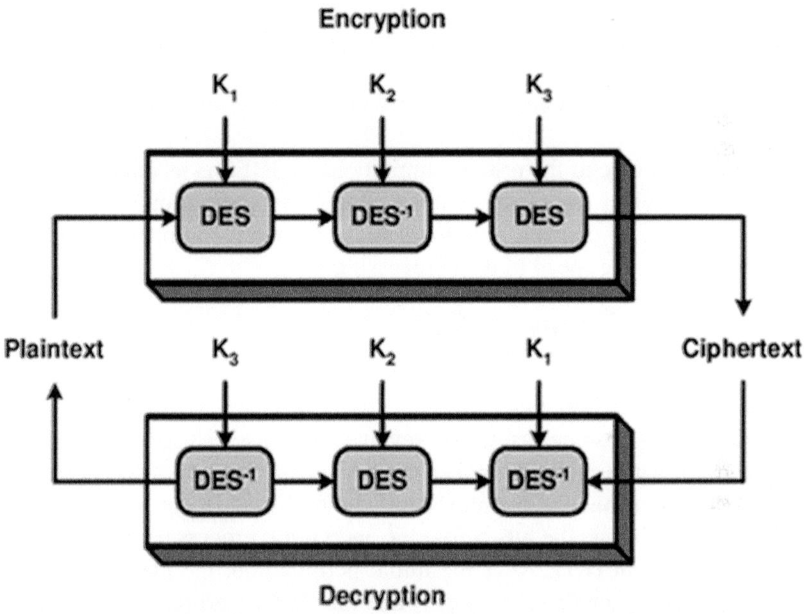

Figure 2: Block diagram for triple DES algorithm.

10.1 Key Features of 3DES (Triple DES)

- **Symmetric Encryption:** 3DES functions as a symmetric encryption technique, employing a single key for both encrypting and decrypting data. Consequently, this indicates that both the sender and receiver utilize an identical secret key to secure the privacy of the information.
- **Triple Encryption:** As the name suggests, 3DES applies the DES encryption process three times in succession. The data is encrypted, decrypted, and then encrypted again, using three different keys. The 3DES encryption offers an elevated level of safety compared to the original DES algorithm.

- **Key Size:** The 3DES employs three 56-bit keys, totaling 168 bits in key size. Nevertheless, the presence of the Meet-in-the-Middle attack vulnerability reduces the effective security to 112 bits.
- **Keying Options:** 3DES offers various keying options, such as two-key and three-key modes. In the two-key mode, the first and third stages employ the same key, whereas the second stage uses a distinct key. In the three-key mode, all three stages utilize different keys.
- **Compatibility:** 3DES is designed to be backward compatible with the original DES. It can process data encrypted with DES, making it suitable for transitioning from DES to a more secure encryption standard.
- **Security:** 3DES was considered secure for many years, and its multiple rounds of encryption provide a considerable level of protection against brute-force attacks. However, due to its relatively slow performance and vulnerabilities, it has become less popular in modern applications, where AES is generally preferred.
- **Data Integrity:** While 3DES provides encryption, it does not inherently include mechanisms for data integrity or authenticity. To ensure data integrity, additional mechanisms like message verification codes (MACs) or digital signatures are required.
- **Performance:** One of the primary limitations of 3DES is its relatively sluggish performance when contrasted with contemporary encryption algorithms such as AES. The triple encryption process adds computational intensity, which can adversely affect the speed of data processing [18].

10.2 Encryption Process of DES

- **Key Selection:** In 3DES, three keys are used for encryption, denoted as Key1, Key2, and Key3. These keys are typically 56 bits each, resulting in a total key size of 168 bits. In some cases, two-key mode can also be used, where Key1 and Key3 are the same, and only two keys are used.
- **Initial Permutation:** The plaintext data is first subjected to an initial permutation (IP) step to rearrange the bits before the encryption process begins.
- **First Encryption (E1):** After the initial permutation, the plaintext undergoes encryption using the first key (Key1) and the DES algorithm. The result of this process is referred to as ciphertext1.
- **Second Decryption (D2):** The ciphertext1 derived from the initial encryption phase is subsequently decrypted using the second key (Key2) and the DES algorithm. These operations successfully back the encryption process, resulting in intermediate plaintext data.
- **Third Encryption (E3):** The intermediate plaintext data from the second decryption stage is encrypted again by applying the third key (Key3) and the DES algorithm. The result of this stage is known as the ciphertext2.
- **Final Permutation:** The ciphertext is subjected to a final permutation (FP) step to rearrange the bits before it is considered the final encrypted output.

10.3 Decryption Process of DES

- **Key Selection:** Just like in the encryption process, the same three keys (Key1, Key2, and Key3) are used for decryption in the reverse order.
- **Initial Permutation:** The ciphertext to be decrypted is first subjected to the initial permutation (IP) step.
- **First Decryption (D3):** The ciphertext is decrypted and applies the third key (Key3) and the DES algorithm. The result of this stage is the intermediate plaintext data.
- **Second Encryption (E2):** The intermediate plaintext data obtained from the first decryption stage is then encrypted by applying the second key (Key2) and the DES algorithm. This reverses the encryption process from the encryption phase and produces intermediate ciphertext data.
- **Third Decryption (D1):** The intermediate ciphertext data obtained from the second encryption stage is decrypted using the first key (Key1) and the DES algorithm. This process successfully backs the last encryption step, yielding the final plaintext output.
- **Final Permutation:** The final plaintext output undergoes a final permutation (FP) step to rearrange the bits and produce the correct decrypted data.

10.4 Advantages of 3DES

- **Enhanced Security:** When compared to DES, the encryption method known as 3DES, which uses three layers, offers a higher level of protection.
- **Widely Used:** When compared to DES, the encryption technique known as 3DES, which makes use of three layers, provides a better degree of security due to the increased number of layers it employs.
- **Customizable Key Sizes:** The fact that 3DES provides various key sizes enables it to better accommodate a wide variety of security requirements.

10.5 Limitations of 3DES

- **Performance:** The triple encryption and decryption process of 3DES involves three rounds of the DES algorithm, which can be computationally intensive and slow compared to more modern encryption algorithms like AES. As a result, 3DES may not be suitable for applications requiring high-speed data processing and performance.
- **Key Length:** Even though 3DES utilizes three keys, its effective key length is diminished to 112 bits because of vulnerabilities associated with the Meet-in-the-Middle attack. As a result of this key length limitation, some may view it as inadequate to provide the same level of security as other cryptographic algorithms with longer key lengths.
- **Compatibility:** While 3DES was designed to be backward compatible with DES, its usage may lead to interoperability issues with modern cryptographic systems that prefer more efficient algorithms like AES. This can be a challenge when integrating with newer applications or services.

- **Vulnerable to Known Attacks:** Over time, cryptanalysis techniques have improved, and certain vulnerabilities in 3DES have been discovered. Although no practical attacks against the full 3DES have been found, the overall security of the algorithm is now considered weaker compared to newer and more secure encryption standards like AES.

10.6 Applications of 3DES

3DES is extensively employed in numerous applications, including but not limited to:

- **Legacy Systems:** Many legacy systems and older hardware may still be using 3DES for encryption due to historical reasons. Upgrading these systems to newer encryption standards like AES could be costly and time-consuming, making 3DES a more practical choice to maintain compatibility.
- **Financial Transactions:** In some financial systems and payment processing applications, 3DES is used for secure data transmission and encryption of sensitive financial information. However, newer systems are increasingly adopting AES or other more modern encryption methods.
- **Smart Cards:** Some smart cards and embedded systems still use 3DES for data protection and authentication. Smart cards often have limited resources, and implementing AES might be more resource-intensive than 3DES, making the latter a viable option.
- **Virtual Private Networks (VPNs):** In certain cases, 3DES may still be employed in older VPN implementations. However, modern VPNs generally prefer stronger encryption algorithms like AES for improved security and performance.
- **Government and Defense:** In specific governmental and defense applications, 3DES may be used due to its historical use and compatibility with older systems. However, in critical and classified operations, more advanced encryption methods are likely preferred.
- **Secure Socket Layer (SSL) and Transport Layer Security (TLS):** Although SSL and TLS protocols predominantly use AES for encryption, some older versions of these protocols may still support 3DES for compatibility reasons. However, modern versions of SSL/TLS should favor AES.
- **Digital Rights Management (DRM):** Some older DRM systems may use 3DES to protect copyrighted content and prevent unauthorized access. However, newer DRM solutions may opt for stronger encryption algorithms.

11. Blowfish

Figure 3 illustrates Blowfish, created by Bruce Schneier in 1993, is a symmetric-key block cipher algorithm well-regarded for its simplicity, speed, and adaptability. It manages 64-bit blocks of data and keeps up variable key lengths, ranging from 32 bits to 448 bits. The algorithm comprises two primary phases: key setup and data encryption/decryption. During the key setup, the input key undergoes a series of transformations to generate subkeys, which are subsequently employed in the encryption and decryption process. Utilizing a Feistel network structure, Blowfish executes multiple rounds of data transformation. Each round involves a combination of substitution and permutation operations. The algorithm's core relies on the use of S-boxes (substitution boxes) and a sequence of modular addition and XOR operations.

While Blowfish was considered secure for many years, its key size started to raise concerns as computing power increased. Therefore, newer algorithms like AES (Advanced Encryption Standard) with larger key sizes have become more popular for securing sensitive data. Nevertheless, Blowfish remains a relevant and valuable algorithm in various applications and is still studied for educational and historical purposes.

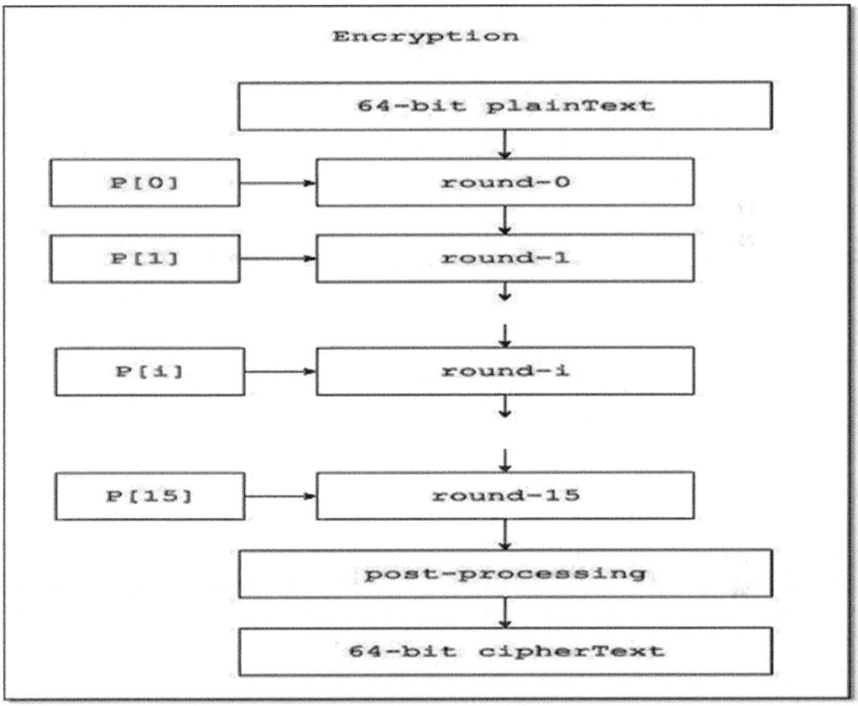

Figure 3: Blowfish algorithm.

11.1 Limitations of Blowfish

- **Key Size:** While Blowfish supports variable key sizes, its largest key size of 448 bits may not be sufficient for fixed high-security applications, especially in the face of increasing computational power and sophisticated attacks. As a result, it may be less suitable for scenarios that demand extremely strong encryption.
- **Vulnerability to Differential Cryptanalysis:** Blowfish is known to be vulnerable to certain differential cryptanalysis techniques. Although it was considered secure at the time of its design, more modern block ciphers like AES have been specifically designed to resist such attacks more effectively.

- **Lack of Hardware Acceleration:** Blowfish's speed and efficiency in software implementations are commendable, but it may not be as well-suited for hardware acceleration as some other algorithms. Modern cryptographic applications often rely on hardware acceleration to achieve faster encryption and decryption, which could be a concern for Blowfish's adoption in certain environments.
- **Limited Adoption:** Blowfish has not been widely adopted in comparison to some other encryption algorithms like AES. This limited adoption might mean that it has seen less scrutiny and review from the cryptographic community, potentially leaving some security vulnerabilities undiscovered.
- **No Longer Standard:** Blowfish is not part of any official cryptographic standard, which could be seen as a disadvantage when comparing it to widely accepted and standardized algorithms like AES.
- **No Forward Secrecy:** Blowfish lacks forward secrecy, implying that if an attacker acquires the key, they can decrypt all previous and future encrypted communications. In contrast, contemporary cryptographic systems frequently adopt methods like ephemeral key exchange to achieve further confidentiality. This makes sure that even if the long-duration key is compromised, past communications continue to exist safeguarding due to the use of temporary, one-time keys for each session.

Due to these limitations and advancements in cryptography, Blowfish is now considered more of a legacy algorithm. While it may still be suitable for certain specific use cases, modern applications tend to prefer more robust and widely studied algorithms like AES.

12. AES Algorithm

Figure 4 describes the AES algorithm. It is a highly prevalent symmetric encryption technique crafted to safeguard susceptible data. In 2001, it was selected by the U.S. National Institute of Standards and Technology (NIST) as the quality encryption algorithm, replacing the aging Data Encryption Standard (DES)[20]. AES operates on fixed block sizes of 128 bits (16 bytes) and provides hold-up three key lengths: 128 bits, 192 bits, and 256 bits. The key length determines the number of rounds (encryption iterations) utilized in the algorithm [21].

- 128-bit key size: there are10 rounds
- 192-bit key size: there are 12 rounds
- 256-bit key size: there are 14 rounds

Both encryption and decryption processes in AES are iterative and involve many rounds. Every round employs a group of transformations on the data utilizing a round key, which is derived from the actual encryption key. These round keys are generated through a key expansion process.

12.1 AES Encryption Process

- Key Expansion involves transforming the initial encryption key into a series of round keys, with each round of encryption having its dedicated key.

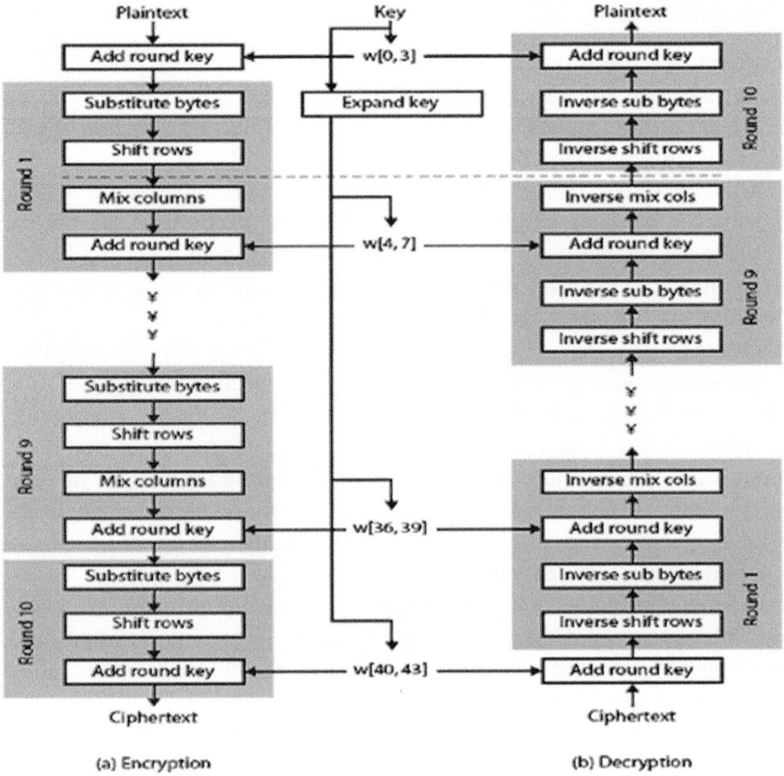

Figure 4: Basic structure of AES.

- During the Initial Round, the algorithm applies substitution and permutation action to the input data, utilizing the first-round key.
- **Main Rounds:** Depending on the key length, AES will repeat a set number of main rounds. Each main round consists of three operations.
- Sub Bytes is a process that entails the nonlinear substitution of each byte within the data state by utilizing an S-box lookup table.
- Shift Rows is a step that involves shifting the rows of the data state to introduce diffusion and enhance the encryption process.
- Mix Columns is a procedure that involves mixing the columns of the data state to introduce diffusion and strengthen the encryption process.
- The Final Round resembles the main rounds but excludes the Mix Columns step, completing the encryption process.
- Once all rounds are completed, the encryption process produces the encrypted data, known as ciphertext. This ciphertext is the final output of the encryption algorithm.
- In essence, AES decryption is the opposite of the encryption process, employing the identical round keys in a reversed sequence.
- Due to its robust security and widespread adoption, AES is used in various applications, including securing communications (e.g., TLS/SSL), protecting files and data at rest, and securing wireless networks (e.g., WPA2).

12.2 Advantages of AES

- **Security:** AES is considered highly secure and has withstood extensive cryptanalysis. Its strength is attributed to its complex mathematical structure and the use of multiple rounds of substitution, permutation, and diffusion operations, making it resistant to various cryptographic attacks.
- **Standardization:** AES is a widely accepted and standardized encryption algorithm. It has been adopted as a federal excellence by the U.S. government and is used globally in various industries, including finance, healthcare, telecommunications, and more. This standardization ensures interoperability and compatibility across different systems and platforms.
- **Efficiency:** AES is designed to be efficient and fast, even on resource-constrained devices like mobile phones and IoT devices. Its symmetric encryption nature enables straightforward implementation, leading to faster encryption and decryption times compared to asymmetric encryption algorithms like RSA.
- **Versatility:** AES provides flexibility in key sizes, offering options of 128, 192, and 256 bits. This enables users to select the desired level of security according to their specific needs, making AES adaptable to a wide range of security requirements and applications.
- **Hardware Support:** AES encryption and decryption can be efficiently implemented in hardware, which provides hardware acceleration for AES operations. Many modern processors and cryptographic hardware include built-in AES instructions, further enhancing its performance.
- **Public Scrutiny:** The AES algorithm selection process involved a public competition, inviting cryptographic experts to analyze and evaluate potential candidates. This extensive public scrutiny and analysis by the global cryptographic community have increased confidence in the algorithm's security.

12.3 Disadvantages of AES

- **Key Management:** For AES, ensuring secure distribution and management of encryption keys is crucial. If the keys are compromised, the security of the encrypted data becomes vulnerable. Proper key management can be intricate and difficult, particularly in extensive systems.
- **Performance Impact:** AES encryption and decryption can be computationally intensive, especially for large volumes of data. As a result, it may introduce some performance overhead, particularly on resource-constrained devices or systems.
- **Limited in Scope:** AES is specifically designed for symmetric encryption, where the similar key is utilized for both encryption and decryption procedure. While this reference is well-suited for numerous situations, it might not be the optimal choice for all use cases. In certain specific tasks, asymmetric encryption schemes, such as RSA, are better suited and more appropriate.
- **Lack of Built-in Authentication:** AES alone does not provide data integrity or authenticity. It only ensures confidentiality by encrypting the data. To ensure the integrity and authenticity of the data, a separate authentication mechanism needs to be employed.

- **Vulnerable to Quantum Computing:** While AES is currently considered secure against classical computing attacks, it is not resistant to quantum computing attacks. As quantum computing develops, it could potentially break AES encryption, leading to the need for quantum-resistant encryption algorithms.

13. RSA Algorithm

Figure 5 illustrates The RSA algorithm, a popular asymmetric cryptographic technique utilized for secure data transmission and encryption, was created in 1977 by Ron Rivest, Adi Shamir, and Leonard Adleman. It is playing a vital role in modern cryptography and provides a foundation for safe communication, digital signatures, and authentication in various applications across the internet and computer networks. However, it is prime to note that the safety of RSA relies on the proper execution and key size, as advances in computing power or mathematical breakthroughs could impact its effectiveness over time. Therefore, using appropriate key sizes and staying up-to-date with security best practices is crucial when employing RSA in real-world scenarios.

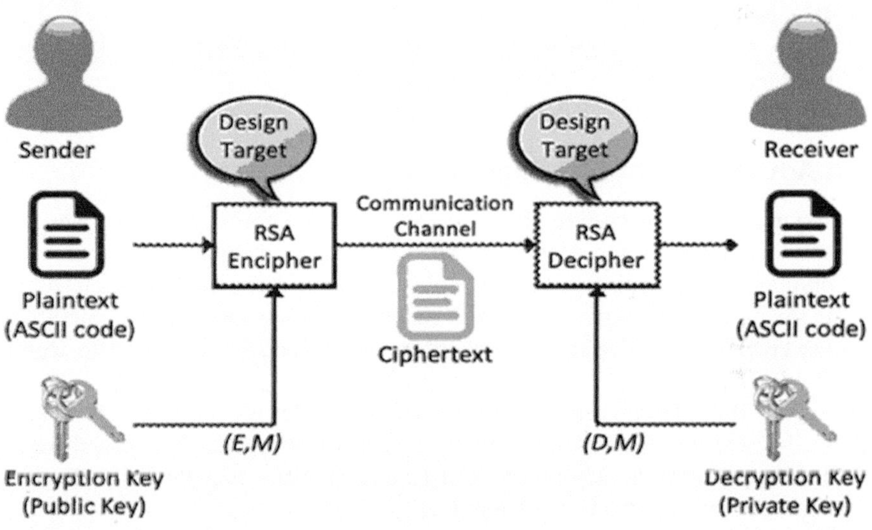

Figure 5: RSA algorithm.

RSA has found extensive application in ensuring secure communications, digital signatures, and key exchanges in various contexts, such as SSL/TLS to safe web communications, PGP (Pretty Good Privacy) for email encryption, and numerous other safe protocols. Nevertheless, with the continuous progress in computing power, it is crucial to periodically enhance the key size to preserve security against potential attacks [22].

13.1 Inherent Characteristics of RSA Algorithm

- The RSA technique is a common method for performing exponentiation over integers, including prime numbers, in settings where the field is finite.
- The integers that are employed in this method are suitably huge, which makes the problem challenging to solve (Tutorials point, 2020).

13.2 RSA Encryption/Decryption

- **Key Generations**
  a. Select two large prime numbers, p and q.
  b. Evaluate the modulus, $N = p * q$.
  c. Evaluate the Euler's totient function, $\varphi(N) = (p - 1) * (q - 1)$.
  d. Select a public exponent, e, such that $1 < e < \varphi(N)$ and $\gcd(e, \varphi(N)) = 1$. Usually, e is a small prime such as 3 or 65537.
  e. Compute the private exponent, d, such that $(d * e) \% \varphi(N) = 1$.
- **Encryption**
  Given a plaintext message, M, the recipient's public key (N, e) is used for encryption.
  Ciphertext, C, is calculated as: $C = M^e \% N$.
- **Decryption**
  Given the ciphertext, C, the recipient uses their private key (d) to decrypt the message.
  Plaintext, M, is calculated as: $M = C^e \% N$.

13.3 Advantages of RSA Algorithm

- **Asymmetric Encryption:** RSA is an encryption algorithm that operates with two distinct keys for encryption and decryption, making it an asymmetric cryptographic technique. This characteristic enables safe communication without the need for both parties to share a secret key in advance. During encryption used recipient's public key, and only the recipient used the private key to decrypt the data.
- **Secure Data Transmission:** RSA offers a robust level of security, rendering it well-suited for safeguarding data during transmission over insecure channels, such as the internet. As long as the private key remains protected, the encrypted data remains impervious to unauthorized decryption.
- **Digital Signatures:** RSA is applicable for digital signatures, permitting a sender to digitally sign a message or document using their private key. Afterwards, the recipient can authenticate and validate the message's integrity by verifying the signature with the sender's public key.
- **Key Exchange:** RSA can enable a secure exchange of keys between two parties. For instance, it is frequently employed in the initial stages of secure communication protocols like SSL/TLS to establish a safe connection between a web browser and a server.
- **Widely Supported:** RSA has been around for several decades and is supported by various programming languages and cryptographic libraries. This widespread support makes it easy to implement RSA in various applications and platforms.

14. Proposed Work

These ten papers examine different aspects of social networking sites (SNSs) and their impact on society. De Wolf, Dhoest, and Ballon [23] investigate how SNSs contribute to the surveillance society by examining the usage of these sites by students in Salzburg. Ling [24] explores how the popularity of SNSs has affected mobile phone use and the ways in which people interact with their surroundings. Hill and Wiggins [25] study how SNSs enable people to create and express their identities within online communities, using linguistic analysis of online football fan forums as a case study. Fisk [26] discusses the use of SNSs by college admissions officers and the potential impact of online profiles on the admissions process. Xu and Kraut [27] examine users' perceptions of privacy and security risks on SNSs and explore the protective behaviors that users adopt to mitigate these risks. Seidman [28] explores the impact of SNSs on romantic relationships, focusing on the effects of these sites on jealousy and relationship happiness. Nilakanta and Chen [29] examine the ethical considerations associated with SNSs, focusing on the privacy policies of these sites and the choices made by users regarding their personal information. Hoffman [30] discusses the impact of SNSs on the social and academic development of adolescents, examining current theories and controversies surrounding this topic. Baptiste, Aubert, and Robert [31] examine the challenges associated with introducing SNSs in organizations and explore strategies for integrating these sites into existing organizational structures. Finally, DiMaggio, Hargittai, Celeste, and Shafer [32] examine the role of SNSs in news consumption, using an empirical analysis of the United States as a case study.

Figures 6, 7, 8 illustrate a proposed novel algorithm for securing social networking sites involves detecting and preventing various security threats such as phishing attacks, malware, and spam. The algorithm is designed to analyze user behaviors and patterns, detect anomalies, and prevent unauthorized access to user accounts. It also uses data encryption and multi-factor authentication methods to secure the confidentiality and integrity of user data. By continuously analyzing and learning from user behavior, the algorithm can adapt to new security threats and provide an effective and reliable security solution for social networking sites:

This research paper examines the utilization of advanced cryptographic algorithms to protect social networks and secure the security and integrity of data. The study explores different cryptographic algorithms, including symmetric key cryptography, asymmetric key cryptography, and hash functions, as potential means for secure communication and data storage. The paper analyzes the advantages and disadvantages of each cryptographic algorithm, discusses their strengths and limitations, and identifies various use cases where they can be applied to enhance data security and integrity. In conclusion, the paper emphasizes the significance of employing advanced cryptographic algorithms to safeguard social networks and emphasizes the ongoing need for research and development in this field.

Proposed Algorithms and Flow Charts

Step 1: From the social networking site sever obtained the string containing user ID and Password.

Step 2: Convert the string into Binary string.
Step 3: Perform the Encryption Algo (describe below).
Step 4: Send the obtained Encryption Text (key) to the public domain.
Step 5: Authorized user will obtain the key from public domain.
Step 6: Decryption Algorithm (described below) is implemented by using the obtained key.
Step 7: Binary string is converted into Text.
Step 8: User ID and Password is obtained.

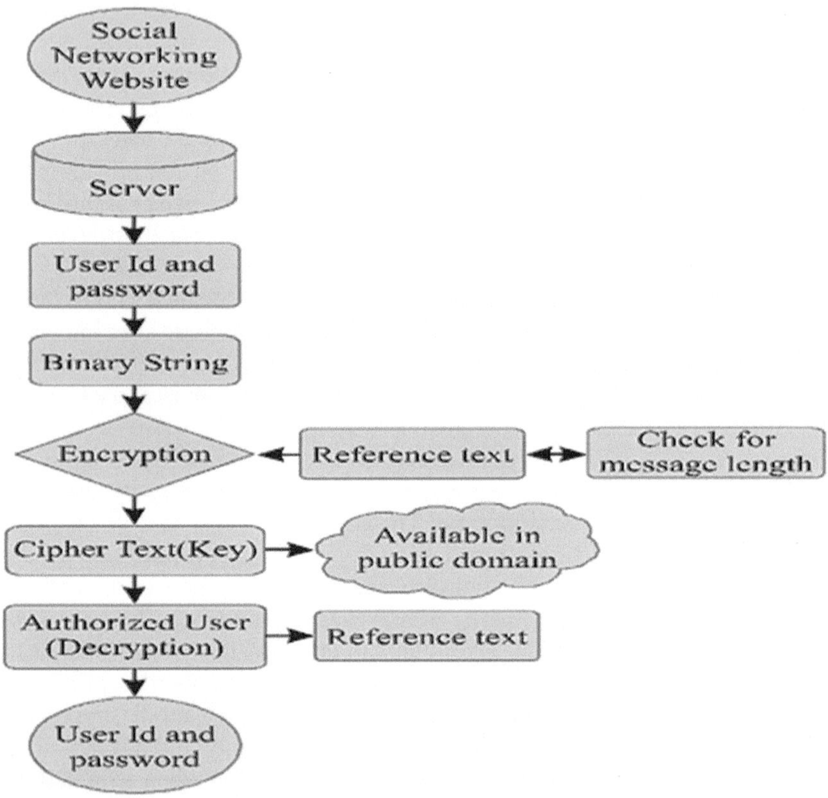

Figure 6: Flow chart of proposed algorithms.

14.1 Implementation

Encryption

- Take any reference text of length bigger than this string.
- Convert this string in binary format.
- Map the binary string with White Space 1 and White space two.
- Encode the above string using reference text.

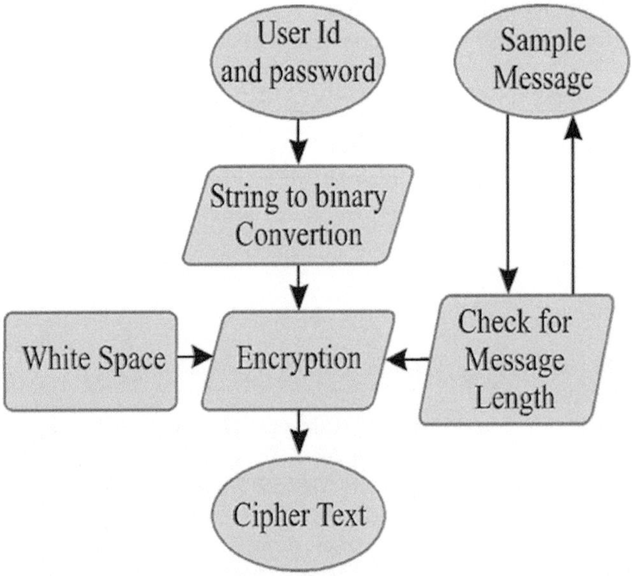

Figure 7: Flow chart of encryption algorithm.

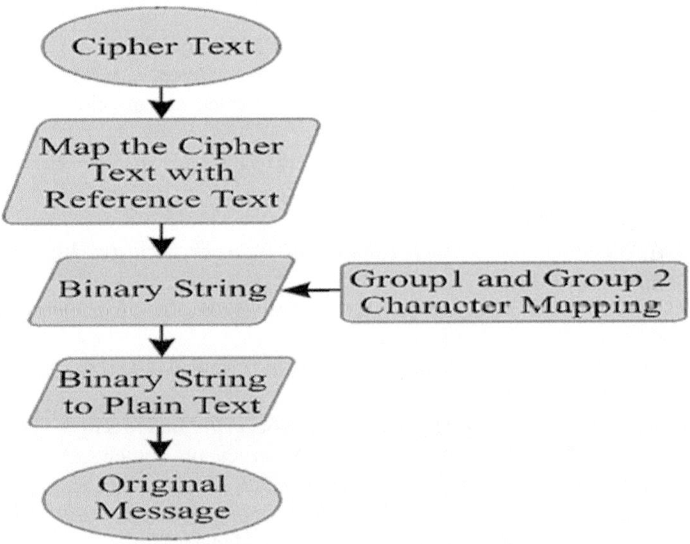

Figure 8: Flow chart of decryption algorithm.

Decryption

- Map the cipher text with reference text used in encryption.
- Again, map the text obtained from above with white space 1 and white space two.

- Convert the binary string to plaintext.
- Plaintext obtained from above is our original message.

Complexity Analysis

- Time complexity: (length of pdf file) + O (length of the extracted text) * 8
- Space complexity: (length of the text extracted from pdf file) * 8

References

1. Stallings, William. (2007). *Network Security Essentials: Applications and Standards*. Pearson Education India.
2. Saranya, K., R. Mohana Priya, & J. Udhayan. (2014). A review on symmetric key encryption techniques in cryptography, *Int. J. Sci. Eng. Technol.*, 3(3), 539–544.
3. Kahate, Atul. (2013). *Cryptography and Network Security*. Tata McGraw-Hill Education.
4. Schneier, B. (1996). Applied Cryptography. *Electr. Eng.*, 1(32), 429–455.
5. Gulzar, N., B. Abbasi, E. Wu, A. Ozbal, & W.Q. Yan. (2013). Surveillance privacy protection. In: *Intelligent Multimedia Surveillance*, 83–105. Springer Berlin Heidelberg.
6. Wang, Cong, Qian Wang, Kui Ren, Ning Cao, & Wenjing Lou. (2012). Toward secure and dependable storage services in cloud computing. *Services Computing, IEEE Transactions*, 5(2), 220–232.
7. Beaulieu, Ray, Douglas Shors, Jason Smith, Stefan Treatman-Clark, Bryan Weeks, & Louis Wingers (2015). The SIMON and SPECK lightweight block ciphers. In: *Proceedings of the 52nd Annual Design Automation Conference*. ACM.
8. Komninos, Nikos. (2012). Morpheus: A word-oriented stream cipher. *International Journal of Computer Research*, 19(2, 3), 220.
9. Cao, N., Wang, C., Li, M., Ren, K., & Lou, W. (2013). Privacy-preserving multi-keyword ranked search over encrypted cloud data. *IEEE Transactions on Parallel and Distributed Systems*, 25(1), 222–233.
10. Stallings, William. (2006). *Cryptography and Network Security*. 4th Edn. Pearson Education India.
11. Schneier, Bruce. (2007). *Applied Cryptography: Protocols, Algorithms, and Source Code*. 2nd Edn. C. John Wiley & Sons.
12. Conti, Greg. (2007). *Security Data Visualization: Graphical Techniques for Network Analysis*. No Starch Press.
13. Kahate, Atul. (2013). *Cryptography and Network Security*. Tata McGraw-Hill Education.
14. Jesudoss, A., & N. Subramaniam. (2014). A survey on authentication attacks and countermeasures in a distributed environment. *IJCSE*, 5(2).
15. Daemen, Joan, & Vincent Rijmen. (2013). *The Design of Rijndael: AES – The Advanced Encryption Standard*. Springer Science & Business Media.
16. Kahate, Atul. (2013). *Cryptography and Network Security*. Tata McGraw-Hill Education.
17. Bellare, Mihir, Kenneth G. Paterson, & Phillip Rogaway. (2014). Security of symmetric encryption against mass surveillance. In: *Advances in Cryptology – CRYPTO 2014*, 1–19. Springer Berlin Heidelberg.
18. Raychev, Nikolay. (2012). Classical cryptography in quantum context. In: *Proceedings of the IEEE 10 (2012): 2015.*

19. Rebeiro, Chester, Debdeep Mukhopadhyay, & Sarani Bhattacharya. (2015). *Modern Cryptography: Timing Channels in Cryptography*. Springer International Publishing. pp. 13–35.
20. https://en.wikibooks.org/wiki/Cryptography/DES.
21. Nilesh, D., & M. Nagle. (2014, January). The new cryptography algorithm with high throughput. In: *Computer Communication and Informatics (ICCCI), 2014 International Conference*, pp. 1–5. IEEE.
22. Kaur, A. (2017). A review on symmetric key cryptography algorithms. *International Journal of Advanced Research in Computer Science*, 8(4), 358–362.
23. https://cyberw1ng.medium.com/triple-des-3des-encryption-features-process-advantages-and-applications-2023-587e5a092789.
24. Berent, A. (2013). *Advanced Encryption Standard by Example*. Document available at URL http://www. networkdls. com/Articles/AESbyExample. pdf (April 1, 2007) Accessed: June.
25. Mohamed, A.A., & A.H. Madian. (2010, December). A modified Rijndael algorithm and its implementation using FPGA. In: *Electronics, Circuits, and Systems (ICECS), 2010 17th IEEE International Conference*, pp. 335–338.
26. Pramstaller, N., F.K. Gurkaynak, S. Haene, H. Kaeslin, N. Felber, & W. Fichtner. (2004, September). Towards an AES crypto-chip resistant to differential power analysis. In: *Solid-State Circuits Conference*. ESSCIRC 2004.
27. Rouse, M. (2021). Techtarget. [Online] Available at: https://searchdisasterrecovery.techtarget.com/definition/business-continuity [Accessed 06 01 2021].
28. De Wolf, R., A. Dhoest, & P. Ballon. (2012). Social networking sites and the surveillance society: A critical case study of the usage of studiVZ, Facebook, and MySpace by students in Salzburg in the context of electronic surveillance. *European Journal of Communication*, 27(1), 34–49.
29. Ling, R. (2008). From social butterfly to urban citizen: The evolution of mobile phone practice. In: A. Kavoori & N. Arceneaux (Eds.), *The Cell Phone Reader: Essays in Social Transformation*, pp. 155–166. Peter Lang.
30. Hill, C.A., & R.W. Wiggins. (2014). Identity and interactivity in online communities: Evidence from linguistic analyses of online football fan forums. *Journal of Broadcasting & Electronic Media*, 58(1), 1–22.
31. Fisk, N. (2012). Social networking sites and college admissions: The case of Facebook. *Journal of College Admission*, 215, 18–25.
32. Xu, H., & R.E. Kraut. (2013). Privacy and security in online social networks: Risk perceptions and protective behaviors. *Journal of the Association for Information Science and Technology*, 64(5), 1018–1030.

8 | Securing Tomorrow: The Transformative Role of IoT in Smart Security Systems

Ashish A. Desai[1,2], S.N. Khan[2], Dr. G.S. Patel[2]

[1] Mechanical Engineering Department, Rajarshi Shahu College of Engineering, Tathawade, Pune, Maharashtra, India

[2] Automation and Robotics Department, Sharad Institute of Technology College of Engineering, Yadrav, Maharashtra, India

1. Introduction

IoT is crucial in today's technology-driven world. With the increasing connectivity and integration of devices in the Internet of Things (IoT) ecosystem, the potential for security breaches and cyber attacks has also grown exponentially. It is essential to understand the various security issues and challenges faced by IoT devices, such as weak authentication protocols, lack of encryption, and susceptibility to malware. By conducting a comprehensive study, researchers can identify vulnerabilities and develop robust security measures to safeguard the privacy and integrity of IoT systems, ensuring a safer and more secure digital environment for users. Additionally, the increasing number of interconnected devices in the IoT ecosystem creates a larger attack surface for hackers to exploit. This poses a significant risk as compromised IoT devices can not only compromise the privacy of individuals but also be used as entry points to infiltrate other systems. Therefore, it is crucial for manufacturers and developers to prioritize security measures, including regular software updates and patches, to prevent potential breaches and protect the overall network. By addressing these security challenges head-on, the full potential of the IoT can be harnessed without compromising user safety [1].

Many researchers found that while there are existing security models, techniques, and tools for the IoT, they are often inadequate in ensuring complete protection. Therefore, it is essential for manufacturers and developers to continuously innovate and improve security measures to keep up with the evolving threat landscape. Additionally, collaboration between industry stakeholders, government bodies, and cybersecurity experts is crucial to establish industry-wide standards and best

*Corresponding author: ashishdesai@sitcoe.org.in

DOI: 10.1201/9781003560012-8

practices that can effectively safeguard IoT devices and networks. Only through such comprehensive efforts can the potential of the IoT be fully realized while maintaining user safety and privacy. By implementing robust encryption protocols, regularly updating software, and conducting rigorous vulnerability testing, manufacturers and developers can enhance the security of IoT devices. Furthermore, raising awareness among consumers about the importance of practicing good cybersecurity hygiene, such as setting strong passwords and avoiding suspicious links, can also contribute to a safer IoT ecosystem. Ultimately, a collective effort from all stakeholders is necessary to address the security challenges posed by the IoT and ensure its successful integration into our daily lives [2].

Kim [3] emphasized the importance of gateway-based security requirements in IoT applications, highlighting the role of secure data transmission, authentication, and access control at the gateway level to protect resource-constrained IoT devices.

Tan et al. [4] discussed key security challenges in IoT systems, including device heterogeneity, scalability, and privacy concerns, and outlined future research directions for developing resilient and adaptive IoT security frameworks.

Al-Fuqaha et al. [5] provided a comprehensive survey of IoT enabling technologies, communication protocols, and applications, stressing the need for standardized security mechanisms to ensure interoperability and trustworthy data exchange across IoT networks.

Kraijak and Tuwanut [6] presented an extensive review of IoT architectures, protocols, applications, and security issues, highlighting real-world implementation challenges and the necessity of robust privacy-preserving and secure IoT system designs. A survey on internet of things architecture, protocols, possible applications, security, privacy, real-world implementation and future trends revealed that while TLS/SSL protocols are widely used, there are still vulnerabilities present in IoT devices due to outdated firmware. Therefore, it is crucial for manufacturers to prioritize regular updates and patches to address these vulnerabilities and enhance the security of their products. Furthermore, the survey emphasized the need for robust authentication mechanisms and encryption protocols to protect sensitive data in IoT systems. Looking ahead, future trends in IoT security include the adoption of block chain technology and the development of artificial intelligence-based threat detection systems to counter emerging cyber threats. These advancements can provide an additional layer of security and transparency to IoT devices, ensuring the integrity and privacy of user data. Additionally, collaboration between manufacturers, government agencies, and cybersecurity experts is essential to establish standardized security measures and regulations for IoT devices. By addressing these issues proactively, the industry can build a more secure and trustworthy IoT ecosystem that benefits both businesses and consumers alike [7].

Patil and Iyer [8] designed an IoT-enabled health monitoring and tracking system for soldiers, demonstrating the application of IoT in military healthcare. Deshpande and Iyer [9] also looked at research paths in the Internet of Every Things (IoET), stressing how important it is becoming in the fields of health and automation.

Sonar et al. [10] created an electronic health record system that uses biometric authentication to keep patient information safe. Martinhoa et al. [11] developed a wireless multiparameter patient monitoring system that facilitated real-time data transmission and analysis. Wcislik et al. [12] also proposed a wireless health monitoring system to enhance remote healthcare delivery.

Bera et al. [13] also looked into hand biometrics in digital forensics and said that it might be useful for safe medical identification. Iyer et al. [14] created an RF sensor with two inputs and two outputs that can be used to keep track of people inside, making it easier to keep track of patients. Valsalan et al. [15] developed an Internet of Things (IoT)-based health monitoring system capable of real-time data collection and analysis of patient information. Sathya et al. [16] discussed the primary challenges associated with IoT-based health monitoring, emphasizing concerns related to data security and system integration. Finally, Kumar and Jasuja [17] presented how to combine IoT and Raspberry Pi to build a system that checks the air quality. This is an example of how healthcare analytics may work with environmental apps.

2. Application IoT in Smart Security Systems

Investigating the integration of IoT technology with smart security systems to enhance overall safety and protection in various applications.

2.1 E-Health

This study proposes a secure and energy-efficient scheme for patient data transmission from wearable IoT sensors to base stations. The proposed scheme addresses security breaches, threats, and energy degradation in resource-constrained IoT sensors. Tested, using a mathematical model and simulation setup, it provides secure, energy-efficient data transmission, addresses issues like availability, reliability, scalability, and limited patient mobility. This innovative approach for e-health applications uses IoT technology. The proposed scheme utilizes a multiple group node concept, where IoT sensors are grouped together based on their proximity and resource capabilities. This allows for efficient and secure data transmission, as nodes within a group can collaborate and share resources to optimize energy consumption. Furthermore, the scheme employs advanced encryption algorithms and authentication mechanisms to ensure the confidentiality and integrity of patient data. Overall, this innovative approach holds great potential for revolutionizing e-health applications by providing a robust and scalable solution for secure patient data transmission.

2.2 Retail and Logistics

By integrating IoT devices with smart security systems, retail, and logistics companies can enhance their supply chain management and improve overall efficiency. Real-time tracking and monitoring of inventory and shipments can help identify and address potential issues or delays, ensuring timely deliveries and reducing costs. Furthermore, this integration can enable seamless communication between different stakeholders in the supply chain, leading to better coordination and increased customer satisfaction.

2.3 Smart Environment

Smart transportation systems, coupled with smart security systems, can greatly improve safety and efficiency in the transportation industry. IoT devices can be used to monitor traffic conditions in real-time, helping to optimize routes and reduce congestion. Additionally, these devices can enhance security measures by detecting potential threats, such as unauthorized access or suspicious activities, and alerting authorities immediately. By integrating smart security systems into transportation infrastructure, the overall transportation experience can be enhanced for both commuters and businesses. IoT devices integrated with smart security systems can greatly contribute to creating a smart environment. For instance, sensors can be used to monitor and control energy usage in buildings, leading to more efficient energy management and cost savings. Additionally, smart security systems can detect and respond to environmental hazards such as fires or leaks, ensuring timely action and minimizing damages. Overall, the integration of IoT devices with smart security systems can lead to a safer, more sustainable, and comfortable environment for individuals and communities.

2.4 Energy Conservation

IoT devices integrated with smart security systems can also contribute to energy conservation efforts. These devices can automatically regulate lighting, heating, and cooling systems based on occupancy and environmental conditions, reducing energy wastage. Additionally, smart security systems can detect and alert for any energy leaks or abnormal energy consumption patterns, enabling prompt action and optimization. This integration of IoT and smart security can help businesses reduce their carbon footprint and contribute to a more sustainable future.

2.5 Smart Home

The Smart Home with IoT Security System emphasizes the need for increased awareness and education about IoT security, including multi-factor authentication and encryption protocols. These measures provide additional protection by requiring multiple forms of identification, making it harder for unauthorized individuals to access systems. Encryption protocols safeguard sensitive data, ensuring a secure smart home environment.

2.6 Environmental Monitoring

The implementation of a robust environmental monitoring system within the IoT security system adds an extra layer of protection. By utilizing sensors and detectors, the system can constantly monitor factors such as temperature, humidity, air quality, and water leaks. In the event of any abnormal readings, immediate alerts can be sent to the homeowners and relevant authorities, allowing them to take necessary actions to prevent any potential hazards or damages. This integration of environmental monitoring with IoT security systems not only ensures the safety of the smart home, but also provides peace of mind to the users. With the ability to detect smoke or gas leaks, the environmental monitoring system can swiftly alert occupants of any potential fire or toxic gas threats. Additionally, by continuously monitoring the air quality, the system can help identify and mitigate health risks caused by poor indoor air quality. Overall, the integration of environmental monitoring with IoT security systems not only enhances the security measures of the smart home but also prioritizes the well-being of its occupants.

2.7 Green Agriculture

Green agriculture practices can be enhanced and made more efficient. Smart greenhouses can be equipped with IoT devices that monitor and control temperature, humidity, and lighting conditions, optimizing crop growth. Compost and irrigation management can also be improved through IoT sensors that track and adjust nutrient levels and water usage, reducing waste and increasing productivity. Furthermore, IoT devices can provide real-time data on soil moisture levels, allowing farmers to make informed decisions and prevent over or under watering. Overall, the implementation of IoT security systems in green agriculture can revolutionize farming practices and contribute to sustainable and environmentally friendly food production.

3. IoT-enabled Biometric Authentication can Bring Substantial Benefits to Various Domain

- **E-Health:** In healthcare settings, IoT-based biometric authentication ensures secure access to electronic health records, restricted areas like medicine cabinets, and facilitates patient identification. It enhances security and confidentiality while streamlining access for authorized personnel.
- **Retail and Logistics:** Biometric authentication in retail can optimize employee access to inventory rooms or sensitive areas, reducing theft or unauthorized access. In logistics, it can ensure secure access to warehouses, track employee attendance, and improve overall security.
- **Smart Environment and Energy Conservation:** In smart environments, IoT-based biometric systems can control access to smart appliances, manage energy consumption based on user preferences, and personalize environmental settings for optimized energy usage.
- **Smart Home Environmental Monitoring:** Biometric authentication enhances security within smart homes, allowing only authorized individuals to control smart devices. It also enables personalized environmental monitoring and adjustments based on user preferences or presence.
- **Green Agriculture:** In agriculture, IoT-based biometric authentication ensures secure access to agricultural facilities, greenhouses, or storage areas. It helps monitor and control sensitive equipment or systems critical for efficient farming practices.

4. Ensuring Patient Safety: Integrating IoT-enabled Smart Security for Enhanced Crime Prevention and Emergency Response in E-health

Biometric authentication algorithms for e-health IoT security systems involve several steps, including data acquisition, preprocessing, feature extraction, template creation, user authentication, matching algorithms, decision-making, continuous authentication, error handling, and security measures. The block diagram of e-health IoT security systems is given in Figure 1.

These steps involve capturing biometric data, normalizing it, creating a template, encrypting it, and deciding whether to grant access or deny entry. For higher security, continuous authentication is optional, and error handling mechanisms are implemented. User feedback is provided to ensure a transparent and user-friendly experience. Data encryption and protection are also essential to maintain confidentiality and prevent unauthorized access. The choice of algorithms and methodologies may vary based on the type of biometric data, system requirements, and desired security and accuracy.

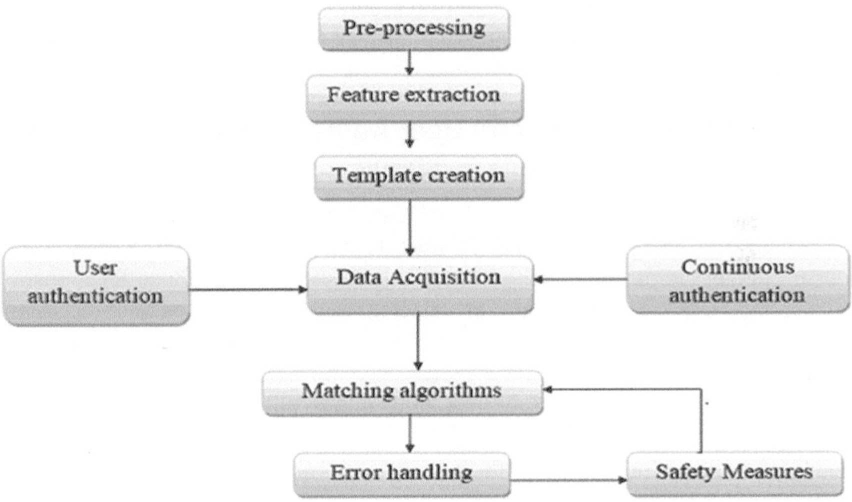

Figure 1: E-health IoT security systems.

4.1 Comparison of Fingerprint Security with Other Authentication Methods

Sensitive data protection and digital system security are greatly enhanced by user authentication monitoring. Organizations can identify any unauthorized access attempts or questionable activity by continuously monitoring user authentication. This enables them to take prompt action to reduce potential risks. The definition and explanation of user authentication monitoring will be covered in detail in this part, along with its benefits and role in preserving security.

Still, fingerprint security is one of the most dependable and effective forms of verification available there. Fingerprint authentication uses the distinct ridges and patterns on a person's fingertips to confirm their identification. Compared to other authentication techniques like passwords or PINs, this method has significant advantages because fingerprints are very difficult to copy or fake. Additionally, fingerprints are always immediately available, reducing the need to remember complex passwords or carry physical tokens.

Fingerprint security offers more accuracy and ease when compared to other types of authentication. In contrast to passwords, which are readily forgotten or compromised, fingerprints provide a biometric factor that is specific to each person. Because it greatly lowers the likelihood of unwanted access, its uniqueness improves the security of digital systems. Additionally, fingerprint authentication streamlines the authentication process and improves user experience by removing the need for users to memorize numerous passwords for various accounts.

Ultimately, the upkeep of digital systems' overall security is contingent upon the execution of user authentication monitoring. By integrating fingerprint security with its strength and ease of use, companies can guarantee a dependable and efficient authentication procedure that shields confidential data from unwanted access. A more thorough explanation of fingerprint security in user authentication will be provided in the parts that follow, which will also examine various user authentication monitoring mechanisms.

4.2 Fingerprint Security and User Authentication Monitoring in E-health IoT Security Systems

To guarantee the best possible levels of data security and usability, enterprises should take into account a number of aspects when adopting fingerprint security for user authentication monitoring in health IoT systems. To reduce false positives or negatives, it is first important to select a fingerprint authentication solution with high accuracy. To guarantee a smooth integration with the current health IoT infrastructure, device compatibility should also be extensively evaluated. Strong encryption methods and safe fingerprint data storage must be implemented in order to meet privacy issues. Companies should give users and patients thorough training procedures to acquaint them with the technology and stress the value of protecting the privacy of their fingerprints. For the fingerprint authentication system to remain secure, regular updates and maintenance are necessary to fix any flaws. A block diagram of the proposed model is given in Figure 2.

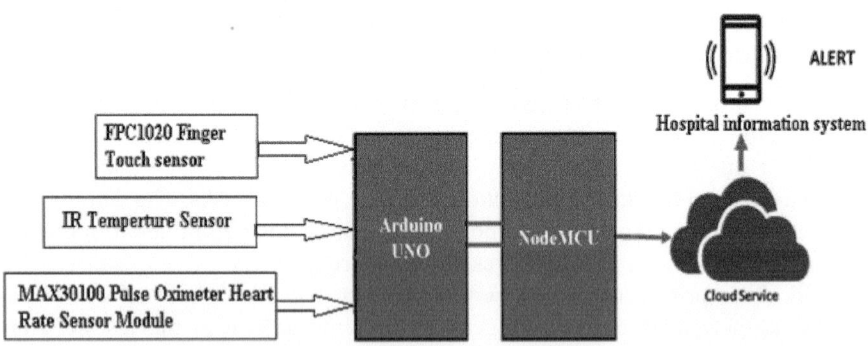

Figure 2: Block diagram of the proposed model.

The usage of sensors such as the FPC 1020 Finger Touch Sensor, IR Temperature Sensor, MAX 30100 Pulse Oximeter Heart Rate, and 20705 Heart Rate Sensor for health tracking is examined in Monitoring with Fingerprint Security. Time series analysis techniques are applied to the collected data to find patterns and anomalies. Based on the study results, the technology develops work patterns for drivers and actively sends alerts to the hospital information system and the emergency alert system.

1. **A Pulse Oximeter Sensor:** Called the MAX30100, it is used in the operation of the pulse oximeter heart rate system. This sensor measures the blood's oxygen saturation levels and heart rate. The Arduino Uno R3 microcontroller then processes the sensor readings. The heart rate and oxygen saturation levels are identified based on the processed data that is shown on a 16x2 LCD screen. The device is able to run off of a power source and is portable.
2. **Time Series Analysis Strategies for Trend Identification:** Learn more about the procedures utilized in the time series analysis examination of the collected data from various sensors. This method aids in spotting trends or patterns linked to medical issues. Patterns or trends pertaining to medical issues can be found by using time series analysis to examine the data collected from the sensors. The heart rate and oxygen saturation can be examined using time series analysis techniques to find any anomalies or irregularities. The pulse oximeter heart rate system is operated by a pulse oximeter sensor known as the MAX30100. This sensor detects the heart rate and blood oxygen saturation levels. The sensor readings are subsequently processed by the Arduino Uno R3 microcontroller. The processed data appears on a 16x2 LCD screen and is used to identify the heart rate and oxygen saturation levels. The device is portable and can be powered by an external source. In levels, making it possible to identify possible health problems early. Improving overall patient care and delivering prompt medical action can both benefit greatly from this knowledge.

   The solution allows the use of cloud computing by gathering and sending sensor data to a centralized cloud-based platform for storage and analysis. Here, trends, patterns, and anomalies in the heart rate etc. data are found with the aid of sophisticated data analysis techniques, such as time series analysis.
3. **Identification of Anomalies in Health Data:** Describe the process by which these sensors are used to gather data, analyze it using appropriate methods, and find anomalies within it. Explain the significance of anomaly detection in healthcare settings and its possible repercussions.
4. **Integration with Hospital Information Systems:** Stressing their integration with hospital information systems, describe how driver work patterns are generated based on the analytical findings from the sensors. Talk about how this integration guarantees timely action based on real-time insights, improving patient care.
5. **Implementation of Emergency Alert Systems:** Examine how technology can be used to notify emergency alert systems of emergencies or serious abnormalities that are discovered by these health-tracking devices. Emphasize how crucial it is to act quickly to intervene or assist during medical situations.

When an irregularity is discovered, the cloud-based platform immediately sends an alarm to the emergency alert system, which subsequently notifies the appropriate authorities or healthcare specialists. This technology is vital in ensuring that persons receive prompt intervention or aid, which can potentially save lives in severe situations. Furthermore, cloud computing enables seamless data storage and processing, making it easier for healthcare providers to track and monitor patients' health problems in real time. When an anomaly is identified, the cloud-based platform immediately sends an alarm to the emergency alert system, which then notifies the proper authorities or healthcare professionals. This technology is critical for ensuring that people receive early intervention or aid, which can potentially save lives in dire situations. Furthermore, cloud computing facilitates smooth data storage and processing, allowing healthcare providers to track and monitor patients' health issues in real time.

5. Conclusion

The oT is transforming smart security systems by providing authentication, increasing trust, and protecting against illegal access. Integrating IoT devices with security systems enables real-time monitoring, data-driven decision-making, remote management, automation, improved user authentication, energy efficiency, and scalability. This not only strengthens the overall security infrastructure, but also allows for seamless coordination among components, resulting in a more efficient and effective security ecosystem. Biometric authentication is a significant improvement, removing the weaknesses associated with traditional password-based systems. IoT technology enables real-time monitoring, networked systems, data-driven decision-making, remote management, automation, stronger user authentication, energy efficiency, and scalability. These advancements are critical for developing strong security infrastructures capable of effectively addressing future threats. By incorporating IoT into smart security systems, it can keep ahead of emerging threats and create resilient security infrastructures for the future.

References

1. Vithya Vijayalakshmi, A., & L. Arockiam. (2016). A study on security issues and challenges in IoT. *International Journal of Engineering Sciences & Management Research* (*IJESMR*), 3(11), 34–43.
2. Raja Benabdessalem, Mohamed Hamdi, & Tai-Hoon Kim. (2014). A survey on security models, techniques, and tools for the Internet of Things. In: *International Conference on Advanced Software Engineering & Its Applications*, pp. 44–48.
3. Kim, J.T. (2016). Requirement of security for IoT application based on gateway system. *International Journal of Security and Its Applications*, 9(10), 201–208. https://doi.org/10.14257/ijsia.2015.9.10.18
4. Tan, Soo Fun, Azman Samsudin, & Suraya Alias. (2019). Internet of Things: Security challenges and its future direction. In: *10th International Conference on Robotics, Vision, Signal Processing and Power Applications*. Springer Singapore. http://dx.doi.org/10.1007/978-981-13-6447-1_61.

5. Al-Fuqaha, Guizani, Mehdi Mohammadi, Mohammed Aledhari, & Moussa Ayyash. (2015). Internet of Things: A survey on enabling technologies, protocols, and applications. *IEEE Communications Surveys & Tutorials*, 17(4), 2347–2376.
6. Surapon Kraijak, & Panwit Tuwanut. (2015). A survey on internet of things architecture, protocols, possible applications, security, privacy, real-world implementation, and future trends. In: *Proceedings of ICCT*, pp. 26–31.
7. Humayun, M. (2020). IoT-based secure and energy-efficient scheme for e-health applications. *Indian Journal of Science and Technology*, 13(28), 2833–2848. https://doi.org/10.17485/IJST/v13i28.861
8. Patil, N., & B. Iyer. (2017). Health monitoring and tracking system for soldiers using internet of things (IoT). In: *International Conference on Computing, Communication, and Automation*, pp. 1347–1352.
9. Deshpande, P., & B. Iyer. (2017). Research directions in the Internet of Every Things (IoET). In: *International Conference on Computing, Communication, and Automation (ICCCA)*, pp. 1353–1357.
10. Sonar, R.A., H.V. Dhande, & H. Ingale. (2019). Implementation of E-health record with biometric authentication. *Int. J. Innovat. Eng. Sci.* (*IJIES*), 4(10), 32–37. ISSN: 2456-3463.
11. Martinhoa, J., L. Pratesa, J. Costa, A. Isel, R.C.E. Navarro, & L. Portugal. (2014). Design and implementation of a wireless multi parameter patient monitoring system. In: *Conference on Electronics, Telecommunications, and Computers* (*CETC*), pp. 542–549. Hosting by Elsevier Ltd.
12. Wcislik, M., M. Pozoga, & P. Smerdzynski. (2015). Wireless health monitoring system. In: *IFAC* (*International Federation of Automatic Control*), pp. 312–317. Hosting by Elsevier Ltd.
13. Bera, A., D. Bhattacharjee, & M. Nasipuri. (2014). Hand biometrics in digital forensics. In: *Computational Intelligence in Digital Forensics: Forensic Investigation and Applications*, pp. 145–163. Springer.
14. Iyer, B., N.P. Pathak, & D. Ghosh. (2015). Dual-input dual-output RF sensor for indoor human occupancy and position monitoring. *IEEE Sens. J.*, 15(7), 3959–3966.
15. Valsalan, P., T.A.B. Baomar, & A.H.O. Baabood. (2020). IoT based health monitoring system. *J. Crit. Rev.*, 7(4). ISSN-2394-5125.
16. Sathya, M., S. Madhan, & K. Jayanthi. (2018). IoT based health monitoring system and challenges. *Int. J. Eng. Technol.*, 7(1.7), 175–178.
17. Kumar, S., & A. Jasuja. (2016). Air quality monitoring system based on IoT using Raspberry Pi. *International Conference on Computing, Communication, and Automation* (*ICCCA*), pp. 1341–1346.

9 | Role of IoT in Smart Security Systems

Manish Kumar Singh[1*], Amit Jain[2], Suruchi Gautam[3]

[1] Department of Computer Science, Shyama Prasad Mukherji College, University of Delhi, India

[2] Department of Electronics, Rajdhani College, University of Delhi, India

[3] Department of Computer, Rajdhani College, University of Delhi, India

1. Introduction

The Internet of Things, or IoT, represents a technological revolution that is turning common things into networked beings with individual voices [1]. Essentially, it creates a network of intelligent, responsive devices by giving commonplace objects the capacity to interact with one another over the internet.

1.1 IoT and Its Integration into Various Domains

The Internet of Things, or IoT, is a technological paradigm shift that seamlessly merges the digital and physical realms [2]. IoT breaks through conventional barriers, expanding its influence over a wide range of industries and changing how we engage with the outside world [3]. IoT applications in healthcare improve patient care and treatment outcomes. Examples include smart medical equipment, data-driven diagnostics, and remote patient monitoring. IoT makes transportation safer and more effective by enabling real-time tracking, vehicle predictive maintenance, and effective traffic control, etc. The block diagram of IoT and its integration into various domains are given in Figure 1.

Through precision farming, which uses smart sensors to monitor crop health, weather patterns, and soil conditions to optimize agricultural operations and resource utilization, the agricultural industry benefits from the IoT? It improves productivity and lowers downtime in industrial environments by streamlining processes with inventory management, quality assurance, and predictive maintenance.

IoT may be found in commonplace items like lighting, thermostats, and security systems in smart homes, providing automation, energy savings, and enhanced security. These instances show how IoT penetrates several domains,

*Corresponding author: manish@spm.du.ac.in

DOI: 10.1201/9781003560012-9

Figure 1: IoT and its integration into various domains.

building intelligent ecosystems that improve productivity, effectiveness, and general well-being.

1.2 Significance of IoT in Revolutionizing Security Systems

The significance of the IoT in revolutionizing security systems cannot be overstated [4]. IoT represents a groundbreaking evolution in technology, empowering security infrastructure with unprecedented capabilities and redefining the landscape of safety measures.

Traditionally, security systems relied on static, localized mechanisms. However, the integration of IoT introduces a dynamic and interconnected framework. This paradigm shift arises from the ability of IoT devices to seamlessly communicate, share data, and respond in real-time. This interconnectedness translates into enhanced situational awareness, allowing security systems to adapt swiftly to evolving threats.

The revolutionary aspect lies in the capacity of IoT to turn inanimate objects into intelligent sensors and actuators. Everyday devices, from cameras and sensors to access control systems, become nodes in a comprehensive security network. This transformation transcends traditional limitations, enabling proactive measures and swift responses to potential risks. Moreover, the significance extends beyond the immediate response to security incidents. IoT introduces a predictive dimension, where data analytics and machine learning empower security systems to anticipate threats based on patterns and trends [5]. This foresight not only fortifies defenses but also facilitates a more efficient allocation of resources.

2. Fundamentals of Smart Security Systems

This section provides definition of smart security systems with respect to the IoT and discusses its main components. Further, it explores how security systems evolved while discussing the need for smarter solutions. Lastly, it presents key features of an ideal security system.

2.1 Definition of Smart Security Systems

Smart Security Systems represent an innovative integration of advanced technologies to create a comprehensive and adaptive approach to safeguarding assets and individuals [6]. Unlike conventional security systems, smart security systems leverage a combination of sophisticated hardware, intelligent software, and connectivity to enhance their functionality. Block diagram of smart security is given in Figure 2.

Figure 2: Smart security system.

2.2 Components of Smart Security Systems

At their core, smart security systems utilize a network of interconnected devices, including surveillance cameras, sensors, access control mechanisms, and communication modules [7]. The intelligence embedded in these systems enables them to go beyond the traditional role of detecting and responding to security threats. Instead, they operate proactively, employing data analytics, machine learning, and real-time monitoring to predict, prevent, and adapt to potential risks.

Smart security systems are designed to offer a dynamic and responsive defense mechanism. They have the capability to learn from patterns, analyze data in real-time, and evolve their strategies to address emerging threats. The integration of these technologies not only fortifies the security infrastructure but also enables seamless communication and coordination between various components of the system.

2.3 Evolution of Security Systems

The evolution of security systems traces a remarkable journey marked by transformative advancements in response to the changing nature of threats and challenges [8]. Traditional security measures, characterized by physical barriers and rudimentary locks, were effective in their time but gradually proved inadequate in the face of increasingly sophisticated risks.

The advent of electronic security systems in the mid-20th century marked a pivotal shift. Alarms and surveillance cameras became prevalent, introducing a level of automation and remote monitoring. However, these systems still operated on a reactive basis, responding to incidents after they occurred.

As technology burgeoned, the integration of computers and digital systems in the late 20th century ushered in a new era of security. Access control systems and digital surveillance emerged, providing more sophisticated means of safeguarding assets. Yet, challenges persisted, necessitating a paradigm shift towards smarter solutions.

The current phase of evolution revolves around smart security systems. These systems leverage the power of interconnected devices, data analytics, and artificial intelligence to create a dynamic and proactive defense mechanism. Unlike their predecessors, smart security systems can predict, analyze, and prevent potential threats in real-time.

The integration of biometrics, smart sensors, and machine learning has brought about a level of sophistication that was once the realm of science fiction. Smart security systems not only respond to incidents but also learn from them, adapting and evolving to anticipate and mitigate future risks. This evolution signifies a departure from reactive measures to a more anticipatory and adaptive security paradigm, reflecting the ongoing commitment to staying ahead in the ever-evolving landscape of security challenges.

Need for Smarter Solutions

The need for smarter solutions in security arises from the evolving nature of threats and the limitations of traditional security measures [9]. Conventional security systems, while effective in their time, often fall short in addressing the complexities of contemporary risks. Several key factors underscore the pressing need for a more intelligent and adaptive approach:

- **Sophistication of Threats:** As technology advances, so do the capabilities of malicious actors. Cyber threats, sophisticated burglaries, and other forms of criminal activity have become more nuanced and evolved. Smarter solutions are essential to counteract these sophisticated threats effectively.
- **Real-time Responsiveness:** Traditional security systems often rely on after-the-fact responses to incidents. In a rapidly changing security landscape, the ability to respond in real-time is critical. Smarter solutions leverage technology to detect and address security breaches as they occur, preventing or minimizing potential damage.
- **Data-Driven Insights:** The need for smarter solutions is fueled by the wealth of data available today. Intelligent security systems can harness data analytics to gain insights into patterns, anomalies, and potential risks. This data-driven approach enables a more proactive stance in identifying and mitigating security threats.

- **Adaptability to Varied Environments:** Traditional security measures may struggle to adapt to diverse and dynamic environments. Smarter solutions incorporate adaptability, utilizing technologies like machine learning to understand and respond to unique security challenges in different settings.
- **Integration of Technologies:** Smarter solutions integrate various technologies seamlessly. The convergence of sensors, artificial intelligence, and connectivity allows for a comprehensive security ecosystem. This integration enhances the overall effectiveness of security measures.

Key Features of an Ideal Smart Security System

An ideal smart security system is characterized by a suite of advanced features designed to provide a comprehensive and intelligent defense against evolving security challenges [10]. These key features distinguish it from conventional security measures:

- **Real-Time Monitoring:** The system employs advanced surveillance cameras and sensors for continuous, real-time monitoring of the secured environment. This ensures immediate awareness of any suspicious activities or potential security breaches.
- **Interconnected Devices:** Smart security systems integrate a network of interconnected devices, including cameras, sensors, and access control mechanisms. This seamless connectivity facilitates efficient communication and coordinated responses to security incidents.
- **Adaptive Learning and Analysis:** Leveraging machine learning algorithms, the system has the capability to adapt and learn from patterns and anomalies. This enables it to enhance its effectiveness over time, providing a more nuanced and precise response to potential threats.
- **Predictive Analytics:** The integration of predictive analytics allows the system to anticipate security risks based on historical data and emerging patterns. This proactive approach enables preventive measures rather than reactive responses.
- **Biometric Access Control:** Advanced access control mechanisms, such as biometrics (fingerprint, retina scans, etc.), enhance security by ensuring that only authorized individuals have access to specific areas. This adds an extra layer of precision to the system.
- **Secure Communication:** Robust encryption and secure communication protocols are integral components, safeguarding the transmission of data within the system. This ensures the confidentiality and integrity of sensitive information.
- **Mobile Accessibility:** A user-friendly interface accessible through mobile devices allows users to monitor and control the security system remotely. This feature enhances convenience and provides real-time access to security information.
- **Automation and Smart Sensors:** The inclusion of smart sensors enables automation of security processes. For example, smart motion detectors can trigger specific responses, and automated alerts can be sent to designated authorities or users.
- **Scalability and Flexibility:** Ideal smart security systems are designed to be

scalable, allowing for easy expansion to accommodate growing security needs. They also exhibit flexibility to adapt to diverse environments and changing security requirements.

- **Integration with Emergency Services:** In the event of a security breach, the system seamlessly integrates with emergency services, ensuring a swift and coordinated response. This feature enhances the overall effectiveness of the security infrastructure.
- **User-friendly Interface:** An intuitive and user-friendly interface simplifies the management of the security system. This includes easy navigation, clear visualizations of security data, and straightforward controls for users.

3. Core Concepts of IoT

This section covers the definition of IoT along with its key principles. Further, it provides details regarding the connectivity mechanism of IoT with devices and the exchange of data between them. Lastly, it presents the overview of IoT protocols as well as communication standards.

3.1 Definition of IoT

The IoT is a transformative paradigm that refers to the interconnection of everyday physical devices and objects to the internet [11]. In essence, IoT extends the power of the internet beyond traditional computing devices, such as computers and smartphones, to a vast array of everyday items, creating an intelligent network of interconnected entities.

3.2 Key Principles of IoT

The following are key principles that ensures the successful implementation and sustainable growth of IoT ecosystems, fostering innovation and improvement across diverse industries and applications [12]:

- **Interconnectivity:** The fundamental principle of IoT is interconnectivity, allowing devices and objects to communicate and share information seamlessly. This interconnected network forms the backbone of the IoT ecosystem, enabling data exchange and collaboration among diverse entities.
- **Sensing and Perception:** IoT devices are equipped with sensors that enable them to perceive and gather data from their environment. These sensors can capture information such as temperature, motion, light, or other relevant parameters, providing real-time insights into the physical world.
- **Data Processing and Analysis:** The collected data undergoes processing and analysis either locally on the device or in the cloud. This step involves extracting meaningful information, identifying patterns, and deriving actionable insights from the raw data generated by IoT devices.
- **Remote Monitoring and Control:** IoT allows for remote monitoring and control of connected devices. Users can access and manage IoT devices from a distance, facilitating real-time adjustments, interventions, or updates. This principle enhances efficiency and responsiveness in various applications.

- **Communication Protocols:** Standardized communication protocols ensure effective data exchange between IoT devices. These protocols define how devices transmit and receive information, promoting compatibility and interoperability within the IoT ecosystem.
- **Security and Privacy:** Security is a critical principle in IoT to protect data and ensure the privacy of users. Implementing robust encryption, authentication mechanisms, and secure communication channels safeguards IoT ecosystems from unauthorized access and data breaches.
- **Scalability:** IoT systems are designed to scale efficiently to accommodate a growing number of devices and users. Scalability ensures that the infrastructure can handle increased data volumes and the addition of new devices without compromising performance.
- **Energy Efficiency:** Many IoT devices operate on limited power sources, emphasizing the importance of energy efficiency. Low-power design, energy harvesting, and optimized communication protocols contribute to prolonged device lifespan and reduced environmental impact.
- **Standardization and Interoperability:** Standardization of protocols and interfaces is crucial for ensuring interoperability among different IoT devices and platforms. This principle facilitates seamless communication and collaboration, allowing devices from various manufacturers to work together cohesively.
- **Adaptability and Flexibility:** IoT systems are designed to adapt to changing conditions and requirements. This adaptability ensures that IoT solutions can evolve to meet new challenges, integrate with emerging technologies, and stay relevant in dynamic environments.
- **Cost-effectiveness:** IoT solutions aim to provide cost-effective implementations. This involves optimizing hardware costs, minimizing energy consumption, and ensuring efficient use of resources to deliver value to users and organizations.

3.3 Connectivity Mechanism of IoT Devices

The following are the connectivity mechanisms that is crucial for designing and deploying effective IoT solutions that align with the specific requirements of diverse applications, ensuring optimal performance, scalability, and interoperability within the broader IoT ecosystem [13]:

- **Wireless Communication Protocols:** IoT devices predominantly leverage wireless communication protocols to transmit data efficiently. Common protocols include Wi-Fi, Bluetooth, Zigbee, and RFID. Each protocol is chosen based on factors such as data transfer speed, range, and energy efficiency, aligning with the specific requirements of the IoT application.
- **Internet Protocols (IP):** IoT devices utilize standard Internet Protocols, such as IPv6, to ensure compatibility and interoperability within the broader internet infrastructure. This enables IoT devices to have unique IP addresses, facilitating direct communication and integration into existing networks.
- **Cloud Connectivity:** Cloud connectivity is a fundamental aspect of IoT systems. Devices often communicate with cloud-based platforms, where data is stored, processed, and analyzed. Cloud connectivity allows for remote management, updates, and accessibility of data from anywhere with an internet connection.

- **Edge Computing:** Some IoT devices leverage edge computing, where data processing occurs closer to the device rather than relying solely on centralized cloud servers. This reduces latency, enhances real-time decision-making, and alleviates bandwidth requirements for certain applications.
- **MQTT (Message Queuing Telemetry Transport):** MQTT is a lightweight and efficient messaging protocol frequently used in IoT applications. It enables devices to publish and subscribe to messages on a broker, facilitating asynchronous communication. This mechanism is particularly useful for scenarios where devices need to exchange data without continuous, direct connections.
- **Sensor Networks:** In scenarios where multiple sensors are deployed, forming sensor networks is a common connectivity mechanism. These networks may use protocols like Zigbee or LoRaWAN to enable communication among sensors, aggregating data before transmitting it to a central hub or cloud platform.
- **Narrowband IoT (NB-IoT) and LTE-M:** For applications requiring cellular connectivity, Narrowband IoT (NB-IoT) and LTE-M are cellular standards optimized for low-power, wide-area IoT devices. They provide reliable, cost-effective connectivity suitable for various IoT applications.
- **RFID (Radio-frequency Identification):** RFID is a wireless communication mechanism that uses electromagnetic fields to identify and track tags attached to objects. It is commonly employed in logistics, inventory management, and supply chain applications.
- **6LoWPAN (IPv6 over Low-power Wireless Personal Area Networks):** 6LoWPAN is a protocol designed for low-power, low-rate IoT devices. It enables the transmission of IPv6 packets over low-power, short-range wireless networks, making it suitable for applications with constrained resources.
- **Device-to-Device (D2D) Communication:** Some IoT devices communicate directly with each other through device-to-device (D2D) communication. This mechanism is particularly useful in scenarios where devices need to collaborate or share information in close proximity.

4. Integration of IoT in Security Systems

This section provides an overview of connecting traditional security devices to the IoT. Further, it explains the benefits of integrating Iot into security infrastructure. Lastly, it presents challenges and considerations followed during the integration process.

4.1 Connecting Traditional Security Devices to the IoT

The integration of traditional security devices into the IoT heralds a new era in the realm of safety and surveillance. This process involves augmenting existing security infrastructure with smart capabilities, enabling enhanced functionality, real-time monitoring, and data-driven insights. Connecting traditional security devices to the IoT not only modernizes existing infrastructure but also unlocks a spectrum of possibilities for a more intelligent, responsive, and adaptive security ecosystem

[14]. It transforms static surveillance into a dynamic and data-driven approach, significantly elevating the capabilities of traditional security systems.

Below elucidates the seamless integration of traditional security devices into the IoT landscape:

- **Smart Sensors and Adapters:** Retrofitting traditional security devices with smart sensors and adapters serves as a foundational step. These sensors can include motion detectors, door/window sensors, and environmental sensors. Adapters act as interfaces, translating the data from traditional devices into a format compatible with IoT protocols.
- **Connectivity Protocols:** The choice of connectivity protocols is crucial in linking traditional security devices to the IoT. Wireless protocols such as Wi-Fi, Bluetooth, or Zigbee are often employed for their versatility and ease of integration. This connectivity enables devices to share data with centralized systems or other smart devices seamlessly.
- **Gateways and Hubs:** Gateways and hubs act as intermediaries, aggregating data from connected traditional devices and transmitting it to the cloud or edge computing platforms. These devices ensure a smooth transition for legacy systems, enabling them to participate in the broader IoT ecosystem.
- **Cloud Integration:** Leveraging cloud platforms is pivotal for real-time data processing and storage. Integrated traditional security devices can transmit data to the cloud, where it is analyzed for patterns, anomalies, and potential security threats. This cloud integration enhances the overall intelligence and responsiveness of the security system.
- **Security and Encryption Measures:** As with any IoT integration, security is paramount. Implementing robust encryption measures and security protocols ensures that data exchanged between traditional security devices and IoT platforms remains confidential and secure, safeguarding against potential vulnerabilities.
- **Data Standardization:** Standardizing the format of data exchanged between traditional devices and IoT platforms is essential for seamless communication. Adopting common data formats and protocols ensures interoperability and facilitates integration with a variety of devices and systems.
- **Firmware and Software Updates:** Ensuring that traditional security devices are equipped with firmware or software update capabilities is vital. This feature allows for the incorporation of new functionalities, security patches, and compatibility enhancements, keeping the devices aligned with evolving IoT standards.
- **Remote Monitoring and Control:** The integration enables remote monitoring and control of traditional security devices through mobile applications or web interfaces. Users can receive real-time alerts, view surveillance footage, and control access remotely, enhancing the flexibility and accessibility of security systems.
- **Machine Learning and Analytics:** Incorporating machine learning algorithms and analytics into the IoT ecosystem enables traditional security devices to evolve beyond mere surveillance. These technologies empower the system to

learn from historical data, identify patterns, and provide predictive insights for proactive security measures.

- **Scalability and Interoperability:** The design should allow for scalability, enabling the integration of additional traditional security devices without compromising system performance. Interoperability ensures that devices from different manufacturers seamlessly communicate within the unified IoT framework.

4.2 Advantages of Integrating IoT into Security Infrastructure

The integration of IoT into security infrastructure elevates traditional systems to new heights, fostering a more intelligent, proactive, and interconnected approach to safeguarding assets and individuals. These advantages collectively contribute to a security landscape that is not only more robust but also more responsive to the dynamic challenges of the modern world.

The following highlights the key benefits of incorporating IoT into security frameworks [15]:

- **Real-Time Monitoring and Alerts:** IoT-enabled security systems provide real-time monitoring of premises through connected devices such as cameras and sensors. This instantaneous data allows for immediate response to security incidents, reducing response times and enhancing overall situational awareness.
- **Proactive Threat Detection:** The integration of IoT introduces proactive threat detection mechanisms. Smart sensors, analytics, and machine learning algorithms analyze data patterns, enabling the system to identify potential security threats before they escalate. This predictive capability enhances the security posture by preventing incidents rather than merely reacting to them.
- **Remote Surveillance and Control:** IoT enables remote surveillance and control, empowering users to monitor security systems from anywhere with an internet connection. This flexibility enhances convenience and responsiveness, allowing users to take timely actions or make informed decisions remotely.
- **Data-Driven Decision Making:** The wealth of data generated by IoT devices contributes to data-driven decision-making. Analytics and insights derived from security data help in understanding patterns, optimizing resource allocation, and formulating strategies to bolster security measures effectively.
- **Integration with Other Smart Systems:** IoT security systems seamlessly integrate with other smart systems in homes, offices, or industrial settings. This interconnectedness allows for a holistic approach to security, where devices like smart locks, access control systems, and environmental sensors collaborate to create a comprehensive security ecosystem.
- **Enhanced Access Control:** Access control systems in IoT security infrastructure leverage biometrics, smart cards, and mobile credentials, enhancing the precision and security of access management. This ensures that only authorized individuals gain entry to secure areas, reducing the risk of unauthorized access.
- **Automation of Responses:** IoT devices enable the automation of security responses based on predefined rules and triggers. For instance, smart cameras can automatically pan to follow motion, and access control systems can lock or

unlock doors based on user permissions. This automation enhances efficiency and reduces reliance on manual interventions.

- **Energy Efficiency and Resource Optimization:** Smart sensors and devices in IoT security systems are designed for energy efficiency. They activate only when necessary, conserving energy and optimizing resource usage. This not only contributes to sustainability but also extends the operational life of devices.
- **Scalability and Flexibility:** IoT security solutions are scalable, allowing for the seamless addition of new devices or the expansion of the system to accommodate evolving security needs. The flexibility of IoT systems ensures adaptability to changing requirements and environments.
- **Cost-Effectiveness:** While initial investments may be required, the long-term benefits of IoT integration include cost-effectiveness. The efficiency gains, reduced response times, and preventive measures contribute to minimizing potential losses and operational costs over time.
- **Improved User Experience:** The integration of IoT enhances the user experience by providing intuitive interfaces, mobile applications, and user-friendly dashboards. This ease of use contributes to better management and utilization of security systems by both professionals and end-users.

4.3 Challenges and Considerations During the Integration Process

While the integration of the IoT into security systems offers numerous benefits, it comes with its own set of challenges and considerations. Understanding and addressing these challenges is crucial for a successful and effective integration process [16]:

A. Compatibility Issues

Challenge: Traditional security devices may operate on legacy systems that are not inherently compatible with IoT protocols.

Consideration: Implementation of adapters, gateways, or middleware can bridge the gap between legacy systems and modern IoT standards, ensuring seamless communication.

B. Security Concerns

Challenge: The increased connectivity introduces new security vulnerabilities, making the system susceptible to cyber threats and attacks.

Consideration: Implementing robust encryption, secure communication protocols, and regular security updates are imperative to safeguard against potential breaches.

C. Data Privacy and Compliance

Challenge: Collecting and processing sensitive data through IoT devices raises concerns about privacy and compliance with data protection regulations.

Consideration: Implementing privacy-by-design principles, anonymizing data, and adhering to relevant regulations ensure ethical data handling and legal compliance.

D. Network Reliability and Bandwidth

Challenge: IoT devices heavily rely on network connectivity, and network outages or bandwidth limitations can disrupt communication.

Consideration: Redundancy measures, load balancing, and optimizing data transmission protocols help mitigate the impact of network-related challenges.

E. Interoperability

Challenge: Ensuring seamless communication between devices from different manufacturers, operating on diverse protocols, can be challenging.

Consideration: Prioritizing standards compliance, adopting open-source solutions, and participating in industry collaborations promote interoperability.

F. Cost of Implementation

Challenge: Integrating IoT may involve upfront costs for hardware, software, and training, which can be a barrier for some organizations.

Consideration: Conducting a cost-benefit analysis, exploring scalable solutions, and considering long-term operational savings help justify the initial investment.

G. Data Overload and Analytics

Challenge: The sheer volume of data generated by IoT devices can overwhelm existing analytics capabilities, leading to information overload.

Consideration: Implementing advanced analytics and machine learning algorithms helps extract actionable insights from data, preventing information overload.

H. Device Management and Updates

Challenge: Managing a large number of IoT devices and ensuring timely updates for security patches can be resource-intensive.

Consideration: Implementing centralized device management systems and adopting Over-The-Air (OTA) update capabilities streamline device maintenance.

I. Power Consumption and Battery Life

Challenge: IoT devices often operate on limited power sources, posing challenges for energy efficiency and battery life.

Consideration: Employing low-power design, optimizing device sleep cycles, and exploring energy-efficient technologies contribute to prolonged battery life.

J. User Resistance and Training

Challenge: Resistance from users accustomed to traditional systems and the need for training on new IoT interfaces can impede adoption.

Consideration: Conducting user training programs, providing user-friendly interfaces, and emphasizing the benefits of IoT integration help overcome resistance.

K. Ethical and Social Implications

Challenge: The use of IoT in security raises ethical concerns related to surveillance, data ownership, and societal implications.

Consideration: Establishing transparent policies, conducting impact assessments, and involving stakeholders in decision-making address ethical and social considerations.

5. IoT Sensors and Devices in Security

This section provides details related to surveillance cameras and smart sensors, door and window sensors, motion detectors and biometric sensors, and smart locks and access control systems.

5.1 Surveillance Cameras and Smart Sensors

Integrating surveillance cameras and smart sensors into IoT security systems brings together the strengths of video surveillance and data-driven insights, creating a robust and responsive security ecosystem [17].

A. Surveillance Cameras

Surveillance cameras, also known as security cameras or CCTV cameras (Closed-Circuit Television), are electronic devices designed to capture and record video footage in a specific area for monitoring and security purposes. In the context of the IoT, these cameras are equipped with additional features for connectivity, real-time data exchange, and integration into smart security systems [18]. An image of a surveillance camera is given in Figure 3.

Figure 3: Surveillance camera.

Components

- **Sensor Element:** Detects and measures specific physical properties (e.g., motion, temperature, light).
- **Processor:** Processes raw sensor data and executes predefined algorithms.
- **Communication Module:** Enables connectivity to IoT networks for data exchange.
- **Power Source:** Provides the necessary energy for sensor operation.
- **Enclosure:** Protects the sensor components from environmental conditions.
- **Control Unit:** Manages the overall operation of the sensor and its integration with other devices.

B. Smart Sensors

Smart sensors are devices equipped with advanced functionalities such as data processing, communication capabilities, and often built-in intelligence. In IoT security systems, smart sensors play a vital role in providing real-time data on various environmental and security parameters [19]. Figure 4 shows a smart sensor.

Figure 4: Smart sensor.

Components

- **Sensor Element:** Detects and measures specific physical properties (e.g., motion, temperature, light).
- **Processor:** Processes raw sensor data and executes predefined algorithms.
- **Communication Module:** Enables connectivity to IoT networks for data exchange.
- **Power Source:** Provides the necessary energy for sensor operation.
- **Enclosure:** Protects the sensor components from environmental conditions.
- **Control Unit:** Manages the overall operation of the sensor and its integration with other devices.

Difference between Surveillance Cameras and Smart Sensors

I. **Purpose**

Surveillance Cameras: Primarily designed for capturing and recording visual information in the form of video footage for monitoring and security purposes.

Smart Sensors: Serve a broader range of purposes, including detecting changes in the environment, monitoring specific parameters (e.g., motion, temperature), and triggering automated responses.

II. **Functionality**

Surveillance Cameras: Focus on capturing visual information through lenses and converting it into video data for monitoring and analysis.

Smart Sensors: Detect changes in the environment or specific parameters, providing real-time data that can trigger actions or be analyzed for insights.

III. Components

Surveillance Cameras: Include components like lenses, image sensors, processors, IR cut filters, infrared LEDs, enclosures, connectivity modules, and power supplies.

Smart Sensors: Components vary based on the type of sensor but generally include a sensor element, processor, communication module, power source, and enclosure.

IV. Data Type

Surveillance Cameras: Capture and process visual data in the form of video footage.

Smart Sensors: Capture various types of data depending on their purpose, such as motion data, temperature data, or environmental conditions.

V. Integration with IoT

Surveillance Cameras: In IoT security systems, cameras are often equipped with IoT features to enable connectivity, real-time monitoring, and integration into a larger smart security ecosystem.

Smart Sensors: Inherently designed for integration into IoT networks, providing real-time data exchange and contributing to a more interconnected and responsive system.

VI. Automation

Surveillance Cameras: Automation is often limited to features like motion detection triggering recording or alerts.

Smart Sensors: Central to automation, as they detect specific events or changes and trigger automated responses, enhancing overall security measures.

VII. Environmental Monitoring

Surveillance Cameras: Primarily focus on capturing visual information and are less geared towards environmental monitoring.

Smart Sensors: Specifically designed to monitor environmental conditions, such as temperature, humidity, or air quality.

VIII. Power Consumption

Surveillance Cameras: Tend to consume more power, especially those equipped with advanced features like high-resolution imaging and continuous video recording.

Smart Sensors: Often designed with energy-efficient features, allowing for longer operational life and suitability for battery-powered setups.

IX. Deployment Locations

Surveillance Cameras: Typically deployed in areas where visual monitoring is crucial, such as entrances, hallways, or outdoor spaces.

Smart Sensors: Deployed in various locations based on their specific detection capabilities, such as motion sensors in hallways or temperature sensors in server rooms.

X. Data Analysis

Surveillance Cameras: Primarily used for recording and monitoring, with some analytics features for video analysis.

- *Smart Sensors*: Provide real-time data that can be analyzed for insights, contributing to data-driven decision-making in security and environmental management.

5.2 Door and Window Sensors

Door and window sensors are devices designed to detect the opening and closing of doors, windows, or other entry points. They are a fundamental component of security systems, alerting users to unauthorized access or providing information about the status of entry points. These sensors play a crucial role in enhancing the security of residential, commercial, and industrial spaces [20]. Figure 5 shows an image of the window and door sensor for clear fathoming.

Figure 5: Door and window sensor.

Components

- **Magnetic Contacts:** Consist of two parts – one attached to the door or window and the other to the frame. When the door or window is closed, the magnetic contacts align, completing the circuit. Opening the door or window disrupts this alignment, triggering the sensor.
- **Sensor Circuit:** The circuit that registers changes in the magnetic field when the door or window is opened or closed.
- **Transmitter:** In wireless systems, the transmitter sends signals to the central control panel when the sensor is triggered.
- **Battery or Power Source:** Provides the necessary power for the sensor's operation. Some sensors are battery-powered, while others may be wired into the electrical system.
- **Control Panel:** Receives signals from the sensors, processes the information, and triggers appropriate responses or alerts.

5.3 Motion Detectors and Biometric Sensors

Both motion detectors and biometric sensors contribute significantly to the effectiveness of security systems, providing detection capabilities and access control mechanisms that enhance overall safety and protection.

A. Motion Detectors

Motion detectors, also known as motion sensors, are devices designed to detect movement within a specific area. As given in Figure 6, they are commonly used in security systems to trigger alarms, lights, or other responses when motion is detected. Motion detectors play a crucial role in enhancing security by providing an additional layer of surveillance and detection [21].

Figure 6: Motion detector.

Components

- **Sensor Element:** Detects changes in infrared radiation or other types of motion-related stimuli.
- **Lens or Fresnel Zone:** Focuses and directs the incoming signals towards the sensor element.
- **Signal Processing Circuit:** Analyzes the signals received from the sensor element to distinguish between normal environmental changes and significant motion.
- **Alarm or Output Device:** Activates an alarm, light, or other response when motion is detected.
- **Power Source:** Provides the necessary electrical power for the sensor's operation.

B. Biometric Sensors

Biometric sensors are devices that capture and measure unique biological characteristics of individuals for the purpose of identification or authentication. These sensors are commonly used in security systems to provide access control based on physiological or behavioral traits that are unique to each person [22] (Figure 7).

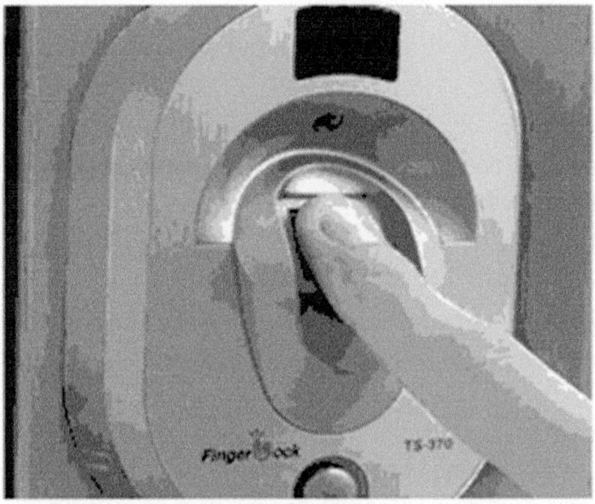

Figure 7: Biometric sensor.

Components

- **Biometric Scanner:** Captures the biometric data, such as fingerprints, facial features, iris patterns, or voice.
- **Processor:** Analyzes and processes the captured biometric data to generate a unique identifier.
- **Database:** Stores and compares the generated identifier with pre-registered biometric templates for authentication.
- **Output Device:** Communicates the authentication result, allowing or denying access based on the match.

Difference between Motion Detectors and Biometric Sensors

I. **Purpose**

Motion Detectors: Primarily designed to detect movement within a specific area. They are commonly used for security purposes to trigger alarms or other responses when motion is detected.

Biometric Sensors: Designed for identification or authentication based on unique physiological or behavioral traits such as fingerprints, facial features, iris patterns, or voice.

II. **Detection Principle**

Motion Detectors: Detect changes in the environment, such as movement or changes in infrared radiation, to trigger a response.

Biometric Sensors: Capture and analyze unique biological characteristics of individuals to verify identity or grant access.

III. **Application**

Motion Detectors: Widely used in security systems for intrusion detection, turning on lights, triggering alarms, or activating surveillance cameras.

Biometric Sensors: Mainly used for access control, ensuring that only authorized individuals with specific biometric traits can gain entry to secure areas.

IV. **Data Captured**

Motion Detectors: Capture data related to movement and changes in the environment.

Biometric Sensors: Capture and analyze unique biological traits for identification, such as fingerprints, facial features, or iris patterns.

V. **Authentication vs. Detection**

Motion Detectors: Focus on detecting changes or motion in the environment but do not authenticate the identity of individuals.

Biometric Sensors: Specifically designed for authentication by matching captured biometric data with pre-registered templates to verify the identity of an individual.

VI. **Unique Identifier**

Motion Detectors: Do not provide a unique identifier for individuals; they are more concerned with the presence or absence of motion.

Biometric Sensors: Provide a unique identifier based on an individual's biological traits, allowing for precise identification.

VII. **Security Level**

Motion Detectors: Contribute to security by detecting movement, but their primary function is not to provide secure access control.

Biometric Sensors: Offer a high level of security as they rely on unique and difficult-to-replicate physiological or behavioral traits.

VIII. **Use Cases**

Motion Detectors: Used in various scenarios, including home security, outdoor lighting systems, and automated environments where motion triggers specific actions.

Biometric Sensors: Commonly used in access control systems, secure entry points, time and attendance tracking, and scenarios where precise identification is crucial.

IX. **Speed of Operation**

Motion Detectors: Provide quick detection of motion, triggering responses almost immediately.

Biometric Sensors: Typically offer fast authentication, allowing quick and efficient access control.

X. **False Positives**

Motion Detectors: Prone to false positives, triggered by non-human movements or environmental factors.

Biometric Sensors: Generally have a lower likelihood of false positives, especially in well-designed systems.

5.4 Smart Locks and Access Control Systems

Both smart locks and access control systems offer advanced solutions for managing and securing access to physical spaces. While smart locks are focused on individual entry points and offer remote control features, access control systems provide centralized management for multiple entry points and integrate various authentication methods.

A. Smart Locks

Smart locks are electronic locks that provide keyless entry and can be controlled and monitored remotely through a smartphone or other connected devices [23]. They offer advanced features such as biometric access, remote locking/unlocking, and integration with smart home systems. A closer look at the smart lock is shown in Figure 8 for easier understanding.

Figure 8: Smart lock.

Components

- **Lock Body:** The physical component of the lock that interacts with the door frame and secures the entry point.
- **Electronic Components:** Include the control circuitry, microcontroller, and communication modules for remote access.
- **Biometric Sensors:** For advanced models, biometric sensors such as fingerprint scanners may be incorporated.
- **Keypad or Touchpad:** Allows users to input PIN codes for entry.
- **Communication Modules:** Enable connectivity to the internet or local networks for remote control.
- **Mobile App:** Provides a user interface for remote control and monitoring.
- **Battery or Power Source:** Powers the electronic components of the smart lock.

B. Access Control Systems

Access control systems manage and monitor entry to a physical space or information system. These systems use various authentication methods to grant or deny access to authorized individuals [24]. An illustration of an access control system for clear fathoming is provided in Figure 9.

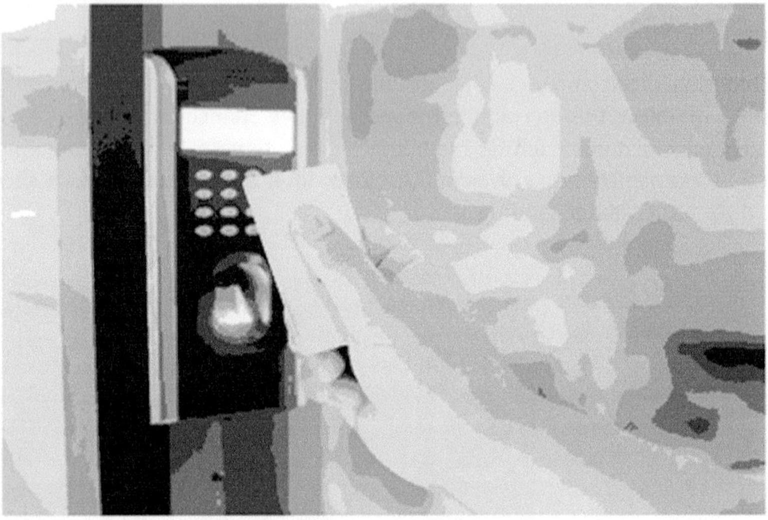

Figure 9: Access control system.

Components

- **Access Control Panel:** Central component that processes authentication information and controls access to entry points.
- **Card Readers or Biometric Scanners:** Devices that capture and verify user credentials.
- **Credentials:** Methods for user identification, such as access cards, key fobs, PIN codes, or biometric data.
- **Electric Locks or Door Strikes:** Physical devices that control the locking and unlocking of doors.
- **Communication Networks:** Enable connectivity between different components of the system.
- **Monitoring and Logging Systems:** Keep records of access events and provide real-time monitoring.
- **Software Interface:** Allows administrators to configure settings, manage user access, and review access logs.

Difference between Smart Locks and Access Control Systems

I. **Scope of Control**
Smart Locks: Typically designed to control access to individual entry points,

such as doors. They focus on providing keyless entry and often offer remote access features.

Access Control Systems: Manage access to multiple entry points within a facility, including doors, gates, elevators, and more. They provide a centralized solution for comprehensive access control.

II. Components

Smart Locks: Include electronic locks, biometric sensors, keypads, communication modules, and mobile apps for remote control.

Access Control Systems: Comprise access control panels, card readers, credentials (cards, key fobs, biometrics), electric locks, communication networks, and monitoring software.

III. Authentication Methods

Smart Locks: Offer various authentication methods such as PIN codes, biometrics (fingerprint scanning), mobile app access, and sometimes traditional keys.

Access Control Systems: Support a range of authentication methods, including access cards, key fobs, PIN codes, and biometrics, depending on the components used.

IV. User Access Management

Smart Locks: Typically allow users to manage access for individual doors and may provide features like temporary access codes for guests.

Access Control Systems: Offer centralized user access management, enabling administrators to define access rules, add or remove users, and set permissions across multiple entry points.

V. Integration

Smart Locks: Can integrate with some smart home systems but are generally designed for standalone applications.

Access Control Systems: Are designed for integration with other security systems such as video surveillance, intrusion detection, and alarm systems, providing a comprehensive security solution.

VI. Scale and Complexity

Smart Locks: Suited for residential or small-scale commercial applications with a focus on simplicity and ease of use.

Access Control Systems: Scale to meet the needs of larger commercial or institutional environments, providing advanced features and complex access control configurations.

VII. Monitoring and Logging

Smart Locks: May provide basic activity logs for individual locks, offering information on when doors were locked or unlocked.

Access Control Systems: Provide comprehensive monitoring and logging capabilities, maintaining detailed records of access events across multiple entry points.

VIII. Remote Management

Smart Locks: Often allow remote locking/unlocking through mobile apps but may have limitations in remote access management for multiple doors.

Access Control Systems: Offer robust remote management capabilities, allowing administrators to control and monitor access to multiple entry points from a centralized location.

IX. Scalability

Smart Locks: Primarily suitable for standalone applications and may not be as easily scalable for larger installations.

Access Control Systems: Are designed to scale to accommodate the needs of facilities with a larger number of entry points and users.

X. Use Cases

Smart Locks: Commonly used in residential settings, small businesses, or individual rooms where simplified access control is sufficient.

Access Control Systems: Suited for commercial and institutional environments, office buildings, apartment complexes, and facilities with multiple access points.

6. Real-time Monitoring and Alerts

This section covers the discussion on utilizing IoT for real-time surveillance, automated alerts, and notifications, and remote monitoring through mobile devices.

A. Utilizing IoT for Real-time Surveillance

The utilization of the IoT in real-time surveillance represents a paradigm shift in the way we monitor and secure various environments. IoT, with its interconnected network of devices and sensors, offers unprecedented capabilities for enhancing surveillance in real-time scenarios [25].

Real-Time Monitoring

In the realm of surveillance, real-time monitoring is a critical aspect that directly influences the effectiveness of security measures. IoT-enabled devices such as cameras, sensors, and actuators play a pivotal role in transforming traditional surveillance into a dynamic, responsive system.

Key Components

a. **Smart Cameras:** Equipped with advanced features such as high-resolution imaging, night vision, and motion detection, smart cameras capture and transmit real-time video feeds.
b. **Sensors and Detectors:** Various sensors, including motion detectors, temperature sensors, and sound detectors, contribute to a comprehensive surveillance ecosystem. These sensors continuously collect data and promptly transmit alerts in response to predefined triggers.
c. **Network Connectivity:** IoT devices are interconnected through robust communication networks, enabling seamless data exchange. This connectivity facilitates the transmission of real-time surveillance data to centralized monitoring systems.

B. Automated Alerts and Notifications

Automated alerts and notifications are integral components of modern systems, particularly in the context of security, monitoring, and management. This functionality, facilitated by advanced technologies, significantly enhances the efficiency and responsiveness of various applications [26].

Definition

Automated alerts and notifications refer to the instant dissemination of predefined messages or warnings triggered by specific events or conditions within a system. These automated processes are designed to promptly inform relevant stakeholders, ensuring timely awareness and swift responses.

Key Components

a. **Event Triggers:** Automated alerts are initiated by predefined events, which can range from security breaches and system malfunctions to environmental changes and user activities.
b. **Notification Channels:** Alerts are delivered through diverse channels, including emails, SMS, mobile applications, and visual or auditory signals, catering to the preferences and accessibility of the intended recipients.
c. **Rule-Based Logic:** The automation of alerts relies on rule-based logic, where predefined conditions and thresholds determine when a notification is triggered. This logic is often customizable to suit the specific needs of the system.

C. Remote Monitoring through Mobile Devices

Remote monitoring through mobile devices has become a cornerstone in the realm of contemporary surveillance and management systems, offering unparalleled flexibility and real-time insights [27]. This innovative approach leverages the ubiquitous presence of mobile devices to enable users to monitor, manage, and respond to various environments and systems from virtually anywhere.

Key Components of Remote Monitoring through Mobile Devices

a. **Mobile Applications:** Purpose-built applications allow users to connect to surveillance systems, access live feeds, and receive real-time data on their mobile devices.
b. **Wireless Connectivity:** Leveraging Wi-Fi, cellular networks, or other wireless technologies, mobile devices establish a seamless connection to surveillance cameras, sensors, and other monitoring devices.
c. **Live Video Feeds:** Users can access live video feeds from surveillance cameras, providing real-time visuals of monitored areas directly on their mobile screens.
d. **Alerts and Notifications:** Mobile monitoring applications are equipped with automated alert systems, notifying users of critical events or triggering conditions. Alerts may include security breaches, environmental changes, or system malfunctions.
e. **Two-Way Communication:** Some systems enable two-way communication, allowing users to interact with monitored areas by sending voice commands or receiving audio feedback.

f. **Geolocation Services:** Mobile devices often incorporate geolocation services, providing information on the current location of the user and the monitored site.

7. Data Analytics and Predictive Maintenance

This section covers the overview of collecting & analyzing security data, predictive analytics for threat detection, and enhancing system efficiency through data-driven insights.

A. Collecting and Analyzing Security Data

The collection and analysis of security data are fundamental pillars in the contemporary landscape of risk management and threat detection. In today's dynamic and interconnected digital environments, organizations rely on robust systems to gather and interpret security data, allowing for proactive measures against potential threats and vulnerabilities [28].

Collecting Security Data

a. **Log Files:** Systems generate log files that record various activities, such as user logins, system changes, and network transactions. Collecting and analyzing these logs provide insights into potential security incidents.
b. **Network Traffic Data:** Monitoring network traffic helps identify abnormal patterns, potential intrusions, or unauthorized access. Network data includes information on data transfers, communication protocols, and connection attempts.
c. **Endpoint Data:** Data collected from individual devices, or endpoints, such as computers, servers, and mobile devices, can reveal patterns of behavior, anomalies, or signs of compromise.
d. **Security Event Data:** Events triggered by security systems, such as intrusion detection or antivirus alerts, contribute valuable data for understanding potential threats.
e. **User Activity Logs:** Tracking user activities, including login times, access permissions, and file interactions, aids in identifying unusual or suspicious behavior.

Analyzing Security Data

a. **Anomaly Detection:** Analyzing security data involves identifying anomalies or deviations from normal patterns. Anomaly detection algorithms can flag unusual activities that may indicate a security threat.
b. **Correlation Analysis:** Correlating data from multiple sources allows for a comprehensive understanding of security events. For example, correlating network traffic with user login data may reveal patterns indicative of a security incident.
c. **Behavioral Analysis:** Studying the behavior of users and systems helps establish baselines and detect deviations that might signify a security breach.
d. **Threat Intelligence Integration:** Incorporating threat intelligence feeds into data analysis enriches the understanding of potential threats by providing

information on known attack vectors, malware signatures, and malicious IP addresses.

e. **Incident Response Planning:** Analyzing security data is a crucial component of incident response planning. It helps organizations develop effective strategies for mitigating and responding to security incidents promptly.

Advantages of Effective Data Collection and Analysis

- **Early Threat Detection:** Proactive data analysis enables the early detection of potential threats, allowing organizations to respond before incidents escalate.
- *Forensic Investigation*: Detailed data records facilitate forensic investigations, helping organizations understand the scope and impact of security incidents after they occur.
- *Continuous Improvement*: Regular analysis of security data contributes to the continuous improvement of security measures by identifying weaknesses, vulnerabilities, or areas for enhancement.
- **Compliance Management:** Effective data collection and analysis aid organizations in meeting regulatory compliance requirements by maintaining detailed records of security-related activities.
- **Risk Mitigation:** By understanding patterns and potential risks through data analysis, organizations can implement targeted risk mitigation strategies to strengthen their overall security posture.

Challenges and Considerations

- **Data Volume and Variety:** The sheer volume and diversity of security data can be overwhelming. Organizations must implement scalable solutions and analytics tools capable of handling large datasets.
- **False Positives and Negatives:** Balancing the identification of real threats while minimizing false positives and negatives is a challenge. Fine-tuning analysis tools is crucial to avoid alert fatigue and ensure accurate threat detection.

B. Predictive Analytics for Threat Detection

Predictive analytics for threat detection is a proactive approach leveraging advanced data analysis and machine learning algorithms to forecast potential security threats before they escalate [29]. By scrutinizing patterns, anomalies, and historical data, predictive analytics enhances the ability to identify and respond to security incidents effectively.

Key Components of Predictive Analytics for Threat Detection

a. **Data Collection:** Comprehensive data sets from various sources, including logs, network traffic, and endpoint activities, are collected to create a robust foundation for analysis.

b. **Machine Learning Algorithms:** Advanced machine learning algorithms, such as supervised and unsupervised learning, are employed to analyze historical data and identify patterns associated with security incidents.

c. **Behavioral Analysis:** Predictive analytics assesses normal patterns of user and system behavior, enabling the identification of deviations that may indicate a potential security threat.

d. **Threat Intelligence Integration:** Incorporating threat intelligence feeds enriches the analysis by providing real-time information on known threats, vulnerabilities, and attack vectors.
e. **Continuous Monitoring:** Predictive analytics operates in real-time or near-real-time, ensuring continuous monitoring of systems and networks for emerging threats.

Advantages of Predictive Analytics for Threat Detection

- **Early Threat Identification:** Predictive analytics enables the identification of potential threats at an early stage, allowing organizations to take preventive measures before incidents occur.
- *Reduced False Positives*: By utilizing machine learning models that learn from historical data, predictive analytics helps reduce false positives and enhances the accuracy of threat detection.
- **Proactive Mitigation:** The ability to predict potential threats empowers organizations to proactively implement mitigation strategies, reducing the impact of security incidents.
- **Efficient Resource Allocation:** Predictive analytics optimizes resource allocation by focusing on areas with a higher likelihood of experiencing security threats, improving overall operational efficiency.
- **Advanced Behavioral Profiling:** Analyzing patterns of behavior over time enables the creation of advanced behavioral profiles, aiding in the identification of anomalies indicative of potential security breaches.

Challenges and Considerations

- **Data Quality and Volume:** The effectiveness of predictive analytics relies on the quality and volume of historical data. Ensuring accurate and sufficient data is available is crucial for meaningful analysis.
- *Model Training and Tuning*: Ongoing model training and tuning are essential to adapt to evolving threats and maintain the efficacy of predictive analytics over time.
- **Interpretability:** Complex machine learning models can pose challenges in terms of interpretability. Understanding and explaining the rationale behind threat predictions is crucial for gaining trust in the system.
- **Privacy Concerns:** Analyzing user behavior raises privacy considerations. Striking a balance between effective threat detection and respecting user privacy is a critical aspect of implementation.

C. Enhancing System Efficiency through Data-driven Insights

Enhancing system efficiency through data-driven insights is a strategic approach that leverages the power of data analysis to optimize operations, improve decision-making, and drive continuous improvement within an organization [29, 30]. By extracting meaningful insights from diverse datasets, businesses can make informed choices, streamline processes, and achieve higher levels of productivity.

Key Components of Enhancing System Efficiency through Data-driven Insights

a. **Data Collection and Aggregation:** Gathering relevant data from various sources, including operational processes, user interactions, and system performance metrics, forms the foundation for deriving actionable insights.
b. **Data Processing and Cleaning:** Preprocessing data involves cleaning, organizing, and transforming raw data into a usable format. This step ensures the accuracy and reliability of the insights derived from the analysis.
c. **Descriptive Analytics:** Descriptive analytics examines historical data to provide a comprehensive understanding of past performance, trends, and patterns within the system. This information serves as a baseline for further analysis.
d. **Diagnostic Analytics:** Diagnostic analytics delves deeper into the reasons behind specific outcomes or issues, identifying the root causes of inefficiencies or bottlenecks within the system.
e. **Predictive Analytics:** Predictive analytics forecasts future trends and potential issues by utilizing machine learning algorithms. This proactive approach allows organizations to anticipate challenges and take preemptive actions.
f. **Prescriptive Analytics:** Prescriptive analytics recommends specific actions based on the insights derived from the analysis. It guides decision-makers on the most effective strategies to enhance system efficiency.

8. Conclusion

This chapter on "Role of IoT in Smart Security Systems" delves into crucial aspects that underline the profound impact of the IoT on contemporary security infrastructure. The following are the key points discussed in the chapter:

- Introduction to IoT's integration into various domains, emphasizing its significance in revolutionizing security systems.
- Exploration of smart security systems, elucidating their components, evolution, and the imperative for intelligent solutions.
- Core concepts of IoT, encompassing its definition, key principles, connectivity mechanisms, and communication standards.
- Integration of IoT into security systems, addressing the challenges and advantages associated with connecting traditional devices.
- In-depth examination of IoT sensors and devices in security, including surveillance cameras, smart sensors, access control systems, and more.
- Insights into real-time monitoring, automated alerts, and the pivotal role of data analytics for threat detection and system efficiency.

Throughout the chapter, the transformative impact of IoT on security systems is evident. The integration of IoT brings about a paradigm shift by introducing real-time monitoring, intelligent analytics, and proactive threat response. The chapter underscores how IoT enhances traditional security measures, making them more adaptive, efficient, and capable of addressing contemporary security challenges. The chapter advocates for a continuous quest to refine existing solutions, embrace emerging technologies, and develop innovative strategies to stay ahead of evolving security landscapes. The encouragement for ongoing research serves as a catalyst for the evolution of smart security systems in an ever-changing technological landscape.

References

1. Greengard, S. (2021). *The Internet of Things*. MIT Press.
2. Abikoye, O.C., A.O. Bajeh, J.B. Awotunde, A.O. Ameen, H.A. Mojeed, M. Abdulraheem, ... & S.A. Salihu. (2021). Application of internet of things and cyber physical system in Industry 4.0 smart manufacturing. In: *Emergence of Cyber Physical System and IoT in Smart Automation and Robotics: Computer Engineering in Automation*, pp. 203–217. Cham: Springer International Publishing.
3. Vermesan, O., P. Friess, P. Guillemin, S. Gusmeroli, H. Sundmaeker, A. Bassi, ... & P. Doody. (2022). Internet of things strategic research roadmap. In: *Internet of Things: Global Technological and Societal Trends from Smart Environments and Spaces to Green ICT*, pp. 9–52. River Publishers.
4. Kumar, A., S. Sharma, A. Singh, A. Alwadain, B.J. Choi, J. Manual-Brenosa, ... & N. Goyal. (2021). Revolutionary strategies analysis and proposed system for future infrastructure in Internet of Things. *Sustainability*, 14(1), 71.
5. Aldahiri, A., B. Alrashed, & W. Hussain. (2021). Trends in using IoT with machine learning in health prediction system. *Forecasting*, 3(1), 181–206.
6. Ali, B., & A.I. Awad. (2018). Cyber and physical security vulnerability assessment for IoT-based smart homes. *Sensors*, 18(3), 817.
7. Madakam, S., & H. Date. (2016). Security mechanisms for connectivity of smart devices in the internet of things. In: *Connectivity Frameworks for Smart Devices: The Internet of Things from a Distributed Computing Perspective*, pp. 23–41. ResearchGate.
8. Ande, R., B. Adebisi, M. Hammoudeh, & J. Saleem. (2020). Internet of Things: Evolution and technologies from a security perspective. *Sustainable Cities and Society*, 54, 101728.
9. N. Komninos, E. Philippou, & A. Pitsillides. (2014). Survey in smart grid and smart home security: Issues, challenges, and countermeasures. *IEEE Communications Surveys & Tutorials*, 16(4), 1933–1954.
10. Indumathi, J., N. Asha, & J. Gitanjali. (2020). Smart security system using IoT and mobile assistance. In: *Emerging Research in Data Engineering Systems and Computer Communications: Proceedings of CCODE 2019*, pp. 441–453. Springer Singapore.
11. Atzori, L., A. Iera, & G. Morabito. (2017). Understanding the Internet of Things: definition, potentials, and societal role of a fast evolving paradigm. *Ad Hoc Networks*, 56, 122–140.
12. Benkhelifa, E., M. Abdel-Maguid, S. Ewenike, & D. Heatley. (2014, November). The Internet of Things: The ecosystem for sustainable growth. In: *2014 IEEE/ACS 11th International Conference on Computer Systems and Applications* (*AICCSA*), pp. 836–842. IEEE.
13. Madakam, S., & H. Date. (2016). Security mechanisms for connectivity of smart devices in the internet of things. In: *Connectivity Frameworks for Smart Devices: The Internet of Things from a Distributed Computing Perspective*, 23–41. ResearchGate.
14. Park, J., H. Kwon, & N. Kang. (2017). IoT–Cloud collaboration to establish a secure connection for lightweight devices. *Wireless Networks*, 23, 681–692.
15. Bagherzadeh, L., H. Shahinzadeh, H. Shayeghi, A. Dejamkhooy, R. Bayindir, & M. Iranpour. (2020, July). Integration of cloud computing and IoT (CloudIoT) in smart grids: Benefits, challenges, and solutions. In: *2020 International Conference on Computational Intelligence for Smart Power System and Sustainable Energy* (*CISPSSE*), pp. 1–8. IEEE.
16. Nizetic, S., P. Solic, P., D.L.D.I. Gonzalez-De, & L. Patrono. (2020). Internet of Things (IoT): Opportunities, issues and challenges towards a smart and sustainable future. *Journal of Cleaner Production*, 274, 122877.

17. Lulla, G., A. Kumar, G. Pole, & G. Deshmukh. (2021, March). IoT based smart security and surveillance system. In: *2021 International Conference on Emerging Smart Computing and Informatics (ESCI)*, pp. 385–390. IEEE.
18. Goold, B., I. Loader, & A. Thumala. (2013). The banality of security: The curious case of surveillance cameras. *British Journal of Criminology*, 53(6), 977–996.
19. Frank, R. (2013). *Understanding Smart Sensors*. Artech House.
20. Eliasson, O. (2017). Monitoring of doors, door handles, and windows using inertial sensors.
21. Borst, A., & M. Egelhaaf. (1989). Principles of visual motion detection. *Trends in Neurosciences*, 12(8), 297–306.
22. Ratha, N.K., & V. Govindaraju. (Eds.). (2007). *Advances in Biometrics: Sensors, Algorithms and Systems*. Springer Science & Business Media.
23. Ho, G., D. Leung, P. Mishra, A. Hosseini, D. Song, & D. Wagner. (2016, May). Smart locks: Lessons for securing commodity internet of things devices. In: *Proceedings of the 11th ACM on Asia Conference on Computer and Communications Security*, pp. 461–472.
24. Benantar, M. (2005). *Access Control Systems: Security, Identity Management, and Trust Models*. Springer Science & Business Media.
25. Kumari, M., A. Kumar, & R. Singhal. (2020, February). Design and analysis of IoT-based intelligent robot for real-time monitoring and control. In: *2020 International Conference on Power Electronics & IoT Applications in Renewable Energy and Its Control (PARC)*, pp. 549–552. IEEE.
26. Wanderer, J.P., W.S. Sandberg, & J.M. Ehrenfeld. (2011). Real-time alerts and reminders using information systems. *Anesthesiology Clinics*, 29(3), 389–396.
27. Heß, D., & C. Rohrig. (2009, September). Remote controlling of technical systems using mobile devices. In: *2009 IEEE International Workshop on Intelligent Data Acquisition and Advanced Computing Systems: Technology and Applications*, pp. 625–628. IEEE.
28. Meneely, A. (2015). Analyzing security data. In: *The Art and Science of Analyzing Software Data*, pp. 215–229. Morgan Kaufmann.
29. Nassar, A., & M. Kamal. (2021). Machine learning and big data analytics for cybersecurity threat detection: A holistic review of techniques and case studies. *Journal of Artificial Intelligence and Machine Learning in Management*, 5(1), 51–63.
30. Fan, C., D . Yan, F. Xiao, A. Li, J. An, & X. Kang. (2021, February). Advanced data analytics for enhancing building performances: From data-driven to big data-driven approaches. In: *Building Simulation* (Vol. 14), pp. 3–24. Tsinghua University Press.

10 | Wireless Network Security Analysis in Optimized Data Preservation Modeling Using Machine Learning Algorithm

Hashim Elshafie[1], Haroon Bengali[1], Mohammed Inamurrahman[2], Shamimul Qamar[2*], Syed Asif Basha[1], Firdouse Banu[3], Ajay Roy[4], Amrita Rai[5]

[1] Department of Computer Engineering, College of Computer Science, King Khalid University, Saudi Arabia

[2] Computer Science & Engineering, College of Arts & Sciences, Dhahran Al Janoub, King Khalid University, Saudi Arabia

[3] Department of Applied Information System, Applied College, Khamis Mushaiyt, King Khalid University, Saudi Arabia

[4] Lovely Professional University, Jalandhar, Punjab, India

[5] Department of Electronics and Communication Engineering, Galgotias College of Engineering and Technology, Greater Noida, India

1. Introduction

Among the most often used wireless communication networks are wireless sensor networks (WSNs), in which sensor nodes serve as the central hub. In terms of configuration, WSNs can feature homogeneous or heterogeneous sensors, ranging in quantity from hundreds to thousands. The majority of WSNs are tailored to specific applications, and typically, their sensor nodes have some fundamental functions including sensing, processing, computation, and communication. Radio frequency electromagnetic pulses are used mostly for communication with nearby nodes [1]. In addition, a base station (BS) functions as a centralised node in the WSN architecture, receiving and transmitting monitored data from sensor nodes at a designated area. WSNs are application-based communication networks, that is, the communication network is constructed and sensors are placed in the monitoring field in accordance with a particular application. Wide-open areas are typically where WSNs are installed for tracking and monitoring purposes [2]. Applications for monitoring include the rubber industry, the chemical industry for hazardous gas monitoring, and

*Corresponding author: sqamar@kku.edu.sa

DOI: 10.1201/9781003560012-10

patient health monitoring. Additionally, WSN technology can be utilized for tracking applications including tracking pets, tracking wild species, and tracking humans. Micro-electromechanical systems (MEMS) are among the hardware that has been released recently [3]. Recent advancements in WNS technology have resulted in more inventive platforms for more economical and effective communication networks. Radio frequency information can be detected, interpreted, and transmitted by sensor nodes (SNs). There are very few BS nodes in WSNs. Their applications are numerous and include weather tracking, front-line tracking, compound smoke examination drug detection, and clinic patient monitoring (risk) [4]. Furthermore, for monitoring and tracking reasons, WSNs are generally helpful in hostile and inaccessible environments where human intervention is either impossible or not possible. Tracking goals include following humans and animals, while checking goals include observing gaseous tension and mixture vapour.

A node's power consumption rises with a WSN's increased security complexity and vice versa. One of the problems that new studies in this subject are tackling is the necessity for both (lowering security and energy consumption), given the demanding settings in which these sensors might function. Moreover, it is necessary to reevaluate the application of the conventional security measures, which are characterized by Confidentiality, Integration, and Authentication (CIA) and are known as the Triangle. Traditional methods also include key exchange and encryption, as well as the process of encrypting data between two communication devices (two nodes) [5]. Furthermore, these technologies require a lot of energy, particularly given the way that network topologies are constantly changing as a result of WSN nodes moving around, as we have just discussed in the previous paragraph. Therefore, the goal is to identify faster and simpler alternative approaches. Artificial intelligence algorithms, for instance, are among the techniques that can be applied in this way. A node can learn how to communicate with neighbouring WSN nodes, recognise and eliminate viruses, examine incoming and outgoing packets, verify node-to-node authenticity, and preserve availability [6].

One of the most well-known applications of AI (artificial intelligence) is ML (machine learning), in which computers create a mathematical method based on a sample of data—referred to as "training data"— to make predictions or judgements without needing to be explicitly taught to do so. The ML aspect of WSNs makes sense for the following reasons: It is impossible to build mathematical frameworks for WSN ecosystems due to their complexity. Furthermore, WSNs exhibit surprising dynamics and behaviours. Lastly, consistent with WSN characteristics, ML algorithms do not necessitate human interaction. Resources as well as computational constraints of nodes, requirement for big data sets for learning, present the two primary obstacles to ML in WSNs. One of the biggest issues with ML algorithms for WSN network security is how hard it is to apply them to integrity as well as confidentiality of security requirements. As a result, machine learning algorithms can aid in improving wireless network security, lowering congestion issues in all their manifestations, facilitating physical layer authentication procedures, assisting with mistake detection. Moreover, ML methods are very advantageous in packet analysis during packet transit between WSN nodes and in node detection [7].

2. Related Work

The majority of current privacy-preserving electricity consumption readings collection techniques described in literature [8] rely on smart metres to provide power consumption readings on a regular basis, even in cases where there hasn't been much of a change in consumption from the last reported reading. To protect privacy of the customers, these schemes aggregate the encrypted readings using privacy-preserving data aggregation techniques. Additionally, Almutairi [9] proposes a viable encryption-based strategy for aggregating customers' readings while protecting their privacy. Since the strategy needs utilizing a new timestamp in each reading, it is also inapplicable in the case of CAT (computerised adaptive testing) method. This is because it cannot use the most recent power consumption reading of an SM (streaming multiprocessor) while consumption remains constant. Thus, while the schemes suggested in [10] concentrated on protecting consumers' privacy by concealing power consumption readings, our goal in this paper is to protect consumers' privacy by concealing data that, in the event that the CAT approach is used, deduced from consumers' transmission patterns. The CAT technique in smart grids has not received much attention in the literature [11]. In order to analyze power consumption of each appliance, some of these works have examined the use of the CAT method in various applications, such as load disaggregation and demand/ response [12]. This approach attempts to extract the power patterns of individual appliances from the aggregated power pattern detected by SM. Other studies [13] go on determining a reasonable value for shift in consumption that makes a reading transmission necessary. CAT-based methods in [14] are susceptible to PPA because they disregard the privacy of their users. PPA has been studied utilizing the CAT technique in work [15]. A defence plan known as "ASP" is put up to prevent PPA by creating fake transmissions. Two heuristic-based techniques—Poisson packet generation as well as history template based generation—have been developed to generate spoofing broadcasts. Average number of power consumption variations across various time intervals when the occupants are at home is stored in SM's memory when using the Poisson packet generating mechanism. Wazid et al. [16] outlined security measures for 5G and beyond. It is now easier than ever to connect practically every aspect of contemporary life to the internet at lightning-fast speeds without any latency thanks to the introduction of 5G wireless networks. Because the network is so vital to our everyday existence, it is essential that all of its users, parts, and services be safeguarded. Methods for Securing Internet of Things Devices Using Deep Learning and Machine Learning were examined in Work [17]. IoT systems span numerous industries and are multidisciplinary, which has created new security challenges. The advantages, drawbacks, and potential applications of ML/ DL (deep learning) techniques for IoT (internet of things) security are then covered by the writers. We talk about the advantages and disadvantages of leveraging ML/ DL to increase IoT security. These opportunities and challenges might serve as sources of ideas for new research directions. Otoum et al. [18] concentrated on the architecture of 5G network security. The mobile sector will witness the emergence of new services, business models, and rivals due to the capabilities of 5G networks. The networks will enable the rapid and low-cost implementation of several services, each targeted at a certain industry niche with particular requirements for security and services and involving a broad spectrum of users. Rehman et al. [19] discussed the possible applications, benefits, and research goals of AI and ML in relation to 5G network security. The fact that 5G networks are currently being widely deployed indicates how valuable the latest architectural and technical advancements in these networks are. The software, cloudification, and virtualization of critical enabling network processes can be credited for improvements in network performance everywhere, from the edge to the core. Next-generation system device discovery: a review of privacy and safety considerations was introduced by author [20]. For 5G and future mobile networks, D2D connections are very attractive because of their high throughput, low latency, low energy consumption, and significant data traffic offload. Sharma et al. [21] provide a thorough examination of 5G privacy and security, both in terms of its present state and its potential. Due to the serious consequences that could arise from any breach, security has now elevated to the top of the priority list in many telecommunications industries. Sensitive data will be transmitted over all tiers of next wireless systems since 5G networks will incorporate core and enabling technologies. Chu et al. [22] looked into the risks associated with and protections against data-driven ML. The desire to increase public knowledge of ML-related security dangers and responses drove the lengthy research for this work. The entire survey of defences against adversarial learning for deep neural network categorization was the main emphasis of the author [23]. They also discuss potential security breaches involving training data privacy. Then, by comparing the results to industry standards, they demonstrate how well different defences perform against TTE, RE, and backdoor DP attacks on images.

3. Wireless Network Data Preservation Model

Malicious activities frequently occur when data are not encrypted during data transmissions, as Figure 1 illustrates. Data encryption may also not be implemented because of performance concerns. As a result, we suggest in this work to selectively encrypt data according to the limitations as well as specifications of related hardware or software. In particular, we represent the hardware/software requirements as restrictions that data encryption must meet before data transmission. For example, longest admissible execution time is set as a timing constraint for a real-time service application. Our suggested model's fundamental tenet is to use the available computational resources to maximize privacy protection levels by creating the best possible solution.

We characterize privacy weight as a classification criterion for privacy protection levels. Degree of privacy protection is positively correlated with the value of privacy weight. For instance, a greater emphasis on privacy is linked to a higher level of privacy weight. $N(D_i) = N^e(D_i) + N^n(D_i)$ exists. Making a binary function $s(i)$ is our aim. When $s(i) = 1$, the encryption approach is used; when $s(i) = 0$, the non-encryption technique is used. The formula for calculating P is given in Eq. (1).

$$P = \sum_{s(i)=1} N^e(D_i) \times W^e(D_i) + \sum_{s(i)=0} N^n(D_i) \times W^n(D_i) \tag{1}$$

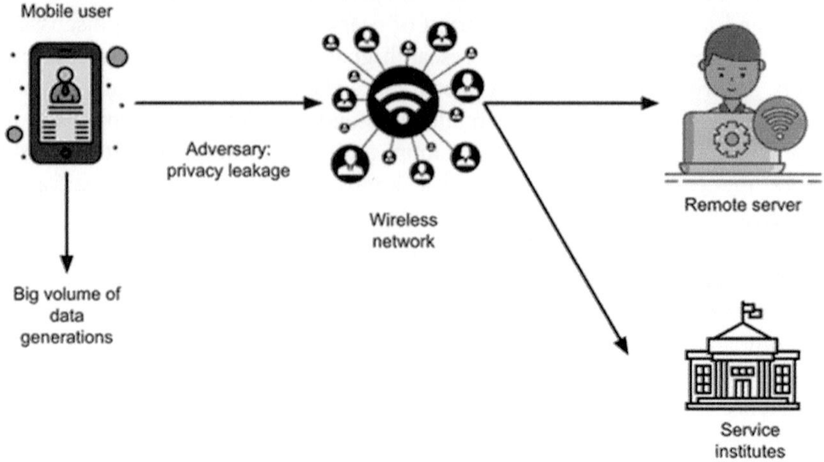

Figure 1: Wireless network data preservation model.

The overall computation cost is represented by C, while the configured constraint is represented by C^s. One way to limit the overall execution time is to apply the timing restriction T^s. A formula for figuring out the overall computation expenses in line with the limitations is given by Eq. (2).

$$C = \sum_{s(i)=1} N^e(D_i) \times C^e(D_i) + \sum_{s(i)=0} N^n(D_i) \times C^n(D_i) \quad (2)$$

The constraint $0 \leq C^s$ governs the scope of C. Our objective is to satisfy the constraint $0 \leq C \leq C^s$ and maximize the value of P. Furthermore, we discover that it is an NPHard task to concurrently satisfy both Eq. 1 and Eq. 2. An undirected connected graph $G(V, E)$ is used to depict the sensor network, with $V = \{1, 2,..., n\}$ representing a set of n sensor nodes as well as E representing a set of m edges. A series of data packets, each consisting of a bit, is used to simulate the sensory input. Referred to as source nodes, some sensor nodes are in close proximity to the event of interest and produce a high volume of data packets, using up all available store capacity. WLOG $V^s = \{1, 2,..., k\}$ contains k source nodes. Storage nodes are the remaining nodes in $V - V^s$. The source node of D_j is represented by $s(j)$ ε V^s, $1 \leq j \leq d$. Let m_i represent the amount of open storage space (in bits) at sensor node i in the range of V. A source node is said to be storage-depleted and to have zero available storage space if $i \in V^s$, as indicated by the value of $m_i = 0$. $M_i \geq 0$ implies that a storage node P_i can store an additional m_i bits of data packets if $i \in V - V^s$. We make the assumption that $n_i = k + 1$ $m_i > d \cdot a$, meaning that the entire number of storage spaces available can hold the total size of overflow data packets.

Let d_i be the number of data packets that overflow when source node I is generated O. Let $D = \{D_1, D_2,..., D_d\}$ represent the collection of these d data packets, and let $d = Pk_i = 1$ d_i represent the total number of overflow data packets. The source node of D_j is represented by $s(j) \in V^s$, $1 \leq j \leq d$. Let m_i represent the amount of open storage space (in bits) at sensor node i in range of V. We make assumption that $n_i =$

$k + 1\ m_i > d \cdot a$, meaning that the entire number of storage spaces available can hold the total size of overflow data packets.

When there isn't a noticeable change, the window will dynamically enlarge; otherwise, it will compress. Let n be W's length, $\hat{\mu}W$ its (observed) elemental average, and μW its (unknown) μt average for t in W. Although these quantities should strictly speaking be indexed by t, t will typically be evident from context. For a partition $W_0 \cdot W_1$ of W, the value of cut is calculated as follows: In order to receive extremely strict performance guarantees, we describe by Eq. (3).

$$m = \frac{1}{1/n_0 + 1/n_1} \text{ (harmonic mean of } n_0 \text{ and } n_1\text{)},$$

$$\delta' = \frac{\delta}{n}, \text{ and } \epsilon_{\text{cut}} = \sqrt{\frac{1}{2m} \cdot \ln\frac{4}{\delta'}} \tag{3}$$

According to the definition of the Hoeffding bound, the estimated mean following k independent observations of range k will not deviate from the true mean by more than ε, with probability $1 - \delta$ by Eq. (4).

$$\varepsilon = \sqrt{\frac{R^2 \ln(1/\delta)}{2n}} \tag{4}$$

Where: $\delta \in (0, 1)$ is a user-defined confidence parameter.

Let's say that W_0 and W_1 represent the two subwindows, with W_1 holding the most recent examples. $|\mu W_0 - \mu W_1| \leq 2\varepsilon$, where ε is the Hoeffding bound and μW_0 and μW_1 are the means of two subwindows, with probability $1 - \delta$ by Eq. (5).

$$P(t): p^*_{P(t)} = \left(p_{i,P(t),}, p_{j,P(t)}, p_{k,P(t)}\right) \in I^3_{++}, l_{P(t)} = \left(l_{i,p(t)}, l_{j,p(t)}, l_{k,p(t)}\right) \in I^3_{++}$$

$$l_{i,p(t)} = \frac{l_{x,P(t)}}{1_x}, l_{j,P(t)} = \frac{l_{y,P(t)}}{1_y}, l_{k,P(t)} = \frac{l_{z,P(t)}}{1_z}$$

$$C: p_C = \left(p_{i,C}, p_{j,C}, p_{k,C}\right) = (1,1,1), l_C = L - \left(L_i, L_j, L_k\right) \in T^3_{++}$$

$$L_i = \frac{L_x}{1_x}, L_j = \frac{L_y}{1_y}, L_k = \frac{L_z}{1_z} \tag{5}$$

Assume μ to be the real mean of W. The Hoeffding bound states that $|\mu W_0 - \mu| <$ ε and $|\mu W_1 - \mu| \leq \varepsilon$ can be obtained independently. It is therefore possible to convert them into $-\varepsilon \leq |\mu W_0 - \mu| \leq \varepsilon$ and $-\varepsilon \leq |\mu - \mu W_1| \leq \varepsilon$. Once these two disparities are added up by Eq. (6).

$$\left|\mu_{W_0} - \mu_{W_1}\right| \leq 2\varepsilon$$

$$\left|\mu_{W_0} - \mu_{W_1}\right| \leq \sqrt{\frac{2R^2 \ln(1/\delta)}{n}} \tag{6}$$

Two subwindows of equal length were created out of the sliding window W: a right subwindow WR and a left subwindow WL. The definition of the Kullback-Leibler distance between X and Y is by Eq. (7).

$$KL(W_L \parallel W_R) = \sum_{x \in X} P_{W_L}(x) \log \frac{p_{W_L}(x)}{p_{W_R}(x)} \tag{7}$$

The operator sc's discrete-window equivalent is represented by s and is described as follows by Eq. (8).

$$s(P(t)) = \{(i^-, j^-, k^-) \in I^3_{++} \mid p_{i,p(t)} \le i^- \le p_{i,p(t)} + l_{i,p(t)} - 1, p_{j,p(t)} \le p_{j,p(t)} + l_{j,P(t)} - 1, p_{k,P(t)} \le k \le p_{k,p(t)} + l_{k,P(t)} - 1\} \tag{8}$$

A confidence number $\delta \in (0, 1)$ and a (potentially infinite) succession of real values $x_1, x_2, x_3, ..., x_t$, are inputs to methods. Only at time t is the value of x_t available. For every t, each x_t is individually produced according to a distribution D_t. When x_t is drawn in accordance with D_t. This can be done with ease by rescaling. Regarding the sequence of distributions D_t, nothing else is known. This can be done with ease by rescaling. Regarding the sequence of distributions D_t, nothing else is known; specifically, for every t, μ_t and σ_{2t} are unknown.

- **Key Generation:** A secret s is sampled utilizing seed from the supplied $E[P]$ value over a Gaussian distribution z. $E[P]$ contains k reduced polynomials, therefore (seeds, seed_{e1}, seed_{e2},..., seed_{ek}) is the definition of the seeds. The seed value must meet the criterion that $|s|$ < RN, or be within the range of lattice polynomials, in order to be checked. To preserve uniqueness, a counter called c is started at 1 and is increased by each session key that is generated. The foundation of secret key S is (K, z). SK is now created using reduced polynomial Pred for n users. Lastly, a secure channel is used to transmit the secret key parameters (SK, IDES, IDAO, and nonce) so that healthcare users can communicate.
- **Signature Generation:** To sign a message M, a polynomial p is selected from RN, and the signature generation parameters 1 and 2 are calculated using the random number ↲ and the SK obtained from the key-creation step. Following each created signature that uses values from the pos_list and sign_list, the number is increased. If $Z < Ry$, [BLE S], the signature is not accepted. Computed signature (S, SK, counter0) is now forwarded to the opposite side for confirmation.
- **Signature Verification:** Every time a message is received with 0 1 ($H(M)$, r_0, K), M and 2 are calculated using values chosen from the arrays pos_list and sign_list. Every sign that is received, 2 C lz is calculated. The sign is then accepted or rejected by comparing it with the original sent values as shown in the figure. If 2(b_1) LE < by/2c Rn, then it is known that the signature matches for any bit string b_0.

4. Optimization of Wireless Network Data Using Grey Wolf Colony Optimization (GWCO)

FA is defined in three main steps: (i) A firefly's attraction is universal and does not depend on a person's gender. (ii) The light of flies corresponds to their magnetic field. Low-brightness flies will be drawn to the luminous ones. The firefly gets closer to one another when the brightness increases. (iii) Lastly, a fitness function is used to map the brightness of fireflies. A firefly with origin brightness Y has the following luminosity expression by Eq. (9).

$$Y(s) = Y_0 e^{-\delta s} \tag{9}$$

Where: δ is the light coefficient that determines luminous intensity and occupation, Y_0 indicates the source of brightness, and s is the distance between two fireflies. Because beauty and brightness are known to be proportionate, attraction T can be written as follows by Eq. (10).

$$T(s) = T_0 e^{-\delta s} \tag{10}$$

T_0 is the attractiveness when $s = 0$. The following is an expression of Firefly l and m's attraction by Eq. (11).

$$P_I^{z+1} = T_0 e^{-\delta \delta_{lm}^2} \left(P_m^z - P_I^z\right) + \varphi(\text{Rand} - 0.5) \tag{11}$$

Where: z is the number of iterations, υ defines the parameter unpredictability, Rand produces a random number between 0 and 1. S_{lm} stands for distance between l_{th} and m_{th} fireflies, and it can be further explained as follows by Eq. (12).

$$s_{lm} = \| P_m - P_l \| = \sqrt{\sum_{k=1}^{K} \left(P_{lk} - P_{mk}\right)^2} \tag{12}$$

The following is the essential update equation for FBGO in this method by Eq. (13).

$$l_j^{h+1} = \text{crossover}\left(l_1, l_2, l_3\right) \tag{13}$$

Between solutions l, m, n, and (l_1, l_2, l_3), which are binary vectors illustrating the effect of wolves migrating towards alpha, beta, delta grey wolves, in that sequence, crossover (l, m, n) is a suitable crossover. Equation (14) can be used to calculate (l_1, l_2, l_3).

$$l_1^t = \{1 \text{ if}\left(l_u^t + \text{bistepa } p_u^t\right) > 1 0 \text{ Otherwise} \tag{14}$$

Where: bistepa p_a^t in dimension t represents the binary step and l_1^t is the location vector. Equation can be used to calculate it by Eq. (15).

$$\text{bistep } P_a^t = \{1 \text{ if costep } p_a^t \geq \text{rand } 0 \text{ Otherwise} \tag{15}$$

Where: costep P_a^t is the continuous value of the size step, and rand is an integer chosen at random from a uniformly distributed ∈ [0, 1]. This can be calculated using the following Eq. (16).

$$\text{costep } I_a^t = \frac{1}{1 + e^{-10\left(X_1^t r_a^t - 0.5\right)}} \tag{16}$$

Where: $\vec{X}$ and $\vec{D}_a$ are calculated using Eqs. (16) and (17), which were then used in the following manner for threshold selection

$$\vec{X} = 2c \cdot \vec{r_1} - c$$

$$\vec{D}_a = \left|\vec{C_1} \times \vec{X_a} - \vec{X}\right|$$

$$I_2^t = \{1 \text{ if } \left(I_b^t + \text{bistep}_b^t\right) 0 \text{ Othervise} \tag{17}$$

Where: $\vec{r_1}$ represents random distribution, c is continuously decreased within range of (2, 0), and X is the updated position of the prey in Eq. (16). Distances of prey from each grey wolf are represented by D_a are in Eq. (18), and the coefficient variable is represented by $\vec{C_1}$. The binary step in Eq. (18) is represented by bistep p_b^t in dimension t, whereas position vector in dimension t is indicated by I_2^t.

Algorithm of FBGO:
Start Step 1: Describe fitness function : $h(x)$, $x = (x_1, x_2, \ldots, x_d)$ Step 2: Produce initial population of fireflies P_h, where $l = 1, 2, 3, \ldots, n$ Step 3: Evaluate Brightness $\gamma(S) = Y_0 e^{-\delta S}$ Step 4: Describe absorption coefficient δ While ($z <$ MaxGeneration) • for $l = 1 : n$ for $m = 1 : l -$ if $(Y_m > Y_i)$ • Vary attractiveness with distance S via e^{-is} • Move firefly l towards m utilizing $P_I^{z+1} = T_0 e^{-\delta s_m^2}\left(P_m^z - P_I^z\right) + \varphi(\text{Rand} - 0.5)$ • Calculate new solutions and update brightness • end if • end for m • end for 1 • Determine latest best Firefly • Entropy-based activation is applied $H(\Phi)$ • Best Optimal Features are choosed $\widehat{\Phi_N^k}$ • end While • Processing results and visualization End

Search method is described as follows by Eq. (18).

$$\Psi_{mf_o} = \left(\Psi_{IP}, \Psi_{UP}, \Psi_{SP}\right) \tag{18}$$

Where: $N = 20$ is population that is randomly generated in first phase, where Ψ_{IP} stands for an initial phase, Ψ_{UP} for an updated phase, Ψ_{SP} for stopping condition.

Fitness function is applied to assess features using following Eq. (19).

$$\text{Fitness}(\vartheta_i) = r \times \text{Error}(\vartheta_i) + (1-r) \times \left(\frac{|\Psi_i|}{Dim}\right)$$

$$\Psi_i = \{1, \text{ for} \frac{1}{1+e^{-\Psi_i}} > V \text{ } 0, \text{ Otherwise} \tag{19}$$

While there is a potential that some significant features may be lost throughout this process, there is also a substantial chance that valuable features are carried over for the following iteration. This formulation is used to upgrade the features by Eq. (20).

$$\Psi_i = d_i e^{lb} \cos(2\pi l) + \text{ Flame}_{(u)} \times w + (1-w) \times u \tag{20}$$

Where: $d\_i = \int$ and i, $u = 1,2,\ldots N\_((u)) - \Psi\_i\sphericalangle$, and $l = [1, -1]$, the flame The new moth positions with respect to flames are updated based on this phrase. In this case, $l = -1$ denotes the new proximity to the flame, whereas $l = 1$ denotes the distance from it by Eq. (21).

$$\Psi_i = \{1, \text{for} \frac{1}{1+e^{-u_p(Y_i)}} > H\left(U_p\left(\Psi_i\right)\right) 0, \text{ Otherwise} \tag{21}$$

Until the iterations are finished, the characteristics that pass this test are once again assessed in the fitness function. Optimized feature vectors, given by $\Psi_i f^1$ and $\Psi_j f^2$ respectively, have lengths of $N \times 1262$ and $N \times 826$. We eventually combined two vectors to create a feature matrix that was more illuminating. Accuracy improvement is the primary goal of feature fusion, however there is a trade-off: longer computation times. We evaluated entropy of shorter length feature vectors based on maximum length as well as applied padding. Following the padding process, we calculated correlation between feature pairs as well as classified only fused vector features with highest correlation. It was expressed mathematically as follows. Assume that we have a classified feature vector $\Psi_{k,}f''$ of dimension $N \times k^3$, where $\Psi_{i,}f^1$ and $\Psi_{j,}f^2$ of dimension $N \times 1262$ and $N \times 826$ by Eq. (22).

$$\text{Max(length)} = \text{Max}\left(\Psi_{i,}f'^1, \Psi_{j,}f'^2\right) \tag{22}$$

It is necessary to adjust the length of additional feature vectors based on the length of the resultant vector, as this Equation yields a maximum length feature vector of dimension $N \times$ klen, where klen = 1262. Typically, zero padding is carried out for feature vectors of equal length; however, we calculated the entropy value of a smaller number of feature vectors before doing padding. Maximum correlation coefficient between pair characteristics (i, j) was evaluated using the formula below by Eq. (23).

$$\Psi(i, j) = Y\tilde{}_{\rho}(\Psi_{i,}f^1, \Psi_{j,}f^2)$$

$$\rho(i, j) = \frac{Cov(i, j)}{\sqrt{\sigma^2(i)}\sqrt{\sigma^2(j)}} \tag{23}$$

Where: Ye is a supremum function, $\Psi_i f^1$, $\Psi_j f^2 \in R$, interval is [−1, 1]. Only chose feature pairs with maximum correlations of one or close to one. Finding ideal values using this procedure primarily depends on the feature pairs that are chosen. The features were chosen in this manner until $Y(i, j)$ was determined for every pair of characteristics (1262 pairs total). Ultimately, the optimized breast cancer that was produced had a dimension of $N \times 1632$ for $\Psi k\,fu$.

5. Network Security Analysis Using Quantum Reinforcement Regressive Encoder Neural Network (QRRENN)

Take Figure 1, for example, which shows an architecture with heterogeneous wireless access technologies. This architecture is able to gather a lot of data from the wireless devices, process it, and feed it into ML algorithms, which produce patterns that can aid in better decision-making for optimizing operating parameters and enhancing network quality-of-service (QoS) and quality-of-experience (QoE).

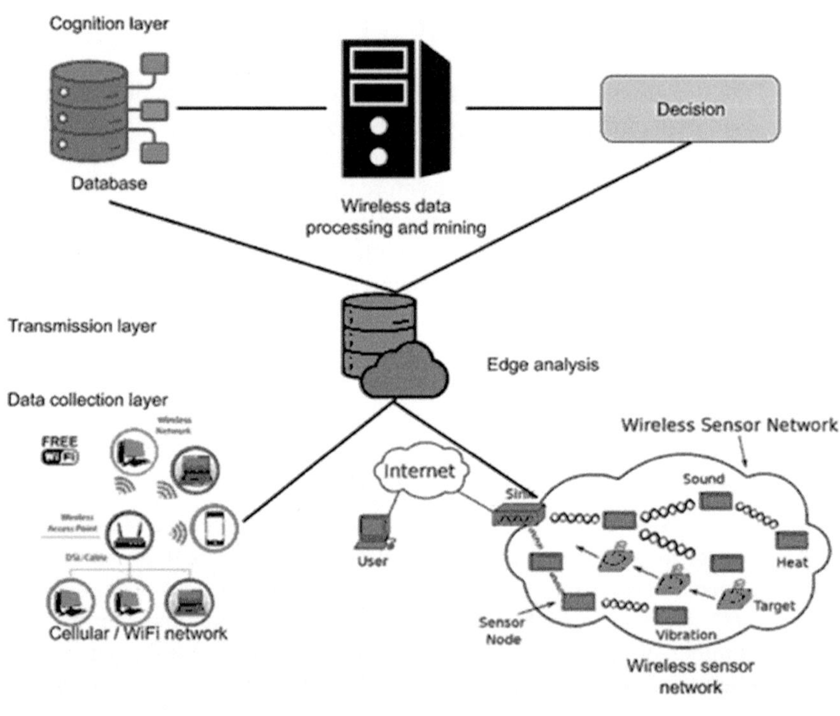

Figure 2: Network security analysis.

Our suggested approach predicts the data for the upcoming period in the secure data sensing and fusion technique (Figure 2). The sensed data and the anticipated data are compared by the sensor node. When the difference in error between them is less than the threshold, the sensor node doesn't need to transmit the data to the sink node, saving energy and accomplishing the data fusion objective simultaneously. In the meantime, the sink node uses the same prediction method to forecast the data for the upcoming period, taking the projected data into account as sensed data for the present period. Finding best course of action to maximize the discounted long-term reward $E\left[\sum_{t=0}^{\infty} \gamma^t r_t \mid \pi\right]$ is the goal, whose value functions can be estimated to solve. Under policy π, the values of *s*'s state and *a*'s state-action value are as follows: $V^{\pi}(s) = E_{\pi}\left[\sum_{t=0}^{\infty} \gamma^t r_t \mid s_0 = s\right]$ and $Q^{\pi}(s,a) = E_{\pi}\left[\sum_{t=0}^{\infty} \gamma^t r_t \mid s_0 = s, a_0 = a\right]$ are definitions of the optimal value functions. Recursively stated as in Eq. (1), the Bellman equation is satisfied by optimal value functions V^* and Q^* by Eq. (24).

$$V^*(s) = \max_{a \in A} Q^*(s,a),$$
$$Q^*(s,a) = r(s,a) + \gamma \sum_{s' \in S} p(s' \mid s,a) V^*(s') \tag{24}$$

Value iteration Bellman can be used to evaluate optimal value function V^* given an arbitrary initial value function V_0 and an iterative update $V_{k+1} = TV_k$, where T is Bellman operator described by Eq. (25).

$$(TV)(s) = max_{a \in A}\left[r(s,a) + \sum_{s' \in S} p(s' \mid s,a) \gamma V(s')\right] \tag{25}$$

Q-learning is an efficient approach to learn by observing surroundings while method is unknown.

$Q(s, a) = (1 - \alpha)\, Q(s, a) + a\, (r + \gamma \max_a{}' Q(s', a'))$ where the learning rate is given by α. Keep in mind that *Q*-learning updates value function utilizing hard max operator, i.e., by Eq. (26).

$$\max(X) = \max_i x_i \tag{26}$$

Log-sum-exp operator is another frequently used operator by Eq. (27).

$$L_\beta(X) = \frac{1}{\beta} \log\left(\sum_{i=1}^{n} e^{\beta x_i}\right) \tag{27}$$

Next, we have Eq. (28).

$$\| (T_{\beta_t} V_1) - (T_m V_2) \|_\infty \le \underbrace{\| (T_{\beta_t} V_1) - (T_m V_1) \|_\infty}_{(I)} + \underbrace{\| (T_m V_1) - (T_m V_2) \|_\infty}_{(II)} \tag{28}$$

For term (I), we have

$$\| (T_{\beta_t} V_1) - (T_m V_1) \|_\infty \le \frac{\log(|A|)}{\beta_t} \tag{29}$$

For term (II), we have

$$\| (T_m V_1) - (T_m V_2) \|_\infty \le \gamma \| V_1 - V_2 \| \tag{30}$$

Combining (29), (30), and (31), we have

$$\| (T_{\beta_t} V_1) - (T_m V_2) \|_\infty \le \gamma \| V_1 - V_2 \|_\infty + \frac{\log(|A|)}{\beta_t} \tag{31}$$

Since max is a contraction mapping, $T_m V^* = V^*$ follows from Banach fixed point theorem [Banach, 1922]. According to Eq. (32)'s definition of DBS value iteration,

$$\| V_t - V^* \|_\infty = \| \left(T_{\beta_t} \ldots T_{\beta_1}\right) V_0 - \left(T_m \ldots T_m\right) V^* \|_\infty \leq \gamma \| \left(T_{\beta_{t-1}} \ldots T_{\beta_1}\right) V_0 -$$

$$\left(T_m \ldots T_m\right) V^* \|_\infty + \frac{\log(|A|)}{\beta_t} \leq \gamma^t \| V_0 - V^* \|_\infty + \log(|A|) \sum_{k=1}^{t} \frac{\gamma^{t-k}}{\beta_k} \ldots \quad (32)$$

If $\beta_t \to \infty$, then $lim_{t \to \infty} \sum_{k=1}^{t} \frac{\gamma^{t-k}}{\beta_k} = 0$. We get $lim_{t \to \infty}^{-} \| V_{t+1} - V^* \|_\infty = 0$ by taking the limit of the right-hand side of Eq. (10). We merely need state-independent parameter β_t to method infinity to ensure convergence while dynamically altering β_t, even though non-expansion property can be broken for some specific values of β.

For any power series $\beta_t = t^p$ $(p > 0)$, let V_0 be an arbitrary initial value function such that $\| V_0 \|_\infty \leq \frac{R}{1-\gamma}$, where $R = max_{s,a} | r(s,a) |$. For any non-negative $\in < 1/4$,

after $\max \left\{ O\left(\frac{\log\left(\frac{1}{t}\right) + \log\left(\frac{1}{1-\gamma}\right) + \log(R)}{\log\left(\frac{1}{2}\right)} \right), O\left(\left(\frac{1}{(1-\gamma) \in} \right)^{\frac{1}{p}} \right) \right\}$ steps, the error $\| V_t - V^* \|_\infty \leq \leq^{-*}$.

An associated collection of intermediate probability distributions is fully described by a set of parameters, *q(Z/X)*, which are mapped from *X* by the encoder. These intermediate distributions are sampled, and the result is a set of latent variables, *Z*. The input for the decoder, which is the next block, is this set of samples. Conditional probability distributions are those that, whilst representing the likelihood of *Xb* and *Z*, depend on their specific inputs, *Z* and *X*, respectively. These are the probability distributions *p(Xb/Z)* and *q(Z/X)*.et of linked probability distributions from which samples will once more be extracted. We are able to learn the probability distributions in a VAE: *q(Z/X)* and *p(Xb/Z)* by using a variational technique that reduces the learning process to a minimization process that is simply defined in terms of stochastic gradient descent (SGD) in a neural network. This distance is commonly represented in terms of the Kullback-Leibler (KL) divergence. All learned distributions are parameterized probability distributions, meaning that they are fully defined by a single set of parameters. This is essential to the operation of the model because these parameters, which are obtained as the values of network nodes, are used to simulate the related probability distributions, *p(Xb/Z)* and *q(Z/X)*. In order to ensure that the fusion of *H*[*t*] for machine learning authentication should be near to the fusion of the initial attribute estimates *H*[*t*], the obfuscation patterns are mainly designed. Information exchange between various network architecture layers is necessary to accomplish this. In order to ensure that the system has enough capacity, the obfuscation pattern superimposed on any property that Alice does not find to be private should be set to zero. In summary, by utilizing masking-based privacy protection strategy in conjunction with spatial as well as temporal aggregation, Bob is not able to access any sensitive information about Alice because all of her attributes are random number series.

6. Results and Discussion

The suggested architecture with fog and cloud nodes is evaluated on a server with a Core E7400 CPU, 3.00 GB of RAM, and a 32-bit operating system working at 2.80 GHz.

Dataset Description: A number of such datasets remain private, primarily due to security concerns, although some are now available to the public, including DARPA 98, KDD99, and UNSW-NB15. Not many actual IoT and network traffic datasets that include new Botnet instances have been developed, despite the fact that many datasets have been created. Furthermore, several databases lack IoT-generated traffic, while others don't incorporate any fresh functionalities.

Table 1: Comparative based on various wireless security datasets

Dataset	Techniques	Training accuracy	QoS	MSE	Scalability	Mean average precision
DARPA 98	SVM	89	59	45	81	82
	SYN-DOS	92	62	44	83	85
	GWCO_ QRRENN	93	63	42	85	88
KDD99	SVM	92	65	48	82	89
	SYN-DOS	94	68	46	84	92
	GWCO_ QRRENN	96	72	44	86	93
UNSW-NB15	SVM	95	58	52	85	85
	SYN-DOS	96	72	50	88	88
	GWCO_ QRRENN	98	74	45	92	92

Based on several harmful attack datasets, the comparison study between suggested and current techniques is displayed in Table 1. The datasets studied in this case are UNSW-NB15, KDD99, and DARPA 98. Training accuracy, quality of service, mean average precision, scalability, and MSE are all considered in the parametric analysis. There are 39,786 entries in all, each of which represents a particular consumer's power usage reading for a given day. Next, two sets of the dataset are created: 80% for training and 20% for testing. Keep in mind that the transmission rate is expressed as "1/x min," where x is the transmission interval and one reading is transferred every x minutes. We construct datasets for the CAT technique using these datasets with thresholds of 1%, 4%, 7%, and 10%.

Feeding features and input data into method layers is the first step in training a DLmethod. Then, over a predetermined number of iterations, these features are progressively mapped into higher-level abstractions via iterative update through intermediate levels of the model. The output layer decision is made using these mapping abstractions. By establishing a cost function and choosing an optimizer, the weight and bias parameters Θ are learned during the model training process. The cost function gradients are utilized to update model weights as well as biases via each iteration of back-propagation method. Model's output values are contrasted with the ideal values to maximize the cost function. To lower cost (loss) function, error is then transmitted back through layers to modify weights of every connection.

Figures 3(a) through (e) compare suggested and current methods for the DARPA 98 dataset. The suggested method achieved 93% training accuracy, 63% QoS, MSE of 42%, 85% scalability, and 88% mean average precision; the current SVM achieved 89% training accuracy, 59% QoS, MSE of 45%, 81% scalability, and 82% mean average precision; SYN-DOS achieved 92% training accuracy, 62% QoS, MSE of 44%, 83% scalability, and 88% mean average precision. From a comparative study, contrasting the suggested and current approaches using the KDD99 dataset. Here, the suggested method achieved 96% training accuracy, 72% QoS, 44% MSE, 86% scalability, and 93% mean average precision; the current SVM achieved 92% training accuracy, 65% QoS, 48% MSE, 82% scalability, and 89% mean average precision; and SYN-DOS achieved 94% training accuracy, 68% QoS, 46% MSE, 84% scalability, and 92% mean average precision. The suggested method achieved 98% training accuracy, 74% QoS, 45% MSE, 92% scalability, and 92% mean average precision; the current SVM achieved 95% training accuracy, 58% QoS, 5% MSE, 85% scalability, and 92% mean average precision; for the UNSW-NB15 dataset, SYN-DOS achieved 96% training accuracy, 72% QoS, 50% MSE, 88% scalability, and 88% mean average precision.

This trend can be attributed to the fact that investigating many qualities increases the authentication accuracy at legitimate devices in complicated time-varying environments, making it more difficult for Spoofer to predict as well as duplicate multiple attributes of Alice. Additionally, it is noted that the intelligent authentication scheme's misdetection rate stays steady and strong as the interval between updates increases, whereas the static authentication scheme's misdetection rate sharply rises. This illustrates how the static authentication scheme's performance will be significantly reduced in intricate, time-varying environments in the absence of situation-aware adaptation, which will restrict its use in 5G as well as beyond wireless networks. Static authentication strategy must continue the authentication procedure by gathering attribute estimations, determining statistical features of attributes, determining a new test threshold, then re-authenticating devices to ensure continuous authentication. Static authentication approach uses more processing power and causes a longer lag by repeating this operation. The existing techniques are one-time, static authentication solutions that depend on landmarks to gather signal RSSI. In contrast, an intelligent scheme that utilizes N attributes—that is, $N = 1$, $N = 2$, and $N = 3$—is continuously adaptive to changing circumstances. The developed intelligent system has a one-time authentication calculation cost of about

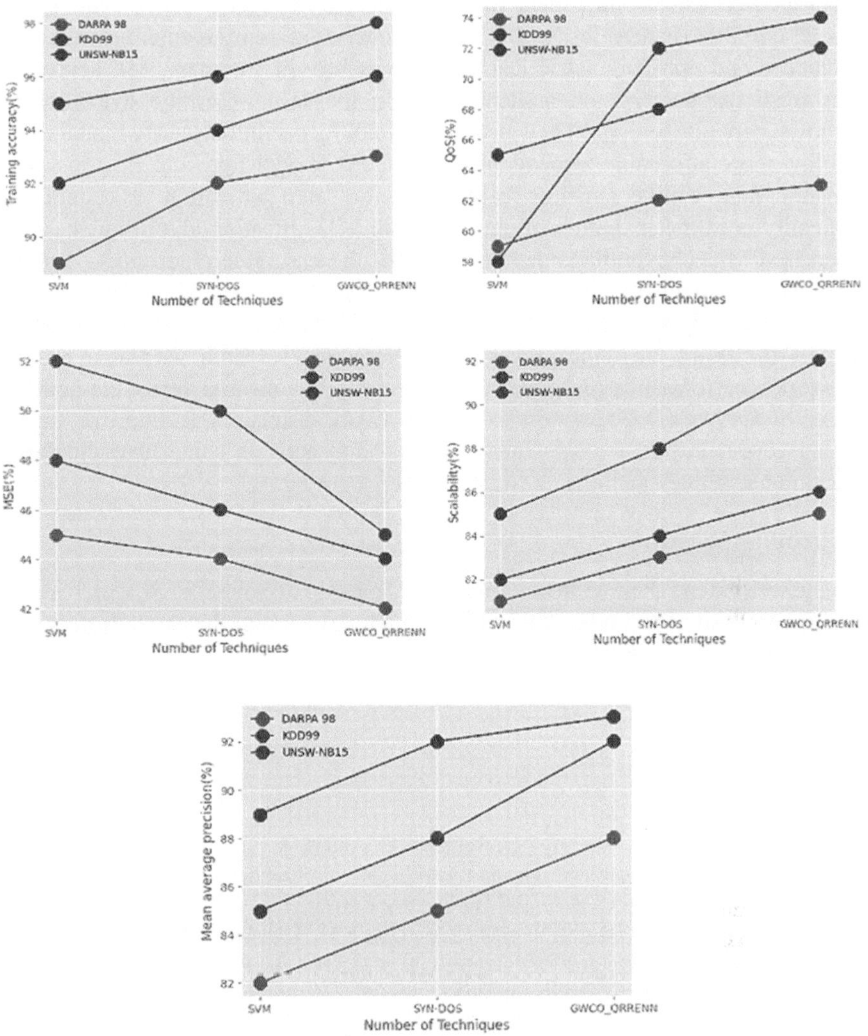

Figure 3: Comparative for DARPA 98 dataset in terms of (a) training accuracy, (b) QoS, (c) MSE, (d) scalability, (e) mean average precision.

400. In contrast, other schemes take many iterations to obtain optimal solutions, resulting in significantly greater computing costs—77,988 in this case.

7. Conclusion

This study presents a novel method to the analysis and optimization of wireless network security combining ML-based grey wolf colony optimization and quantum reinforcement regressive encoder neural networks, together with data retention. The goal of the intelligent authentication design was to improve wireless network security in 5G as well as beyond. Then, ML methods for intelligent authentication were divided into three categories: supervised, unsupervised, reinforcement learning, and parametric and non-parametric learning approaches. In summary, ML approaches offer fresh perspectives on authentication in the face of erratic dynamics and unknown network settings. They also infuse intelligence into security management, enabling more affordable, dependable, continuous, model-free, and situation-aware authentication. Unlike existing feature selection and generation procedures, the originality is in the invention of network traffic classification algorithms based on supervised ML. Our findings demonstrate that the ensemble algorithms—Random Forest and Gradient Boosting—perform better than the previously employed single ML classifier. When we used both VPN and non-VPN traffic, the classifier produced the best results and the highest accuracy. In subsequent research, we plan to examine our work's performance using alternative security models and verify the ability of Denial of Service (DoS) assaults to cause network distortion. To improve our trial findings even further, we also intend to take into account some heuristic feature selection techniques with the use of some deep learning.

Acknowledgment

The authors extend their appreciation to the Deanship of Scientific Research at King Khalid University for funding this work through large group Research Project under grant number RGP2/469/44.

References

1. Waqas, M., S. Tu, Z. Halim, S.U. Rehman, G. Abbas, & Z.H. Abbas. (2022). The role of artificial intelligence and machine learning in wireless networks security: Principle, practice, and challenges. *Artificial Intelligence Review*, 55(7), 5215–5261.
2. Gupta, C., I. Johri, K. Srinivasan, Y.C. Hu, S.M. Qaisar, & K.Y. Huang. (2022). A systematic review on machine learning and deep learning models for electronic information security in mobile networks. *Sensors*, 22(5), 2017.
3. Kshirsagar, P.R., H. Manoharan, H.A. Alterazi, N. Alhebaishi, O.B.J. Rabie, & S. Shitharth. (2022). Construal attacks on wireless data storage applications and unraveling using machine learning algorithm. *Journal of Sensors*, 2022(1), 9386989.
4. Kathamuthu, N.D., A. Chinnamuthu, N. Iruthayanathan, M. Ramachandran, & A.H. Gandomi. (2022). Deep Q-learning-based neural network with privacy preservation method for secure data transmission in internet of things (IoT) healthcare application. *Electronics*, 11(1), 157.
5. Keserwani, H., H. Rastogi, A.Z. Kurniullah, S.K. Janardan, R. Raman, V.M. Rathod, & A. Gupta. (2022). Security enhancement by identifying attacks using machine learning for 5G Network. *International Journal of Communication Networks and Information Security*, 14(2), 124–141.
6. Kamruzzaman, M.M., & O. Alruwaili. (2022). AI-based computer vision using deep learning in 6G wireless networks. *Computers and Electrical Engineering*, 102, 108233.
7. Boopathi, M., S. Gupta, A.M. Zabeeulla, R. Gupta, V. Vekriya, & A.K. Pandey. (2023). Optimization algorithms in security and privacy-preserving data disturbance for

collaborative edge computing social IoT deep learning architectures. *Soft Computing*, 1–13.

8. Farooq, M.S., S. Khan, A. Rehman, S. Abbas, M.A. Khan, & S.O. Hwang. (2022). Blockchain-based smart home networks security empowered with fused machine learning. *Sensors*, 22(12), 4522.
9. Almutairi, M.S. (2022). Deep learning-based solutions for 5G network and 5G-enabled Internet of vehicles: Advances, meta-data analysis, and future direction. *Mathematical Problems in Engineering*, 2022, 1–27.
10. Khan, S., V.N.G.C. Saravanan, T.J. Lakshmi, N. Deb, & N.A. Othman. (2022). Privacy protection of healthcare data over social networks using machine learning algorithms. *Computational Intelligence and Neuroscience*, 2022.
11. Yazici, I., I. Shayea, & J. Din. (2023). A survey of applications of artificial intelligence and machine learning in future mobile networks-enabled systems. *Engineering Science and Technology, An International Journal*, 44, 101455.
12. Mijwil, M., I.E. Salem, & M.M. Ismaeel. (2023). The significance of machine learning and deep learning techniques in cybersecurity: A comprehensive review. *Iraqi Journal for Computer Science and Mathematics*, 4(1), 87–101.
13. Wang, H., X. Zhang, Y. Xia, & X. Wu. (2022). A differential privacy-preserving deep learning caching framework for heterogeneous communication network systems. *International Journal of Intelligent Systems*, 37(12), 11142–11166.
14. Wang, X., Y. Wang, Z. Javaheri, L. Almutairi, N. Moghadamnejad, & O.S. Younes. (2023). Federated deep learning for anomaly detection in the internet of things. *Computers and Electrical Engineering*, 108, 108651.
15. Kumar, P.M., B. Rawal, & J. Gao. (2022, January). Blockchain-enabled privacy preserving of IoT data for sustainable smart cities using machine learning. In: *2022 14th International Conference on Communication Systems & Networks* (*COMSNETS*) (pp. 1–6). IEEE.
16. Wazid, M., A.K. Das, V. Chamola, & Y. Park. (2022). Uniting cyber security and machine learning: Advantages, challenges, and future research. *ICT Express*, 8(3), 313–321.
17. Firdaus, M., & K.H. Rhee. (2022, August). A joint framework to privacy-preserving edge intelligence in vehicular networks. In: *International Conference on Information Security Applications*, pp. 156–167. Cham: Springer Nature Switzerland.
18. Otoum, S., N. Guizani, & H. Mouftah. (2022). On the feasibility of split learning, transfer learning, and federated learning for preserving security in ITS systems. *IEEE Transactions on Intelligent Transportation Systems*, 24(7), 7462–7470.
19. Rehman, M.U., A. Shafique, Y.Y. Ghadi, W. Boulila, S.U. Jan, T.R. Gadekallu, ... & J. Ahmad. (2022). A novel chaos-based privacy-preserving deep learning model for cancer diagnosis. *IEEE Transactions on Network Science and Engineering*, 9(6), 4322–4337.
20. Zhang, J., X. Li, Z. Shi, & C. Zhu. (2022). A reputation-based and privacy-preserving incentive scheme for mobile crowd sensing: A deep reinforcement learning approach. *Wireless Networks*, 1–14.
21. Sharma, B., L. Sharma, C. Lal, & S. Roy. (2023). Anomaly based network intrusion detection for IoT attacks using deep learning technique. *Computers and Electrical Engineering*, 107, 108626.
22. Chu, H.C., C.Y. Chang, & H.C. Chao. (2022). Mapping deep learning technologies for mobile networks with the Internet of Things. *Human-centric Computing and Information Sciences*, 12, 59.
23. Fadlullah, Z.M., B. Mao, & N. Kato. (2022). Balancing QoS and security in the edge: Existing practices, challenges, and 6G opportunities with machine learning. *IEEE Communications Surveys and Tutorials*, 24(4), 2419–2448.

11 | Preserving Techniques in Big Data: A Comparative Analysis

Manish Kumar Gupta[1], Ashok Kumar Rai[2], Vipul Narayan[1*], Swapnita Srivastava[1]

[1] Department of Computer Science & Engineering, Madan Mohan Malaviya University of Technology, Gorakhpur - 273010, India

[2] Bennett University, Greater Noida

1. Introduction

Big Data (BD) has become a ubiquitous term in today's data-driven world. It refers to large volumes of complex and diverse datasets that are generated at a high velocity, often in real-time. The term "big data" also encompasses the technologies, tools, and processes used to store, manage, and analyze these massive datasets. BD is characterized by the three V's: volume, velocity, and variety as shown in Figure 1. The volume of BD is typically too large to be processed by traditional data processing tools, the velocity of data creation and transmission is very high, and the variety of data types and formats is very diverse. The analysis of BD can provide valuable insights and business intelligence for organizations, such as identifying patterns and trends, understanding customer behavior, and improving operational efficiency. However, BD also presents significant challenges in terms of data storage, processing, and analysis, as well as concerns over data privacy and security (P & S). According to IDC (Internet Data Centre), the amount of data generated worldwide is expected to grow from 33 zettabytes in 2018 to 175 zettabytes by 2025. This exponential growth of data is driving the demand for BD technologies and solutions, such as Hadoop, Spark, and NoSQL databases.

BD refers to the huge volume of structured, semi-structured, and unstructured data that is generated by various sources, such as social media, sensors, and transactions. BD poses significant challenges in terms of collection, storage, processing, and analysis, as traditional data processing tools and techniques are often inadequate for handling the size and complexity of big data. BD analytics involves the use of advanced techniques such as Machine Learning (ML), data mining, and natural language processing to extract insights, patterns, and trends from BD [33]. The analysis of BD can provide valuable insights and business

*Corresponding author: vipulupsainian2470@gmail.com

DOI: 10.1201/9781003560012-11

Figure 1: Three V's concept in big data.

intelligence for organizations, such as identifying patterns and trends, understanding customer behavior, and improving operational efficiency. However, BD also presents significant challenges in terms of data storage, processing, and analysis, as well as concerns over data privacy and security.

BD has had a profound impact on current IT (information technology) trends, shaping the way organizations store, process, and analyze data. Here are some relevant journal citations that discuss how BD has changed current IT trends:

1. **Cloud Computing:** BD has led to the rise of cloud computing, which allows organizations to store and process large volumes of data more efficiently and cost-effectively [27].
2. **Data Analytics:** BD has led to the development of new data analytics tools and techniques, such as ML and artificial intelligence that can extract insights from large and complex datasets [28].
3. **Cybersecurity:** BD has also led to new cybersecurity challenges and the need for more sophisticated cybersecurity solutions to protect data from breaches and cyber attacks [53].
4. **Internet of Things (IoT):** BD has also contributed to the growth of IoT, which involves the collection and analysis of data from connected devices such as sensors and wearables [1].

These trends are continuing to evolve as BD becomes more prevalent and organizations seek new ways to harness its potential for business insights and innovation.

This paper examines the newest advancement in Privacy Preservation (PP) technology based on BD and PP locations (Figure 2). We examine and categorize the fundamental ideas, metrics, and privacy-related research directions as well as the features of privacy preservation. Access control, encryption, anonymous protection, data auditing, and differential privacy protection are some unique PP aspects that are covered in depth. We also discuss the PP issue about its legal and societal ramifications. The challenges and unresolved problems are also listed in this paper to help the researcher with future studies.

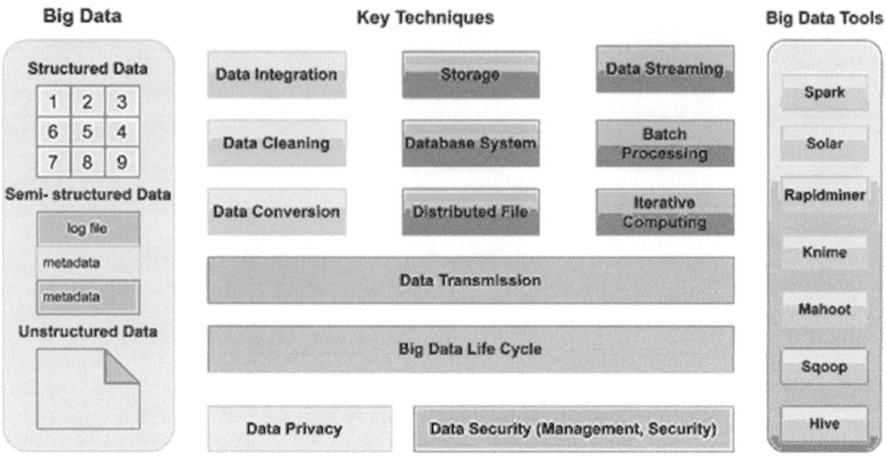

Figure 2: Technology framework for big data.

The remainder of the paper is structured as follows. The infrastructure of BD is introduced in Section 2. It also describes the BD life cycle, sources of big data, challenges of big data, and Privacy in different phases of BD in Section 3. The primary focus of Section 4 is privacy-preserving (PP) techniques in big data. Section 5 provides related works to the date. Section 6 identifies areas for Conclusion and Future Work.

2. Big Data Infrastructure

We need to create efficient and effective systems to process large amounts of data arriving at very high speeds to handle various dimensions of BD in terms of volume, velocity, and variety of paces derived from various sources. As seen in Figure 3, the life cycle of BD involves several stages. These days, data is dispersed, and new technologies are being created to store and process huge data repositories. For instance, techniques for large data processing and storage in the cloud, such as Hadoop MapReduce, are being investigated. This section provides an overview of BD life cycle along with the source of BD and the challenges of big data.

2.1 BD Life Cycle

The BD life cycle refers to the series of stages that data goes through from its initial creation or acquisition to its ultimate deletion or archiving. The stages of the BD life cycle typically include data acquisition, data storage, data processing, data analysis, and data visualization as shown in Figure 3. A key aspect of the BD life cycle is that it is iterative, meaning that the output of one stage can inform and influence subsequent stages [50].

Data Acquisition: In this stage, data is collected from various sources such as sensors, social media, and transactional systems. Data can be structured, semi-structured, or unstructured [36].

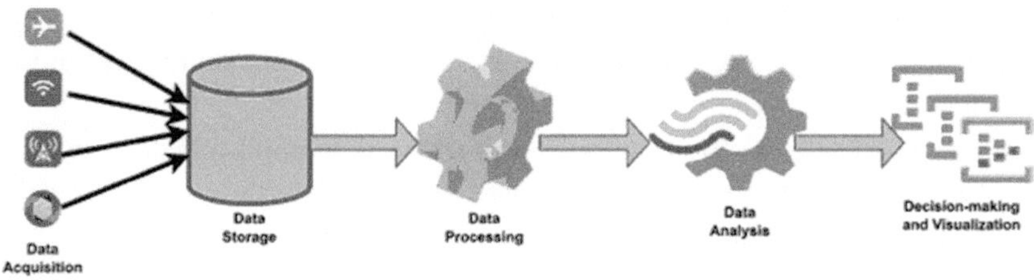

Figure 3: BD life cycle.

Data Storage: In this stage, data is stored in a suitable storage system, such as Hadoop Distributed File System (HDFS), NoSQL databases, or cloud-based storage systems [54]. In addition to distributed storage systems, big data applications may also use in-memory data storage solutions such as Apache Spark or Apache Ignite. These systems allow data to be stored and accessed in memory, providing faster access to data and more efficient data processing.

Data Processing: In this stage, data is processed and cleaned to remove any inconsistencies or errors. Data processing can be batch or real-time, and it involves techniques such as MapReduce, Spark, and Flink [44].

Data Analysis: In this stage, data is analyzed using various techniques such as ML, data mining, and natural language processing to extract insights, patterns, and trends [9].

Decision-making and Visualization: In this stage, the insights and results of data analysis are used for decision-making and visualization. Data visualization tools such as Tableau, Power BI, and D3.js can be used to visualize the results [18].

Effective decision-making and visualization in big data requires careful planning and execution to ensure that the insights and recommendations generated are relevant, accurate, and actionable. This can involve using specialized tools and technologies, such as data visualization tools like Tableau, Power BI or QlikView, and dashboard creation tools such as SAP Lumira or IBM Cognos Analytics. These steps in the life cycle of BD are iterative and ongoing, and they involve a range of stakeholders, including data scientists, IT professionals, business analysts, and decision-makers.

2.2 Sources of BD

The sources of BD are diverse and can come from various domains, including social media, scientific research, business transactions, and government records. Understanding the sources of BD is important for managing and analyzing large datasets and extracting valuable insights [35]. BD is generated from various sources, including social media, mobile devices, sensors, and transactional systems. Some relevant journal citations that discuss the sources of big data are:

Social Media: Social media platforms such as Facebook, Twitter, Instagram, and LinkedIn generate vast amounts of user-generated content that can be analyzed for insights and trends [80].

Mobile Devices: Mobile devices such as smartphones and tablets generate large volumes of data, including location data, search queries, and aPP usage data [73].

Sensors: Sensors embedded in various devices such as cars, home aPPliances, and wearables generate data on various parameters such as temperature, humidity, and movement patterns [34].

Transactional Systems: Transactional systems such as point-of-sale systems and customer relationship management systems generate data on customer behavior, preferences, and purchase history [10].

2.3 Technical Framework of BD

In accordance with the data processing life cycle, a big data process system includes big data acquisition, preprocessing, storage, and administration. Big data mining, big data analysis, big data visualization, and big data privacy and security are all aspects of the big data computing paradigm and system. Figure 2 displays a schematic of the big data technology's primary framework.

3. Challenges and Issues in BD

BD has become increasingly important in many domains, including business, science, health care, and government. Large datasets can provide valuable insights and enable better decision-making, as well as facilitate the development of new products and services [58]. BD management and analysis pose various challenges that need to be addressed to extract valuable insights from large datasets. Here is a journal article that discusses some of the key challenges of big data [67]:

- **Data Quality:** Ensuring that the data is accurate, complete, and consistent.
- **Data Privacy and Security:** Protecting sensitive data from unauthorized access and ensuring compliance with regulations.
- **Data Integration:** Integrating data from multiple sources to enable comprehensive analysis.
- **Scalability:** Managing and analyzing large datasets in a timely and efficient manner.
- **Data Analysis and Visualization:** Developing techniques for analyzing and visualizing complex datasets. Managing and analyzing BD poses several challenges that need to be addressed to extract valuable insights from large datasets [11].

The article identifies several types of challenges associated with big data, including:

- **Technical Challenges:** Managing and analyzing large and complex datasets, developing algorithms and models to extract insights, and ensuring data privacy and security.
- **Organizational Challenges:** Managing the cultural and organizational changes required to implement BD projects, building cross-functional teams to collaborate effectively, and ensuring adequate funding and resources.
- **Data Quality Challenges:** Ensuring that data is accurate, complete, and consistent, dealing with missing or incomplete data, and identifying and mitigating biases in the data.

- **Social and Ethical Challenges:** Balancing the potential benefits of BD with concerns about data privacy, security, and the potential for discriminatory or unethical uses of data.
- **Data Quality and Trust Issues:** Ensuring the quality and trustworthiness of BD is a challenge due to the variety, volume, and velocity of data. Data can be incomplete, inconsistent, and inaccurate, leading to unreliable insights and decisions [18].
- **P & S Issues:** BD often contains sensitive personal and business information, which can be vulnerable to unauthorized access, theft, and misuse. Ensuring data P & S is a critical challenge in the era of BD [8].
- **Data Processing and Analysis Issues:** Processing and analyzing BD require significant computational resources and expertise. Traditional data processing tools and techniques are often inadequate for BD due to the size and complexity of the data [14].
- **Data Integration and Interoperability Issues:** Integrating and interoperating heterogeneous BD sources is a significant challenge due to the lack of standardization and semantic heterogeneity [24].
- **Legal and Ethical Issues:** BD collection, processing, and analysis can raise legal and ethical concerns related to privacy, discrimination, and accountability. Ensuring legal compliance and ethical considerations is a challenge in the era of BD [4].

4. Privacy in Different Phases of BD

Privacy in BD refers to the protection of personal information that is collected, stored, and analyzed as part of BD initiatives. Here is a relevant journal citation that provides a definition of privacy in big data: According to Kshetri and Voas [38], privacy in BD can be defined as "the ability of individuals or groups to control, manage, and protect information that pertains to them, their transactions, and activities from unauthorized access, use, or disclosure by others" [37]. Privacy in BD is a complex issue that involves a range of technical, legal, and ethical considerations. As organizations collect and analyze more data, there is a growing need to ensure that personal information is handled responsibly and transparently. Privacy regulations such as the General Data Protection Regulation (GDPR) and the California Consumer Privacy Act (CCPA) have been introduced to protect individuals' privacy rights and regulate how personal data is collected and processed in BD initiatives. Privacy in BD refers to the protection of personal information and ensuring that sensitive data is not misused or exposed to unauthorized access. Here is a reference for a journal article that discusses privacy in the context of BD [18]. BD often involves the collection of large amounts of personal data, which can be used for various purposes, including marketing, research, and analysis. However, this also raises privacy concerns, as individuals may not be aware of what data is being collected, how it is being used, and who has access to it. Storing large amounts of personal data requires secure systems and processes to ensure that data is not lost or stolen. In addition, measures must be put in place to prevent unauthorized access to sensitive data. BD analytics involves processing large amounts of data to extract insights and patterns. This can lead to concerns about privacy, as individuals may not want their data used for these purposes. In addition, sharing of data between organizations can also raise privacy concerns, as there may be a risk of data being misused or shared without consent.

4.1 Privacy in the Data Generation Phase

Privacy in the data generation phase refers to the protection of personal information during the collection and creation of data [71]. This phase involves the gathering of raw data from various sources, such as surveys, sensors, and social media, which can include personal information about individuals. It is important to ensure that this information is collected in a manner that preserves the privacy and confidentiality of the individuals involved. Table 1 shows the comparison of privacy techniques in the data generation phase.

Several techniques can be used to ensure privacy in the data generation phase, including:

- **Anonymization:** Removing any identifying information from the data, such as names, addresses, and social security numbers, so that the data cannot be linked back to an individual. This can be done by either removing the information entirely or replacing it with a non-identifiable code. For example, instead of collecting the name of an individual, a unique ID can be assigned to them, which cannot be traced back to their real name. Anonymization helps to prevent the re-identification of individuals in the data and protects their privacy.
- **Pseudonymization:** Replacing identifying information with a pseudonym or code, which can still be used for analysis but does not reveal the identity of the individual. Pseudonymization is the process of replacing identifying information with a pseudonym or code. Unlike anonymization, which completely removes identifying information, pseudonymization allows data to be associated with a unique identifier that cannot be linked to an individual's real identity. This technique can be useful for research studies that require tracking of individuals over time, while still protecting their privacy.
- **Data minimization:** Collecting only the minimum amount of data necessary to achieve the research objectives, reducing the risk of collecting unnecessary or sensitive information. This reduces the amount of sensitive information collected, reducing the risk of privacy breaches. For example, instead of collecting a person's full name, address, and date of birth, only their age and gender may be needed for a particular study.
- **Encryption:** Encoding data so that it cannot be read or accessed by unauthorized individuals, protecting the data during transmission and storage. Encryption can be used to protect data during transmission and storage, such as encrypting data that is transmitted over the internet or storing data in an encrypted format on a secure server. This technique helps to prevent unauthorized access to sensitive information.
- **Consent:** Obtaining informed consent from individuals before collecting their data, informing them of the purpose and intended use of the data, and giving them the opportunity to opt-out or withdraw their consent at any time. This involves informing individuals of the purpose and intended use of the data, the parties that will have access to the data, and the risks and benefits of participating in the

study. Individuals should also be given the opportunity to opt-out or withdraw their consent at any time. Consent ensures that individuals are aware of how their data will be used and have given explicit permission for its collection and use.

Table 1: Comparison of privacy techniques in the data generation phase

Techniques	Major advantage	Major disadvantage	Major techniques
Anonymization	Protects individual privacy by removing identifying information	Reduces the usefulness of data for analysis	Remove or replace identifying information with non-identifiable codes
Pseudonymization	Protects individual privacy while still allowing data to be linked over time	Can still potentially identify individuals if additional information is collected	Replace identifying information with a pseudonym or code
Data minimization	Reduces the amount of sensitive information collected, reducing the risk of privacy breaches.	May not provide enough data for certain types of analysis	Collect only the minimum amount of data necessary to achieve the research objectives
Encryption	Protect data during transmission and storage from unauthorized access	Can be resource-intensive to implement and maintain	Encode data so that it cannot be read or accessed by unauthorized individuals
Consent	Ensures individuals are aware of how their data will be used and have given explicit permission for its collection and use	Can be difficult to obtain meaningful Consent, especially for complex studies	Obtain informed consent from individuals before collecting their details

4.2 Privacy in the Data Storage Phase

Privacy in the data storage phase refers to the protection of personal information during the storage and management of data [12]. This phase involves the preservation of data in a secure and confidential manner to prevent unauthorized access, use, or disclosure of the information. Table 2 shows the comparison of privacy techniques in the data storage phase. Several techniques can be used to ensure privacy in the data storage phase, including:

- **Access Controls:** This involves restricting access to the data by implementing user authentication and authorization protocols. This ensures that only authorized

Table 2: Comparison of privacy techniques in the data storage phase

Techniques	Major advantage	Major disadvantage	Major techniques
Access controls	Restricts access to the data, reducing the risk of unauthorized access	Can be time-consuming to manage and may require significant resources to implement.	Implement user authentication and authorization protocols, such as passwords or biometric authentication
Encryption	Protects data from unauthorized access or theft, ensuring data confidentiality	Can be resource-intensive to implement and maintain	Use encryption algorithms such as AES or RSA to encrypt data at rest or in transit
Secure storage	Physically secures data, reducing the risk of theft or physical damage	Can be expensive to implement and may require dedicated resources	Store data in a locked room or secure server protected by firewalls and other security measures
Data backup and recovery	Ensures that data can be recovered in the event of a disaster or security breach	Can be time-consuming and resource-intensive to implement and maintain	Regularly backup data to a secure location and implement procedures for recovering lost or corrupted data
Data retention and disposal	Ensures that sensitive information is not retained for longer than necessary, reducing the risk of privacy breaches	Major disadvantage: Can be difficult to manage and may require dedicated resources	Establish data retention schedules and data destruction procedures to ensure that data is properly disposed of when it is no longer needed

individuals have access to the data, and limits the potential for unauthorized access or misuse. This can include measures such as requiring users to enter a password or using biometric authentication, such as fingerprint scanning. Authorization protocols can limit access based on job roles and responsibilities, ensuring that only those with a legitimate need to access the data are able to do so.

- **Encryption:** This involves encoding the data so that it cannot be read or accessed by unauthorized individuals. This helps to protect the data in the event of a security breach or unauthorized access. This can be done using algorithms such as AES or RSA, which use a key to encrypt and decrypt the data. Encryption can be used to protect data at rest, such as encrypting data stored on a hard drive, or data in transit, such as encrypting data being transmitted over the internet.

- **Secure Storage:** This involves storing the data in a secure location, such as a locked room or a secure server, that is only accessible to authorized individuals. This helps to prevent physical access to the data. This can include storing the data in a locked room or using a secure server that is protected by firewalls and other security measures. Physical security measures such as security cameras and access control systems can also be used to protect the data.
- **Data Backup and Recovery:** This involves regularly backing up the data and implementing a disaster recovery plan to ensure that the data can be recovered in the event of a security breach, natural disaster, or other unexpected event. This can include measures such as regular backups to a secure location, using redundant storage systems, and implementing procedures for recovering lost or corrupted data.
- **Data Retention and Disposal:** This involves establishing policies and procedures for the retention and disposal of data, to ensure that sensitive information is not retained for longer than necessary and is properly disposed of when it is no longer needed. This can include measures such as data retention schedules, data destruction procedures, and ensuring that all backups and copies of the data are properly destroyed when they are no longer needed.

4.3 Privacy Preserving in the Data Processing

Privacy in the data processing phase refers to the protection of personal information during the analysis and manipulation of data [78]. This involves minimizing the risk of unauthorized access or disclosure of sensitive data during the processing phase. Table 3 shows the comparison of privacy techniques in the data processing phase. Several techniques can be used to ensure privacy preserving in the data processing phase, including:

Differential Privacy: This involves adding random noise to the data before processing it, to prevent the disclosure of sensitive information. This technique ensures that the processed data does not reveal any information about individual records in the dataset. The amount of noise added is carefully calibrated to ensure that the results of the data analysis remain statistically accurate while ensuring that individual records cannot be identified.

Secure Multiparty Computation: This involves dividing the dataset among multiple parties and performing computations on the data without revealing the individual data records to any of the parties. This technique is particularly useful when working with sensitive data that cannot be shared with a third party. This ensures that the data remains confidential and is particularly useful when working with sensitive data that cannot be shared with a third party.

Homomorphic Encryption: This involves encrypting the data in such a way that computations can be performed on the encrypted data without decrypting it. This technique ensures that the data remains confidential during the processing phase. This ensures that the data remains confidential during the processing phase and is particularly useful when working with data that cannot be shared or processed in plain text.

Data Masking: This involves removing or replacing sensitive data with non-sensitive data before processing it. This technique ensures that the sensitive data is not exposed during the processing phase. For example, replacing a person's name with a pseudonym or replacing their age with an age range. This ensures that sensitive data is not exposed during the processing phase.

Federated Learning: This involves training a machine learning model on multiple devices without sharing the raw data. The model is trained locally on each device, and the results are aggregated to create a global model. This technique ensures that the raw data is not exposed during the training process.

Table 3: Comparison of privacy techniques in the data processing phase

Techniques	Major advantage	Major disadvantage	Major techniques
Differential privacy	Provides strong privacy guarantees for individual records in the dataset	Can reduce the accuracy of the data analysis	Use techniques such as Laplace noise or randomized response to add noise to the data
Secure multi-party computation	Enables data analysis on sensitive data without sharing the data with a third party	Can be computationally expensive and difficult to implement	Use techniques such as secret sharing or garbled circuits to perform computations on the data without revealing the data to any of the parties
Homomorphic encryption	Enables data analysis on sensitive data without decrypting the data	Can be computationally expensive and difficult to implement	Use techniques such as fully homomorphic encryption or partially homomorphic encryption to perform computations on the encrypted data
Data masking	Protects sensitive data during the processing phase	Can reduce the accuracy of the data analysis	Replace sensitive data with non-sensitive data or pseudonyms before processing the data
Federated learning	Enables data analysis on sensitive data without sharing the raw data	Major disadvantage: Can be computationally expensive and may require significant resources	Use techniques such as horizontal or vertical federated learning to train machine learning models on distributed data

4.4 Matrices of Privacy

The concept of "matrices of privacy" refers to the different dimensions or aspects of privacy that must be considered when dealing with personal data. Here is a reference for a journal article that discusses matrices of privacy in the context of BD [40]:

Data Privacy: Protection of personal data from unauthorized access, use, or disclosure. Data privacy involves ensuring that personal data is collected and stored securely and that it is only used for legitimate purposes.

Communication Privacy: Protection of personal information during communication or transmission. Communication privacy involves ensuring that personal data is encrypted during transmission and that it is only transmitted to authorized recipients.

Processing Privacy: Protection of personal information during processing or analysis. Processing privacy involves ensuring that personal data is only processed by authorized individuals or systems and that it is processed in a way that protects individual privacy.

Location Privacy: Protection of personal information related to an individual's location. Location privacy involves ensuring that personal location data is collected and used only for legitimate purposes and that it is protected from unauthorized access or disclosure.

Social Privacy: Protection of personal information related to an individual's social interactions or networks. Social privacy involves ensuring that personal data related to an individual's social interactions is collected and used only for legitimate purposes and that it is protected from unauthorized access or disclosure.

5. Privacy Preserving Techniques in BD

PP techniques are essential in BD analytics to protect sensitive information and ensure that personal data is not exposed to unauthorized access or misuse. Table 4 shows the comparative analysis of different PP techniques. Here are some common techniques for preserving privacy in big data:

Differential Privacy (DP): DP is a widely used technique for preserving the privacy of individuals in BD analytics [15]. Differential privacy is a technique that involves adding noise to data to protect individual privacy. It works by adding random noise to data before analysis, which makes it difficult for an attacker to identify an individual's data in the dataset. The idea behind DP is to provide a mathematical guarantee that the analysis of the data will not reveal any private information about the individuals who contributed to the data. This is achieved by adding noise to the data in a controlled way, which ensures that even if an attacker knows some information about a specific individual in the dataset, they cannot use this information to infer any additional information about that individual. DP has become increasingly important in the age of big data, where large datasets are often used to train machine learning models or perform other types of data analysis. By using DP, organizations can ensure that the privacy of individuals is protected, while still being able to draw meaningful insights from the data. DP is not without its limitations, however. Adding noise to the data can reduce the accuracy of the analysis, and it can be difficult to find the right balance between privacy and accuracy. Additionally, there are still open questions around how to implement DP in practice, and how to measure the privacy guarantees provided by different DP mechanisms. Nonetheless, DP is an important tool for protecting the privacy of individuals in the age of big data. Figure 4 displays the concept of DP.

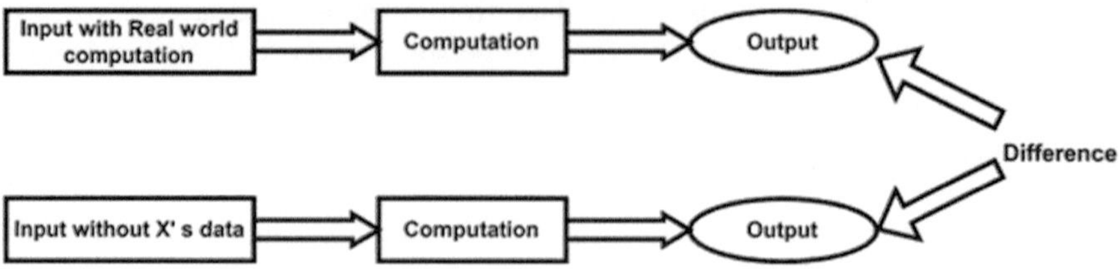

Figure 4: Differential privacy.

Homomorphic Encryption (HE): HE is a technique that allows computations to be performed on encrypted data, without first decrypting it, thereby preserving privacy [20]. In other words, HE allows for data to be processed in its encrypted form, providing a way to preserve the privacy and security of the data throughout the computation process. HE is based on mathematical operations that enable the encrypted data to be manipulated in a way that preserves the meaning of the original data. There are different types of HE, such as Fully Homomorphic Encryption (FHE), Partially Homomorphic Encryption (PHE), and Somewhat Homomorphic Encryption (SHE), which differ in the types of computations that can be performed. HE has a wide range of applications, such as secure cloud computing, secure data processing, and secureML. By using HE, sensitive data can be securely processed by third-party providers without the need for decrypting the data, which can help to protect the privacy and security of the data. However, HE is still an emerging technology and comes with its own challenges, such as computational overhead and potential security risks. Figure 5 shows the working process of Homomorphic Encryption.

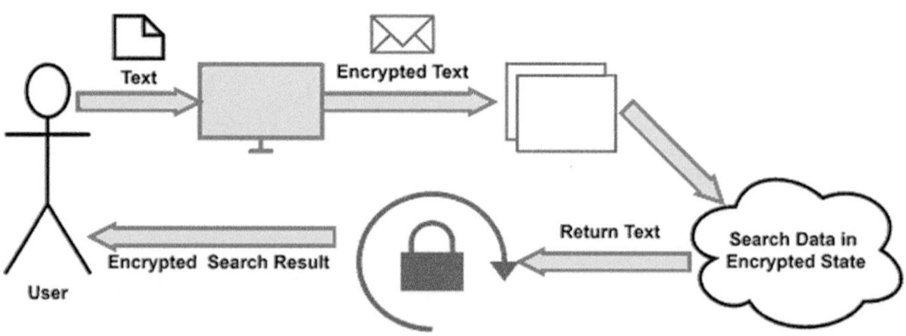

Figure 5: Homomorphic encryption.

Secure Multiparty Computation (SMPC): SMPC is a technique that allows multiple parties to jointly compute a function over their private data without revealing the data to each other [84]. This technique involves dividing the data between different parties and performing computations in a way that keeps the data confidential. SMPC involves distributing the computation of a function across multiple parties, each of whom holds a portion of the data required for the computation. The parties work together to perform the computation, without any party being able to access the entire input dataset. This ensures the privacy of each party's data, while still allowing the computation to be performed correctly. It typically involves the use of cryptographic protocols, such as secure multiparty computation protocols, to ensure that the privacy of each party's input is preserved. These protocols allow the parties to communicate and collaborate on the computation without revealing any sensitive information to each other.

Privacy Preserving Data Mining (PPDM): PPDM techniques include k-anonymity, l-diversity, t-closeness, and others, which aim to protect individual privacy while still allowing useful data analysis [64]. It involves mining data without revealing sensitive information. This technique involves encrypting data, randomizing data, or obscuring data to protect sensitive information. PPDM involves the use of various cryptographic techniques such as encryption, secure multiparty computation, and data anonymization to protect sensitive information from being revealed during the data mining process. These techniques ensure that the data remains confidential and cannot be accessed by unauthorized users. There are several techniques used in PPDM, including:

Data Anonymization: This involves modifying or removing identifying information from the data to prevent it from being traced back to individuals. Techniques such as k-anonymity, l-diversity, and t-closeness are commonly used for data anonymization.

Differential Privacy: This is a technique that adds noise to the data before mining it to prevent the identification of individual data points. Differential privacy ensures that the results of the data mining process are accurate while preserving the privacy of individuals.

Homomorphic Encryption: This is a technique that allows computation to be performed on encrypted data without decrypting it. This ensures that the data remains secure during the data mining process.

Secure Data Aggregation (SDA): SDA techniques aim to preserve the privacy of individual data sources while still allowing aggregate data analysis [51]. SDA involves a number of cryptographic techniques, such as encryption, secure multiparty computation, and data obfuscation, to ensure the privacy and security of individual data sources. The main goal of SDA is to aggregate data in such a way that the resulting aggregate data is as informative as possible, while at the same time preserving the privacy of individual data sources.

Obfuscation: Obfuscation techniques involve modifying the data in ways that preserve useful information while making it difficult to trace back to the original data [26]. Obfuscation refers to the process of making something unclear or difficult to understand, often intentionally, to prevent others from gaining access to or understanding sensitive information. In computer science, obfuscation is often used to protect software or algorithms from being reverse-engineered or to hide vulnerabilities from potential attackers.This techniques involve modifying code or data in such a way that it becomes difficult for someone to understand its underlying structure or purpose. For example, code obfuscation involves modifying the source code of a software program to make it difficult to read or decompile. This can be achieved through various methods, such as renaming variables, inserting useless or redundant code, or encrypting the code. Data obfuscation, on the other hand, involves modifying the data in a way that makes it difficult to interpret. This can be achieved through various techniques, such as data masking, data perturbation, or data shuffling. Data obfuscation is often used to protect sensitive data, such as personal information or financial data, from being accessed by unauthorized users. Obfuscation techniques can be used in combination with other security measures, such as encryption and access control, to provide additional layers of protection. However, it is important to note that obfuscation does not provide complete security and can be bypassed by determined attackers who have access to the right tools and techniques. Therefore, obfuscation should be considered as one of many security measures used to protect sensitive information.

Data Masking: Data masking involves replacing sensitive data with non-sensitive data while preserving the structure and format of the original data [61]. Data masking is a technique used to hide or replace sensitive data in a database or other data storage system with non-sensitive data, while retaining the data's original structure and functionality. Data masking is often used to protect sensitive data from unauthorized access or misuse by limiting the exposure of sensitive data to only authorized individuals. It involves modifying the original data by substituting sensitive data with fictitious but realistic data that does not reveal the original data's identity. For example, a credit card number might be masked by replacing some of the digits with asterisks or other symbols, making it difficult for unauthorized users to read or use the information. Data masking can be applied to various types of sensitive data, including personal information, financial data, healthcare information, and intellectual property. Some common techniques used for data masking include:

Substitution: In this technique, sensitive data is replaced with fictitious but realistic data, such as replacing a name with a similar-sounding name or replacing a phone number with a similar-looking number.

Shuffling: This technique involves rearranging the order of the data records, so that the sensitive data is not associated with its original record.

Encryption: In this technique, sensitive data is encrypted using an algorithm, and only authorized users with the correct decryption key can access the data.

Tokenization: Tokenization involves replacing sensitive data with randomly generated tokens, which can be used in place of the original data for analysis purposes [41]. Tokenization is a technique used to protect sensitive data by replacing it with a non-sensitive equivalent, known as a token. The token is a randomly generated string of characters that does not contain any sensitive information but serves as a reference to the original data. Tokenization is commonly used in the payment industry to protect credit card information. When a customer makes a payment using a credit card, the credit card number is replaced with a token that is stored in the payment gateway or merchant's database. This token is used to process future transactions and is associated with the customer's credit card information on the payment gateway or merchant's secure servers. Tokenization is a more secure alternative to storing sensitive data in plain text or using encryption, as it eliminates the risk of data exposure in case of a security breach. In addition, tokenization allows merchants to store customer information for longer periods without the risk of exposing sensitive data, as the tokenized data is not considered sensitive and is not subject to regulatory compliance requirements.

Anonymization: Anonymization involves removing or obscuring identifying information from data, while still preserving its utility for analysis [55]. The goal of anonymization is to protect individuals' privacy while still allowing the data to be used for analysis or research purposes. Anonymization techniques involve replacing or removing PII from the data, such as names, addresses, social security numbers, and other identifying information. Common anonymization techniques include:

- **Aggregation:** This technique involves combining multiple data records to create summary statistics, such as averages or totals, while removing identifying information.
- **Masking:** This technique involves replacing PII with a generic or randomized value, such as replacing a name with "Person A" or a phone number with a random set of digits.

Table 4: Comparative analysis of different PP techniques

Technique	Description	Features	Key challenges
Differential Privacy	A statistical technique that masks individual data to protect privacy.	Provides provable privacy guarantees.	Balancing privacy and data utility.
Homomorphic Encryption	Encryption technique that allows computation on encrypted data while maintaining privacy.	Maintains privacy by allowing computation on encrypted data.	Limited aPPlicability due to high computational costs.
SMPC	A technique that enables multiple parties to jointly compute a function over their private data without revealing data to each other.	Allows computation on private data while preserving privacy.	Scalability and complexity issues.
PP Data Mining	Techniques that protect individual privacy while still allowing useful data analysis.	Protects individual privacy while enabling useful data analysis.	Difficulty in maintaining privacy while still allowing useful analysis.
Secure Data Aggregation	Techniques that preserve the privacy of individual data sources while still allowing aggregate data analysis.	Preserves privacy of individual data sources while allowing aggregate data analysis.	Ensuring the security and accuracy of aggregated data.
Obfuscation	Modifying data to preserve useful information while making it difficult to trace back to the original data.	Protects data by modifying it to make it difficult to trace back to the original data.	Balancing privacy and data utility.

(Contd.)

Table 4: (*Contd.*)

Technique	Description	Features	Key challenges
Data Masking	Replacing sensitive data with non-sensitive data while preserving the structure and format of the original data.	Replaces sensitive data with non-sensitive data while preserving structure and format.	Limitations in preserving the structure and format of the original data.
Tokenization	Replacing sensitive data with randomly generated tokens for analysis purposes.	Maintains data privacy by replacing sensitive data with random tokens.	Potential re-identification of data through token analysis.
Anonymization	Removing or obscuring identifying information from data while preserving its utility for analysis.	Protects privacy by removing or obscuring identifying information.	Difficulty in balancing privacy and data utility.

- **Generalization:** This technique involves replacing specific information with more general information, such as replacing an exact age with a range of ages, or replacing a specific location with a larger geographic area.

The performance summary of privacy-preservation techniques are given in Table 5.

Table 5: Performance evaluation of privacy-preserving techniques.

Technique	Privacy preserving scale	Computing cost	Data missing	Data dependency	Communication overhead
Differential Privacy	H	M⊛H	M⊛H	M⊛H	M⊛H
Homomorphic Encryption	H	H	M	M⊛H	H
SMPC	H	M⊛H	M⊛H	M⊛H	H
PP Data Mining	H	M⊛H	M⊛H	M⊛H	M⊛H
Secure Data Aggregation	H	M⊛H	M⊛H	M⊛H	H
Obfuscation	H	H	L⊛M	L⊛M	L⊛M
Data Masking	L⊛M	L⊛M	L⊛M	L⊛M	L⊛M
Tokenization	H	L⊛M	L⊛M	L	L⊛M
Anonymization	H	L⊛M	L⊛M	L	L⊛M

Notes: L: Low, M: Medium, H: High , L⊛M Low to Medium, M⊛H Medium to High.

6. Related Works

Various researchers and scholars have published various research and review papers related to privacy and security related in the terms of big data. Tables 6 and 7 provide a comparative analysis of various survey papers and research papers, respectively. Wang X. et al. [69] provide a comprehensive survey of the security issues in big data. The authors examine various threats to data security and discuss different techniques and aPProaches to mitigate them, including encryption, access control, and anomaly detection. Zaidi et al. [80] provide an overview of the security and privacy (S & P) challenges associated with big data. The authors discuss various S & P protection mechanisms that can be used to address these challenges, including encryption, access control, and anonymization. Wu J. et al. [70] give a comprehensive survey of the security issues associated with big data. The authors discuss various types of security threats and vulnerabilities that can occur in the context of BD and examine different security protection mechanisms that can be used to mitigate these threats. Zikopoulos, P. et al. [81] provide a comprehensive overview of BD and its associated technologies. The authors discuss various S & P challenges that arise in the context of BD and examine different APProaches and techniques that can be used to address these challenges. Bao, R. et al. [63] provide a review of the S & P challenges associated with big data. The authors discuss various S & P protection mechanisms that can be used to address these challenges, including encryption, access control, and data anonymization. Zhang, Y. et al. [82] examine the challenges and OPPortunities for BD S & P protection. The authors discuss various types of S & P threats that can occur in the context of BD and provide recommendations for how to mitigate them. Wu, J. et al. [71] focus on the S & P issues that arise in cloud computing, particularly concerning big data. The authors discuss various types of attacks and vulnerabilities that can occur in the cloud, as well as the different S & P protection mechanisms that can be used to mitigate them. Almishari, S. et al. [2] examine the S & P issues that arise in the context of BD in healthcare. The authors discuss the challenges of protecting sensitive medical data and provide an overview of the different S & P protection mechanisms that can be used to address these challenges. Ye, F. et al. [76] provide a survey of the different S & P preservation techniques that can be used in the context of big data. The authors examine various data protection methods, such as encryption and access control, and discuss their strengths and weaknesses. Alomari, M et al. [3] provide a survey of the different S & P issues that arise in the context of BD in cloud computing. The authors discuss various threats and attacks that can occur in the cloud and examine the different S & P protection mechanisms that can be used to address these threats. Ahmad, S et al. [4] provide a comprehensive review of the current challenges and research oPPortunities in the field of BD S & P . They discuss the key issues in BD security, including data breaches, unauthorized access, and data theft. Ali, A. et al. [5] present a comprehensive review of the state-of-the-art research on BD S & P. They examine the key challenges and issues in BD S & P, including data confidentiality, integrity, and availability, as well as privacy preservation. The paper also discusses the various techniques and tools that have been developed to address these challenges. Bujlow, T et al. [7] present a survey of the major S & P challenges associated with big data. They discuss the various threats and risks to data S & P, including data breaches, data theft, unauthorized access, and the compromise of data confidentiality, integrity, and availability. Eslami, M. et al. [16] present a survey on the key S & P challenges associated with BD in healthcare. They examine the various threats and risks to data S & P in healthcare, including data breaches, data theft, and unauthorized access. Guo, Y. et al. [17] present a comprehensive survey of BD security, covering various aspects such as privacy, confidentiality, integrity, availability, data breaches, data theft, and unauthorized access. Jana, P.K. et al. [29] present a comprehensive survey of S & P issues in big data. The paper discusses the various threats and risks associated with BD security, including data breaches, data theft, unauthorized access, and the compromise of data confidentiality, integrity, and availability. The authors review the techniques and tools that have been developed to address these challenges, including encryption, access control, and authentication mechanisms. Khosravi-Far et al. [31] present a systematic review of the P & S challenges associated with big data. The paper discusses the various threats and risks to BD privacy and security, including data breaches, data theft, unauthorized access, and the compromise of data confidentiality, integrity, and availability. The authors also review the techniques and tools that have been developed to address these challenges, including encryption, access control, and intrusion detection mechanisms. S. Kim et al. [32] discuss the S & P challenges faced in the BD environment, including the risks associated with data breaches, cyber attacks, and unauthorized access. T. Liu et al. [45] explore the various P & S issues in big data, including privacy threats, data protection, and access control. S. Kim et al. discuss different techniques for PP data analysis in the context of big data, including differential privacy and homomorphic encryption. X. Lin et al. [46] provide an overview of the S & P challenges in big data, including data protection, access control, and PP techniques. S.S. Park et al. [60] discuss the unique S & P challenges in the healthcare industry, including the sensitive nature of healthcare data and the need for secure data storage and transmission. W. Jia et al. [30] provide an overview of the security challenges in big data, including data protection, privacy, and access control. R. Li et al. [47] provide a survey of privacy preservation techniques for big data, including k-anonymity, l-diversity, and t-closeness. D. Zhang et al. [83] provide an overview of the S & P challenges in big data, including data protection, access control, and PP techniques. Y. Liu et al. [52] discuss the S & P challenges in big data, including data protection, access control, and PP techniques. J. Yang et al. [77] provide a comprehensive review of the security challenges in big data, including data protection, access control, and PP techniques. Y. Zhang et al.'s [82] paper discusses the S & P challenges in big data, including data protection, access control, and PP techniques. K. Xie et al. [73] the S & P challenges in BD and cloud computing, including data protection, access control, and PP techniques. D. Wang et al. [68] explore the S & P challenges in healthcare big data, including data protection, access control, and PP techniques.

W. Lin et al. [49] propose a hybrid encryption scheme for secure BD transmission in the cloud. The scheme combines symmetric and asymmetric encryption techniques to achieve a balance between security and efficiency in transmitting large amounts of data. Y. Xue et al. [74] present a multiparty computation aPProach to preserve data privacy in BD analytics. The aPProach allows multiple parties to perform

Table 6: Comparative analysis of various survey papers

Citation	Confidentiality	Integrity	Availability	Data breaches	Data theft	Unauthorized access	Data encryption	Access control	Intrusion detection mechanisms	Cyber attack	Data protection	Privacy-preserving
Ahmad S. et al. [4]	×	×	×	✓	✓	✓	×	×	×	×	×	×
Ali A. et al. [5]	✓	✓	✓	✓	×	✓	×	×	×	×	×	×
Bujlow T. et al. [7]	✓	✓	✓	✓	✓	✓	×	×	×	×	×	×
Eslami M. et al. [16]	✓	✓	✓	✓	✓	✓	✓	✓	×	×	×	×
Guo Y. et al. [17]	✓	✓	✓	✓	✓	✓	×	×	×	×	×	×
Jana P.K. et al. [29]	✓	✓	✓	✓	✓	✓	✓	✓	×	×	×	×
Khosravi-Far et al. [31]	✓	✓	✓	✓	✓	✓	✓	✓	×	×	×	×
S. Kim et al. [32]	×	×	×	×	✓	×	✓	×	×	✓	×	×
T. Liu et al. [45]	×	×	×	×	×	×	×	✓	×	×	×	×
S.S. Park et al. [60]	×	×	×	×	×	✓	✓	×	×	×	✓	×
X. Lin et al. [46]	×	×	×	×	×	×	×	✓	×	×	✓	✓
S.S. Park et al. [60]	×	×	×	×	×	✓	×	✓	×	×	✓	✓
W. Jia et al. [30]	×	×	×	×	×	×	×	×	×	×	×	✓
R. Li et al. [47]	×	×	×	×	×	×	×	✓	×	×	✓	✓
D. Zhang et al. [83]	×	×	×	×	×	×	×	✓	×	×	✓	✓
Y. Liu et al. [52]	×	×	×	×	×	×	×	✓	×	×	✓	✓
J. Yang et al. [77]	×	×	×	×	×	×	×	✓	×	×	✓	✓
Y. Zhang et al. [82]	×	×	×	×	×	×	×	✓	×	×	✓	✓
K. Xie et al. [73]	×	×	×	×	×	×	×	✓	×	×	✓	✓
D. Wang et al. [68]	×	×	×	×	×	×	×	✓	×	×	✓	✓

computations on shared data without revealing the data itself, thus protecting sensitive information while enabling data analysis. An efficient and secure data-sharing model has been developed for big data analytics in the cloud. The framework uses a combination of encryption, access control, and auditing mechanisms to ensure data confidentiality, integrity, and availability in a multi-tenant cloud environment. J. Wang et al. introduce a blockchain (BC)-based secure data-sharing system for BD analytics. The system uses BC technology to create an immutable ledger of data access and sharing activities, ensuring transparency and accountability while protecting data privacy. Z. Hu et al. [24] present an efficient and secure

Table 7: Comparative analysis of various research papers.

References	Method used	Key features	Challenges	Future scope
W. Lin et al. [49]	Hybrid encryption scheme for secure BD transmission in the cloud.	Combination of symmetric and asymmetric encryption, parallel processing, data partitioning, data compression, key management, and access control mechanisms.	Balancing security and efficiency, handling large-scale data transmission, and ensuring key management and access control mechanisms are robust.	Further research on optimizing the hybrid encryption scheme for different types of BD and cloud environments, exploring the potential of using BC technology for key management and access control.
Y. Xue et al. [74]	Multiparty Computation (MPC) aPProach for preserving data privacy in BD analytics.	Secure MPC protocols, data perturbation, and shuffling techniques for privacy preservation.	Balancing privacy and computation efficiency, secure key management, handling large-scale data processing, and selecting aPPropriate MPC techniques.	Optimizing MPC for different BD analytics tasks, using advanced MPC techniques, and integrating MPC with other PP technologies.
M. Alshaikh et al.	Secure and efficient data-sharing framework for BD analytics in the cloud.	Encryption-based data sharing, fine-grained access control, data integrity, and authenticity assurance, scalable architecture with parallel processing, efficient search and retrieval mechanisms.	Balancing security and efficiency, ensuring robust access control mechanisms, handling large-scale datasets, and addressing potential vulnerabilities in the cloud environment.	Optimizing the framework for different cloud environments and BD analytics tasks, exploring the potential of using BC technology for secure data sharing, and integrating the framework with other PP technologies such as differential privacy.

J. Wang et al.	BC-based secure data sharing system for BD analytics.	Decentralized data sharing, secure data storage, and retrieval, immutable audit trail, fine-grained access control, and data privacy preservation.	Ensuring scalability and efficiency, addressing potential security vulnerabilities in the BC environment, managing complex access control policies, and handling large-scale datasets.	Further research on optimizing the BC -based system for different BD analytics tasks, exploring the potential of using smart contracts for automated access control and data sharing, integrating the system with other PP technologies such as homomorphic encryption.
Z. Hu et al. [24]	Efficient and secure data sharing scheme for BD aPPlications in the Internet of Things (IoT).	Encryption-based data sharing, data partitioning, data compression, access control, secure key management, and lightweight encryption for IoT devices.	Ensuring security and efficiency in IoT environments, handling large-scale datasets, managing complex access control policies, and addressing potential vulnerabilities in IoT devices.	Further research on optimizing the scheme for different IoT environments and BD aPPlications, exploring the potential of using BC technology for secure data sharing in IoT, and integrating the scheme with other PP technologies such as differential privacy.
Li et al. [47]	BC-based secure data storage scheme for big data.	Maintains integrity and immutability of data, Merkle tree-based structure to store big data, access control for privacy protection.	Limited scalability due to the high computational and storage overhead of BC, possible privacy issues in the public BC.	Optimizing the use of BC in BD storage, exploring the use of private BC or other distributed ledger technologies for better scalability and privacy protection.
Zhang et al. [82]	Secure BD storage and sharing scheme using BC and ciphertext-policy attribute-based encryption (CP-ABE).	Ensures data integrity and fine-grained access control, dynamic revocation mechanism to revoke unauthorized access.	High computational and storage overhead of CP-ABE, scalability issues with the use of BC.	Exploring the use of more efficient and scalable attribute-based encryption schemes, optimizing the use of BC to address scalability issues.

(Contd.)

Table 7: *(Contd.)*

References	Method used	Key features	Challenges	Future scope
Zhang et al. [82]	Secure data storage and sharing scheme for BD based on BC and attribute-based encryption (ABE).	Ensures data integrity and fine-grained access control, dynamic revocation mechanism to revoke unauthorized access	High computational and storage overhead of ABE, scalability issues with the use of BC.	Exploring the use of more efficient and scalable ABE schemes, optimizing the use of BC to address scalability issues.
Jia, R. et al.	BC-based data-sharing mechanism.	PP BD storage and analysis.	Scalability of BC -based systems.	Improve scalability and explore other PP technologies such as differential privacy.
Wen, X. et al.	Homomorphic encryption.	Secure BD storage, and data processing in encrypted form.	Computational overhead, security of homomorphic encryption scheme.	Improve efficiency and security of homomorphic encryption, explore other secure multiparty computation techniques.
Xia, W. et al.	ML	Anomaly detection for BD security.	Need for a large amount of training data, selection of aPPropriate features	Explore deep learning techniques and other unsupervised learning methods.
Hua, S. et al.	Secret sharing and cloud computing.	Security enhancement for BD storage.	Loss of data availability, the overhead of secret sharing.	Explore other secure multiparty techniques.
Li et al. [47]	PP ML.	BD security with privacy preservation.	Accuracy and efficiency of the ML model.	Explore federated learning and other PP techniques.
W. Shen et al.	BC technology.	Ensures the integrity and confidentiality of data Enables secure sharing among different parties Uses smart contracts for automatic execution of data access policies.	High computational and storage requirements Limited scalability.	Integration with other emerging technologies such as ML and IoT Enhancement of scalability and performance.

S. Xu et al.	Attribute-based encryption and pseudonymization.	Ensures the P & S of shared data Enables data sharing among multiple parties with different access levels SuPPorts flexible access control policies.	Key management and distribution Potential performance overheads.	Integration with other privacy-enhancing technologies such as homomorphic encryption Enhancement of scalability and performance.
Y. Wang et al. [67]	Homomorphic encryption	Enables data aggregation while protecting the privacy of individual data contributors SuPPorts both linear and nonlinear functions Provides efficient computation and communication overhead.	Limited scalability for large-scale data sets Key management and distribution.	Integration with other privacy-enhancing technologies such as differential privacy Enhancement of scalability and performance.
X. Wu et al.	Lightweight encryption algorithm	Ensures the integrity and confidentiality of data during transmission. Provides efficient computation and communication overhead SuPPorts mutual authentication between data senders and receivers.	Potential vulnerabilities to attacks such as replay and man-in-the-middle attacks Key management and distribution.	Enhancement of security against known vulnerabilities Integration with other authentication and access control technologies such as biometrics.

(*Contd.*)

Table 7: (*Contd.*)

References	Method used	Key features	Challenges	Future scope
Y. Liu et al. [52]	Lightweight encryption algorithm.	Ensures the integrity and confidentiality of data during transmission Provides efficient computation and communication overhead SuPPorts real-time data transmission in smart grid environments.	Potential vulnerabilities to attacks such as replay and man-in-the-middle attacks Limited scalability for large-scale datasets.	Integration with other emerging technologies such as BC and edge computing. Enhancement of scalability and performance.

data-sharing scheme for BD aPPlications in the Internet of Things (IoT). The scheme uses a distributed access control mechanism to enable secure data sharing among IoT devices while preventing unauthorized access and ensuring data confidentiality and integrity.

Li et al. [47] present a BC-based secure data storage scheme for big data. The proposed scheme uses BC to maintain the integrity of the stored data and ensure the immutability of the transactions. The authors used a Merkle tree-based structure to store the big data, and the proposed scheme also provided access control to ensure the privacy of the stored data. Zhang et al. [82] proposed a secure BD storage and sharing scheme using BC and ciphertext-policy attribute-based encryption (CP-ABE). The proposed scheme used BC to maintain the integrity of the stored data and CP-ABE to provide fine-grained access control to the stored data. The authors also proposed a dynamic revocation mechanism to revoke the access rights of unauthorized users. Zhang et al. [82] proposed a secure data storage and sharing scheme for BD based on BC and attribute-based encryption (ABE). The proposed scheme used BC to ensure the integrity of the stored data and ABE to provide fine-grained access control to the stored data. The authors also proposed a dynamic revocation mechanism to revoke the access rights of unauthorized users. Jia, R. et al. present a BC-based method for PP BD storage and analysis. The method uses smart contracts to control data access and data sharing. The authors also discuss the challenges of scalability in BC-based systems and suggest future work to improve scalability and explore other PP technologies such as differential privacy. Wen, X. et al. give a novel aPProach for securing BD storage based on homomorphic encryption. The authors use homomorphic encryption to process data in encrypted form, ensuring that data is kept secure during storage and processing. The authors also discuss the challenges of computational overhead and security of the homomorphic encryption scheme and suggest future work to improve efficiency and explore other secure multiparty computation techniques. Xia, W. et al. present an anomaly detection method for BD security using ML techniques. The authors use ML to identify anomalous data points and suggest that this can be used to detect security threats. The authors also discuss the challenges of needing a large amount of training data and selecting aPPropriate features and suggest future work to explore deep learning techniques and other unsupervised learning methods. Hua, S. et al. propose a security enhancement method for BD storage based on secret sharing and cloud computing. The authors use secret sharing to divide data into multiple parts and distribute them to different cloud servers, ensuring that data is kept secure during storage. The authors also discuss the challenges of loss of data availability and overhead of secret sharing and suggest future work to explore other secure multi-party techniques. Li, Q. et al. [47] propose a PP ML method for BD security. The authors use differential privacy to ensure that the privacy of individuals is not compromised during M . The authors also discuss the challenges of accuracy and efficiency of the ML model and suggest future work to explore federated learning and other PP techniques. W. Shen et al. propose a novel aPProach to secure BD storage and sharing based on BC technology. The proposed scheme ensures the integrity and confidentiality of data while enabling secure sharing among different parties. S. Xu et al. proposes a secure data-sharing scheme for BD aPPlications in cloud computing in 2018. The proposed scheme uses attribute-based encryption and pseudonymization to ensure the P & S of shared data. S. Xu et al. present a PP data aggregation scheme for BD aPPlications. The proposed scheme enables the aggregation of data while protecting the privacy of individual data contributors. Y. Wang et al. [67] present an authentication protocol for BD aPPlications that are both secure and efficient. The proposed protocol uses a lightweight encryption algorithm and ensures the integrity and confidentiality of data during transmission. Y. Liu et al. [52] propose a secure and efficient data transmission scheme for BD aPPlications in smart grids. The proposed scheme uses a lightweight encryption algorithm and ensures the integrity and confidentiality of data during transmission, while also minimizing communication overhead.

7. Conclusion

While big data can provide valuable insights, it also poses significant challenges. One of these challenges is protecting personal privacy in the era of big data. Privacy has become a critical issue, especially as it relates to customers. This article outlines the concept of big data, the importance of privacy-preserving techniques, specific challenges, and various approaches to protect privacy in big data. Additionally, it highlights the significance of laws and regulations in addressing privacy concerns.

Despite the existence of privacy-preserving techniques, current methods are not yet mature enough to fully address privacy concerns in big data. However, combining different technological methods, policies, and laws could provide a more comprehensive solution to the problem. By taking an integrated approach, we can more effectively preserve privacy in the context of big data.

References

1. Atzori, L., A. Iera, & G. Morabito. (2010). The internet of things: A survey. *Computer Networks*, 54(15), 2787–2805.
2. Almishari, S., & S. Alfayez. (2018). A comprehensive survey of BD S & P issues in healthcare. *Journal of Healthcare Engineering*, 2018.
3. Alomari, M., & I. Alsmadi. (2019). A survey on BD S & P in cloud computing. *Journal of Cloud Computing*, 8(1), 1–17.
4. Ahmad, S., & S. Pandey. (2020). BD S & P challenges: Review and research opportunities. *Journal of Network and Computer Applications*, 153, 102548.
5. Ali, A., N. Haider, I. Shafi, & M.H. Memon. (2020). BD S & P: A review. *Journal of Ambient Intelligence and Humanized Computing*, 11(1), 127–142.
6. Gupta, A., & M.K. Gupta. (2022). Prediction of diseases using different machine learning approaches. In: *2022 3rd International Conference on Intelligent Engineering and Management (ICIEM),* London, United Kingdom, pp. 712–717, doi: 10.1109/ICIEM54221.2022.9853132.
7. Bujlow, T., & T. Dehling. (2021). A survey of BD S & P challenges. *BD Research*, 25, 100186.
8. Bowers, K.D., P.R. Juels, & A. Oprea. (2014). Hacking blind. In: *Proceedings of the 2014 ACM SIGSAC Conference on Computer and Communications Security*, pp. 80–91.

9. Carvalho, A., J. Cardoso, & G. Marques. (2020). Big data analytics: A comprehensive survey. *ACM Computing Surveys* (*CSUR*), 53(2), 1–34.
10. Chen, H., R.H. Chiang, & V.C. Storey. (2012). Business intelligence and analytics: From big data to big impact. *MIS Quarterly*, 1165–1188.
11. Chen, M., S. Mao, & Y. Liu. (2014). Big data: A survey. *Mobile Networks and Applications*, 19(2), 171–209. https://doi.org/10.1007/s11036-013-0489-0.
12. Chen, Q., & X. Zhao. (2017). Privacy protection in big data storage. *Journal of Network and Computer Applications*, 88, 34–42. https://doi.org/10.1016/j.jnca.2017.04.010.
13. Ching, J., J. Sander, & S. Kumar. (2018). Data-driven discovery of models. *SIAM Review*, 60(2), 267–307.
14. Chen, Y., R. Gopal, H. Liu, & L. Raghunathan, L. (2019). Big data and analytics in healthcare: Introduction to the special section. *Information Systems Frontiers*, 21(5), 939–943.
15. Dwork, C. (2014). A tutorial on differential privacy. *Foundations and Trends in Theoretical Computer Science*, 9(3–4), 211–407.
16. Eslami, M., & M. Ahmadzadeh. (2020). A survey on BD S & P in healthcare. *Journal of Medical Systems*, 44(12), 209.
17. Guo, Y., Y. Gao, C. Liu, & W. Lu. (2020). BD security: A comprehensive survey. *Journal of Network and Computer Applications*, 148, 102472.
18. Gantz, J.F., & D. Reinsel. (2012). The digital universe in 2020: Big data, bigger digital shadows, and biggest growth in the far east. *IDC iView: IDC Analyze the Future*, 2007(2012), 1–16.
19. Gupta, M., & R.K. Dwivedi. (2023, Oct.). Fortified MapReduce layer: Elevating security and privacy in big data. *EAI Endorsed Transactions on Scalable Information Systems*, 10(6). DOI: https://doi.org/10.4108/eetsis.3859.
20. Gentry, C. (2010). Computing arbitrary functions of encrypted data. *Communications of the ACM*, 53(3), 97–105.
21. Gupta, A., & M.K. Gupta. (2017). HIVE-processing structured data in Hadoop. *International Journal of Scientific & Engineering Research*, 8(6), 45–48.
22. Gupta, M., & R.K. Dwivedi. (2023, Jun.). Blockchain-based secure and efficient scheme for medical data. *EAI Endorsed Transactions on Scalable Information Systems*, 10(5). DOI:https://doi.org/10.4108/eetsis.3235.
23. Han, Y., S. Liu, Y. Zhang, & Q. Li. (2018). Big data security and privacy: Challenges and countermeasures. *Journal of Cyber Security and Mobility*, 6(2), 81–107.
24. Hu, S., L. Deng, X. Liu, & Q. Li. (2020). A survey on big data integration. *Journal of Big Data*, 7(1), 1–31.
25. He, W., Y. Li, J. Li, Y. Li, & Y. Liu. (2019). Research on big data security and privacy protection technology. *Journal of Physics: Conference Series*, 1168(1), 012031.
26. Holohan, N., & M. Schellekens. (2017). Obfuscation techniques and software piracy. *Journal of Cybersecurity*, 3(1), 29–38.
27. Islam, M.S., M.R. Islam, & D. Kwak. (2017). The rise of cloud computing: A review of current and future trends. *Journal of Supercomputing*, 73(3), 1102–1137.
28. Janssen, M., Y. Charalabidis, & A. Zuiderwijk. (2012). Benefits, adoption barriers, and myths of open data and open government. *Information Systems Management*, 29(4), 258–268.
29. Jana, P.K., & N.C. Debnath. (2021). S & P issues in big data: A comprehensive survey. *Journal of Big Data*, 8(1), 1–30.
30. Jia, W., Q. Zhang, Y. Zhang, & J. Wang. (2021). A survey on BD security. *Journal of Supercomputing*, 77(2), 1149–1179.

31. Khosravi-Far, R., S.M. Hassan, & M. Ghahramani. (2021). BD P & S challenges: A systematic review. *Journal of Ambient Intelligence and Humanized Computing*, 12(5), 4955–4970.
32. Kim, S., C. Lee, & J. Kim. (2021). S & P challenges in big data. *Information Systems Frontiers*, 23(2), 259–263.
33. Kankanhalli, A., J. Hahn, S. Tan et al. (2016). Big data and analytics in healthcare: Introduction to the special section. *Inf. Syst. Front.*, 18, 233–235. https://doi.org/10.1007/s10796-016-9641-2.
34. Khan, A.M., Y.K. Lee, & S. Lee. (2019). Big data analytics in smart manufacturing: Current status and future prospects. *International Journal of Precision Engineering and Manufacturing – Green Technology*, 6(3), 401–420.
35. Kitchin, R. (2014). Big data, new epistemologies, and paradigm shifts. *Big Data & Society*, 1(1), 1–12.
36. Kwon, O., & H. Kang. (2019). A survey on big data processing: Stages, platforms, and methodologies. *Information Systems Frontiers*, 21(5), 959–987.
37. Kshetri, N. (2014). Privacy in the big data era: A review. *Journal of Business Research*, 67(11), 2147–2155. https://doi.org/10.1016/j.jbusres.2014.03.024.
38. Kshetri, N., & J. Voas. (2018). Big data governance: An emerging research agenda. *Computer*, 51(8), 50–57.
39. Kshetri, N. (2018). Blockchain's roles in meeting key supply chain management objectives. *International Journal of Information Management*, 39, 80–89.
40. Kouhizadeh, M., & J. Sarkis. (2018). Big data and privacy: A technological perspective and review. *Journal of Cleaner Production*, 172, 2199–2217. https://doi.org/10.1016/j.jclepro.2017.11.156.
41. Kantarcioglu, M., & C. Clifton. (2004). Privacy-preserving distributed mining of association rules on horizontally partitioned data. *IEEE Transactions on Knowledge and Data Engineering*, 16(9), 1026–1037.
42. Liu, J., M.T. Ozsu, & S. Zhao. (2019). The big data lifecycle: A survey of state-of-the-art research and open challenges. *ACM Computing Surveys*, 52(5), 1–34.
43. Lu, Y., Q. Li, Y. Li, & Y. Liu. (2019). Secure data sharing in big data era. *Journal of Physics: Conference Series*, 1233(1), 012056.
44. Lu, Y., Y. Wen, & G. Li. (2020). A survey on big data processing frameworks. *Journal of Parallel and Distributed Computing*, 143, 1–18.
45. Liu, T., M. Zhang, Z. Zhang, & Q. Xie. (2021). A survey on BD privacy and security. *IEEE Transactions on Big Data*, 7(2), 343–362.
46. Lin, X., Y. Gao, & L. Ma. (2021). A survey on BD S & P. *Journal of Big Data*, 8(1), 1–22.
47. Li, R., J. Li, & L. Zhang. (2021). A survey of BD privacy preservation techniques. *Journal of Network and Computer Applications*, 184, 1–20.
48. Liu, Y., S. Wang, & D. Yu. (2021). A survey on BD S & P protection. *IEEE Access*, 9, 43903–43916.
49. Lin, W. et al. (2021). A hybrid encryption scheme for secure BD transmission in the cloud. *IEEE Transactions on Services Computing*, 14(4), 689–702.
50. Liu, J., M.T. Ozsu, & S. Zhao. (2019). The big data lifecycle: A survey of state-of-the-art research and open challenges. *ACM Computing Surveys*, 52(5), 1–34.
51. Li, N., T. Li, S. Venkatasubramanian, & Y. Mao. (2007). Secure data aggregation in wireless sensor networks: A survey. *Journal of Computer Security*, 15(6), 643–668.
52. Liu, Y., Y. Zhu, M. Gao, & Y. Dai. (2017). Security and privacy in big data. *ACM Transactions on Big Data*, 3(4), 1–34.
53. Mahmood, Z., M.H. Rehmani, & N. Riaz. (2018). Big data for cyber security: A systematic literature review. *Journal of Big Data*, 5(1), 1–40.

54. Mohanty, S.P., J.M. Jagadeesh, & S.K. Srivatsa. (2019). Big data: A review of storage, processing, and security issues. *ACM Computing Surveys* (*CSUR*), 51(5), 1–36.
55. Machanavajjhala, A., D. Kifer, J. Gehrke, & M. Venkitasubramaniam. (2006). l-diversity: Privacy beyond k-anonymity. *ACM Transactions on Knowledge Discovery from Data* (*TKDD*), 1(1), 3.
56. Majumder, P., & M. Islam. (2018). Security and privacy challenges of big data: A review. *Journal of Big Data*, 5(1), 164.
57. Gupta, M.K., S.K. Pandey, & A. Gupta. (2022). HADOOP: An open source framework for big data. In: *2022 3rd International Conference on Intelligent Engineering and Management* (*ICIEM*), London, United Kingdom, pp. 708–711. doi: 10.1109/ICIEM54221.2022.9853179.
58. Obermeyer, Z., & T.H. Lee. (2017). Lost in thought: The limits of the human mind and the future of medicine. *New England Journal of Medicine*, 377(13), 1209–1211.
59. Park, S.S., S. Lee, & S.H. Park. (2021). Privacy-preserving data analysis for big data: A review. *Journal of Big Data*, 8(1), 1–22.
60. Park, S.S., & S. Kim. (2021). BD S & P issues in the healthcare industry: A review. *Journal of Medical Systems*, 45(1), 1–17.
61. Ramya, T., & A. Amuthan. (2018). A survey on data masking techniques for privacy-preserving data mining. *Journal of Ambient Intelligence and Humanized Computing*, 9(4), 1145–1161.
62. Shukla, S., & S. Singh. (2016). Security and privacy in big data: A review. *Procedia Computer Science*, 78, 491–496.
63. Bao, R., Chen, Z., & Obaidat, M.S. (2018). Challenges and techniques in Big data security and privacy: A review. *Security and Privacy*, 1(4), e13.
64. Sweeney, L. (2002). K-anonymity: A model for protecting privacy. *International Journal of Uncertainty, Fuzziness and Knowledge-Based Systems*, 10(05), 557–570.
65. Tang, X., Y. Wu, & X. Lu. (2019). Big data security and privacy protection: Status and challenges. *Journal of Communications and Information Networks*, 4(2), 43–55.
66. Wang, Y., L. Chen, Y. Li, Y. Li, & Q. Wu. (2019). Protecting privacy in the data generation phase: A review. *Journal of Computer and System Sciences*, 101, 135–151. https://doi.org/10.1016/j.jcss.2018.11.011.
67. Wang, Y., L. Huang, & Y. Zhang. (2018). A review on big data challenges and opportunities. *Journal of Information Processing Systems*, 14(4), 861–874. https://doi.org/10.3745/JIPS.04.0072.
68. Weng, J., E.P. Lim, J. Jiang, & Q. He. (2017). Twitter user geolocation prediction using a unified text and network model. *ACM Transactions on Intelligent Systems and Technology* (*TIST*), 8(1), 1–21.
69. Wang, X., Y. Qian, H. Liang, & W. Xu. (2016). A survey on security in big data. *Journal of Big Data*, 3(1), 1–21.
70. Wu, J., T. Wu, & L. Zhu. (2017). A survey of security issues in big data. *IEEE Access*, 5, 27417–27438.
71. Wu, J., N. Xie, & W. Huang. (2018). Data S & P protection issues in cloud computing. *Journal of Network and Computer Applications*, 103, 1–13.
72. Wang, D., Z. Li, W. Li, X. Sun, & X. Guan. (2021). A survey of BD P & S technologies in healthcare. *Journal of Healthcare Engineering*, 2021, 1–13.
73. Xie, K., J. Zhang, X. Qian, H. Song, & L. Chen. (2021). A survey on BD S & P preservation in cloud computing. *Journal of Ambient Intelligence and Humanized Computing*, 12(6), 5451–5468.
74. Xue, Y. et al. (2021). Preserving data privacy in BD analytics: A multi-party computation approach. *IEEE Transactions on Services Computing*, 14(2), 285–298.

75. Xiang, Z., Q. Du, Y. Ma, & W. Fan. (2017). A comparative analysis of major online review platforms: Implications for social media analytics in hospitality and tourism. *Tourism Management*, 58, 51–65.
76. Ye, F., R. Bai, & X. Zhang. (2019). A survey on BD S & P preservation. *Journal of Ambient Intelligence and Humanized Computing*, 10(5), 1935–1952.
77. Yang, J., H. Gao, Z. Wu, & F. Liu. (2021). A comprehensive review on BD security. *IEEE Transactions on Industrial Informatics*, 17(1), 124–137.
78. Yang, J., J. Li, & J. Wu. (2019). Privacy preserving in big data processing: A survey. *Journal of Network and Computer Applications*, 127, 48–63. https://doi.org/10.1016/j.jnca.2018.11.021
79. Yao, A.C. (1982). Protocols for secure computations. *Proceedings of the IEEE*, 70(6), 728–741.
80. Zaidi, S.A.R., M.Z. Shafiq, & S.A.A. Shah. (2017). Big data security and privacy: A review. *Journal of Big Data*, 4(1), 1–20.
81. Zikopoulos, P., C. Eaton, D. DeRoos, T. Deutsch, & G. Lapis. (2016). *Understanding Big Data: Analytics for Enterprise Class Hadoop and Streaming Data*. McGraw Hill Professional.
82. Zhang, Y., X. Liu, & X. Zhou. (2019). BD S & P protection: Challenges and opportunities. *Journal of Cybersecurity*, 5(1), tyz005.
83. Zhang, D., J. Li, L. Li, Y. Li, & J. Li. (2021). S & P in big data: A survey. *International Journal of Distributed Sensor Networks*, 17(1), 1–19.
84. Zhang, Y., J. Ma, S.S. Park, & X. Wu. (2021). A survey of BD P & S challenges. *Future Generation Computer Systems*, 119, 1–16.

12 | Investigating Nanorobotics: Metamorphosing Healthcare with Manufactured Insights and Efficient Data Preservation

Deepika Yadav[1*], Amrita Rai[2]

[1] EEE Department, SRM University, Delhi NCR-Sonipat

[2] Department of Electronics and Communication Engineering, Galgotias College of Engineering and Technology, Greater Noida, India

1. Introduction

Nanotechnology, which works at the atomic and molecular level, investigates uses that go beyond theory to real-world application. The scale of this scientific frontier is encapsulated in a nanometer, which is a billionth of a meter, or around 1/80,000th of the diameter of a human hair or ten times that of a hydrogen atom. Accurately measuring, manipulating, and assembling matter on a scale of 1–100 nm is the crucial difficulty. Achieving cost-effectiveness in nanotechnology hinges on the automation of molecular manufacturing. This necessitates the deployment of robotic devices known as nanorobots. This review delves into the burgeoning field of nanorobotics, its applications, and the unique properties and dynamical laws that differentiate it from its macro-scale counterpart. While some concerns about nanorobots capable of uncontrolled replication have surfaced, proponents argue that such scenarios are not inherent to productive nanotechnology. The emphasis switches to molecular robots, which are modeled after the nanoscale machinery found in nature. The possibilities of employing biological components such as proteins and DNA to produce dependable and effective nanodevices are investigated. The potential for developing nanorobotics for a variety of uses lies in the synthesis of natural elements in synthetic environments.

Nanotechnology operates at the atomic and molecular scale, investigating applications that extend beyond theoretical frameworks to practical implementations. This scientific frontier is defined by the nanometer, a billionth of a meter, which is approximately 1/80,000th the diameter of a human hair or ten times that of a

*Corresponding author: deepika.y@srmuniversity.ac.in

DOI: 10.1201/9781003560012-12

hydrogen atom. A primary challenge in this field lies in the precise measurement, manipulation, and assembly of matter within a range of 1–100 nm. Achieving cost-effectiveness in nanotechnology is largely contingent on the automation of molecular manufacturing, which necessitates the use of robotic devices known as nanorobots.

This review explores the rapidly evolving domain of nanorobotics, its diverse applications, and the unique properties and dynamical principles that distinguish it from its macro-scale counterparts. Recent studies highlight advancements in the design of biomimetic nanorobots capable of targeted drug delivery, significantly improving therapeutic outcomes in cancer treatment and other diseases. Additionally, researchers have been investigating the integration of machine learning algorithms in nanorobotics to enhance the efficiency and precision of these devices in real-time healthcare applications.

While concerns regarding the potential for uncontrolled replication of nanorobots persist, advocates argue that such risks are not intrinsic to the advancement of productive nanotechnology. The focus is increasingly shifting toward molecular robots inspired by the nanoscale machinery found in biological systems. Ongoing research emphasizes the utilization of biological components, such as proteins and DNA, to create reliable and efficient nanodevices. This chapter aims to highlight the transformative potential of nanorobotics in healthcare, underscoring the synthesis of natural elements within synthetic environments and their implications for efficient data preservation and innovative healthcare solutions.

1.1 Nanorobots in Medicine: Improving Care and Preserving Information

Nanorobots have the potential to completely transform medical care by providing patients suffering from a variety of illnesses with innovative remedies. This promises cutting-edge treatment interventions and represents a major turning point in medical history. The latest developments in biomolecular computing are a promising first step toward more complicated nano processors in the future. Research is now being conducted in two areas: biosensor development and the development of nanokinetic devices that are necessary to enable the movement and operation of medical nanorobots.

These initiatives promise increased accuracy and effectiveness in the diagnosis and treatment of a variety of medical diseases, and they hold the key to realizing the full potential of nanorobots in the medical field. As these technological frontiers develop, the combination of medical science and nanorobots becomes a powerful force that has the potential to completely change the healthcare industry and bring about a period of previously unheard-of medical breakthroughs [1–4]. Nanorobot deployment has the potential to advance biological interventions by enabling less invasive surgical techniques.

These little robotic agents may play a key role in providing patients with proactive healthcare by continuously monitoring critical body systems. Furthermore, they can greatly improve the efficacy of treatment by facilitating the early identification of potentially dangerous illnesses, which leads to quicker and more effective therapeutic actions [5]. For example, nanorobots can be used to attach to migratory white blood cells or inflammatory cells, which will enable them to get to the inflammatory areas faster and aid in the healing process.

In the realm of chemotherapy, nanorobots offer a precise method for administering chemical dosages to combat cancer, and a similar strategy could be employed for the targeted delivery of anti-HIV drugs. Additionally, nanorobots hold the potential to execute specific chemical reactions within the human body, functioning as auxiliary devices for the treatment of injured organs. Nanorobots could potentially be employed to monitor diabetes and regulate glucose levels in patients [6]. They could be deployed to locate and disintegrate kidney stones. Additionally, a crucial prospective function of medical nanorobots involves identifying atherosclerotic lesions in narrowed blood vessels, particularly in the coronary circulation, and addressing them through mechanical, chemical, or pharmacological means. Organic nanorobots, also known as bio-nanorobots, operate based on ATP and DNA molecular machines [7]. In this scenario, the concept involves advancing ribonucleic acid and adenosine triphosphate devices, and even employing modified microorganisms to accomplish biomolecular computation, sensing, and actuation for nanorobots. An alternative avenue for creating molecular machines is through inorganic nanorobots, the development of which relies on tailored nano electronics. Compared to bio-nanorobots, inorganic nanorobots could attain significantly greater complexity in integrated nano-scale components. Several studies explore methods to facilitate the fabrication of inorganic nanorobots. One potential approach involves utilizing new diamonded rigid materials, which could contribute to the development of novel materials for inorganic nanorobots. Our approach in this work centres

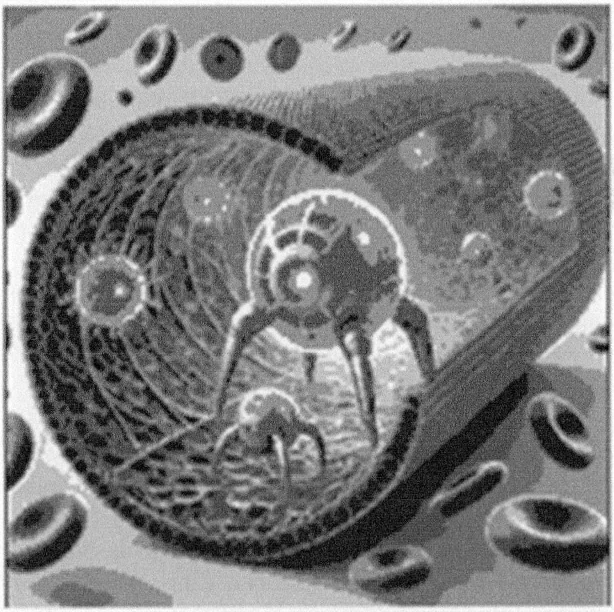

Figure 1: An approach to targeted medical applications using nanobots that navigate through blood vessels.

on the Nano-Build Hardware Integrated System (Nanobhis) [8, 9]. It signifies a collaborative compilation of established methodologies and novel approaches within nanotechnology, with the objective of producing nanorobots [10]. It involves utilizing 3D simulation and design for manufacturing, incorporating analyses of integrated nano electronics. The complexity of nanorobot manufacturing may arise from innovative methods in fabrication, computation, sensing, and manipulation. Real-time 3D prototyping tools play a crucial role in aiding nanotechnology development and can significantly influence the adoption of innovative manufacturing techniques. Simulation allows the anticipation of the performance of emerging nano devices and contributes to the design of nano mechatronics, facilitating the testing of control and automation strategies.

Figure 1 illustrates nanobots traveling through a blood vessel, showing their potential for advanced medical applications. In these microscopic machines, drugs are delivered directly to diseased cells, blockages are cleared, or tissues are repaired. In addition to minimizing side effects, their precision enhances treatment effectiveness. In terms of nanotechnology and how it is incorporated into healthcare, this concept represents a significant leap forward.

2. Metamorphosing Cancer Treatment: The Role of Artificial Intelligence and Data Storage in Nanorobotics

The early detection and diagnosis of cancers pose significant challenges, often resulting in high mortality rates when detected at later stages. To address this issue, there is an urgent need for the development of more sensitive and effective diagnostic and therapeutic methods for cancer treatment. Nanobots, emerging as a promising application of nanomedicines, are at the forefront of interdisciplinary research, leveraging nanotechnology to create functional molecular/nanosized machines. Particularly in the realm of cancer diagnosis and treatment, nanobots have progressed from theoretical concepts to practical applications, transitioning from *in vitro* experiments to *in vivo* implementations. This review explores recent advancements in the application of nanobots for cancer treatment, focusing on key features such as drug delivery, tumor sensing, diagnosis, targeted therapy, and minimally invasive surgery. Notwithstanding these advancements, there are still obstacles to overcome, and we go over possible avenues for future study to advance the use of nanobots to transform cancer therapies. More advanced medical nanobots with several functions, like real nano submarines roaming the bloodstream, are anticipated in the future.

Nanorobots have a wide range of possible medical uses, from treating diseases like Alzheimer's disease to reducing the negative effects of chemotherapy. Sensors, energy supply, and data transfer are just a few of the systems that researchers have greatly improved over the last ten years and are essential to the practical development of nanorobots. Looking ahead a few generations, cancer patients may be offered a ground-breaking substitute for conventional chemotherapy.

Patients might be injected with specialized nanorobots rather than suffering the extensive damage that radiation therapy does, which affects both cancer and healthy cells. By identifying and eliminating cancer cells specifically, these nanorobots would successfully eradicate the disease at its source without endangering healthy cells. A straightforward injection would be the only invasive procedure required of the patient, and the molecular devices functioning inside them would quickly improve their health without the patient even realizing they were there.

Early diagnosis, particularly the identification of cancer before metastasis, is crucial to the efficacy of cancer treatment. Creating focused medication delivery strategies to reduce chemotherapy side effects is another essential component of a successful course of treatment. Because of their ability to navigate, nanorobots—which function as blood-borne devices—are essential in tackling these cancer therapy-related issues. In particular, nanorobots with chemical biosensors integrated into them can help identify tumor cells in a patient's body early on.

Utilizing integrated nano sensors, these nanorobots aim to identify the intensity of E-cadherin signals. To facilitate this application in cancer therapy, a hardware architecture based on nano bioelectronics is proposed. The effectiveness of this model is assessed through real-time 3D simulation, providing valuable insights and conclusions.

This idea emphasizes how robotics and nanotechnology driven by AI might be used to identify and treat cancer is shown in Figure 2. AI improves diagnostic accuracy by using sophisticated imaging and data processing to detect cancer cells early. The development of microscopic robots or particles that can target and eliminate cancer cells while preserving healthy tissue is made possible by nanotechnology.

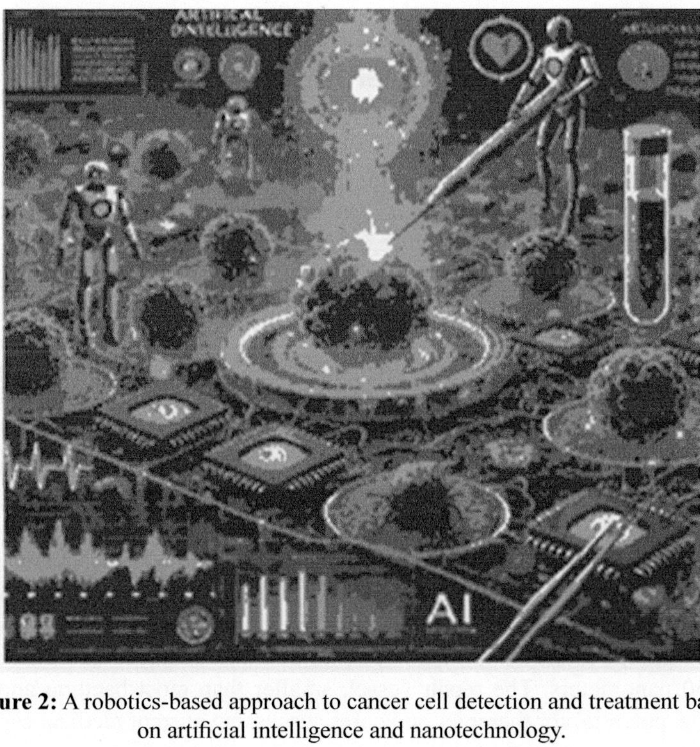

Figure 2: A robotics-based approach to cancer cell detection and treatment based on artificial intelligence and nanotechnology.

When combined, these technologies provide a revolutionary method of effective and individualized cancer treatment.

The blood-brain barrier (BBB) holds significant importance for clinicians aiming to maintain homeostatic function in health and deliver theranostics for brain cancer and various neurological diseases. Efforts to replicate the structural hierarchy and *in situ* biochemical signalling of the BBB neurovascular unit within *in vitro* modules have been prominent. Advancements in micro engineered perfusion systems and the development of 3D cellular and organoid cultures have significantly propelled BBB research in neuropharmacology. This review delves into the re-examination of nanoparticles based on biomolecular engineering, transforming them into nanorobots or nanobots capable of maneuvering, controlling, targeting, and delivering theranostic payloads across the cellular BBB. Case studies exploring payload delivery in brain tumors and neurological disorders (e.g., Alzheimer's disease, Parkinson's disease, multiple sclerosis, etc.) are briefly outlined. The review also addresses opportunities and challenges in nanorobot development and design. Additionally, it discusses the potential partnership of computationally powered machine learning (ML) tools and artificial intelligence (AI) with robotics to predict and design the next generation of nanorobots capable of interacting and delivering across the BBB without causing damage, toxicity, or malfunctions. This review serves as a valuable reference for multidisciplinary professionals, including clinicians, roboticists, chemists, and bioengineers involved in cutting-edge pharmaceutical design and BBB research [11, 12].

3. Metamorphosing Gene Therapy: Enhancing Treatment with AI-Powered Nanorobots and Data Security

Medical nanorobots exhibit the capability to effectively address genetic diseases by comparing the molecular structures of DNA and proteins within cells to predefined reference structures. Upon identifying irregularities, nanorobots can correct them or implement desired modifications directly. Chromosomal replacement therapy, in certain cases, proves more efficient than traditional methods for repair. Operating within the nucleus of a human cell, an assembler-built repair vessel conducts genetic maintenance. The nanomachine extends a super coil of DNA between its lower arms, gently pulling the unwound strand through an opening in its prow for detailed analysis. Simultaneously, the upper arms detach regulatory proteins from the chain, placing them in an intake port for further manipulation. This intricate process showcases the precision and potential of nanorobots in genetic therapy [13, 14].

The comparison of molecular structures in both DNA and proteins involves referencing a database stored in a larger nanocomputer situated outside the nucleus and linked to the cell-repair vessel through a communications link. Any irregularities detected in either structure are corrected, and the proteins are reattached to the DNA chain. This results in the DNA chain recoiling into its original form, with a diameter of only 50 nanometers. The repair vessel, smaller than most bacteria and viruses, exhibits the potential for therapies and cures surpassing current medical capabilities.

With trillions of these nanorobots circulating in a patient's bloodstream, "internal medicine" gains new significance, enabling the molecular-level targeting of diseases such as cancer, viral infections, and arteriosclerosis.

Genetic engineering and DNA manipulation are revolutionized by AI-powered robotics, which automates intricate procedures with unmatched accuracy as shown in Figure 3. With the use of technologies like CRISPR, these systems are able to accurately modify genetic data, identify certain gene sequences, and evaluate genetic data. By forecasting results and reducing mistakes, AI increases productivity and opens the door to advances in synthetic biology, crop resilience, and the treatment of genetic illnesses. Innovation in genetic research and applications is accelerated by this combination of robots and AI.

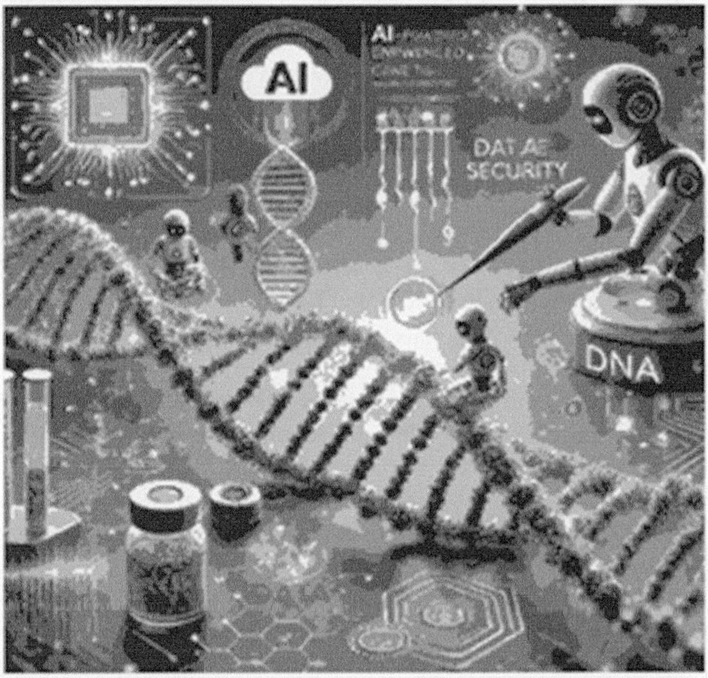

Figure 3: Genetic engineering and DNA manipulation with AI-powered robotics.

Gene therapy, involving the introduction of nucleic acids like DNA and RNA into host cells, is poised to revolutionize the treatment of various diseases. The development has been accelerated by the discovery of CRISPR/Cas technology, allowing precise genome editing. Despite advancements in gene delivery and various viral and non-viral vectors, the challenge lies in efficient non-viral systems with low cellular toxicity. The application of cutting-edge technologies, including AI, presents an opportunity to address this challenge. In this review, we explore the potential of AI, includingML, neural networks, expert systems, deep learning, computer vision, and robotics, in designing targeted gene delivery vehicles. We discuss AI's role in overcoming extracellular and intracellular barriers using viral mimicry strategies, enhancing CRISPR/Cas systems, developing novel nanobots, and optimizing mRNA vaccine carriers. The emerging sector of computational nanobiosensing aims to improve *in vivo* targeting and understanding of protein-induced biological gradients, requiring expertise in medical imaging, sensing, natural and evolutionary computing, micro- and nanorobotics, and nanomaterial-based pharmaceutical development.

4. Metamorphosing Brain Aneurysm Treatment: AI-Driven Nanorobots and the Significance of Data Preservation

The nanorobot developed for brain aneurysm prognosis leverages computational nanotechnology for the prototyping of medical devices. The process involves three primary aspects: Equipment prototyping, manufacturing approach, and inside-body transduction. Computational nanotechnology serves as a crucial tool in rapidly and effectively developing nanorobots, facilitating thorough investigations into key aspects of medical instrumentation and device prototyping. This approach draws parallels with the methodologies employed in various industries, including the construction of racing cars, airplanes, submarines, integrated circuits (ICs), and medical devices [15]. This approach can now be employed to advance the development and research of medical nanorobots [16–18]. The manufacturing technology for nanorobot production should be integrated as a biochip device. This involves incorporating new materials, photonics, and nanobioelectronics into the nanorobot architecture. Inside-body transductions rely on parameters such as cell morphology, microbiology, and proteomics to determine nanorobot morphology and interaction within the body. Changes in chemical gradients and telemetric instrumentation are employed for medical prognosis, activating nanorobots based on proteomic overexpression [19]. As outlined in the paper, these three elements form the essential components needed to progress the development and application of medical nanorobotics. In brain aneurysm prognosis, nanorobots must monitor vascular endothelial injuries before a subarachnoid hemorrhage transpires. These alterations in chemical concentration serve as cues for guiding nanorobots to identify brain aneurysms in their early stages of development. Given the minuscule size of biomolecules, they are challenging to reliably detect. Hence, the nanorobot relies on chemical nanobiosensor contact to detect these biomolecules [20]. The primary morphological characteristics associated with brain aneurysms are considered as the basis for modeling the investigation of nanorobot sensing and interaction within the distorted blood vessel [21, 22]. Intracranial concentrations of NOS are minimal, and false positives can occur due to positive functions of N-oxide with semicarbazone (pNOS). Cells and nanorobots continuously enter one end of the workspace along with the fluid flow. The nanorobots must identify protein overexpression, and the setup for sensing and control activation can be adjusted for different values, such as modifying the detection thresholds. Any nanorobots not responding within the workspace are treated as if they did not detect any signal, allowing them to flow with the fluid as it leaves the workspace. If the nanorobot's electrochemical sensor detects

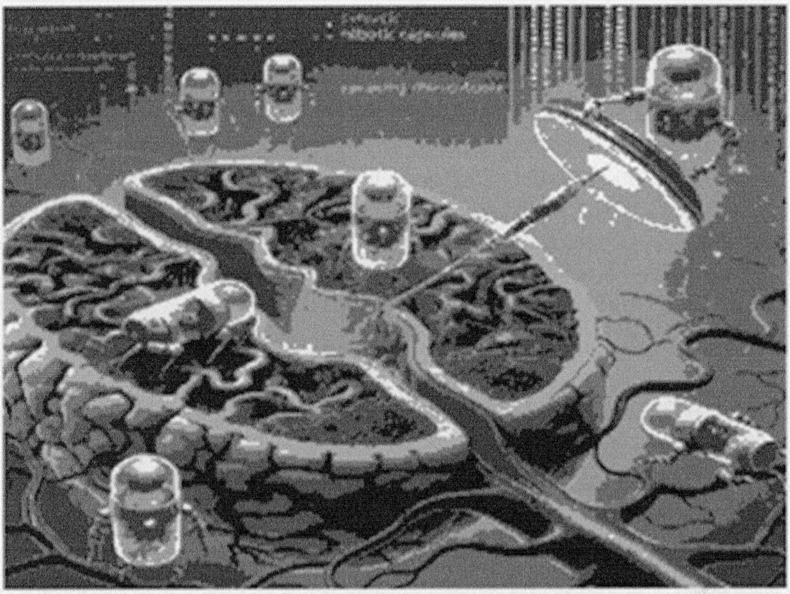

Figure 4: A new approach to healthcare at the microscopic level using nanorobotics.

NOS in low quantities or within a normal gradient, it generates a weak signal lower than 50 nA. [23–25].

By working at the minuscule level to solve medical problems with previously unheard-of precision, nanorobotics is transforming the healthcare industry. These tiny devices can move through the body to carry out precise surgical procedures, targeted medicine distribution, and real-time diagnostics. Nanorobotics has the potential to revolutionize disease management and make revolutionary strides in customized medicine possible by reducing harm to healthy tissues and improving treatment precision as shown in Figure 4.

In this scenario, the nanorobot disregards the NOS concentration, assuming it falls within the expected levels of intracranial NOS. For practical threshold determination in medical prognosis, aiming to avoid noise distortions and achieve higher resolution, the model interprets each instance where the cell phone has received at least a total of 100 nanorobots with higher proteomic signal transduction as strong evidence of intracranial aneurysm. Upon activation, the nanorobots' sensors also indicate their respective positions at the moment of detecting a high NOS protein concentration, providing valuable information about the vessel bulb location and dimensions. Cerebral aneurysms pose potential life-threatening risks and are traditionally treated with catheter-guided coiling or neurosurgical clipping interventions. This study proposes a helically shaped magnetic micro-robot that can be untetheredly steered by magnetic fields, offering a novel coiling approach. Experimental navigation of the micro-robot through an additively manufactured phantom of a human cerebral aneurysm is demonstrated. Magnetic fields are applied using a magnetic particle imaging (MPI) scanner, allowing navigation and tomographic visualization within the same machine. MPI provides a visualization accuracy of 0.68 mm during the actuation process, enabling angiograms without radiation exposure. First *in vitro* phantom experiments showcase the potential of robot-conducted treatment for cerebral aneurysms. Additionally, an innovative architecture for medical nanorobots is proposed as a precise tool for brain aneurysm instrumentation. Nanotubes with nanometer diameters and unique properties are studied for controlled activity at room temperature on dissociated cortical cultures, supporting a cerebral aneurysm. The study reveals that neurons and glial cells incubated with multi-walled carbon nanotubes (MWCNT) exhibit interconnected networks following the pattern of the MWCNT templates. The bridging involves axons or bundles of axons and dendrites, showcasing the potential of MWCNT in facilitating cellular connections for brain aneurysm treatment.

5. Metamorphosing Dentistry: Precision and Efficiency through AI-Enhanced Nanorobots with Data Preservation

The increasing interest in the future of dental applications has given rise to a new field known as Nano dentistry. Nanorobots play a role in oral analgesia, desensitizing teeth, manipulating tissue to realign and straighten irregularly positioned teeth, and enhancing the durability of teeth. The chapter elaborates on the applications of nano robots in preventive, restorative, and curative dental procedures [26, 27]. Nano dental techniques encompass various tissue engineering procedures for significant tooth repair. One key aspect involves the nanorobotic manufacturing and installation of a biologically autologous whole replacement tooth, incorporating both mineral and cellular components, thereby offering a comprehensive solution for dentition replacement therapy. Nano dentistry has introduced nano-structured composite materials, such as sapphire, which contribute to increased tooth durability and enhanced appearance. The upper enamel layers can be replaced with covalently bonded artificial materials, such as sapphire [28]. This material exhibits a hardness and failure strength 100–200 times greater than ceramic. Similar to enamel, sapphire is somewhat susceptible to acid corrosion. [29]. Sapphire serves as an excellent standard for a whitening sealant and cosmetic alternative. A novel restorative nanomaterial for enhancing tooth durability is nano-composites. These are created by aggregating discrete nanoparticles in a nanoscale manner, ensuring homogeneous distribution within resins or coatings to generate nano-composites [30, 31]. The nano-filler comprises alumina silicate powder with an average particle size of approximately 80 nm and a 1:4 ratio of alumina to silica. Possessing a refractive index of 1.503, the nano-filler exhibits superior hardness, modulus of elasticity, translucency, esthetic appeal, excellent color density, high polish, and a 50% reduction in filling shrinkage. These properties make them outperform conventional composites and seamlessly integrate with the natural tooth structure. AI stands as a transformative force in the medical field, bringing advancements that extend into dentistry. By improving preciseness and minimizing errors in dental operations, the incorporation of AI-driven technology has enabled computers to perform better than surgeons. Despite not yet being fully integrated into the dental industry, robotic devices have the potential to improve accuracy and creativity. The smooth integration of these technologies remains a problem for dentistry research, despite notable progress in other medical domains. Robotics has a significant impact on dentistry and is bringing forth modifications in treatment and diagnostic procedures.

Through accuracy, creativity, and automation, AI-powered dentistry is poised to revolutionize oral healthcare. Advanced AI algorithms may accurately interpret dental scans, and robotic equipment can help with precision operations like orthodontic corrections and implant insertion. By decreasing errors, enhancing treatment results, and optimizing workflows, these technologies improve patient care. A new age of efficiency and innovation in dental treatment is promised by this forward-thinking strategy as illustrated in Figure 5.

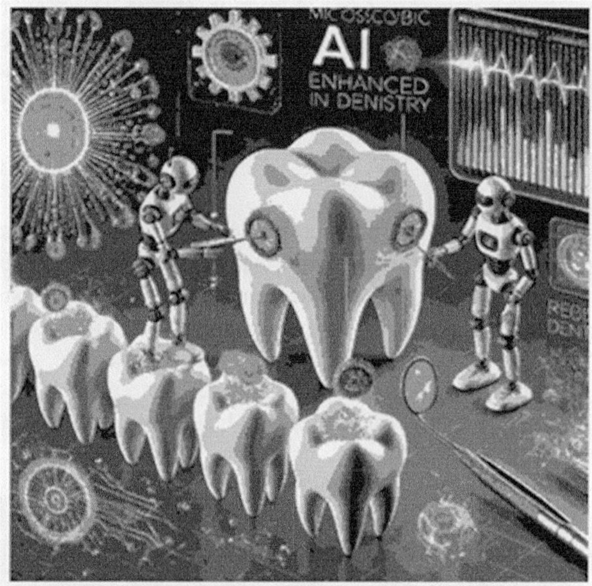

Figure 5: Dental Robotics and AI in the Future: Precision and Innovation.

Particularly in dental implantology, oral and maxillofacial surgery, prosthetics, restorative dentistry, endodontics, orthodontics, oral radiography, and dental education, autonomous robotic devices that can carry out activities on their own are transforming patient care. While acknowledging the promise, it's critical to address the existing constraints and project how dental robots will affect oral healthcare and the dental field in the future.

Another era in healthcare is being ushered in by the convergence of robotics and AI in dentistry. These quickly developing technologies improve decision-making, expedite processes, and increase practitioner and patient confidence. The use of ML in dentistry has sped up decision-making, resulting in less invasive and time-consuming procedures. The foreseeable future of dentistry will be shaped by AI's continued benefits in improving complete patient care and enabling precision, despite persistent misconceptions about the technology.

In conclusion, dentistry is poised for a revolution thanks to the rapidly evolving fields of robotics and AI. These technologies have the potential to enhance diagnostic precision, streamline processes, and deliver superior patient care when integrated into dental practices. Even while there are still issues, there are still efforts to go over them and move dentistry into a future where technology is essential to improve patient outcomes and innovation.

6. Metamorphosing Knee Replacement: The Role of Artificial Intelligence and Data Preservation in Nanorobot Technology

Nanotechnology is the manipulation of matter at the atomic, molecular, and supramolecular levels, and it has applications in many scientific fields, including molecular biology, health and medicine, materials, electronics, transportation, drugs and drug delivery, chemical sensing, space exploration, energy, the environment, sensors, diagnostics, microfabrication, organic chemistry, and biomaterials. Its effects extend to surgical specialties, altering the treatment of medical and surgical diseases.

The combination of data diagnostics and AI-driven nanorobotics is reshaping medicine and paving the way for revolutionary improvements in healthcare. AI-powered nanorobots can move through the human body to mend tissues, administer tailored therapies, or identify cellular illnesses. AI-driven diagnostics, on the other hand, use enormous volumes of medical data to deliver precise, real-time insights and predictive analytics. When combined, these technologies are opening the door to more proactive, effective, and individualized healthcare solutions as illustrated in Figure 6.

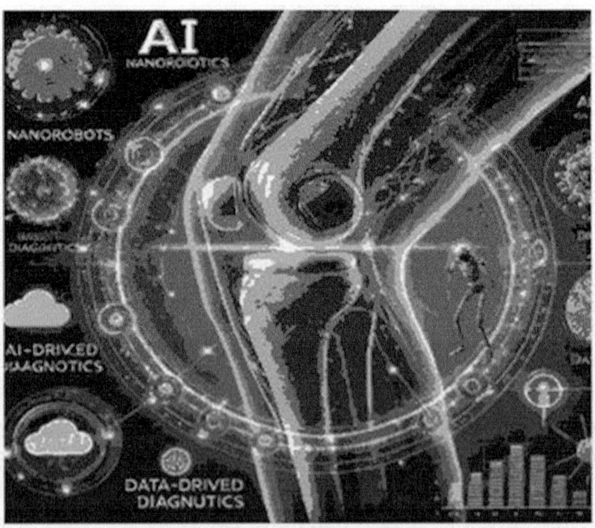

Figure 6: A look at the future of medicine using AI-driven nanorobotics and data diagnostics.

Advanced suture materials, imaging technologies, targeted drug therapy, novel visualization techniques, wound healing procedures, and surgical equipment are just a few of the clinical applications of nanotechnology in surgery.

Burn wounds and scar management are significant areas benefiting from nanotechnology. In orthopedic surgery, nanotechnology plays a crucial role in the prevention, diagnosis, and treatment of various conditions, contributing to functional recovery. In knee arthroplasty, AI-based tools enhance decision-making, surgical planning, and the accuracy and repeatability of procedures. While these advancements show promise, further clinical evidence is necessary to validate their benefits fully. Nanotechnology holds immense potential for sustained positive outcomes in various surgical specialties, including orthopedic surgery, in the years ahead.

7. Metamorphosing Drug Delivery: Artificial Intelligence and Data Preservation in Nanorobot Technology

Nanobots, equipped with precise navigation capabilities, efficiently deliver drugs to targeted or affected areas within the body, offering a potent treatment approach for various diseases. Their ability to penetrate tissues enhances their therapeutic effectiveness [30]. Typically, these nanobots are propelled and guided by either internal (endogenous) or external (exogenous) stimuli, directing them toward the specific area of interest within the body [31]. Wire-shaped magnetoelectric nanobots, crafted and designed, exhibit the capability to be precisely guided to specific locations through wireless magnetic fields. These nanobots are equipped to execute on-demand drug release to cells with the assistance of magneto-electric mechanisms [32]. Nanowire motors powered by ultrasound have been developed, utilizing a nanoporous gold segment.

Innovative breakthroughs like precision drug delivery and nanotechnology-based solutions are being propelled by the AI revolution in medicine. Targeted drug delivery methods that reduce side effects and increase efficacy are made possible by nanotechnology, while AI algorithms evaluate patient data to create customized treatment regimens. These developments guarantee that drugs precisely target particular cells or regions as illustrated in Figure 7.

The study demonstrated that the nanoporous gold structure can facilitate drug release controlled by Near-Infrared (NIR) light, leveraging photothermal effects [33]. A DNA nanobot was engineered with the capability to deliver molecular payloads to cells. Controlled by an aptamer-encoded logic gate, these nanobots exhibited responsiveness to a diverse range of signals, including cell surface markers [34]. Gold nanowires, when coupled with a cytokine-like tumor necrosis factor-alpha, can be precisely transported along a defined trajectory or orientation. This movement is achieved through electrophoretic and dielectrophoretic forces, enabling targeted delivery to a specific location with subcellular resolution. This capability promotes the control of signalling events at the single-cell level, showcasing the potential for advanced manipulation in cellular environments [35].

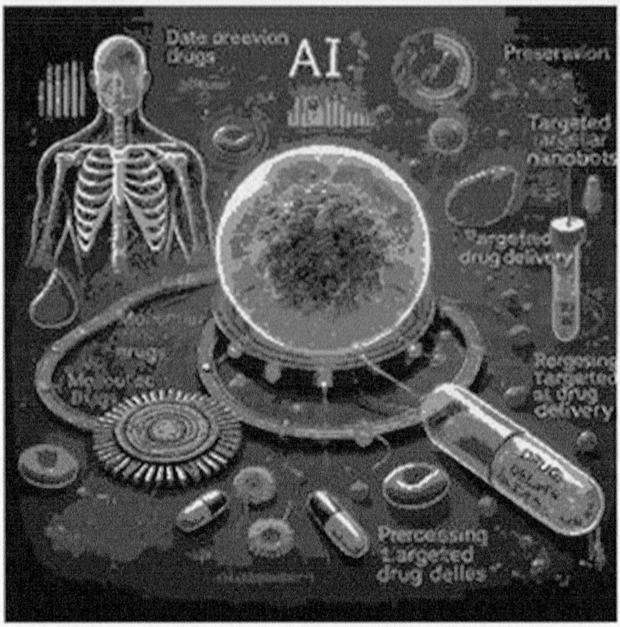

Figure 7: AI Disruption in Medicine: Nanotech Solutions and Precision Drug Delivery.

8. Metamorphosing Surgery: Artificial Intelligence-Powered Nanorobots with Enhanced Data Preservation

Robots were introduced as a solution to problems associated with complex surgical procedures, and for extending the capabilities of human surgeons. Robot-assisted surgery is a rapidly evolving field that allows doctors to perform a variety of minimally-invasive procedures with high precision, flexibility, and control [36, 37]. Nanobots target many specific health problems as they can navigate to tissues which are hard to reach in the human body. For addressing the limitations of the current surgical procedures and for precision surgery, recent nanobots have shown big promises [38, 39]. Untethered nanorobotic tools, ranging from nanodrillers to microgrippers and microbullets, offer unique capabilities for minimally invasive surgery. Nanobots offer major advantages for high precision minimally invasive surgery since their size is compatible with the small biological entities that they treat. The moving nanobots with nanoscale surgical components are powered by diverse energy sources and are able to directly penetrate or retrieve cellular tissues for precision surgery. They can navigate through the body's narrowest capillaries and perform procedures down to the cellular level. A set of responsive microgrippers have been developed that can be actuated autonomously by diverse environmental factors and used as minimally invasive microsurgical tools [40]. These can subsequently move out of the capillary tube with the captured cells in its grasp, demonstrating its strength for performing an *in vitro* tissue biopsy. Acoustically-triggered vaporization of perfluorocarbon fuel was used for developing tubular microscale cannons capable of loading and firing nano bullets at remarkable speeds [41]. These could be used to eject high speed nano bullets and shoot a wide range of payloads deep into diseased tissues. By choosing appropriate propulsion methods and using real-time localization and mapping with a robust control system, surgical nanobots can be improved so that they penetrate through the tissues and sense specific targets.

AI-driven nanorobotics, which provide previously unheard-of control and precision, is poised to transform surgery and healthcare. Under AI guidance, these tiny robots can carry out intricate surgical procedures with less invasiveness, speeding up recuperation and enhancing results. They can move around the body to remove tumors, restore tissues, or administer medications directly to the afflicted areas. This technology has the potential to completely transform healthcare in the future by improving the effectiveness, efficiency, and personalization of treatments as illustrated in Figure 8.

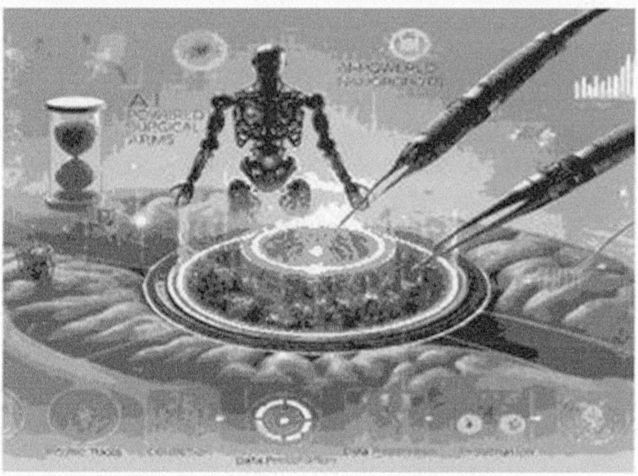

Figure 8: AI-Driven nanorobotics: The future of healthcare and precision surgery.

9. Metamorphosing Medical Applications: The Role of Artificial Intelligence-based Nano Robots in Data Preservation

In our current era, approximately one-third of the global population grapples with various healthcare challenges, necessitating early and accurate diagnoses crucial for effective medical interventions. Existing image processing algorithms, despite their prevalence, often fall short in delivering highly effective results for nerve and material detection. There are possible hazards associated with the introduction of sensor-based technologies that use nanosensors placed inside the body. A breakthrough technology that is incredibly small is suggested as a solution to these issues. A revolutionary method for providing thorough and effective treatments is provided by the use of nanorobots into medical applications.

The difficulties with traditional methods are addressed by nanorobots, which are delivered via single injections. Their installation guarantees early diagnosis, averting preventable fatalities.

Furthermore, subject to design considerations, nanorobots are notable for their flexible cost of components and ease of installation. The use of nanorobots enables people to remotely check on their health, which is very useful in hectic situations. Nanorobotic technology improves the efficacy of medical tests and devices, primarily focusing on monitoring factors associated with tissue loss, and opens the door to a revolution in healthcare.

Advances in data security, age reversal, and cellular repair are being propelled by the AI revolution in healthcare. By encouraging the healing of damaged cells and tissues, AI algorithms are facilitating advances in regenerative medicine and may even be able to reverse the effects of aging. Simultaneously, AI improves data security by protecting patient data and guaranteeing privacy through sophisticated monitoring and encryption methods. When combined, these developments are opening the door to a healthcare system that is more secure, individualized, and robust as illustrated in Figure 9.

Figure 9: Artificial intelligence upheaval in medical services: Cell fix, maturing inversion, and information security.

Robotics, driven by AI, is revolutionizing diagnostics and precision medicine by providing unparalleled efficiency and accuracy. Large volumes of medical data can be analyzed by these intelligent systems, allowing for early disease identification and patient-specific treatment strategies. By increasing surgical precision, robotics lowers risks and improves results. AI is influencing the direction of medicine by fusing robotic accuracy with data processing power to create more efficient, timely, and tailored treatments as illustrated in Figure 10.

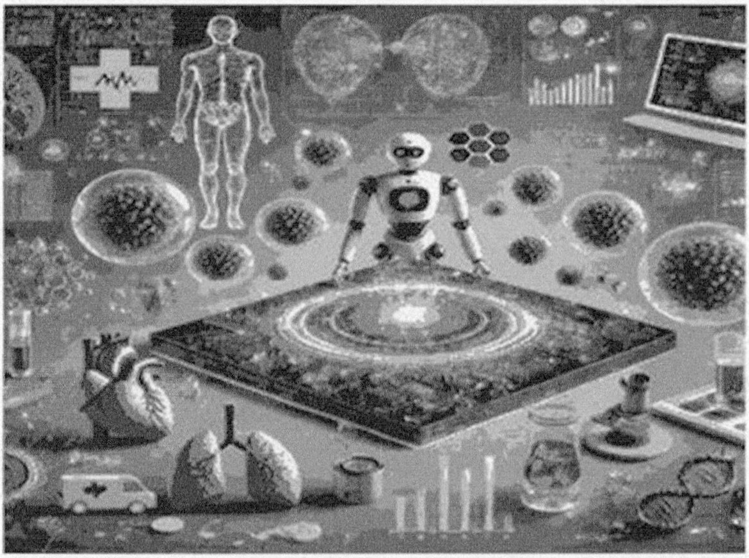

Figure 10: Artificial intelligence fuelled advanced mechanics: The eventual fate of accuracy medication and diagnostics.

10. Concluding Reflections: Pioneering the Future with AI-Integrated Nano Robots and Data Preservation

A paradigm shift driven by improvements in manufacturing technologies is represented by the incorporation of nanotechnology into medical diagnostics and treatments, especially in the treatment of diabetes and cancer. This chapter has highlighted the inventive potential of nanorobots, which hold forth the hope of reversing cellular-level aging processes and curing diseases. Nanorobots are emerging as potential industrial applications in addition to medical ones, offering customized therapies with improved effectiveness and fewer adverse effects.

In the near future in which nanorobots are essential, the continued growth of molecular nanotechnology is the key to improving the speed, comfort, and efficacy of medical treatments while also minimizing danger, expense, and invasiveness. Nanorobots have enormous potential to transform healthcare and the treatment of disease, despite the fact that the idea may sound like science fiction. This area creates new opportunities for extensive research, changing the dynamics of the industry and encouraging cooperation between the biotech, pharmaceutical, diagnostic, and healthcare sectors.

Nanotechnology is anticipated to have a big impact on product development and marketing interactions in the healthcare sector, as well as on human life. Nanomedicine holds the promise of earlier diagnosis, better treatment, and improved follow-up care by emphasizing on important diseases that affect the aging population, such as diabetes, cancer, cardiovascular disease, and neurological disorders. Using a thorough molecular understanding of diseases, nanomedicine's transformative promise extends to a more individualized approach. The incorporation of AI-powered nanorobots is a trailblazing development that is poised to transform healthcare and usher in a new era of medical advancement.

References

1. Ummat, A., A. Dubey, G. Sharma, & C. Mavroidis. (2005). Bio-nanorobotics: A field inspired by nature. In: Y. Bar-Cohen (Ed.), *Biomimetics: Biologically Inspired Technologies* (pp. 483–523). CRC Press.
2. Wang, J. (2009). Can man-made nanomachines compete with natural biomotors? *ACS Nano*, 3(1), 4–9.
3. Cale, T.S., J-Q. Lu, & R.J. Gutmann. (2008). Three-dimensional integration in microelectronics: Motivation, processing, and thermomechanical modeling. *Chemical Engineering Communications*, 195(8), 847–888.
4. Couvreur, P., & C. Vauthier. (2006). Nanotechnology: Intelligent design to treat complex disease. *Pharmaceutical Research*, 23, 1417–1450.
5. Cavalcanti, A., R.A. Freitas, Jr., & L.C. Kretly. (2004). Nanorobotics control design: A practical approach tutorial. In: *Proc. ASME 28th Biennial Mechanisms and Robotics Conference*, Salt Lake City, Utah, USA.
6. Cui, Y., Q. Wei, Q., H. Park, & C.M. Lieber. (2001). Nanowire nanosensors for highly sensitive and selective detection of biological and chemical species. *Science*, 293, 1289–1292.
7. Freitas, Jr. R.A. (2005). Current status of nanomedicine and medical nanorobotics. *J. Comput. Theor. Nanosci.*, 2, 1–25.
8. Cavalcanti, A., B. Shirinzadeh, R.A. Freitas Jr., & T. Hogg. T. (2008). Nanorobot architecture for medical target identification. *Nanotechnology*, 19, 015103.
9. Cavalcanti, A., B. Shirinzadeh, M. Zhang, & L.C. Kretly. (2008). Nanorobot hardware architecture for medical defense. *Sensors*, 8, 2932–2958.
10. Chau, R., B. Doyle, S. Datta, J. Kavalieros, & K. Zhang. (2007). Integrated nanoelectronics for the future. *Nature Materials*, 6, 810–812.
11. Fisher, B. (2008). Biological research in the evolution of cancer surgery: A personal perspective. *Cancer Research*, 68, 10007–10020.
12. Hill, C., A. Amodeo, J.V. Joseph, & H.R.H. Patel. (2008). Nano- and microrobotics: How far is the reality? *Expert Review of Anticancer Therapy*, 8, 1891–1897.
13. Adleman, L.M. (1996). On constructing a molecular computer. DNA based Computers II: Dimacs Workshop, Jun. 10–12. *Dimacs Series in Discrete Mathematics and Theoretical Computer Science*, 44. American Mathematical Society, 1–21.
14. Hamdi, M., A. Ferreira, G. Sharma, & C. Mavroidis. (2008). Prototyping bio-nanorobots using molecular dynamics simulation and virtual reality. *Microelectronics Journal*, 39, 190–201.
15. Genov, R., M. Stanacevic, M. Naware, G. Cauwenberghs, & N.V. Thakor. (2006). 16-Channel integrated potentiostat for distributed neurochemical sensing. *IEEE Transactions on Circuits and Systems I—Regular Papers*, 53, 2371–2376.
16. Cavalcanti, A. (2003). Assembly automation with evolutionary nanorobots and sensor-based control applied to nanomedicine. *IEEE Transactions on Nanotechnology*, 2, 82–87.
17. Hogg, T. (2007). Coordinating microscopic robots in viscous fluids. *Auton Agent Multi Agent Syst.*, 14, 271–305.

18. Cavalcanti, A., & R.A. Freitas, Jr. (2002). Autonomous multi-robot sensor-based cooperation for nanomedicine. *Int'l. J. Nonlinear Science Numerical Simulation*, 3, 743–746.
19. Buchanan, J.R., & C. Kleinstreuer. (1998). Simulation of particle-hemodynamics in a partially occluded artery segment with implications to the initiation of microemboli and secondary stenoses. *J. Biomech. Eng.*, 120, 446–454.
20. Casal, A., T. Hogg, & A. Cavalcanti. (2003). Nanorobots as cellular assistants in inflammatory responses. In: *Proc. IEEE BCATS Biomedical Computation at Stanford 2003 Symposium*, IEEE Computer Society, Stanford CA, USA.
21. Elder, J.B., D.J. Hoh, B.C. Oh, A.C. Heller, C.Y. Liu et al. (2008). The future of cerebral surgery: A kaleidoscope of opportunities. *Neurosurgery*, 62, 1555–1582.
22. Elder, J.B., C.Y. Liu, & M.L.J. Apuzzo. (2008). Neurosurgery in the realm of 10_9, Part 2: Applications of nanotechnology to neurosurgery-present and future. *Neurosurgery*, 62, 269–285.
23. Freitas, R.A. Jr. (2005). What is nanomedicine? *Nanomedicine: Nanotechnology Biology and Medicine*, 1, 2–9.
24. Fukuda, S., N. Hashimoto, H. Naritomi, I. Nagata, K. Nozaki et al. (2000). Prevention of rat cerebral aneurysm formation by inhibition of nitric oxide synthase. *Circulation*, 101, 2532–2538.
25. Fukuda, T., A. Kawamoto, F. Arai, & H. Matsuura. (1995). Steering mechanism and swimming experiment of micro mobile robot in water. *Micro Electro Mechanical Systems*, 300–305.
26. Cavalcanti, A. (2003). Assembly automation with evolutionary nanorobots and sensor-based control applied to nanomedicine. *IEEE Transactions on Nanotechnology*, 2, 82–87.
27. Martel, S., M. Mohammadi, O. Felfoul, Z. Lu, & P. Pouponneau. (2009). Flagellated magnetotactic bacteria as controlled MRI-trackable propulsion and steering systems for medical nanorobots operating in the human microvasculature. *International Journal of Robotics Research*, 28, 571–582.
28. Cavalcanti, A. (2009). Nanorobot Invention and Linux: The Open Technology Factor: An Open Letter to UNO General Secretary. *CANNXS Project 1*.
29. Vaughn, J.R. (2006). Over the horizon: Potential impact of emerging trends in information and communication technology on disability policy and practice. *National Council on Disability*, 1–55.
30. Drexler, K.E. (1992). *Nanosystems: Molecular Machinery, Manufacturing, and Computation*. Wiley & Sons.
31. Fishbine, G. (2001). *The Investor's Guide to Nanotechnology & Micromachines*. Wiley & Sons.
32. Freitas, Jr. R.A. (1999). *Nanomedicine: Basic Capabilities* (Vol. I). Landes Bioscience.
33. Ekpan, F.M., M.O. Ori, H.S. Samuel, & O.P. Egwuatu. (2024). The synergy of AI and drug delivery: A revolution in healthcare. *International Journal of Advanced Biological and Biomedical Research*, 44–66.
34. Douglas, S.M., I. Bachelet, & G.M. Church. (2012). A logic-gated nanorobot for targeted transport of molecular payloads. *Science*, 335(6070), 831–834.
35. Fan, D. et al. (2010). Sub-cellular resolution delivery of a cytokine via gold nanowires. *ACS Nano*, 4(7), 4744–4750.
36. Yang, G., Y. Zhang, J. Yang, Z. Sun, X. Ding, & H. Liu. (2017). Review of robot-assisted minimally invasive surgery systems: From the perspective of industrial design. *Robotics and Computer-Integrated Manufacturing*, 44.
37. Satava, R.M. (2002). Surgical robotics: The early chronicles of a revolution. *Surgical Clinics of North America*, 83(6), 1495–1504.

38. Kim, P.C.W., M. Marcus, & R. Seifabadi. (2020). Current status and future directions of robot-assisted surgery in clinical practice. *Annals of Biomedical Engineering*, 48(2), 557–572.
39. Martel, S., M. Mohammadi, O. Felfoul, Z. Lu, & P. Pouponneau. (2009). Flagellated magnetotactic bacteria as controlled MRI-trackable propulsion and steering systems for medical nanorobots operating in the human microvasculature. *International Journal of Robotics Research*, 28(4), 571–582.
40. Li, J., B. Esteban-FernÃindez de Ãtvila, W. Gao, L. Zhang, & J. Wang. (2017). Micro/nanorobots for biomedicine: Delivery, surgery, sensing, and detoxification. *Science Robotics*, 2(4), eaam6431.
41. Ceylan, H., I.C. Yasa, O. Yasa, A.F. Tabak, J. Giltinan, & M. Sitti. (2019). Translational prospects of untethered medical microrobots. *Progress in Biomedical Engineering*, 1(1), 012002.

Index

P

Q

R

S

T

V

W

About the Editors

Dr. Brajesh Kumar Singh has a B.Tech in Electronics and Communication Engineering from Delhi Technological University, New Delhi (Formerly DCE, Delhi University) and, M.Tech and PhD both from Guru Gobind Singh Indraprastha University (GGSIPU), New Delhi. He is Assistant Professor in the Department of Electronics, Rajdhani College, University of Delhi, India. He has more than 14 years of teaching experience and has published several research papers in international journals, international conferences, and has 3 patents in the field of Image processing, Biometrics Systems, Machine Learning, Communication Technology and IoT.

Dr. Amrita Rai has a B. Tech. (Electronics) degree from College of Engineering Chandpur (Nagpur University), a M.Tech (Power electronics and electrical drives) as university topper from Maharishi Dayanand University, Rohtak and a PhD (Signal Processing) from Thapar University Patiala (previously Thapar Institute of Engineering and Technology), India in 1998, 2007 and 2015 respectively. She possesses more than 20 years of experience in teaching, research and administration. She is Head of Department and Professor at Department of Electronics and Communication Engineering, Galgotias College of Engineering and Technology, Greater Noida, India. Her areas of interest are adaptive filter design and signal processing with very large-scale integration implementation, IOT and Sensors for Industrial Applications. She had published several reputed International/SCI papers and attended various IEEE conferences. She has guided more than 20 PG and 100 UG theses and currently guiding two PhD Scholars. She has recently published a book "Paradigms of Smart and Intelligent Communication, 5G and Beyond". She has written a book "Principles of VLSI and CMOS Integrated Circuits" and 6 chapters. She is a reviewer of reputed journals and conferences. She has published 13 patent and has grants for 2 more, and delivered expert lectures on smart sensors transform healthcare systems, IoT and sensors and adaptive signal processing in many universities and colleges. She has chaired sessions and delivered invited talks in various international conferences which include "ICCI 2023 Sardar Vallabhbhai National Institute of Technology, Surat, India and CISES-2023 GLBITM, Greater Noida, India". She served as senior member of IEEE Delhi section society and reviewer of many international/SCI journals and conferences.

Dr. Shamimul Qamar is a professor and an eminent scholar in the field of Computer Science & Engineering. He has a B.Tech from MMMTU Gorakhpur, M.Tech from AMU, Aligarh and a PhD in Computer Science & Engineering from IIT Roorkee with highly honourable grade. Prof. Qamar has extensive teaching experience in various engineering colleges. He has research interests in computer network & multimedia, networking & security, artificial intelligence. He has published several research papers in reputed journals and conferences. He served as consultant at Jackson State university, USA. He is a reviewer of IEEE/Elsevier/MDPI/EUROSIP/ IJCSIS, USA. He has written some textbooks and chapters in the field of electronics & computer engineering. He is also a technical programme committee member in various international conference. He is a life time member of International Association of Engineers and a life member of Indian Society of Technical Educational. His technical depth and interest resulted in setting up a research lab according to latest technical innovations. Along with this, he has actively participated in various technical courses workshops, seminar etc. at the IITs.

Dr. Ravinder Kumar is chairperson and associate professor of Skill Department of Computer Science & Engineering. He did his PhD from USIC&T Guru Gobind Singh Indraprastha University and Indian Institute of Technology Delhi (IITD) jointly under the supervision of Prof. Pravin Chandra and Prof. M. Hanmandlu. He has more than 20 years of teaching experience in the field of Computer Science, IT, Electronics etc. He has published 50 research papers in international journals, 65 international conferences and 15 chapters in edited books in the field of Image processing, Biometrics, Machine Learning, Blockchain, Privacy preservation etc. He has supervised 4 PhDs in the domain of Computer Vision, Multimodal Biometrics, Stock Proce Prediction and Privacy preservation of Electronic Health Record.

Dr. Anil Kumar has a Doctor of Philosophy (PhD) in Computer Science and Engineering from the esteemed GGS IPU Delhi State University, India in School of USIC&T with specialization in Privacy and Security of Electronic Health Record using soft computing techniques. Currently he is working as an Assistant Professor in the department of Computer Science and Engineering in GLBITM, Greater Noida, India. Throughout his career, he has garnered rich experience in both industry and academia. He has nearly 15 years of experience in the field of education and 3.5 years of experience in industry. He has published numerous research SCI/Scopus papers in reputed journals and conferences. His area of interests are PRIVACY and Security, Blockchain, Cloud Computing, Soft Computing and Human Computer Interface. He has published many patents. He is a renowned author of Data Mining and Warehouse.

For Product Safety Concerns and Information please contact our EU representative GPSR@taylorandfrancis.com Taylor & Francis Verlag GmbH, Kaufingerstraße 24, 80331 München, Germany